RELATIONSHIP
MORALITY

RELATIONSHIP
MORALITY

J. KELLENBERGER

THE PENNSYLVANIA STATE UNIVERSITY PRESS
UNIVERSITY PARK, PENNSYLVANIA

Library of Congress Cataloging-in-Publication Data

Kellenberger, James.
    Relationship morality / J. Kellenberger.

        p.   cm.
    Includes bibliographical references (p.   ) and index.
    ISBN 0-271-01404-0 (cloth)
    ISBN 0-271-01405-9 (paper)
    1. Interpersonal relations—Moral and ethical aspects.   2. Ethics.
    I. Title.
    HM132.K4   1995
    177—dc20   94-15347
                                                                CIP

Published by The Pennsylvania State University Press,
University Park, PA 16802-1003

It is the policy of The Pennsylvania State University Press to use acid-free paper for the
first printing of all clothbound books. Publications on uncoated stock satisfy the
minimum requirements of American National Standard for Information Sciences—
Permanence of Paper for Printed Library Materials, ANSI Z39.48–1992.

To Anne,
and our special relationship

Contents

Preface

"Never send to know for whom the *bell* tolls; it tolls for *thee*." After Hemingway these words are recognized by many. They are from John Donne's Devotion XVII, where we find Donne reflecting: "No man is an *Island*, intire of it selfe; every man is a piece of the *Continent*, a part of the *maine*; if a *Clod* bee washed away by the *Sea, Europe* is the lesse, as well as if a *Promontorie* were, as well as if a *Manner* of thy *friends* or of *thine owne* were; any mans *death* diminishes *me*, because I am involved in *Mankinde*." While Donne's reflections, even in this devotion, embrace more than the sentiment of these lines, these lines provide a poetical expression of the heart of what I am going to call "relationship morality."

"No man is an *Island*," says Donne. Each person is "involved in *Mankinde*." Each is related to each. This moral insight, echoed in religious sensibility and given in individual moral experience, embraces the foundation of all morality; that is a main thesis to be developed in the pages of this book. Morality is a complex whole that ramifies into obligation, justice, virtue, rights, and goods. It is not merely obligation or a matter of determining what is right, as many might come to think, studying philosophical theories of obligation. Yet, this first thesis asserts, the entirety of this complex of morality rests upon the relationship of each to each, discoverable by each in individual moral experience.

In another way, though, "morality" is not one entity, simple or complex, but a series of different morality forms, not all of which give a place to obligation or virtue or rights. Here is a way of thinking about morality that is not that common in philosophical reflection, but essential to consider. Relationship morality, under this aspect of reflection, becomes but one morality form. Even so, it can be seen to underlie or account for more of our moral lives than other forms, and this is a second main thesis of this book.

Some of the material in this book has appeared previously in other forms. Material used in Chapters 10, 11, and 12 was drawn from my *God-Relationships With and Without God*, which was published by The Macmillan Press Ltd. in its Library of Philosophy and Religion, edited by John Hick, and copublished in the United States by St. Martin's Press. I gratefully acknowledge permission from Macmillan to use material from *God-Relationships With and Without God*. In one part of that book I was concerned with a religious form of relationship morality, a form in which a believer's individual relationship to God is a source of individual religious obligations. In the present book I am concerned with relationships between persons and with their foundational role for morality, independent of whatever relationships to God individuals may or may not have. However, in one part of my discussion, I shall undertake to relate these two forms of relationship morality one to the other.

Some material used in Chapter 1 originally appeared in "Ethical Relativism," *The Journal of Value Inquiry* 13, no. 1 (1979): 1–20. I would like to thank the editor and copyright holders of the *Journal of Value Inquiry*, Kluwer Academic Publishers, for permission to use this material, reprinted by permission of Kluwer Academic Publishers. Some of the material used in Chapters 9 and 16 originally appeared in "A Defense of Pacificism," *Faith and Philosophy* 4 (1987), and is reprinted with the permission of the editors.

Chapter 3 has been adapted from my "The Death of God and the Death of Persons," originally published in *Religious Studies* 16 (1980).

I am grateful for support in the form of reassigned time provided by California State University, Northridge, the School of Humanities and the Department of Philosophy. As in the past, the chair of the Department of Philosophy, Daniel Sedey, was particularly helpful in giving me reassigned time and propitious class schedules.

For his editorial support, and for his unflagging understanding of my project, I am grateful to Sanford Thatcher, the director of The Pennsylvania State University Press; and I thank Keith Monley for his sensitive copyediting of the manuscript.

My thanks go to Keith Ward for useful comments on an earlier version of Chapter 14, to Lance Stell for comments about rights, to Crerar Douglas, James Maffe, and Anne Kellenberger for helpful notes on different parts of the manuscript, and to Rita Manning and John Kekes for their comments on the manuscript as a whole.

Introduction

It is possible to see morality as a free-floating aberration of human habit or proclivity. Perhaps such a view has some appeal to some postmodern intellects. But for a long time in the history of moral reflection it has been strongly sensed that our morality must in some way be grounded. In order to have the serious and binding nature we take it to have, it must rest upon some foundation. It must have a source other than our delusions, a basis other than wish fulfillment. So it has been felt by many. And many have spoken to this concern, in one way or another identifying, or recommending to our acceptance, some foundational stratum for morality.

Often one part of morality has been felt to be morally prior to and underlying the other elements of morality, as when virtue is taken to be the bedrock of morality. Similarly, right action (or moral obligation) can be, and has been, taken to be the more fundamental element of morality, underlying and defining virtue. The first intuition was at home in Aristotle's thinking four centuries before the Common Era. The second intuition is shared by those who, like John Stuart Mill in the last century, see as fundamental to ethics a standard that defines right action.

Once the main concern focuses on right action, the issue between Immanuel Kant and the utilitarians arises. According to Kant's ethical thinking, the foundation of the moral law is the internal coherence of moral action, and he proposed a test for such moral coherence. According to utilitarian thinking, exemplified by the views of Mill and Hastings Rashdall, it is not an action's internal nature that determines its moral rightness; rather, the good consequences of an action determine its moral rightness and provide the foundation for morality. And, especially in reaction to utilitarian thinking, there are the counterpoised and opposite intuitions about the good and the right. For one intuition, the good, or some definite moral goods, are prior to the right (right action): the good is foundational to the right. For the other intuition, right action is prior to, or independent of, the good.

Again, from a rather different perspective, it has been possible to see yet another element of morality as basic and foundational: not virtue, not right action, not the good, but the moral rights of individuals. This, roughly, was the perspective of moral thinking in the Enlightenment.

Nor should we fail to mention that strain of religious ethical reflection, reaching back from the present day to the Middle Ages and beyond, that regards God's commands as foundational to and the establishment of morality.

In this book I shall pursue a different and, I think, new perspective on the foundation of morality, although it will accommodate, or at least explain, and draw strength from many of the views just recited.

This book is an enquiry into the extent to which relationships between persons are foundational in morality. It is an effort to discover how relationships between persons underlie the various parts of morality that I mentioned—moral rightness, virtue, the good, and the rights of individuals—and, indeed, the entire complex phenomenon of human morality. As I see it, there are two main avenues down which such an enquiry can be pursued.

First, one might divide ethics into its parts and try to show how each part rests upon human relationships. Following this avenue, I shall look at the various parts—or, better, the various mansions—of ethics: these include moral obligation, its determination and source, moral principles, justice, the good, moral virtue, and moral rights. In this movement of our enquiry we shall concentrate on obligation.

A second avenue of enquiry is necessary, however, because morality as a human phenomenon is circumscribed neither by the philosophical discussion of the source of obligation nor by the expanded discussion that embraces justice, the good, virtue, and rights. It has other dimensions that do not neatly fit into such a schema. We come at ethics in quite another way by reflecting on the character of moral failure and moral success. Doing so presents us with a second main avenue of enquiry; and, following its line of sight, I shall contrast relationship morality (as it may be called), in which moral failure stems from violating a relationship, with shame morality, in which moral failure is marked by one's being ashamed, and with guilt morality, in which moral failure is violating a duty, as opposed to violating a relationship.

This is not to say that our enquiry falls neatly into two parts, for, despite their importance, these two avenues are not the only ways into our enquiry and following them alone is not sufficient. The issue posed by this book has ramifications amounting to other byways that will have to be followed as well, such as the implications of relationship morality for an understanding of religious duty to God, and implications for the status of our obligations to animals. The book divides into six parts.

In Part I we shall follow the avenue of enquiry that seeks the foundations of the different mansions of morality. Specifically, in Chapter 1, we shall begin with an examination of moral obligation and its connection with human relationships. Though not the whole of ethics, obligation is a not unimportant part of ethics. In the first chapter I shall try to show that human relationships between individuals are what clarify and give specific form to various particular obligations, such as the obligation to honor one's spouse, and to various general obligations, such as the obligation not to lie. Also in the first chapter I shall try to show that, furthermore, relationships between persons are the source of such particular and general obligations (a rather different claim). In this connection I shall begin to bring out how other contenders for the basis of obligation, namely good effects and the internal moral coherence of actions (important to utilitarian and deontological theories of obligation respectively), themselves must heed relationships between persons.

At this point the question arises, What, if anything, is the difference between relationship morality and the moral perspective, developed in feminist thought and called an "ethic of care," that focuses on relationships as opposed to competing rights and moral principles in considering what ought to be done? There are differences, as well as similarities, and I want to bring out both in Chapter 2.

The concern of the first chapter is limited to various particular and general obligations. In this book, however, I want to explore the extent to which all obligations, not just various particular and general obligations, rest on relationships between persons (and, finally, the extent to which all the elements of ethics rest on relationships). In Chapter 3 we take up the broader concern as it relates to obligation. At the root of relationship morality, in contrast with utilitarian and deontological theories of obligation in their pure forms, and with feminine ethics, is the perception of what I call "the person/person relationship" between each and every person. For relationship morality, it is this relationship that is the ultimate source of obligation, and I shall expend some effort in trying to clarify it. In Chapter 3 I shall discuss the nature of one's discovering this relationship to persons, how this discovery amounts to coming into the presence of persons, and how that phenomenon has distinguishable parts.

In Part II, I shall explore the internal logic of the person/person relationship. This ultimate relationship, as I shall try to bring out in Chapter 4, obtains not only between each person and every other person but also obtains between each person and himself or herself. In Chapters 5 and 6 I shall examine various other features of the logic of coming into the presence of persons, for as we shall see, a definite logic governs this moral phenomenon.

The importance of the person/person relationship, which is of course between persons, makes it hard to avoid the question, What is a person? This is a knotty question with a long history, a question that has invited confusions and that has recently, in the age of bioethics, assumed a new aspect of relevance. I shall, in Chapter 7, offer a resolution of it adequate for the needs of relationship morality.

So far the discussion will have focused on obligation and how human relationships, significantly the person/person relationship, determine obligations. But there are other elements of ethics, and at this point (in Part III, in Chapters 8 and 9) I shall broaden the discussion to include the other mansions of morality—moral principle, justice, goods, virtue, and rights. With Chapter 9 the journey down the first main avenue of the book's enquiry will be completed.

In Part IV we shall turn to the second main avenue of enquiry into the extent that relationships are foundational to ethics. In the first nine chapters relationship morality is contrasted with theories of obligation and philosophical theories of the virtues and rights. Pursuing the second main avenue of our enquiry involves contrasting relationship morality not with competing theories of morality but with other identifiable forms of morality: shame morality and guilt morality. Each of these forms of morality has its own internal coherence, and each has its own form of moral failure and success. In Chapter 10 I shall show that there are various morality forms and then focus on guilt morality. In Chapter 11 I shall present and discuss a very different form of morality: shame morality. Then, in Chapter 12, I shall bring out how relationship morality is sin morality (in one central understanding of "sin"); and I shall try to show how relationship morality provides us with a more adequate picture of the complex phenomena of human morality than either guilt morality or shame morality.

In Part V I shall relate human sin morality to religious sin morality. In human sin morality, a moral fault is a violation of a human relationship and so a sin against a human person. In religious sin morality, sin against God is a violation of a relationship to God. The two forms of sin morality are distinct, but I shall argue in Chapter 13 that they are compatible and that, indeed, the one is "continuous" with the other. Also in Chapter 13 I shall try to show how the notion of sin central to sin morality underlies various other notions of sin.

Using the previous discussion of shame morality and sin morality, in Chapter 14 I shall analyze the Genesis story of Adam and Eve and the loss of innocence in order to show how the categories of shame and sin enhance our understanding of that charged and revelatory moral myth.

Part VI will explore the implications of relationship morality (or of sin/relationship morality) for our moral lives. What of our obligations to animals if the root of morality is relationships between persons? We do have obligations to animals, I would insist, and we do even if nonhuman animals are not persons. How, nevertheless, relationship morality accounts for these obligations, and does so most reasonably, I shall try to show in Chapter 15.

Finally, in Chapter 16, I shall try to project possible fruits of relationship morality in the form of further practical implications. More exactly, since my thesis is that fully realized morality is in fact relationship morality, though this may be only dimly appreciated by many, my rumination will be on the fruits of our coming to a more explicit understanding of the character of the morality we live and its grounding in relationships.

In brief summary these are the avenues and byways down which the enquiry of this book will be pursued. At the end I hope that I shall have made it fairly clear that relationships between persons are foundational to morality. There is perhaps one small possible confusion that I ought to obviate just here before we get to our effort. While I am seeking the foundations of ethics in what I deem the most substantive sense, I am not looking for a foundation in the sense of a principle or psychological truth that can be used "rationally" to support ethics or one's being ethical with an appeal to direct or indirect self-interest. Several, of course, have looked for a foundation of ethics in this sense—in effect an answer to that desperate but not always adolescent question, Why should I be moral? So it is that Henry Hazlitt, for instance, says "the aim of each of us to satisfy his own desires, to achieve as far as possible his own highest happiness and well-being, is best forwarded by a common means, Social Cooperation, and cannot be achieved without that means. Here, then, is the foundation on which we may build a rational system of ethics."[1] And, of course, Mill thought that the principle of utility, or "the greatest happiness principle," for him the primary principle of ethics, could be given a sort of proof by appealing to what people desire: since individuals desire their own happiness, so the general happiness is desired by "the aggregate of all persons," he reasoned, and he went on to conclude that since only what is a means or part of happiness is capable of being desired, happiness "must be the criterion of morality."[2] In this way he sought to rest morality on what the individual desires.

It may be that moral individuals act in accord with their deepest desires and are happiest, but it may not be too; for in many cases a moral decision brings with it burdens and sorrow that a more pragmatic and accommodating nature would opt to avoid. In any case my effort is not to seek a pragmatic basis for moral behavior. It is not to show the wary individual newly suspicious of what appear to be the constraining demands of morality that being ethical really does have a rather large return or is really an extension of one's personal desire.

Our not seeking a pragmatic basis for morality or for being moral, and even our denial of such a basis (if we cared to make that denial), of course does not reject the point Plato has Socrates make in the *Crito* (47d) that one who does what is evil thereby wounds his soul and one who does what is just or right thereby upbuilds his soul, or the point in the *Republic* (444e) that virtue is a kind of health and beauty of the soul. But these perceptions do not provide an exterior pragmatic reason for enduring the burdens of being moral; they proceed from a standpoint from which the inherent value—the beauty, Plato would say—of moral action is evident. This standpoint, unalloyed, rejects not only the need but the appropriateness of seeking a pragmatic reason for being moral.[3] One's valuing beauty or a moral act only because it pays to do so, it may be said, presents a prima facie case that one does not value beauty or morality at all, at least not for their own sake.

Yet, though we reject seeking a pragmatic reason for being moral, we are

---

1. Henry Hazlitt, *The Foundations of Morality* (Princeton: D. Van Nostrand, 1964), 14.

2. John Stuart Mill, *Utilitarianism* (Indianapolis: Hackett, 1979), 34–38.

3. Elsewhere in the *Republic*, it must be admitted, Plato does give a sort of pragmatic reason for being just: the unjust soul will not do as it wishes (577e), and the just soul will have the sweetest pleasure (583a).

not left in a position where we must say one's being moral is a matter of will, not reason, a matter of making a sheer commitment to principles, a matter of a choice, or a decision, for which no supportive, as opposed to pragmatic, reason can be given. There may yet be a foundation to ethics in the sense pertinent to this enquiry, and it is the concern of this enquiry to examine the extent to which relationships form that foundation.

PART I

RELATIONSHIPS WITH PERSONS AND OBLIGATIONS TOWARD PERSONS

1

Relationships and Obligations

Relationships between persons—that is, for our present concern, human relationships—are foundational to morality in more than one way. One way they are foundational, and the easiest to grasp, I think, relates to their function in clarifying the form of various obligations as they exist for individuals.

I shall assume that we human beings have moral obligations, something that few would utterly deny. All except those who embrace an extreme ethical nihilism would grant that we human beings have obligations of various sorts to other persons. There may be some disagreement about how certain obligations are incurred, or how they arise, and about the underlying principles that govern obligation, but for most of us it is simply an undeniable fact of our moral lives that obligations exist. This perception, in some form shared by the cultures of the world, is in the West common to the religious traditions of Judaism, Christianity, and Islam, as well as to intellectual positions that stand outside religion, such as those of the Enlightenment. It of course is the ineluctable nature of this perception that provides the starting place for both casuistry and philosophical theories of obligation. So let us grant that we human beings are faced with obligations of various sorts as a part of our moral lives. Not that obligation is the whole of morality, for it is not—a matter of some importance for our enquiry later on—but obligation is an inescapable element of morality. This brute fact of human existence we take as a part of our starting point in this chapter.

Moreover, let us allow that many of these obligations are discernible to untutored moral sensibility, that is, to persons of mature age who have not undertaken any formal study of ethics, although they may have received moral instruction from parents and others. One need not read Immanuel Kant or John Stuart Mill or even the Bible to have the sense that it is wrong to lie or to steal and that something is owed to one's parents and to one's spouse. My point here is not that each discernment of obligation by every person is accurate, but only that, if it came to it, each of us, or most of us, could begin a list of moral rules that embodied obligations. True, about some of these rules some persons might be more confident than others, and some lists might lack rules prominently featured on others. There could well be differences in formulation, as well. I suspect, however, that there would be a nucleus of moral obligations commonly recognized. Be that as it may, I shall assume that we have some notion of what our various obligations are.

Given our sense that we have obligations, and our further sense of what many of these obligations are, it still may be unclear what actions will fulfill a specific obligation in a particular setting. It is just here that human relationships play a primary role. One of the ways that relationships are foundational to ethics is that they clarify or determine the individual forms of the obligations we recognize. The extent and the way that relationships clarify or determine our obligations, and the implications of this being so, form our first concern in this chapter. In order to pursue this concern it is useful to distinguish between obligations to particular persons—such as one's obligation to one's spouse, one's obligation to one's parents, or one's obligation to one's children—and general obligations—such as the obligation to tell the truth, the obligation not to steal, or the obligation to keep promises. Let us start with particular obligations, for the role of relationships between persons in defining the requirements of obligations emerges most clearly regarding these.

Consider the obligations of parents toward their children. Parents must, in the moral, obligatory sense of "must," love and care for their children. In order to care for their offspring parents must provide for their needs. Some of the needs of children can be stated in a general way: food, clothing, shelter, and so on. But some of the subtler needs of children are more individual and can vary immensely in growing children. One child may be as adventurous as Huck Finn, another as sedate as a gentlemany Prince of Wales. One may be an Esau, another a Jacob. Esau, who grew into "a skillful hunter, a man of the field," in his youth, we can imagine, developed athletically, grew physically adept, and became accomplished in animal husbandry. Jacob grew into "a quiet man, dwelling in tents." In his youth we should imagine him as less active, more reflective, inclined to be bookish, perhaps; a contemporary Jacob might become a dweller of libraries.[1] Some children are quite verbal early on; others are not. For some children, artistic ability may begin to emerge naturally and easily. These various tendencies and incipient abilities create individual needs.

The forms of dependence and expectation such individual needs create are determined by the relationship the child has to his or her parents. Accordingly, the parents' duty to the child to meet these needs, with their particular forms of dependence and expectation, is determined by the particular relationship with the child. The duty is not created by the need alone. For one thing, parental duty is not created in nonparents, in any form (although this of course is not to say that nonparents have no duties toward children). For another thing, it is not just the parental relationship to a child, shared by a father and a mother, that determines the individual form of parental duty that a parent has. In the case of a child's emerging artistic sense, say, it may be that one parent more than another is better at encouraging its development. Which parent has this primary responsibility will depend not merely on which parent has artistic skill but also on the factors of dependence and expectation, and these are determined by the relationship, or relationships, between the child and his or her parents. So one parent may have a greater obligation than the other to meet certain needs of the child precisely because of the particular relationship between that parent and that child. A particular father may be better able than a particular mother to encourage a son's sense of accomplishment by taking him on camping trips, or, conversely, a particular mother may be better able to encourage a son's sense of accomplishment by stimulating his interest in soccer or knitting.

As the relationship between parent and child can determine the form of a parent's duty toward offspring, so an offspring's relationship to his or her parent can determine the form of the obligation to honor a parent. Allowing that there are general, even universal, forms of filial honor—such as paying heed and showing gratitude—pretty clearly in many instances, regarding the particular form that an offspring's honor takes, what honors one person's parent may not honor another person's parent. In one case a parent may be honored by an honesty on the part of a son or daughter that might seem ruthless to many outside the relationship, such honesty honoring the parent by recognizing his or her courage. In another relationship such honesty

1. Gen. 25.27. All references to the Bible, unless otherwise indicated, are to the Revised Standard Version.

could be gratuitous and hurtful, and proper honor would take the form of a respectful silence. A parent may be honored by the nearly constant solicitude of offspring, while for another parent such attention may seem oppressive. Here again, as with the obligation to children, needs are important in determining the form of the obligation, although again it is not the need alone, but the need as understood in a particular relationship, that gives the obligation its form. Also important here are the wishes of parents, and in a clear way parents' wishes will often relate not to all their offspring generally, but to one offspring rather than another. A father may wish his son to come to him with his personal, social, or business problems without wishing his daughter to do so, or in another possible relationship he may wish his daughter to do so without wishing this from his son. Of course, a father may wish all of his offspring to bring their problems to him, and there may be a question here about what the father ought to do, even about what he ought to wish. The present point, however, is that the wish of a parent can operate in determining the form of the obligation to honor one's parent in a particular child-parent relationship.

Other factors can operate as well, of course. Noah's son Ham dishonors Noah when he views him in his nakedness, while his other sons, Shem and Japheth, honor him by covering him with a garment, averting their eyes as they do so.[2] In our own time, in many relationships, though not all, no dishonor would attach to a son's seeing his father naked, as when a father and son shower together in a public facility after a tennis match. Here we may note a social factor, but it expresses itself in the individual relationship and not invariably in the same way.

In a similar way the form of various other sorts of obligations to particular persons is determined or clarified by the relationships that exist between persons. This is so regarding the marital relationship between husband and wife. The husband-wife relationship requires each to respect and honor the other; this is a marital obligation (even though in many marriages the obligation may be lightly borne and not be a burdensome duty or feel like an obligation). Though husbands and wives have the obligation to respect and honor each other, the form such respect and honor come to take in a particular marital relationship depends not only on the personalities of the spouses but importantly on the relationship that evolves between the spouses. The expression of respect may or may not take the form of giving little gifts and sharing dinners out. The expression of honor may take the

2. Gen. 9.22–25.

form of each reading the other's diary as a way of sharing thoughts, or it may take the form of each refraining from reading the diary of the other, this as a way of respecting the privacy of the other. True, the respect and honor required have certain general features. They may be said to involve paying attention, being there to listen, and, in general, acknowledging the valuable presence of one's spouse. But, again, this acknowledgment may in one relationship take the form of entertaining, light conversation, while in another it may take the form of serious discussion of professional issues relating to the profession of one or both spouses. It could, in some relationships, take the form of sharing avocations, ranging from coin collecting to parachute jumping, or such a shared activity may not be important at all as a way of acknowledging the valuable presence of the other. Very often one spouse's telling embarrassing stories about the other would violate the marital obligation they have to each other, but not so if the two are a team of husband-and-wife comedians and such persiflage is a part of their routine. In short the range of ways that husbands and wives can honor and respect each other, and so meet their marital obligation to one another, is nearly limitless.

We could cite other examples of different particular obligations in order to illustrate further the role human relationships play in clarifying the form of particular obligations, obligations between particular persons. We could, for instance, bring in relationships between friends or employer-employee loyalty relationships and use them to substantiate the point further. I believe, though, that the point has been sufficiently established regarding particular obligations, and so let us turn our attention to various general obligations, the obligations that persons have to other persons generally.

Most of the moral rules that we can call to mind as moral imperatives embody general obligations: "Do not lie," "Do not steal," "Do not cheat," "Keep your promises," and so on. How are such general obligations clarified or determined by human relationships? To be sure, they are not determined by particular relationships between particular human beings in just the way the obligations so far discussed are. This, however, is not to say that they are not clarified by any human relationships, or even that they are not in some ways clarified by certain particular relationships. Consider the obligation not to lie, or, in its positive expression, the obligation to tell the truth. This obligation requires us to tell the truth in contexts in which information is imparted. It does not require us to refrain from telling jokes and stories or never to use irony. What counts as an information-imparting context depends in great part on the expectations of one's hearers. These expectations are a part of the social arrangement, we might say. That is, they are a function of the general relationship a person has to other persons in that arrangement, including both acquaintances and strangers. If a stranger asks me the way to the nearest hospital, I am required to give information, to tell the truth to the best of my ability. If at the semiannual meeting of the Liars Club I am asked to tell of my greatest feat, that is another matter, as it is when the comedian husband tells his audience stories about his comedian wife. What counts as a bona fide lie, and hence as a violation of one's general obligation to tell the truth, is in these cases determined by one's general relationship to one's hearers. Particular relationships also can come into the determination, as in some cases of irony. When one tells a knowing other that the project one is working on is "going smoothly, as always," the other will recognize this as one's wonted irony, while a stranger might well be deceived.

Something similar holds for the obligation not to steal. Stealing is morally forbidden, but borrowing is not. Stealing is taking the property of another without the other's permission, while borrowing is taking with permission. Permission is often implicitly granted, but what counts as implicit permission is, once again, a matter of the social arrangement that prevails, that is to say, a matter of one's relationship to others in that social arrangement. On the American frontier in the last century, one man's taking the axe or wagon of another in his absence and temporarily using it without explicit permission might well not have been regarded as stealing in various rural communities. So too with trespass, a near cousin of theft. Until quite recently cabins in wilderness settings would be left open, while the owner was gone, so that travelers could use them. Given the general relationship holding between persons in the past, as the first was taking with implicit permission and thus not stealing, so the second was entry with implicit permission and thus not trespassing.

The obligation to keep promises is also clarified or determined by our general relationship to others in a social arrangement. We incur the obligation to do what we promised when we explicitly make a promise, but also when we implicitly make a promise. But whether we have implicitly promised, and so incurred such an obligation, is once again a matter of the social arrangement.[3] What I have said so far regarding other general obligations implies that the social arrangement, that is, a person's relation-

---

3. Sir David Ross subsumes the obligation to tell the truth under the obligation to keep implicit promises. W. D. Ross, *The Right and the Good* (Oxford: Clarendon Press, 1930), 21. Whether he is or is not correct in doing so does not affect the present argument.

ship to others in that social arrangement, can change. It can also vary in different societal settings. What constitutes making an implicit promise in one society may not do so in another. This is a point that is sometimes missed. One author, writing about Eskimo society, says that for Eskimos a promise "means merely that a man tells you what he feels like doing at that particular moment," and if he changes his mind, the agreement is dissolved.[4] This makes it sound as though Eskimos lightly make promises and constantly break them without a qualm. It does not occur to this author that what an Eskimo is doing in saying, "Yes, I'll do it," is not promising, but rather saying, "Yes, I'll do it unless I change my mind." In the author's society most often saying that one will do something implies a promise, makes an implicit promise, but these words, or their counterpart in another language, in Eskimo society may well not be used to do so.

It should at this point be clear that human relationships play a role in determining the form of a number of obligations. This clarifying role may vary somewhat from obligation to obligation, and certainly different relationships between persons are involved in making clear the forms of the different particular obligations we have. However, I believe that it has emerged that human relationships are foundational in ethics at least to the extent that they clarify or determine the form of various particular and general obligations. Let me emphasize that my claim relates to various, and not all, obligations—a point to which I shall return. Now, though, let us look at some of the implications of what we have so far seen, as well as some of what is not implied.

The foundational role of human relationships that I have argued for, it should be noted, is independent of the source of the various particular and general obligations that we have examined. This means that this specific role does not, in itself, imply the correctness or incorrectness of any theory of obligation. It does not matter whether the source of these various obligations is utilitarian or deontological or the natural rights of persons; still, the individual form these various obligations take will be clarified or determined in the way we have seen. However such obligations are created, whatever the criterion of obligation that may establish them, there will be this clarifying role for human relationships. This is so even though it may be that human relationships are foundational to ethics, and to obligation specifically, in other ways that impinge on theories of obligation (which is the case, as we shall see shortly).

4. Vihjalmur Stefansson, *My Life with the Eskimo* (New York: Collier Books, 1962), 270–71.

At the same time, this foundational role of human relationships does, in ways beyond what we have yet seen, carry certain positive implications for the various obligations it touches. It implies that there is a moral necessity to know the persons toward whom one is obligated and with whom one stands in a human relationship, although the sort and depth of knowledge that is necessary can vary with the relationship and the obligation. So it is that in order for one's relationship to a parent to clarify the obligation to honor that parent, one must know the parent. One must have some understanding of the parent's wishes, sensibilities, expectations, and so on. Again, with the obligation of parents toward their children, in order for their relationship to their child to clarify that obligation they must know their child—his or her capacities, potential, and so on. An analogous point holds for the obligation of one spouse to another and the clarifying role of the marital relationship. Here it is critical for each to have some understanding of the character of the other in order for each to honor the other. If the husband or the wife operates without knowledge of the other, then, even with good intentions, it will be hard, perhaps impossible, to honor the other. In Ibsen's A Doll's House we find this point brought home with great force. As Ibsen's play progresses, it becomes clear that Torvald hardly understands his wife, Nora, just as she hardly knows her husband. Each projects a dream version of the other and reads the actions of the other in terms of that projection. Torvald regards Nora as his "lark," his "squirrel," his "little Nora," and does not imagine the sort of courage she can muster. For Nora, Torvald is a hero who, when he discovers her forgery, will do what is "wonderful" and take the blame himself. Neither projection is realistic. Both Nora and Torvald try to respect the obligations of their marital relationship, and both think that they are doing so. Yet, since neither knows the other, neither finally knows how to honor the other.

Of course not all relationships are as intimate as the marriage relationship. And the depth and degree of knowledge of others is less morally demanding in other relationships, although it never reaches a vanishing point. It exists even within those general relationships between individuals and others that give form to general obligations like the obligation to tell the truth. Here, where one has a general obligation that extends to those one has never met, it is not necessary to have knowledge of the other's character. But it is necessary to have knowledge of others as they stand in the relevant relationship—as hearers to whom one is related as speaker, in the case of the obligation to tell the truth, and mutatis mutandis for the other general obligations discussed.

Next, let us note something further that is not implied by the foundational role of human relationships that we have before us. I have tried to show how human relationships play a necessary role in clarifying or determining the form of various obligations. Given this role, it manifestly behooves us to be conscious of our relationships to others, especially our particular relationships, in considering how to fulfill our obligations. However, it does not follow that each individual who takes seriously his or her relationships to others will judge rightly what is morally demanded, or morally allowed, by the obligations determined by those relationships. In fact we have already seen a foreshadowing of this point: Ibsen's Nora and Torvald take their marriage relationship seriously, yet each misjudges the demands of that relationship. Pére Goriot in Balzac's novel takes seriously, almost too seriously, his relationship to his daughters and ends up by indulgently ruining them. In Shakespeare's play Hamlet heeds his father's wish; as delivered to him by his father's ghost, it is a wish for revenge. And ultimately Hamlet gains revenge by killing his uncle, the murderer of his father. However, although Hamlet has taken seriously his filial duty to his father and acted on his wish, it does not follow from the foundational role for human relationships I have argued for that he has acted in accord with the moral demands of his filial obligation.

It is an implication of what I have argued for, however, that what is demanded morally in one relationship may not be demanded in another of the same type. What is morally demanded of a husband or wife in one marital relationship may not be demanded in another, for instance. Some of the examples I used earlier established this fairly clearly, I believe. But it is not a further implication of this, or a direct implication of the role of human relationships for which I have argued, that to meet the obligations of some particular relationship it is sufficient that each in the relationship knows what the other is doing and does not object. In *The Leopard*, a novel by Giusseppe di Lampedusa about a nineteenth-century Sicilian aristocrat and his family, the protagonist, Don Fabrizio, in lucid moments appreciates that in keeping a mistress in the town he is violating his obligation to his wife, even though she knows or guesses and does not register an overt objection. Again, it is not implied by the foundational role for human relationships that I have tried to establish that a relationship morally allows those in the relationship to do as they wish merely because they have agreed their relationship allows them to do so. The lubricious husband who smilingly announces that he and his wife have agreed that "our relationship allows each of us to cheat" proclaims a moral stance that is conceptually and morally incoherent. Nothing in my argument entails that it is otherwise.

We can see, then, that the role for human relationships in determining obligations, the role that I have argued for, does not entail moral relativism, where moral relativism is the view that the beliefs or attitudes of individuals or groups of individuals determine moral rightness. True, there may be a societal factor in determining the form an obligation takes, as there may be individual factors, in ways that we have seen. However, this point does not amount to moral relativism in the sense that I have identified.[5] This is so even though societal differences can appear to be morally radical. It is reported that in Eskimo societies husbands offer to male guests the sexual favors of their wives, and this is approved by custom. Here, one might think, either we must embrace moral relativism, or, if we regard our own view of the demands of the marital relationship as right and reject relativism, we must regard the Eskimo practice as wrong. But not so. Let me supply a modicum of background. In traditional Eskimo societies married couples form an economic unit: the man hunts; the woman dries her husband's clothes, mends his boots, and sews any tears in his clothing (life-and-death matters in the polar region); she also prepares the skins and dries the meat of any animals he kills, thus giving him more time to hunt. Sometimes, if a man's wife is sick or has a baby to care for and he is going on a hunting trip where a woman is needed to warm the igloo that is built, to dry his clothes, to scrape skins, and so on, he will take another woman, with the husband's understanding. And on these occasions it is understood that there will be sexual relations. Does this mean that the Eskimos approve of "wife trading"? I think not. One author who has reported on this practice among the Eskimos observes that Eskimo married people generally remain devoted to each other throughout their lives.[6] The difference between Eskimo societies and the predominant society of, say, the United States or Europe is *not* that a lack of devotion, consideration, and fidelity are considered permissible in one society and not considered permissible in the other, or that "being true" is counted morally right in one society and not in the other. Rather, the difference is over the role of sex in devotion. In some societies, for better or worse, devotion assumes an expression that is essentially, though not exclusively, sexual. In these societies a husband's sharing his wife's

5. Might there be some other variants of moral relativism that the role of human relationships I have argued for in this chapter entails? I suppose that there might be. Some might count it relativistic that different *forms* of an obligation are allowed and insisted upon.

6. Peter Freuchen, *Book of the Eskimo* (New York: World Publishing Company, 1961), 81.

sexual favors hits at the devotion required by the marital relationship. In other societies, like the Eskimo, it does not. In each of these societies it may be that the same thing is counted right, namely, respecting and honoring one's spouse. But the way this is done, or can be done, may vary from one society to the other, depending on cultural beliefs, perhaps unspoken beliefs, about the significance of sex.

On this account, then, though the form of the marital obligation to respect and honor one's spouse may vary from social setting to social setting, moral relativism is not entailed. For the same thing is right and obligatory in each society: respecting and honoring one's spouse. However, I shall not insist that the Eskimo society is right in the case presented—that marital devotion allows the form of infidelity countenanced in Eskimo society. Strictly, the foundational role for human relationships in determining individual forms of various obligations, that role for which I have argued, leaves this matter open. I have already emphasized that this role does not imply that no mistakes in judgment can be made.

Moreover, there is another reason that the role for human relationships I have tried to establish, and the social factors sometimes associated with it, should not be seen as entailing moral relativism. For, arguably, the form of some general obligations are not determined, at least not wholly determined, by our general relationship to others within a social arrangement. They are, I would say, wholly determined by our relationships to other persons—but not wholly determined by our general relationship to persons within a social arrangement. Consider the general obligation to prevent harm. We are generally obligated to prevent harm, even when there is some cost to ourselves. But what counts as harm? Curtailment of freedom or deprivation often would, but not when they are deserved and proper punishment. What is *considered* to be proper punishment, and so not harm, varies from society to society, or from nation to nation. This much must be conceded. But this does not mean that cutting off a hand for theft is proper punishment in one place and not in another or that capital punishment is proper in some countries and not in others. This issue of proper punishment, and with it the cognate issue of harm, transcends societies and nations. It is for this reason that a body like the United Nations can meaningfully raise and debate the question of what is proper punishment.

Something similar may be said about our general obligation to be just. There are, of course, many forms or departments of justice, one being retributive justice, which is concerned with the issue of proper punishment. However, a primary form of justice is what is often called distributive justice, the species of justice that has to do with fairness in the comparative treatment of others. A main part of our obligation to be just is the requirement that we treat others fairly. Limiting our present concern to distributive justice, I think that we can see that this obligation too is not completely determined by our relationship to others within a social arrangement, but rather by our general relationship to others across the societal and national boundaries of the world. The reason for this is not precisely because our obligation to treat others fairly extends to people in other lands. It does, of course, but so do other general obligations, the form of which *is* determined by our relationship to others within a social arrangement, such as the obligation to tell the truth. No, the reason, as with the issue of proper punishment and unlike the question of what is a joke or irony or borrowing, is that the issue of just treatment of others is not wholly culturally determined.[7] This is indicated, again, by the meaningfulness of international debate about the requirements of distributive justice. Thus, for this reason also the foundational role for human relationships in determining the form of various obligations does not entail moral relativism, at least not in the strong sense I have cited. That role, regarding a number of general obligations, relies upon social factors; and I have argued for it here in terms of just such obligations, obligations that are importantly socially determined. However, my general thesis—or the moral perspective I want to explore—does not require that all obligations are determined by our human relationship to others within a social setting. Fully developed, it does require that ultimately the *source* of all our obligations, including our obligations to prevent harm and to be just, is in our relationships to others. And I hope that I will have made such a view highly credible well before we are through with this enquiry.

We turn now to a second way that human relationships are foundational to the elements of ethics, or, more exactly, foundational to the element of obligation. To what extent are human relationships the *source* of our obligations, the ground on which our obligations rest? Once again we shall focus on various particular and general obligations that are familiar to most of us.

We have discussed several particular obligations in order to show how

---

7. This is not to deny that cultural or societal factors cannot, *within limits*, determine the form of distributive justice. We shall consider the extent of what may be called "communitarian" influence on the form of distributive justice in Chapter 8.

human relationships clarify or determine the form of these obligations: the obligation of parent to child, the filial obligation of child to parent, and the marital obligation of spouse to spouse. Friendship also, I suggested, illustrates the first foundational role for human relationships regarding obligation. In our present effort to see how human relationships are foundational to ethics in a second way, in being the source for our obligations, it is useful to begin by considering all of these various particular obligations together. For they share a common feature that allows us to address them as a type. Particular obligations, of course, are obligations that obtain between particular persons—a son's obligation to his father, a husband's obligation to his wife, and so on—as opposed to one's various obligations to other persons in general, such as the obligation to tell the truth. This being the case, it becomes evident fairly quickly that the source of particular obligations must be some human relationship. This is so regarding particular obligations as a type for the simple reason that without the pertinent human relationship there would not be the particular obligation in question. Clearly, if parents have no offspring, they have no parental obligation to any offspring; if one has no parents, one has no filial obligation; and if one is not married, one has no marital obligation. These relationships, once entered, or once they come to exist, create their respective obligations. And they do so not merely as necessary conditions. In order for some particular person to have an obligation to some other particular person, it is necessary that both individuals exist. Such a condition—the existence of each—is a necessary condition for the obligation of the one to the other, but the bare fulfillment of this condition tells us nothing about the character of the obligation. On the other hand, the relationship between two individuals defines the type of particular obligation that obtains and that is created with the emergence of the relationship. In this way they are the source of the obligations they entail.

Turning this point, we find another way to see that relationships between particular persons are the source of the particular obligations attendant upon those relationships. Why is it that the obligations of a daughter to her parent are different in type from the obligations of a wife to her husband? And why is it that the obligations that hold in friendship are different in type from those that hold in other kinds of relationships, such as that between employer and employee? Is it not because the relationships are different in type and, being different, create different types of obligations? The point here is distinct from the point argued earlier. Earlier it was argued that human relationships clarify or determine the *individual form* that particular obligations take, so that the specific marriage relationship between two particular individuals would determine the form that their respecting and honoring one another would take. Here the point is that, even before we know anything about the particular individuals in a marriage relationship and the particularities of that relationship, we know that the attendant obligations are different *in type* from those that offspring have to their parents. Even if in both marital and child-parent relationships there is an obligation to respect and honor, still in an evident way different types of respect and honor are required. Why? Because the relationships are different in type and create different types of obligations.

The obligations of a relationship between persons, we may say, are a function of the relationship that creates them. In fact, it seems that keeping the obligations of a relationship is, or is an essential part of, maintaining that relationship. In a marriage relationship, if one spouse is unfaithful, he or she vitiates or may even destroy the relationship. Quite irrespective of its legal status, the moral status of their relationship may change. A similar comment may be made regarding the child-parent relationship. If a parent feels that filial duty is severely violated by an offspring, that parent may say, "I no longer have a son." Again, such a comment may be essentially correct morally, irrespective of the unchanged biological relationship. The point is perhaps clearer regarding friendship, where there is no legal or biological correlate to be confused with the moral relationship. Thus the particular relationships we have been discussing not only determine the specific form of the obligations associated with them, but these relationships create the obligations in the first place. The fact that one person is related to another as a child to a parent creates the obligation of filial piety, and the further fact that the child and parent are the persons they are, with certain expectations, desires, and so on, in a specific child-parent relationship, determines the individual form of that obligation. Clearly, we would not get to the latter without the former. The latter is the first way that relationships are foundational to obligation, while the former is the second way. In a clear way, then, at least regarding these particular obligations, the second way that relationships are foundational to obligation underlies the first way.

Let us now turn our attention to various general obligations, for I would maintain that human relationships are their source as well. The point is a little harder to see here, perhaps, until we remind ourselves that we stand in various general human relationships to others, as we have seen. Take the general obligation to tell the truth. This is an obligation that speakers have to hearers, and, as I have argued, its specific form depends on socially determined expectations among a speaker's hearers. But, moreover, it is the general relationship between speaker and hearers that is the source of the obligation. This is so even regarding the special case of being truthful to oneself, wherein one is related to oneself as speaker to hearer. If there were no such general relationship between speaker and hearers, there would be no obligation of speakers to tell the truth. More carefully put, if persons were not related so that speakers were called upon to impart information to hearers, there would be no obligation to tell the truth. True, it is hard to imagine such a world and its severely truncated form of human communication, but if we grant the antecedent we must grant the consequent.

The same point can be seen regarding the general obligation not to steal. This obligation has its source in the general relationship that we have to property owners. If we lived in a social arrangement in which nothing was privately owned, in which all property was communally owned, then we would have no such relationship to others and no taking of property would constitute stealing. In such a society there might well be obligations that regulated the use of property and amounted to obligations to share what was commonly owned. However, such obligations are distinct from the obligation not to steal, which forbids taking the property of another without permission, and they would have their source in a different general relationship.

I think that we can say something similar about various other general obligations, such as the obligation to keep promises and obligations of civility. These obligations, too, appear to have their source in some general relationship between human beings, and in their case as well, that relationship exists within some social arrangement. Is it always the case that the general relationship that creates a corresponding general obligation is embedded in a social arrangement? I think not. Consider once more the general obligations to prevent harm and to be just. The individual form of these obligations, I argued earlier, is not determined societally. Analogously, the source of these obligations may not be a general relationship within a society. However, if this is so, it still may be that the source of these obligations is in general human relationships, just not general relationships within and defined by a society.

What emerges from these reflections, then, is this: the source of various particular and general obligations is human relationships. In fact, regarding the particular obligations discussed, such as the obligation to respect and honor one's spouse, keeping the obligation is, or is a part of, maintaining the relationship. And something similar could be argued for various general obligations. Keeping one's obligation to tell the truth is at least a part of maintaining one's general relationship to one's hearers. The case I have presented, once more, embraces various obligations, not all. Still, even if I have not shown that all obligations have their source in human relationships, if the argument presented so far is right, it has been shown that at least some obligations are created by, have their source in, human relationships. This is enough to put relationship morality at odds with traditional theories of obligation, and I think that it would be well to say something about that opposition at this point.

If the source of our obligations, or at least of various of our obligations, is human relationships, then neither John Stuart Mill nor Immanuel Kant was quite right. For if the source of at least some of our obligations lies in our relationships, then our obligations are not created by the maximizing of happiness, as Mill held, nor is their source in the moral law, in Kant's understanding of the moral law. That neither Mill nor Kant was quite right should not be shocking. Both Mill's utilitarian and Kant's deontological ethical theories have problems independent of my reflections. I do not want to discuss at length the faults of these ethical theories: that ground has been well trod. However, one or two reminders of their faults may be in order, to make it clear it is no great deficit for relationship morality that it is not in accord with either. At the same time, it seems to me, both utilitarian and deontological ethical intuitions respond to significant features of our moral lives; and I shall also want to bring out the consanguinity between the pair of these informing intuitions and relationship morality. But first a reminder of one or two faults of utilitarianism and deontological ethics considered as theories of obligation.

In his *Groundwork of the Metaphysic of Morals* Kant illustrates the working of his categorical imperative by applying it to several personal maxims and in a famous passage argues that the personal maxim that one can make a promise without the intention to keep it fails the test of universalizability.[8] Hence, for Kant, it is always wrong to make promises with such an intention. Pretty clearly, Kant's point can be extrapolated to lying, which he closely associates with making false promises.[9] Transferring Kant's reason-

---

8. Immanuel Kant, *Groundwork of the Metaphysic of Morals*, Akademie edition, 422; H. J. Paton, *The Moral Law, or Kant's Groundwork of the Metaphysic of Morals*, 3d ed. (New York: Barnes & Noble, 1956), 89–90.

9. Kant, *Groundwork of the Metaphysic of Morals*, Akademie edition, 402–3; in Paton's *The Moral Law*, 70–71.

ing to lying leads us to the conclusion that it is always and everywhere wrong to lie, a conclusion that has seemed morally preposterous to many.[10] The sort of case that raises a problem for Kant is that involving a person ill and in danger of dying who asks an unhappy question, a truthful answer to which might be traumatic. One can imagine the details. A man precariously recovering from a heart attack asks about his daughter, who, it so happens, has just been in a terrible accident and is herself near death. He expectantly looks for a reply. The truth, however, might literally kill him. Later we can tell him, but not now. Yet Kant seems to be in the position of insisting that we "dutifully" tell him the truth, regardless of the consequences. To many, Kant's rigid absolutism in this instance seems wooden. It stands in contrast with the understanding of the spirit of the moral law that allows one to remove one's sheep from a pit on the sabbath.[11]

Mill does better here. In his *Utilitarianism* he actually considers a case of someone who is "dangerously ill" and argues that in such a case there is an exception to the rule of veracity.[12] But Mill is not quite right, it seems. The reason why it is wrong to tell the truth in this sort of case, for Mill, is that "expediency" requires us not to tell the truth. That is, in such cases, Mill argues, not telling the truth maximizes happiness. However, this does not seem to be quite right. In the case of the heart attack patient it is not maximizing his happiness or the general happiness that justifies, even requires, us to withhold the truth from him. Rather, what does so is, roughly, the moral importance of our not endangering his life. Even if we somehow knew that our telling him the truth and his resultant death would greatly increase the happiness of others, we still ought to withhold the truth from him.

Moreover, beyond these considerations, there are counterexamples to Mill's hedonistic utilitarianism, as well as further counterexamples to Kant's deontological ethical theory. Mill, for instance, is committed to giving moral sanction to the happy sadist whose pleasure outweighs the pain he inflicts, and so on. For Kant, it can be argued, many morally irrelevant "maxims" will pass the test of the categorical imperative and qualify as moral duties. For instance, there seems to be no impossibility or contradiction in willing as a universal law the maxim "Tie your left shoestring first,"

10. See, for instance, A. C. Ewing, *Ethics* (New York: Macmillan, 1965), 58.
11. Matt. 12.12.
12. John Stuart Mill, *Utilitarianism* (Indianapolis: Hackett, 1979), 22.

which accordingly would become a duty on Kant's view as he seems to understand it.[13]

So, as we remind ourselves, there are problems with both Mill's and Kant's ethical theories; and hence, it is no great embarrassment that relationship morality denies each. (There are of course other versions of such theories, and in Chapter 3 we shall look at a different construction of Kant's theory and in Chapter 8 return to other, nonhedonistic versions of utilitarianism.) Still, in spite of their difficulties, Mill and Kant each highlight an important, and opposite, aspect of morality: one the moral relevance of good effects for obligation, the other the moral irrelevance of good effects for obligation. More to our present point, each in his ethical thinking points toward relationship morality.

For Mill, the primary principle of moral action is the greatest-happiness principle, or the principle of utility, which tells us that right actions are those that produce the greatest amount of happiness. As Mill makes clear, the happiness he means is the general happiness, that is, the happiness of all those affected by the action in question. On Mill's view, then—although Mill does not say so—each of our actions puts us into a moral relationship with all those it affects. For Kant, the test for right action is embodied in the categorical imperative and is the test of consistent universalizability: if a personal maxim cannot without self-defeating contradiction be willed a universal law, acting on it is wrong; and if it can be willed a universal law, acting on it is a duty. At least Kant seems to have understood his categorical imperative such that we have an obligation to perform the action of a maxim that passes his test (the alternative is that such actions are permissible). In any case, for Kant, the application of the test of universalizability requires us to ask, What would happen if everyone followed my personal maxim of action? In effect, then, the application of Kant's categorical imperative requires us to consider the relationship between ourselves, in the pursuit of our personal maxims, and others, should they follow such a maxim. Thus both Mill and Kant in their very different ways look at the moral relationship between one person and others that is created by one's real or contemplated action. What is common to both their approaches is a moral appeal that considers the relationship between a person as a moral agent and other persons. It is in this way that the ethical theories of each point toward relationship morality, even if somewhat indirectly.

13. This is one of William Frankena's criticisms of Kant's theory. Frankena, *Ethics*, 2d ed. (Englewood Cliffs, N.J.: Prentice-Hall, 1973), 32.

Furthermore, it is arguable that a consideration of human relationships implicitly underlies the ethical theories of both Mill and Kant. For one thing, as we have just seen, Mill, in making the maximization of the general happiness the criterion of moral rightness, implicitly looks to human beings in relationship to all others who are affected by their actions. For another thing, for Mill, happiness is the presence of pleasure and the absence of pain, and it is human relationships that often determine what is painful or pleasant (as when they determine what is embarrassing or what hurts one's feelings). Kant's view even more clearly must consider human relationships. Perhaps Kant's clearest illustration of the working of the categorical impera-tive is contained in his discussion of making false promises. He argues that the personal maxim that one can make a promise without the intention to keep it cannot be generalized without contradiction. What is the contradic-tion? It is that if everyone made promises without the intention of keeping them, promise making would carry no weight and would lose its point: the generalized maxim is contradictory in that it is self-defeating or pointless. But, clearly, this pointlessness arises from expectations changing because the social relationship involved in promise making changes.

So, although relationship morality, strictly, is at odds with the ethical theories of both Mill and Kant, both Mill and Kant in their respective ways give us some reason to look to relationships as the source of obligation. But they did more than provide an account of the source of obligation (or its "foundation," to use a word they share).[14] They also provided a "criterion" for obligation, or right action, in the sense in which Mill understands this term (which he uses interchangeably with "standard").[15] For Mill, the "criterion" for right action would provide the common feature of all right actions and, more than that, their necessary and sufficient condition (as opposed to what others, following Wittgenstein, have come to mean by "criterion," namely, one of several strong indications, which may neverthe-less not be definitive in certain cases).[16] Both Mill and Kant, then, take up the old Socratic quest for the single defining characteristic of right action, the presence of which makes actions right and the absence of which makes

14. Mill regards the greatest-happiness principle as the "foundation of morals" (*Utilitarianism*, 7). The work in which Kant gives us the categorical imperative is of course entitled the *Groundwork [Grundlegung] of the Metaphysic of Morals.*

15. Mill, *Utilitarianism*, 1 and 3.

16. Wittgenstein says, for instance, that "in different circumstances we apply different criteria for a person's reading." *Philosophical Investigations*, sec. 164.

actions not right.[17] Each provides a principle that embodies a test, or criterion, for moral rightness, or obligation. And it is their proposed criteria for moral rightness that suffer the various counterexamples that critics bring forward. Moreover, their criteria are hard to apply at times. Mill's criterion requires us to consider the effects of our actions, but sometimes it is very hard to assess in advance the effects of our actions. Kant's criterion requires us to test our personal maxims of action. But which ones? It has been pointed out that if we test, *not* the personal maxim "I will make promises with the intention of breaking them when it suits me" (as Kant did), but rather the personal maxim "When breaking a promise is required in order to help someone, I will break it—if the promise is not crucially important and the help is," then Kant's criterion will allow as right some instances of promise breaking.[18]

These two problems relating to Mill's and Kant's proposed criteria—counterexamples and indefiniteness of application—may arise, not because they propose the wrong criteria, but because they propose some criterion. It may be that there is no criterion in Mill's strong sense, that there is no single defining feature of moral rightness. It is, in any case, a rather large Socratic assumption that there is, and it is one to which relationship morality is not committed. Relationship morality maintains that the *source* of various obligations is in human relationships, but it proposes no *criterion*, that is, no single defining feature, for moral rightness that will settle all questions of obligation. True, it in effect says, Look to your relationships. But this hardly amounts to a criterion for right action, for it is the substance of our many particular and general human relationships that does the work of determining the type and form of our obligations. Relationship morality provides guidance and an understanding of the ground of obligation, and may thereby help individuals to come to moral decisions, but it does not provide a working understanding of individual relationships, which, on its own view, is what is needed to determine obligation.

If what has been argued in this chapter is correct, it still may be that we can keep our obligations for prudential or pragmatic reasons. However, we have already seen enough, I think, to justify the judgment that it would be far better to keep our obligations to others with an awareness of the source of those obligations in the net of human relationships that embraces us all.

---

17. Socrates, in the *Euthyphro*, wants to know what piety is (5d), that is, for him, what "makes all pious actions pious" and will enable him to "say that any action of yours of another's that is of that kind is pious, and if it is not that it is not" (6d–e).

18. Frankena, *Ethics*, 32.

2
Relationship Morality and a Feminist Ethic of Care

At this point we must ask the question, What, if anything, is the difference between relationship morality and an ethic of care? That there is an ethic of care is recognized by many feminist thinkers, and they have done much to describe such a morality and to hone its conception. This is not to say that all feminists agree that an ethic of care can be equated with feminist ethics, for some argue that not only can they not be equated, but an ethic of care is not a feminist ethic at all.[1] Nevertheless a number of feminist thinkers have identified in their own moral experience a distinctive form of ethics that centrally embodies caring. For them, an ethic of care is a feminine ethic grounded in women's experience, and it is an ethic that focuses on relationships as opposed to rights and principles in considering what ought to be done. How, then, does such an ethic compare to relationship morality? There are differences, as well as similarities, and I want to bring out both in this chapter.

One author who early on reflected on a distinctive feminine ethic of care is Carol Gilligan. She finds that there is a difference between the morality of men and the morality of women. As Gilligan sees it, the morality of men centers on a concern with competing rights and the principled resolution of such conflicts, while for women morality is more a matter of caring and centers around responsibility and relationships. The first is a morality of

---

1. Rita C. Manning makes this point, although she herself argues for an ethic of care. Manning, *Speaking from the Heart: A Feminist Perspective on Ethics* (Lanham, Md.: Rowman & Littlefield, 1992), 137. A feminist who criticizes an ethic of care is Sarah Lucia Hoagland; see her "Some Thoughts About 'Caring,'" in *Feminist Ethics*, ed. Claudia Card (Lawrence: University Press of Kansas, 1991).

rights in which there is a paramount concern not only with the exercise of one's own rights but also with not interfering with the exercise of the rights of others. The second is a morality of relationships in which there is a greater concern with omission, a concern about not helping those with whom one shares a relationship, to whom one has a responsibility.[2]

A good part of Gilligan's concern is with psychological investigations of moral development. A notable example of such work is Lawrence Kohlberg's study of the moral development in children, which led him to postulate that there were some six stages in moral development. The highest two of these six stages are characterized by an appeal to universal principles of justice, in accord with what Gilligan sees as the masculine conception of rights-centered morality. When Kohlberg's sequence of six stages is used as a basis of evaluation, women, Gilligan observes, appear to be deficient in moral development. However, she suggests, this may be the result of Kohlberg's conceiving of moral development solely in masculine terms. The empirical study that led to his six-stages theory followed the development of eighty-four boys over a twenty-year period. No girls were included. Gilligan believes that if "one begins with the study of women and derives developmental constructs from their lives," one will find a second, relationship-oriented conception of morality and come to a very different understanding of moral development.[3]

Gilligan did in fact undertake such a study, and in it she found indications of just these two different conceptions of morality, the one masculine and the other feminine. This difference emerges, for instance, in her interviews of two eleven-year-old children called Amy and Jake. Kohlberg's method involved interviewing his subjects, asking them questions about how they would deal with certain moral problems. One such problem devised by Kohlberg is what might be called the Heinz dilemma, and Gilligan uses it in her own study. The dilemma as it is presented to Amy and Jake is this: Heinz's wife is dying; he cannot afford the life-saving drug she needs; and the druggist will not reduce its price. After being presented with the dilemma, both Amy and Jake are asked, "Should Heinz steal the drug?" Jake, Gilligan tells us, is clear that Heinz should steal the drug. He sees the dilemma as a conflict between "the values of property and life" and reasons that life is worth more than money. That is, although Gilligan does not bring this out, he implicitly sees the issue as one about the conflict of rights,

2. Carol Gilligan, *In a Different Voice: Psychological Theory and Women's Development* (Cambridge: Harvard University Press, 1982), 17–23.

3. Ibid., 19.

the druggist's right to property and Heinz's wife's right to live, and he is clear which takes priority. Asked about the circumstance that Heinz would be breaking the law, Jake says, "The laws have mistakes." Jake sees the moral dilemma, in his words, to be "sort of like a math problem with humans," with a clear resolution. While Gilligan thinks that Jake's moral thinking would be placed at stages three and four on Kohlberg's scale, she also observes that Jake's ability to bring logic to bear, and his seeing the difference between morality and law, point "toward the principled conception of justice that Kohlberg equates with moral maturity."[4]

Amy's response is quite different. She does not think that Heinz should steal the drug. When she is asked why he should not, she does not consider property or law, Gilligan says, but instead the possible effects that stealing could have on the relationship between Heinz and his wife. (Amy says, "If he stole the drug, he might . . . have to go to jail, and then his wife might get sicker. . . . So, they should really just talk it out.") Amy, Gilligan observes, does not see the dilemma as having an internal structure with a clear resolution, as Jake did. "Seeing a world comprised of relationships," she finds the difficulty to be in the druggist's not responding to the wife's needs. The solution she proposes is to make the druggist more appreciative of the wife's need or, if that fails, to appeal to others for help.[5]

A number of other interview cases are brought forward by Gilligan to fill out and substantiate her claim that there is a distinct women's morality, and in the course of her discussion she identifies several features of her understanding of feminine ethics that bear on our particular concern. For instance, Gilligan says that Amy construes the Heinz dilemma in terms of "a network of connection, a web of relationships that is sustained by a process of communication."[6] Amy's concern with relationships between human beings, then, is with close relationships, with relationships between persons who are at least acquainted, for it is such relationships that are sustained by communication. Again, another subject, Karen, who is eight years old, when asked to think about the moral question which friends she should play with, "describes a network of relationships that includes all of her friends."[7] The relationships here are, once more, close relationships, relationships with friends or acquaintances. Another subject, a twenty-five-year-old law student, is asked, "Is there really some correct solution to moral

4. Ibid., 25–27.
5. Ibid., 27–29.
6. Ibid., 32.
7. Ibid., 33.

problems, or is everybody's opinion equally right?" She answers that she does not think that everybody's opinion is equally right and goes on to say that in seeking a right answer it is important to consider what helps us to live in harmony with everybody else. In response to a follow-up question she says, "There are certain things that you come to learn promote a better life and better relationships and more personal fulfillment."[8] Here too the relationships of moral importance seem to be close, even personal, in nature. Are the human relationships that are central to feminine ethics just those that one has with friends, relatives, and people one is acquainted with? One can get that impression. However, at one point, Gilligan says, "The moral imperative that emerges repeatedly in interviews with women is an injunction to care, a responsibility to discern and alleviate the 'real and recognizable trouble' of this world."[9] And this strongly suggests that the morally relevant relationships in women's morality, as Gilligan sees it, include relationships that the individual has to persons never met. Another signal aspect of feminine ethics is emphasized in this quotation: the place of caring. Gilligan sees it as the essential element of feminine ethics, and, for Gilligan, the central place of caring is what distinguishes the moral perspective of women from that of men. Hence, within the morality of women she finds an "ethic of care."[10] In fact, though, Gilligan allows that there are two "images" deeply involved in human morality and its development. One is the image of a web, or network, which relates to women's experience of interconnection, and it is this experience that gives rise to an ethic of care. The second image is that of hierarchy, which relates to the experience of inequality; this experience gives rise to an ethic of justice and fairness.[11] The first correlates with the moral point of view of women; the second with that of men. But both, Gilligan comes to conclude, are involved in moral maturation. She observes that the men and women in a study of college students she conducted, though they start from "the different ideologies of justice and care," come to "a greater understanding of both points of view and thus to a greater convergence in judgment."[12] In the end the two modes of moral experience are "connected," and "both perspectives converge."[13]

8. Ibid., 20–21.
9. Ibid., 100.
10. Ibid., 174.
11. Ibid., 62–63.
12. Ibid., 167.
13. Ibid., 174. It is interesting to note that Kohlberg came to hold a similar view. For him the final stage of moral development involves an "integration of justice and care that forms a single moral principle." Lawrence Kohlberg, *The Psychology of Moral Development*, vol. 2 of *Essays on*

Several issues have come into, or returned to, prominence following Gilligan's research. These include the issue of the extent to which gender (what counts as feminine or masculine) is socially determined and the issue of the extent Gilligan's findings hold only for white middle-class women and men but not for women and men of other groups.[14] Such issues are not to be dismissed. However, given our precise concern we can set such issues to one side. We can because our concern is to compare an ethic of care that focuses on relationships with relationship morality in the conception we are developing. And this concern remains whether an ethic of care, as Gilligan presents it, is distinctly feminine or not and whether what is feminine is socially determined or not; and this concern remains whether or not an ethic of care is feminine across ethnic boundaries.

Still, it may serve our purposes to be clear on the extent to which Gilligan and others see an ethic of care as a *feminine* ethic. As I observed, not all feminist thinkers regard an ethic of care as a feminist ethic. In fact, since the publication of Gilligan's *In a Different Voice*, there have been, among feminists, both negative and positive critical reactions to the idea of a feminine ethic of care. Among those who have tried to develop the conception of an ethic of care in a positive way are, for instance, Nel Noddings and Rita Manning.[15] Another feminist thinker who has critically and helpfully commented on Gilligan's idea of a feminine ethic of care, or a "female ethic," as she calls it, is Jean Grimshaw.[16] She agrees that Gilligan's work, and that of others, has provided evidence "that women often perceive the maintenance of relationships as very important in their lives, and see it as a moral priority."[17] However, she urges us to be cautious in drawing conclusions from Gilligan's evidence. It does not allow us to conclude that no men have the perspective of an ethic of caring and

---

Moral Development (San Francisco: Harper & Row, 1984), 344; quoted by Lawrence Blum in "Gilligan and Kohlberg: Implications for Moral Theory," in *An Ethic of Care: Feminist and Interdisciplinary Perspectives*, ed. Mary Jeanne Larrabee (New York: Routledge, 1993), 57. Blum goes on to observe that, even so, "the general tenor of [Kohlberg's] work makes it clear that he regards care as very much the junior partner in whatever interplay is meant to obtain between the two moral perspectives" (57).

14. Carol B. Stack, "The Culture of Gender: Women and Men of Color," in *An Ethic of Care*, 108–11.

15. Nel Noddings, *Caring: A Feminist Approach to Ethics and Moral Education* (Berkeley and Los Angeles: University of California Press, 1984); Manning, *Speaking from the Heart*.

16. Jean Grimshaw, *Philosophy and Feminist Thinking* (Minneapolis: University of Minnesota Press, 1986).

17. Ibid., 210.

relationships, nor that all women do.[18] But this caveat is offered as a clarification, not as a criticism, for Grimshaw is sure that Gilligan would agree. Gilligan's claim, properly understood, Grimshaw points out, is that women more commonly have what Gilligan has identified as a feminine approach to moral problems. Gilligan does say that "the different voice I describe is characterized not by gender but theme."[19] And in a work published four years after *In a Different Voice* Gilligan says explicitly that "the care perspective in my rendition is neither biologically determined nor unique to women," though she adds that "the focus on care in moral reasoning, although not characteristic of all women, is characteristically a female phenomenon" in the populations she studied.[20] Allowing, then, that Grimshaw has rightly understood Gilligan's claim, as it seems she has, the idea of a feminine ethic of care remains intact.

Still, as Grimshaw sees it, the difference between men's and women's moral perspectives may be hard to describe. And it may be that Gilligan has not altogether correctly characterized that difference. For Gilligan, the use of moral principles to resolve a moral problem is associated with a masculine rights ethic. Against this idea, Grimshaw argues that women too operate with moral principles. As Kohlberg distinguished between rules and universal principles, so Grimshaw distinguishes between rules and principles. For Grimshaw, a principle is best expressed as "Consider . . ." "Consider whether your action will harm others" is a principle. Rules are more specific, such as the moral rule against killing. While rules require reflection, as on what counts as killing, they require relatively little compared to principles. Moral principles, in contrast to rules, invite contextual reflection and consideration of the particular. Grimshaw allows that there is no hard distinction between moral rules and principles, but still, she holds, there is a distinction. In the light of that distinction she maintains that it is superficial and wrong to say that men uphold moral principle, while the " 'weaker' (and female) task of maintaining relationships" falls to women. In order to support her point she brings forward a case from her own background. Both her father and mother believed that it was wrong for a woman and a man to live together when they were not married, she tells us. When her sister did just this, her father would no longer visit her, for he felt that his doing so would condone her behavior. He would allow her to visit him, but only in the absence of the man she was living with.

18. Ibid., 193.
19. Gilligan, *In a Different Voice*, 2.
20. Carol Gilligan, "Reply to Critics," reprinted in *An Ethic of Care*, 209 and 212.

Grimshaw's mother's response was different. Concerned with maintaining care and her relationships with her daughter and her children, Grimshaw's mother continued to visit the sister in her home. One may be tempted to see Grimshaw's father as a person of principle here, while her mother is not, but this would be wrong, Grimshaw observes. Her father had a principle that strongly guided his action: Consider whether your behavior will condone that which you think to be morally wrong. Her mother also had this principle. But her mother had another principle as well: Consider whether your behavior will stand in the way of maintaining care and relationships. The latter principle overrode the former when Grimshaw's mother saw that she could not both express disapproval of her daughter's action and maintain her relationship with her. It is not the case that Grimshaw's father upheld principle and her mother did not, on this analysis. The difference is that they gave different priorities to their principles. Grimshaw insists upon this interpretation, which brings out the role of moral principles in her mother's ethic, because it corrects the idea that women act "intuitively" without any clear process of moral reasoning.[21] To this extent, then, Grimshaw qualifies Gilligan's description of the difference between men's and women's ethical approaches. However, she has no quarrel with the claim that women give "moral priority" to maintaining relationships. In fact this is a prominent feature of her mother's moral reflection.

Now let us compare relationship morality with both Gilligan's ethic of care and Grimshaw's construction of women's—or at least her mother's—moral reflection. I shall begin by comparing relationship morality with Gilligan's thinking and Grimshaw's thinking taken separately and then go on to compare relationship morality with two important elements of their shared thinking. Gilligan sees that there is a kind of feminine ethical development that heeds relationships with friends and others and sees as paramount maintaining this web of relationships. Several of her subjects, following this moral perspective, try not to offend or to exclude others and in this way maintain a network of friends or create harmony in their close relationships. Two comments are in order. First, relationship morality, in the conception I am developing, is not a morality that gives paramount importance to maintaining in a harmonious way friendships and close personal relationships. To be sure, such relationships are important for relationship morality, but there are other sorts of human relationships as

21. Grimshaw, *Philosophy and Feminist Thinking*, 207–11.

well, general relationships, which, for relationship morality, are equally foundational. Second, Gilligan sees masculine ethics as seeking a reasonable resolution of moral conflicts in accord with moral principles, while feminine ethics does not rely upon principle in this way. This, I think, is or points toward a signal element of similarity between the moral development of women as presented by Gilligan and relationship morality in my conception. For what I mean by relationship morality is a morality that does not put principle first in that it does not regard principle as the ground or foundation of morality. (I shall have more to say about moral principles and acting on principle in Chapters 3 and 6.) I do not mean to say that relationship morality excludes any role for moral principles, and it may be that an ethic of care, in Gilligan's conception, gives no or too little role to principles. Still, I think that there is an important area of agreement here, as against much ethical theorizing.

Grimshaw, of course, as we have seen, argues that women in their ethical thinking use moral principles as much as men. She may well be correct, and I do not wish to deny her assertion. Her offered distinction between rule and principle is understandable (and would remain so even if some moral principles should turn out to demand, "Do such and such," instead of "Consider such and such," as I think some do). Accordingly, her reconstruction of her mother's moral reasoning in the case she considers is coherent. Also, Grimshaw's reconstruction is not at odds with relationship morality, even if it does oppose Gilligan's analysis. However, what Grimshaw characterizes as her mother's ethic is not a filled-out relationship morality in my sense. For one thing, the relationships that are important in it seem once again to be close personal relationships—the relationship between mother and daughter being the one that figures in the case Grimshaw discusses. In the case of her mother's moral principle, maintaining relationships seems to amount to keeping on friendly terms with those with whom one has certain close relationships, as opposed to keeping obligations to those with whom one has either particular or general relationships. And keeping obligations generated by both particular and general relationships is, for relationship morality, involved in maintaining relationships. For another thing, there is no indication that relationships determine obligations or their form; rather, Grimshaw sees two principles in conflict in her mother's ethical thinking, and one principle—maintaining relationships—overrides the other.

Gilligan and Grimshaw, though they may have their differences, agree on two important elements of the ethical approach of women, which together nearly constitute a feminine ethic of care. Both of these elements invite significant comparison with relationship morality. One has to do with the place of human relationships in an ethic of care; the other has to do with the central place of caring in that ethic. I shall discuss them in order.

The place of human relationships in morality. Both Gilligan and Grimshaw agree that, for women, maintaining relationships with others is important in their lives and that women see this as a "moral priority." Relationship morality agrees with Gilligan and Grimshaw that human relationships do indeed have a moral priority (setting aside possible differences about what "maintaining" relationships entails). I believe that it is quite possible that Gilligan and Grimshaw are right that giving moral priority to human relationships is an element of a feminine ethic of care, that is, of an ethical approach that has been culturally assigned to women. But this cultural assignment does not make it any less properly basic to human morality, the morality of human beings, male and female, although such a cultural assignment may of course make it harder to appreciate the universal moral priority that is to be given to relationships. It remains, then, that relationship morality is in significant agreement with this element of an ethic of care, as Gilligan and Grimshaw present it. Still, regarding this element, relationship morality differs from or goes beyond Gilligan and Grimshaw in two noteworthy respects.

First, it does so in the way it spells out this moral priority. There are two subsidiary points here: (1) For relationship morality, relationships are important in that specific relationships determine the individual form of the obligation appropriate to the relationship in question (a concern of Chapter 1) and also in that they are the very source of the type of obligation that obtains (also a concern of Chapter 1). (2) For relationship morality, it is not only relationships to those near us that have moral priority; to the extent Gilligan and Grimshaw mean close personal relationships, relationships to those we know, there is a difference between the conception of a feminine ethic that emerges in their work and relationship morality. To what extent do they mean such close relationships? At least to some extent, as we have seen. But also, as we have seen, there is some indication that relationships to other people of the world beyond our immediate ken are included. Other feminist authors, it may be noted, more clearly recognize that our relationships to persons who are not in our ken have moral priority. I believe that Rita Manning, for one, sees this. She says that "when we are committed to an ethic of care, we see ourselves as part of a network of care and our obligations as requiring a caring response to those who share these networks and to those whose need creates an obligation to respond."[22] Later, when she discusses "caring for persons," while she mostly considers caring for those with whom we have a close personal relationship (our children, our friends, our enemies), she is very clear that caring extends to the homeless.[23] Many of the homeless will be strangers to us, and to strangers, she says, we are related "metaphorically" and "metaphysically."[24] On the other hand, Nel Noddings sees caring as possible only in close and intimate relationships in which the care given is acknowledged.[25] And others, in their discussions of Gilligan's work, assume that, for Gilligan, "care morality is about the particular agent's caring for and about the particular friend or child with whom she has come to have this particular relationship."[26] Relationship morality is closer to an ethic of care when such an ethic allows a moral priority to relationships with those half a world away as well as to those we know intimately.

The second way that relationship morality goes beyond Gilligan and Grimshaw, regarding the place to be given to human relationships, is this: relationship morality sees human relationships as foundational to *all* of morality, including the moral rights of others—or, put more circumspectly, it is concerned to determine the extent to which human relationships are foundational to all of morality. This is a difference between a feminine ethic of care and relationship morality even though, as we have noted, Gilligan gives a place in full moral development to both (feminine) caring for others in relationships and (masculine) justice, with its concerns for rights. I have two comments to make on Gilligan's synthesis: (1) She makes it for good reason, for both caring for others in relationships and respecting the rights of others are parts of the coherent whole of ethics; and if they were at odds, there would be, not just a practical moral dilemma of the sort that can arise in the lives of individual persons, but an unresolvable tension between some main elements of morality. My allowing this, it should be appreciated, is not tantamount to saying that relationship morality gives equal status to relationships and rights. For relationship morality, relationships remain morally prior to rights (in a way we shall come to see in Chapter 9). (2) Ironically, Gilligan *does* give something like equal status to rights and

22. Manning, *Speaking from the Heart*, xiv.
23. Ibid., 89 ff, and 96–97.
24. Ibid., 102.
25. Noddings, *Caring*, 69.
26. Blum, "Gilligan and Kohlberg," 51; and cf. Owen Flanagan and Kathryn Jackson, "Justice, Care, and Gender: The Kohlberg-Gilligan Debate Revisited," in *An Ethic of Care*, 70.

relationships, to justice and caring, since for her they are two converging parts of our mature moral development. Thus she finally mitigates or even rejects the idea that relationships have a moral priority, as relationship morality does not. For relationship morality, moral rights are a part of morality, to be sure, as is virtue, human good, and obligation. But if relationship morality, fully formed, is correct, then human relationships are prior to rights because they are foundational to all of these elements of ethics, including rights (as I shall argue in Chapter 9).

The importance of caring in morality. Gilligan and Grimshaw tend to agree on the importance of caring in morality, which, for both, is involved in maintaining relationships. Grimshaw may be a bit more tentative than Gilligan, and, to be sure, she has reservations about the form of caring (whether it must be "maternal").[27] Still, there is fundamental agreement between them. To the extent that a feminine ethic of care regards caring as basic to respecting relationships, relationship morality is in essential accord with a feminine ethic of care. As a feminine ethic of care sees a deep place for caring in the morality of women, so relationship morality sees a deep place for caring, or a like attitude, in all of morality. Why this is so for relationship morality, and must be so, we shall discuss at some length in succeeding chapters. For the present let it be sufficient to note the parallelism between a feminine ethic of care and relationship morality regarding caring, with two further brief comments. First, for relationship morality, there is a deep place in morality for caring or for some attitude in the *range* of caring. Later (in Chapter 5) we shall enquire into what other attitudes might be in this range. Second, relationship morality recognizes that there are forms of morality that are not animated by caring or by any like attitude. How this can be, if morality is at bottom relationship morality, it must be allowed requires some explanation (and it is to be given in Chapter 3 and at greater length in Part IV).

In the light of what we have seen in this chapter, it is fair to say that there are significant similarities between relationship morality and what feminists call an "ethic of care." In each there are cognate perceptions of the moral importance of relationships and caring (or a like attitude). In many ways there is a deeper consanguinity between relationship morality and a feminine ethic of care than between relationship morality and, say, a utilitarianism that takes as primary in morals something like the principle of utility. However, this does not deny the differences between relationship

27. Grimshaw, *Philosophy and Feminist Thinking*, 252.

morality and a feminine ethic of care, such as the difference over general relationships and the difference over the foundational role of relationships in determining obligations and rights. There is one further difference between feminine ethics, as discussed by Gilligan, Grimshaw, and others, and relationship morality that I should mention here. For relationship morality, the ultimate grounding of obligation, and finally of all morality, is a single but universal relationship between each and all, involving every human being. While I think a feminine ethic of care need not deny such an ultimate grounding, there is, as far as I know, no discussion of it by feminist authors. The nature of this underlying relationship, and its place in morality, we shall begin to take up in the next chapter.

3

Relationship Morality and the Person/Person Relationship

For relationship morality, the source of various particular and general obligations lies in the various human relationships that hold between people. Moreover, the ultimate grounding of all obligations, and finally of all morality, is a relationship between each and all, involving every person. It is time now to look at this ultimate relationship.

In this chapter I want to bring out, first, how this relationship, if it exists at all, exists between each person and all persons; second, how it is the ultimate ground of obligation; and third, how it is to be realized, the mode of discovery involved in its being realized. The postulated relationship before us is of course not a particular relationship (like that between a husband and wife) or even a general relationship (like that between a speaker and his or her potential hearers). It does not exist by virtue of one's being a spouse or speaker or by virtue of any other such "role," and it is not discernible in the way these more conventional relationships are. Yet, as I shall try to show, it is credible that there is such an ultimate relationship, for, arguably, it is discoverable.

Coming to a realization that one has this ultimate relationship to other persons, and that it is morally ultimate, is involved in a phenomenon of human experience that I shall call coming into the presence of persons. Coming into the presence of persons, in the sense I intend, is not a matter of being admitted into the presence of a personage, or a matter of encountering persons socially, or a matter of being physically near any person. Rather, coming into the presence of persons, in the definite sense I intend, involves coming into a realization of the inherent worth of persons. But there are other elements as well. In fact the phenomenon has four interlocking but distinct elements. We come into the presence of persons in this sense when (1) we attain an awareness of the moral necessity of treating persons not merely as a means; (2) we attain an awareness of a kind of personal relationship to those persons as persons; (3) we come to a sense of respect or reverence, of caring or love, for them as persons, or to some other affective attitude in this range; and (4) we realize the worth that they have by virtue of being persons and that we are related to them by virtue of their worth as persons. To come into the presence of a person, or of persons, in this sense, it is not necessary to come into any person's bodily presence. In fact, it is not necessary to have others clearly in mind as individuals. For in this sense one can come into the presence of a person, of some persons, or of all persons. However, this will take some showing. Furthermore, while there are these four distinct elements, the first three are contained in the fourth. Again, this will take some showing. In any case, each of the four elements is distinguishable. All four require some discussion.

1. The first element is, in essence, the awareness of the validity of a moral principle, "the ends principle": It is wrong to treat persons merely as means and not as ends. While there might be some debate over the exact formulation of this principle, it is nevertheless one that strikes most of us as having an apparent moral point. In moderately complex societies, if not in the human condition, it is necessary to rely upon others as means to various ends. This the principle allows. What it forbids is using others as a means only. What it forbids is "using" people to gain some end with no consideration of them beyond their usefulness as a means to that end. It allows us to call upon the plumber to fix our plumbing, but it forbids us to treat him merely as a mechanical implement. As I say, most of us, I believe, are aware of this principle's validity in one way or another, and we draw upon it when we countenance such condemnatory judgments as "You were just using her" and "You shouldn't treat anyone like a thing."

Kant formulated this principle as the "practical imperative." In his words, "Act in such a way that you always treat humanity, whether in your own person or in the person of any other, never simply as a means, but always at the same time as an end."[1] We should note that as Kant has formulated the principle it extends to all persons, including oneself—not just to other

1. Immanuel Kant, *Groundwork of the Metaphysic of Morals*, Akademie edition, 429; H. J. Paton, *The Moral Law, or Kant's Groundwork of the Metaphysic of Morals*, 3rd ed. (New York: Barnes & Noble, 1956), 96.

persons.[2] To some, perhaps, it may not be clear what treating oneself as a means comes to. Examples would be degrading or brutalizing oneself with no thought for one's own moral or other well-being. There is, I think, an important lack of symmetry between treating others merely as a means and treating oneself merely as a means: the ignoble act of sacrificing others for one's own end may well be treating others merely as a means, while the noble act of sacrificing oneself for the sake of others may well *not* be treating oneself merely as a means. When this lack of symmetry is brought into consideration, Kant's formulation of the principle to include oneself can be seen to be absolutely right. It is based on the accurate perception that all persons, including oneself, are equally persons.

Also in the *Groundwork of the Metaphysic of Morals* Kant of course formulated the categorical imperative. This principle, as we have seen (in Chapter 1), is open to various criticisms, even though it may be that we regularly use some principle rather like it in moral reasonings—as when we reason that what someone did was wrong because it obviously would be wrong if everyone did it. Some have thought that, for Kant, the categorical imperative and the practical imperative were different but equivalent expressions of the same moral law. And, it has been argued, they are equivalent at least in the sense that, while the categorical imperative may count as duties, or rule out as wrong, some actions to which the practical imperative does not apply, still, where they both apply they do not conflict.[3] Strictly, however, this issue is not part of our concern. Our present concern, rather, is solely with the principle that Kant formulated as the practical imperative. It is this principle that is widely recognized among ethical thinkers, even if its status and implications are debated. And this principle, in some form, is incorporated into our moral lives, although many have not explicitly formulated it any more than they have explicitly formulated the grammar of their speech. The first element of coming into the presence of persons, then, is the awareness that this basic moral principle applies to persons, all those we recognize as persons, by virtue of their being persons.

2. The second element of coming into the presence of persons is an

2. Actually, as Kant put his principle, it extends to all *human* persons. Paton observes in a footnote that given Kant's thinking, strictly, the formulation should be in terms of "rational nature as such," and not in terms of "humanity." Kant formulated the practical imperative in this way, Paton suggests, because the only persons we are acquainted with are human.

3. For a development of this point, see John E. Atwell's "Are Kant's First Two Moral Principles Equivalent?" *Journal of the History of Philosophy* 7 (1969).

awareness of a kind of personal relationship to persons. This element, while related to the first, is different from it. The relationship that figures here stands opposed to those relationships we have to others by merit of some official presence. We have official relationships to the president qua president and to the grocery clerk and the plumber qua grocery clerk and plumber. But while these relationships can be important for etiquette and, in accord with our earlier argument (in Chapter 1), for the recognition of certain moral obligations, they remain impersonal relationships in a significant sense. While these are relationships we have to persons, they are not relationships we have to persons qua objects of personal attitudes. As relationships between persons they can generate certain obligations, just as the relationship between speaker and hearer does, but like the latter, these relationships can exist in the absence of any personal attitude. Of course, grocery clerks and plumbers need not be regarded only as grocery clerks and plumbers, and the stranger to whom one imparts information need not be regarded in an impersonal way, but to the extent that they are, the relationships to them as persons is that of indifference. On the other hand, the kind of personal relationship that is of concern to us here is, in some way, the foundation of personal attitudes. The recognition of this relationship forms the basis of—or, better, finds expression in—those personal attitudes that are antithetical to indifference. This relationship is not identical with that defined by having respect for persons; rather, having respect for persons is one form or expression of a recognition of this relationship. And its recognition may also be expressed by the relationships defined by other personal attitudes, such as love and hate. It is a paradox of personal relations that one who hates another at least treats the other as a person, while one who is simply indifferent does not.[4]

An awareness of this kind of personal relationship to other persons is, of course, not unrelated to seeing them as persons in the first place. If it is destroyed or undetermined, then it becomes much easier to treat persons in ways that otherwise would be seen as inhuman. Thus, when a nation goes on a war footing, an effort may be made to dehumanize the enemy. Such an effort may involve substituting a neologism for a nationality or constantly and consistently characterizing the enemy as bestial. The same dehumanization may occur in various departments of life, but it is most obvious on a national scale during a war or the occupation or colonization of a territory.

4. This observation has been made more than once, as, for instance, by J. A. Brook in "How to Treat Persons as Persons," in *Philosophy and Personal Relations*, ed. Alan Montefiore (London: Routledge & Kegan Paul, 1973), 69.

Just here let me raise a question: If one appreciates the moral necessity of treating persons, or at least certain persons, not merely as a means, will one then be aware of this kind of personal relationship to them as persons? The answer to this question, I think, is no, not necessarily. Also, conversely, it may be that one can appreciate having this kind of personal relationship to others, as evinced in one's having a personal attitude toward them, and yet fail to see the moral necessity of not treating them merely as a means. On the one hand, it is possible for one to appreciate that others, as persons, are subsumed under the principles of morality and that therefore, *for the sake of the moral law,* it is necessary to treat them not merely as a means but such a recognition of our moral obligation to persons as persons requires no sense of kinship with them or even concern for them as persons. On the other hand, it is possible for one to come to feel that the ends principle does not fully apply to certain others—slaves or serfs or immigrants, for instance—and at the same time to have a personal attitude toward them, a sense of comradeship with them, because circumstances of war or oppression or societal vagary makes one a comrade with them in suffering, prejudice, or the like.

What emerges from reflecting on these possibilities is that there is an identifiable distinction between being indifferent to persons qua objects of morality and being indifferent to persons qua objects of personal attitudes. Overcoming each indifference involves, in part, attaining an awareness of the applicability of a specific truth. But they are different truths. To see that one truth applies to others is to see that a moral principle applies to them. To see that the other truth applies to others is to see that one stands in a kind of personal relationship to them as persons, a relationship the recognition of which may find expression in concern or love or hate, but not in indifference to them as persons.

Characterizing this relationship further, following P. F. Strawson, we might say that to recognize this relationship to other persons is to recognize an *involvement* with other persons. Strawson speaks of an "involvement or participation with others in inter-personal relationships," and he contrasts this involvement with "the objective attitude (or range of attitudes)."[5] We bring an "objective attitude" to the grocery clerk qua grocery clerk or the plumber qua plumber. Such an objective attitude opposes but does not exclude involvement: while having commerce with grocery clerks and

5. P. F. Strawson, "Freedom and Resentment," in *Studies in the Philosophy of Thought and Action,* ed. P. F. Strawson (New York: Oxford University Press, 1968), 79.

plumbers is different from knowing and liking them, the two attitudes do not exclude each other. Strawson's category of objective attitude embraces regarding others as objects of social policy or as objects of training or treatment. And, we should add, it includes, or can include, regarding others as objects of justice.

"Involvement or participation with others," on the other hand, includes "resentment, gratitude, forgiveness, anger [and] the sort of love which two adults can sometimes be said to feel reciprocally for each other." However, while Strawson's distinction is helpful, it is not clear that the kind of personal relationship we are seeking to characterize necessitates involvement in Strawson's sense. Involvement, for Strawson, it would seem, requires personal acquaintance. It is true that there is a strong sense of "personal relationship" that we reserve for long and thorough personal acquaintance. It was just this sense that appeared to be important for a feminist ethic of care. So far as this sense is concerned, it is right that individual acquaintance is required. But there are also personal relationships in another sense, closer to the sense we want, for which individual acquaintance is not required, which nevertheless are personal relationships that persons might conceivably have, and feel they have, toward others, even all others. For this sense, a personal relationship is indicated by a personal reaction or attitude, and for this sense, Strawson's "involvement or participation with others," if it requires personal acquaintance, is not necessary. Generals in charge of far-flung theaters of operation can feel a comradeship with the troops in their command without being acquainted with each. Nationalists typically have a sense of comradeship with all those of their nationality. In fact, if we look at the attitudes of involvement that Strawson lists, we find included resentment, gratitude, forgiveness, and anger, which, very often, individuals manifest toward those they have not personally met. Only the last attitude on the list—the sort of love that two adults can sometimes be said to feel reciprocally for each other—necessitates personal acquaintance.

The notion of involvement may be of some help to us, but perhaps not in Strawson's sense, not if his sense requires personal acquaintance. Involvement in such a conception, with such a requirement, contrasts with "the objective attitude," but so does involvement in a wider conception, which, I think, may provide us more help. I have in mind John Donne's sense when he wrote, Any man's *death* diminishes *me*, because I am involved in *Mankinde;* And therefore never send to know for whom the *bell* tolls; it tolls for *thee*."[6] Let us observe that in Donne's sense of "involvement" his relationship of involvement can be, and is asserted to be, to all persons, or to all of "Mankinde."

3. The third element of coming into the presence of persons is the attainment of reverence or respect for persons, of a sense of caring for them, of love for them, or of some other positive affective attitude in the respect/ love range. These attitudes constitute the affective dimension of coming into the presence of persons. Each, it seems initially, is a possible concomitant of the recognition of the intrinsic worth of persons.

In *The Religious Aspect of Philosophy* Josiah Royce discussed what amounts to just such a recognition of the intrinsic worth of persons.[7] He was concerned to distinguish between such a "moral insight" and "the mere tender emotion of sympathy." For Royce, there is to be found at the heart of moral conduct "no sentiment, no gush of pity, no tremulous weakness of sympathy, but a calm, clear insight."[8] Royce is of course correct to insist upon a distinction between our recognition of a moral truth about others and our sympathetic feelings toward others. An insight, or recognition, as such, is cognitive, being productive of belief or knowledge, while feelings of sympathy or pity, as such, are not. Yet, at the same time, while we should appreciate Royce's point, we should correct the impression it can create that the moral insight is totally independent of our feelings. A recognition can have an affective side or concomitant that is more than accidentally associated with it. In fact in some cases a lack of affection, or the wrong feelings, can be very strong, perhaps even conclusive, evidence that *no* recognition has taken place. And this, at a minimum, is the case with the moral insight. A lack of any affective response in the range of respect or sympathy toward persons strongly indicates that there has been no recognition of their worth as persons. Thus, tightly associated with the recognition of the intrinsic worth of persons is some affective response in this range.

4. The final element of coming into the presence of persons is linked to the third. It is the cognitive aspect of the recognition that persons have value by virtue of being persons, which we can abstract from the affective concomitant even if the two should in fact be inseparable. This fourth element is a recognition of the intrinsic worth of persons as persons, as opposed to their usefulness or worth for certain purposes we may have, be

6. Devotion XVII.

7. Josiah Royce, *The Religious Aspect of Philosophy* (New York: Harper & Brothers, 1968), 155–62.

8. Ibid., 155 and 157.

those purposes moral or immoral, exalted or prosaic. It is a recognition of the intrinsic worth that persons have as persons, as opposed to their moral worth or merit, or their esthetic worth, or indeed any earned or genetically endowed worth that persons may or may not have. As we shall see, this fourth element serves as the keystone to the other three, or, perhaps better, it contains the other three, ordering them as elements of its own structure.

More than one philosopher has placed near the center of morality a recognition of the inherent worth of persons. Royce did, and arguably, Kant did. But not all have understood this recognition of the inherent worth of persons in the same way. For Royce, the moral insight of which he spoke was a recognition that one's neighbor is a "self" as much as one is oneself. While the insight lasts—and it is an ephemeral thing for Royce—"the illusion of selfishness vanishes," and we see clearly that "The Other Life is as My Life." The way we come to the moral insight, for Royce, is through finally appreciating that others have experiences like our own. We realize that our neighbor, too, is "a mass of states of experiences, thoughts and desires, just as real as thou art," that our neighbor is in fact as real to us now as the experiences of "thy future self." That is, for Royce, integral to our realization of the worth of others is an appreciation of their existence as conscious beings, as experiencers, who hate, love, and feel pain just as we do. Kant, on the other hand, would regard the realization of the inherent worth of others rather differently. For Kant, persons, as rational beings, exist as ends in themselves. They are inherently valuable because they are rational beings capable of morality.[9] In Kant's view only rational beings can be fully moral. In short, for Kant, the realization of the intrinsic worth of persons is through, or identical with, a realization of persons' rationality and their consequent capacity to participate in the moral life.

There are, I think, reasons for not accepting either Royce's or Kant's construction of the moral perception of the worth of person (reasons we shall discuss in Chapter 7). Still, though Royce and Kant may differ regarding *how* the recognition of the intrinsic worth of persons is made, and regarding the analysis of that intrinsic worth, it remains that they agree on the recognition itself: the recognition that persons, by virtue of being persons, have an intrinsic worth.

Here, then, are the four elements of coming into the presence of persons. Now let me raise a question that will help us better understand how these

---

9. *Groundwork of the Metaphysic of Morals*, Akademie edition, 435; in H. J. Paton's *The Moral Law*, 102.

four elements are related to one another. How does the recognition, or realization, of the intrinsic worth of persons relate to the awareness that persons ought to be treated as ends and not merely as means? That is, how does the fourth element of coming into the presence of persons relate to the first element? Earlier we saw that one might appreciate the validity of the ends principle, the first element of coming into the presence of persons, and so treat persons as ends, and yet remain indifferent to persons as persons, as objects of personal relationships, and so lack the second element, an awareness of a personal relationship to others. Now, however, our question, put one way, is this: Is our acknowledging that persons ought to be treated as ends, the first element, tantamount to our realizing the intrinsic worth of persons, the fourth element? It is pertinent here to recognize that persons can be treated as ends out of a sense of moral duty. Clearly, if we treat persons as ends out of a sense of moral duty, we have acknowledged that they ought to be treated as ends. But have we thereby acknowledged the inherent value of persons? In fact, it has been suggested, to act out of a sense of duty is *not* to act for the sake of another.[10] Is this true?

Most of us, I suspect, would feel that there was a certain deficiency in human warmth on the part of a person who helped another person in need begrudgingly and solely out of a sense of duty. In the possible case we imagined earlier, in our discussion of the second element and its relation to the first, we postulated an individual who treats others as ends not begrudgingly, but solely out of a sense of duty. C. P. Snow, in his novel *The Affair*, provides a different sort of example. In Snow's novel a young academic has been accused of scientific fraud and dismissed from his university post. At a certain point a senior colleague, Skeffington, who had thought him guilty, comes to believe him innocent in the light of new evidence. Skeffington has no feeling of kindness toward the young academic. He does not perceive his value as a human being. He has no brotherly emotion toward him—only contempt, contempt toward an inferior who has had the bad taste to become the victim of an injustice. Recognizing the applicability of the ends principle to certain persons is distinct from, and does not require, having a personal attitude toward them, as we have seen. It of course *allows* having a personal attitude toward them, but the personal attitude may not be a positive one. As in Skeffington's case, it may be contempt. Skeffington and the sort of individual we postulated earlier are distinguishable. The individual we postulated earlier is aware of no personal attitude toward others but treats

10. Brook, "How to Treat Persons as Persons," 71.

them as ends out of a sense of duty. Skeffington treats the young academic as an object of justice—as deserving to be treated as an end, let us allow—and he has a personal attitude toward him, but it is contempt. Each, we might feel, exhibits a moral or human deficiency. We must, I think, respect the individual we postulated earlier and Skeffington as just individuals. And yet it is precisely in regard to such actions as theirs that we quite correctly are inclined to say that acting out of a sense of duty is *not* acting for the sake of others. It is acting for the sake of a principle.

It emerges that one can treat others as ends out of a sense of duty and so, in one way, be in accord with the first element of coming into the presence of persons (and, furthermore, do so even with *some* personal attitude: the second element), while *not* having realized the inherent worth of persons, that is, while lacking the fourth element. Treating others as ends in this way, though, is not to act for the sake of others. Some might see Kant as endorsing just such action as the only action of moral worth, given his apparent insistence that actions must be performed for the sake of duty in order to have moral worth.[11] What should we say of Kant here? Kant was acutely aware of the value of persons, of their "dignity." But as we have just reminded ourselves, he also seems to have thought that morality required acting out of a sense of duty. Would Kant then rush to embrace Skeffington? I suggest that he would not or need not. While the intricacies of Kant's moral thought are not altogether clear, and while his categorical imperative has its attendant problems, it is fairly easy to interpret his view consistently so that he would not sanction either Skeffington's moral demeanor or that of the individual who acts for the sake of the moral law with no personal attitude toward others. To do so we must distinguish between two conceptions of a sense of duty. We act out of a sense of duty in the first conception when we recognize the validity and applicability of the ends principle and treat others as ends only because the principle requires it. One can act out of a sense of duty in this conception without fully appreciating the inherent worth of persons or, indeed, while believing those persons one is treating as ends lack inherent worth. It is out of a sense of duty of this sort that Skeffington and our postulated individual act. We act out of a sense of duty in the second conception when we recognize the validity and applicability of the ends principle and so treat others as ends, *but* we recognize the validity and applicability of the ends principle precisely because we recognize

11. *Groundwork of the Metaphysic of Morals*, Akademie edition, 398; in H. J. Paton's *The Moral Law*, 66.

the inherent worth of others. A sense of duty of this sort is grounded in a realization of the worth of persons as persons and is impossible without the ground of such an awareness. When Kant says that for an action to have moral worth, it must be done from duty, as I would like to read him, he means a sense of duty in this latter conception.

Royce similarly thought that "the beginning of the real knowledge of duty to others" lay in a reflective process that leads to our appreciation of the value of others.[12] And now, I think, we can see the relationship between a recognition of the validity of the ends principle and a realization of the inherent worth of persons. The former is possible without the latter. But the latter sustains the former. One can recognize the ends principle as a valid principle given only a general sense of the requirements of morality, especially the requirements of justice. However, in order to see why the principle ultimately is valid, one must perceive beneath the varied forms of obligation the essential worth of persons.

At this point we are able to address two of the main concerns of this chapter. If persons, all persons, have intrinsic worth, then we have a relationship to persons, to all persons, that is a relationship to beings with intrinsic worth. And to realize the intrinsic worth of persons is to realize that we stand in this relationship to them. In Kant's terms, persons constitute a "kingdom of ends." This relationship might be called "the worth relationship," since it exists by virtue of the intrinsic worth of persons as persons. Or, because it exists between persons as persons, as opposed to persons as, say, spouses or parents or offspring, it might be called "the person/person relationship," and so I shall call it. Clearly, this relationship is one we have to all persons, since we have it to others simply by virtue of their being persons. This is the first main point I wanted to make in this chapter. Moreover—and this is the second main point I wanted to establish in this chapter—this relationship provides the ultimate ground for all obligation. The person/person relationship, as the relationship we have to beings of intrinsic worth, provides the ground for our obligations to such beings. A realization of our person/person relationship to others creates not a mere sense of duty toward others but a sense of duty grounded in a recognition of the intrinsic worth of persons—a sense of duty in the second conception attributable to Kant. The person/person relationship gives us not only the reason why the ends principle is valid but, as well, the reason why our varied and more specific obligations have moral force. Persons, as

12. Royce, *The Religious Aspect of Philosophy*, 155.

beings of intrinsic worth, *deserve* to be treated fairly and to be treated in all ways morally, as our ultimate relationship to them requires.

We have a third concern in this chapter, relating to the mode of realization, or discovery, that is involved in coming to see that we have the person/person relationship to others. Before I take up that concern, though, let me explore further the interrelationships between the elements of coming into the presence of persons. Our doing so, I believe, will help us further to appreciate the role of the person/person relationship in morality. What I want to bring out before we go on to our third concern is that the fourth element of coming into the presence of persons contains the other three elements.

Let us begin by looking at the relationship between the fourth element, which we may now characterize as a realization of the person/person relationship to others, and the second element, having an awareness of a kind of personal relationship to others. A recognition of our person/person relationship to others should, of course, be distinguished from a recognition of some kind of personal relationship to others (which would fulfill the second element). If a person feels contempt for others, he or she will be aware of a personal relationship to them, but not of their inherent worth. On the other hand, one's awareness of one's having the person/person relationship to others will be reflected in an affective attitude toward them in the respect/love range of personal attitudes, and such an attitude also expresses an awareness of a personal relationship to them. An awareness of the person/person relationship to others requires an awareness of a personal relationship to them, but not the other way around.

Next, let us reflect on the relationship between the fourth and the third element, between realizing the person/person relationship to others and coming to have an affective response to others such as respect or reverence or some like attitude in the respect/love range. Respect or love, or a personal attitude in their range, I think it must be allowed, expresses an awareness of the person/person relationship to those persons toward whom one has such an attitude. We can appreciate our responsibility to and for others, and that others are proper objects of moral obligation, compatibly with having indifference or even contempt for them as persons. However, to respond to others with respect or care or love for them as persons, we must in some sense appreciate their intrinsic worth as persons. Such an attitude toward others is the affective expression of an awareness of their worth as persons, and such an attitude, accordingly, indicates the recognition of the worth of those others, that is, of one's person/person relationship to them. But, conversely, does this recognition require such an attitude? Is it possible to recognize the worth of persons without feeling respect or love or having some other such attitude toward them? Although Skeffington did not recognize the inherent worth of the young academic as a person, could he have while feeling only contempt for him? Earlier I said that lacking a positive attitude, an attitude in the respect/love range, is at a minimum strong, and perhaps even conclusive, evidence that no such recognition had been made. But is it, in fact, a necessary condition? This is a perplexing question. W. G. Maclagan suggests that the recognition of the worth of persons and the response that expresses this recognition should be thought of as "integrated." For Maclagan, the response is always Agape, and Agape and the recognition of the worth of persons are "only different facets of a single experience."[13] On this view, as he says, "it is *in* Agape that we see the significance of persons." However, this thesis may be too strong. It may be, alternatively, that the recognition of the worth of persons *leads to* Agape (or some other attitude in the respect/love range). If so, there may be a stage at which there is the recognition and, as yet, no fully developed positive affective attitude. After the passage of time, though, it could be that the lack of a response in the respect/love range showed conclusively that no recognition had been made, regardless of the regularity of pious mouthings about the inherent worth of one's neighbor. In any case, surely this much is correct: an attitude contrary to Agape—like contempt or indifference—is evidence of a *lack* of awareness of the worth of persons. And it also remains that one who recognizes the value of another would feel the fittingness of respecting, revering, or loving the other; and to the extent this tendency is not manifested in one's actions and feelings, the indications are that no such recognition has been made. In this way, or these ways, an affective attitude in the Agape, or respect/love, range is a part of the recognition of the worth of persons.

Now I think we are in a position to make out how the first three elements of coming into the presence of persons are related to the fourth—how, in fact, the first three are contained in the fourth.

To recognize the intrinsic worth of persons is (1) to recognize the validity and the applicability of the ends principle precisely because the intrinsic worth of persons is recognized; and it is (2) to recognize one's person/person relationship to persons, which entails, or makes inescapable, a recognition

13. W. G. Maclagan, "Respect for Persons as a Moral Principle I," *Philosophy*, 35 (July 1960): 208. Maclagan's article is published in two parts in the July and October issues of volume 35.

of a kind of basic personal relationship to persons, which in turn, in this case, is expressed by (3) Agape, or an affective attitude in the respect/love range.

In this way a realization of the inherent worth of persons, of one's person/person relationship to persons (the fourth element), contains in itself a recognition of the ends principle (the first element), a realization of a basic personal relationship to them that is marked by some personal attitude (the second element) and that, moreover, is a positive affective attitude (the third element).

And when the person/person relationship to *all* persons is realized, we may say with John Donne, or go beyond John Donne in saying, send not for whom the bell tolls, for you are involved in all of humanity, not just in having a kind of personal relationship to all persons, but in being related to all persons as being worthy of your concern, even as you are. This is the ultimate personal relationship, foundational to obligation, that is postulated by relationship morality.

Before I turn to our third main concern in this chapter, the mode of discovery involved in realizing the inherent worth of persons, let me return briefly to a matter I raised at the end of Chapter 2. There I called attention to a difference between relationship morality and an ethic of care over the place of a universal relationship between persons that is foundational to morality. That foundational relationship is of course the person/person relationship. Gilligan, Grimshaw, and others do not deny such an ultimate human relationship, but, on the other hand, they do not explicitly acknowledge it, let alone give an account of it. And Gilligan's and Grimshaw's respective discussions do not necessitate it. Thus Grimshaw does not ground the moral principles she cites in anything like the person/person relationship. Even the principle that commands consideration of whether our behavior will stand in the way of maintaining care and relationships[14] need not be understood as being grounded in the inherent worth of persons. Such a principle could be adopted merely as a prudential matter, with no grounding beyond the wish to be comfortable in one's relations with others. This, of course, is not to say that either Gilligan or Grimshaw would think of the importance of maintaining relationships in such prudential terms, nor, again, is it to say that either is committed to denying an ultimate moral relationship between persons as persons. But as things are, it remains that

14. Jean Grimshaw, *Philosophy and Feminist Thinking* (Minneapolis: University of Minnesota Press, 1986), 209.

they do not ground even an ethic of care in the inherent worth of persons or, what is the same thing, the ultimate human relationship persons have to persons as persons, the person/person relationship.

In this chapter, I said, I wanted to bring out, first, how this relationship, if it exists at all, exists between each person and all persons; second, how it is the ultimate ground of obligation; and third, how it is to be realized, the mode of discovery involved in its being realized. The first two of these concerns have been addressed. It is now time to take up the third.

Relationship morality postulates the person/person relationship between each and every person. This, of course, is not just the relationship of class inclusion that one acknowledges by saying glibly, "Well, I am a person, and so is everyone else." The person/person relationship exists between persons by virtue of the intrinsic worth of each, and to acknowledge this relationship is to acknowledge the intrinsic worth of those in the relationship. But why should we think that there is such a relationship between persons? The short answer to this question is, because we human beings are capable of realizing or discovering that we stand in such a relationship to other persons. However, this answer is too short. For many would ask if there really is such a realization to be made. If there is, why is it that many have not made it, and why is it that many even deny that persons have inherent worth simply by virtue of being persons? In order to address these questions fully, it is necessary to look at the mode of discovery involved in the realization of the intrinsic worth of persons.

Our effort will be to identify the *mode* of discovery, or the discovery type, that would be involved in discovering the worth of persons as persons and our consequent person/person relationship to them. Our concern, at present, is not to identify what it is about persons that allows us to identify such beings as persons. Nor is it to identify what it is about persons that endows them with intrinsic worth and so creates the basis of the person/person relationship between persons. That is, our concern, at present, is not to address either (1) What makes persons persons? or (2) What makes persons inherently valuable as persons? These admittedly are important questions, especially for relationship morality, and they are questions that, from the viewpoint of relationship morality, are closely related. They deserve to be addressed and will be addressed in Chapter 7, after we have explored further the character of the person/person relationship in the next three chapters.

But now we need to look at the mode of discovery that our discovering a person/person relationship to others presupposes or that, if it is not presupposed, it is at least a discovery type that makes the possibility of such a discovery understandable. What *kind* of discovery is the discovery of the worth of others and of our consequent person/person relationship to them? Let us begin by asking, If persons have inherent worth, why do human beings fail to recognize the inherent worth of other human beings? Why do we fail to make this discovery, to have what Royce called "the moral insight"? Or, as Royce would put the question, why do we fail to retain the moral insight? His answer is that passion clouds the insight. "It is," he says, "as impossible for us to avoid the illusion of selfishness in our daily lives, as to escape seeing through the illusion at the moment of insight."[15] Royce is, I believe, essentially right when he says that *passion clouds* the moral insight. A failure to realize the inherent worth of others is not due to a failure of investigation; it is due to an inability to see the significance of what is already before us. It is indeed a cognitive failure of sorts to fail to attain (or, for Royce, to preserve) the moral insight, if there is such an insight to be attained. However, the cognitive deficiency here is not a failure to verify a thesis. It is a failure to realize a truth that, as it were, stares us steadily in the face, which we nevertheless cannot see. It is a failure to make what may be called a *realization-discovery* of the worth of persons. Realization-discoveries are a definite type of discovery that can be fairly well delineated. Their hallmark is that they occur when the significance of the familiar is realized. Such discoveries occur when a kind of blindness is lifted and we see the significance of facts that have long been familiar to us. They are not a matter of gathering new facts; they are a matter of seeing the significance of old facts. They are not a matter of gathering evidence (to verify a suspicion or hypothesis); they are a matter of seeing the significance of the already-familiar as evidence, we may say. Such discoveries are not the outcome of intellectual enquiry. They are not the outcome of empirical investigation (fact gathering), or of logical argument, or even of an intellectual ordering of familiar facts to settle an issue. They should, then, be distinguished, in particular, from the models of issue settling discussed by John Wisdom.[16] They, in short, are not the product of any kind of enquiry. They can, on the contrary, descend upon us so that we realize the last thing we would have thought is true.

Such discoveries, though not the product of enquiry, have a logic that can be enquired into, a part of which I have just sketched. Much more could be said to illustrate that logic and to bring into greater relief the

---

15. Royce, *The Religious Aspect of Philosophy*, 155.
16. John Wisdom, "Gods," in *Philosophy and Psycho-analysis* (Oxford: Blackwell, 1964).

contrast between realization-discoveries and a range of other types of discoveries that follow upon enquiry. I hope, however, that enough has been said to convey a sense of their nature (elsewhere I have provided a fuller discussion).[17] In any case, realization-discoveries, I submit, are not uncommon and sound mysterious, if they do, only because we most easily think of discoveries that occur as a result of conscious enquiry of some sort. The man who, after years of denying it even to himself, realizes that he looks upon other men with eyes of desire makes such a discovery, as does the man who realizes what he never suspected, that he is jealous of his own children, and as does the woman who, contrary to what she would have confessed even to herself, realizes a subtle animosity toward her sister.

Now let us apply the mode of realization-discovery, or as much of it as we have seen, to the discovery of the person/person relationship. On the realization model of discovery, a failure to make a discovery of the person/person relationship is a failure to realize the significance of the familiar. On this model, the evidence of the worth of persons is all about us in the familiar presence of persons. Discovering our person/person relationship to others is not a matter of discovering some hidden fact about human psychology or capability, or some new fact about our common human physiology. It is a matter of discovering the *significance* of the far-from-arcane, already familiar facts of the personhood of others, which would bring us to see the intrinsic worth of others as persons.

Our failure to make such a discovery is not due to a lack of rigor in our investigative technique. It is not that we have failed to verify a hypothesis. It is not that we have failed to construct an attainable logical proof or even failed intellectually to order certain familiar facts that would settle the issue. Our failure occurs because our moral vision is "clouded," as Royce says. Royce does not speak of self-deception in this connection. Rather, he speaks of passion. However, he could as well, and perhaps better, have spoken of self-deception or the kind of blindness that self-deception creates.

If self-deception is operative in preventing the realization of the worth of others, then the role of selfishness that Royce mentions is clarified. It is generally agreed by philosophers who have written on self-deception that

17. For a fuller discussion of realization-discoveries, see my *The Cognitivity of Religion: Three Perspectives* (London: Macmillan; Berkeley and Los Angeles: University of California Press, 1985); see pages 104–7 for a discussion of the realization-discovery type as a type; see pages 107–17 for a discussion of the "religious discovery," a realization-discovery of God's presence; and see pages 117–30 for a discussion of the logic of the issue of whether religious realization-discoveries have been made. For an earlier discussion of what I later came to call "realization-discoveries," see my *Religious Discovery, Faith, and Knowledge* (Englewood Cliffs, N.J.: Prentice-Hall, 1972), 12–26.

we can with point seek a motive or reason for a person's self-deception. This recognition has been expressed several ways. The self-deceiver, it has been said, "persuades himself to believe contrary to the evidence in order to evade [an] unpleasant truth" relating to his "personal identity."[18] Or, the self-deceiver has an "interest . . . associated with preserving his identity, the sort of person he is, or conceives himself to be,"[19] or he deceives himself "out of concern for truth or moral and personal integrity [or] in order to avoid facing up to some truth that is painful or as a result of fear and/or desire."[20] Self-deception, then, is intentional and motivated. This is a conceptual feature.[21] For Sartre, human beings practice self-deception regarding their freedom ("bad faith") because they want to avoid the anxiety of freedom and responsibility. A similar motive is generated by selfishness. If we come to realize that other persons are inherently valuable, then we shall have to admit the moral necessity of treating them as ends in themselves in accord with the ends principle, and, more than that, we shall have to admit the moral necessity of responding to them with respect and even Agape or love. Agape, or some like attitude, is demanded by the moral insight, and, for relationship morality, it is demanded by morality itself. To be sure, many who strive toward attaining such an attitude toward other persons may fail in its perfect expression. And, too, there may be forms of morality, coherent in their ways, that embody no such attitude toward persons. It may be that morality in some forms can be used as an escape, as by the individual who refuses help to those of a certain ethnic background

18. Herbert Fingarette, *Self-Deception*, Studies in Philosophical Psychology, ed. R. F. Holland (New York: Humanities Press, 1969), 28 and 67 (emphasis deleted).

19. Amelie O. Rorty, "Belief and Self-Deception," *Inquiry* 15 (1972): 395.

20. Alan Drengson, "Critical Notice: Herbert Fingarette, *Self-Deception*," *Canadian Journal of Philosophy* 3 (1974): 482.

21. Not that this is the only conceptual feature of self-deception. Another is that it invites a paradoxical description of itself, in that one and the same person, regarding some specific belief, is both the self-deceiver and the self-deceived, or both believes and does not believe, or both knows and does not know. Whether self-deception *must* be described in some such paradoxical way—a way that posits a bifurcation of the self, as it were—is a question at issue. I confess that I am not overly bothered by the notion that the human breast may harbor different levels of consciousness not in communication with one another: such a state of affairs may be both paradoxical and possible. On the other hand, the role of self-deception of concern to us, its role in blinding one to a realization of the significance of the familiar, does not require that it take some form of paradoxical description. Robert Audi, in several different papers, has developed an account of self-deception that is not ultimately paradoxical; and, he has suggested to me, his account is not at odds with my treatment of the concept. For Audi's analysis of self-deception see his "Self-Deception, Action, and Will," *Erkenntnis* 18 (1982) and his "Self-Deception and Rationality," in *Self-Deception and Self-Understanding: New Essays in Philosophy and Psychology*, ed. Mike W. Martin (Lawrence: University of Kansas Press, 1985).

who are in need, with the announcement: "My principles dictate that I not help persons like you." I shall have more to say about the possibility of such moralities in Chapter 6, but for the present we should note and acknowledge that such a morality need not give any place to Agape or a like attitude. However, if the discovery of the presence of persons is made, if we discover our person/person relationship to others, this will not be the morality we come to. If this discovery is made, Agape, or a response to others in its range, with its full demands on our moral emotions and energy, will stand forth as a requirement of morality. Such a response to others many do not care to make and even regard as incompatible with a proper commitment to their own survival. In this way, our ego-survival, in resistance to the demands of a response to others in the Agape or respect/love range, provides a motive for self-deception.

The presence of such a possible motive does not in itself show that those who have not discovered the presence of persons are self-deceived. It is not my argument that they are self-deceived or suffer blindness, nor have I tried to show that there *is* a realization-discovery of the person/person relationship to others. Rather, what I have tried to show is that *if* there is such a discovery to be made and some have made it, the reason that those who have not made this discovery have not is the kind of blindness that is caused by self-deception.

This analysis of the *mode* of discovery involved in realizing our person/person relationship to others, then, explains both how such a discovery can be made merely through, or as a part of, being in the presence of others and how it is that perhaps many have failed to make this discovery. Still, it may be said, there is no proof of this person/person relationship to others. In fact, on my view, if it is only discoverable by the mode of discovery I have put forward, then there must be no proof. For any such proffered "proof" would have to cite the familiar facts of the personhood of others, which, on the one hand, provide no proof to those who are blind to their significance and, on the other hand, present a redundancy to those who have realized that significance. In either case no proof is given. The only "proof" would be in the seeing. John Stuart Mill, in trying to show that his principle of utility was subject to a "sort of proof," said that the only proof that things are desirable is that they are actually desired.[22] Notoriously, since what he meant by "desirable" is "morally desirable," his claim embodies an egregious lapse. However, we can with more safety allow that if the person/person

22. Mill, *Utilitarianism*, 34.

relationship to others is seen, then it is not only discoverable but has been discovered.

In any case, for relationship morality, the person/person relationship is the foundation of all morality. Relationship morality posits the person/person relationship as the ultimate basis, not only of human obligation but of all of ethics. More has to be said about how this relationship underlies all the various departments of ethics. Before I undertake to do so (as I shall do in Part III) let me say more about various features of the person/person relationship and its discovery: about the scope of this relationship, about the affective dimension of its discovery, and about some main implications of this relationship and its discovery. These we take up in the next three chapters, in Part II.

PART II

THE LOGIC
OF THE
PERSON/PERSON
RELATIONSHIP

4

The Two Scopes of the Person/Person Relationship

The person/person relationship has two distinct kinds of scopes. It has one scope that consists of all those persons in the relationship. It has another that consists of all the actions of those persons in the relationship that come under the moral purview of the relationship. All the various kinds of human relationships that exist between persons have both sorts of scopes. We ask about the first sort when we ask, for instance, "Who is his spouse?" or "Who is their child?" or "Who are my friends?" And we implicitly refer to the second sort of scope when we remark to ourselves, for instance, "I ought to give my wife more help," or "I ought to be more patient with the children," or "I ought to know better how to aid my friends." In general we specify the first scope of a relationship when we answer the question, What persons are in the relationship? And we specify the second scope of a relationship when we answer the question, What actions are covered by the relationship? Accordingly, we may call the first a relationship's person-scope and the second a relationship's action-scope. In this chapter we want to clarify further the person/person relationship by examining both its person-scope and its action-scope.

Let us start with the first kind of scope it has, its person-scope. Our first question, then, is, What persons are in the person/person relationship? Different relationships of course may have different person-scopes by virtue of their type. The marital relationship between spouse and spouse is by its nature two-person in scope. It is, I think, even in a polygamous setting, where, if the husband has several wives, as is allowed in Islam, the husband still is in a two-person relationship with each wife. In such a setting there may also well be a relationship that includes the polygamous husband

and all of his wives, but that is an additional relationship. Friend-friend relationships also are two-person in scope. True, three or more individuals may form a three-person friendship relationship between themselves. Such a relationship does not, or need not, displace the two-person relationships that may yet hold between each pair of friends. It again constitutes another relationship. An example of a three-person relationship is that of an offspring to his or her mother and father. Family relationships, as the class of relationships between an individual and all the members of his or her family, provide examples of relationships that may have a scope of few or many persons, even very many persons, as when the family is the extended family. Relationships that are larger yet in person-scope are those of the individual to his or her community and to his or her society.

So much is fairly clear, I would suppose. In each case the relationship type is familiar, as is the basis of the relationship, that by virtue of which it exists—marriage, friendship, family, community membership. The basis of the person/person relationship is perhaps not so familiar, but it is nevertheless at times, and not all that infrequently, alluded to, as when reference is made to "the family of man" or "our neighbors," or, in the way I would read him, as when John Donne advises us not to send for whom the bell tolls. The basis of the person/person relationship is simply and precisely the shared personhood of persons. The person-scope of the person/person relationship, then, is all persons. In fact, in effect, we saw this in the last chapter, although we had not yet introduced the notion of person-scope. For there we saw that the person/person relationship involves all persons just because it exists between persons by virtue of nothing other than their being persons.

However, before we turn to the action-scope of this relationship, there is a bit more to say about its universal person-scope. For one thing, observe that the person/person relationship has a universal person-scope not only in that it exists between me, a particular individual, and each and every person, but also in that it exists between each and every person and each and every person. Of course, if it is universal in the second way, it will also be in the first way. But some relationships can be universal in the first way without being universal in the second way. An example is provided by the relationship that the thoroughly principled and consistent misanthropist puts himself or herself into. The principled misanthropist, by feeling ill will toward all, posits and thereby enters a universal relationship between himself or herself and all persons, although no relationship between the next individual and each and every person is thereby created.

Also note that the universal person-scope of the person/person relationship is not a product of any person's attitude. The person/person relationship does not come into existence through being posited by an attitude but, like many relationships, exists independently of human attitudes. In this it is unlike the misanthropist's universal relationship to others, since the basis for such a relationship may be nothing other than a bilious nature. The person/person relationship has a basis of quite another type, namely the personhood of all persons, which, according to relationship morality, is in principle discoverable.

This brings us to a third and more important point regarding the first scope of the person/person relationship. This scope of the person/person relationship should not be confused with what may be called the scope of the *discovery* of the person/person relationship. The scope of the discovery can vary, while the scope of the relationship itself is fixed. Though our person/person relationship, if it exists at all, is to all persons without exception, our discovery of our person/person relationship to others may be a discovery of our relationship to all or to many or to only a few persons. While the relationship itself is universal, one's discovery of the relationship may or may not be universal in scope. We discover our person/person relationship to others when we come into the presence of others and so realize their worth as persons, and we may come into the presence of all others or many others or only a few others. To be sure, the discovery can be universal. Coming into the presence of others in the relevant sense does not require coming into their bodily presence, and, accordingly, it is possible to come into the presence of all persons, to realize the inherent worth of all persons without exception. Occasionally, it seems to me, we find allusions in literature to such a universal discovery of the worth of others. Arguably, Donne's saying that he is "involved in *Mankinde*" carries such an allusion. Another instance, I suggest, is to be found in Dostoyevsky's *The Brothers Karamazov*. In Dostoyevsky's novel Markel, the elder brother of the ten-year-old boy who would become Father Zossima, expresses a similar sense of involvement with the lives of all others. Markel tells his mother joyfully that "every one is responsible to all men for all men and for everything."[1] His words announce a realization that comes to him only weeks before his death, in a time of spiritual peace; and they, like Donne's words, seem, in the context of Dostoyevsky's novel, to evince an awareness of the inherent

1. Fyodor Dostoyevsky, *The Brothers Karamazov*, trans. Constance Garnett (New York: Modern Library, n.d.), pt. 2, bk. 6, I, "Father Zossima and His Visitors," 301.

worth of all persons without exception, even though his reflection is explicitly about his (and our) responsibility to and for all others. In the novel Markel's words are recalled by Father Zossima late in his life, but they are echoed in what Father Zossima himself says earlier than the time of his recollection. The monk living in seclusion, he says, must realize "that he is responsible to all men, for all and everything, for all human sins, national and individual. . . . This knowledge is the crown of life for the monk and for every man. [And] only through that knowledge, our heart grows soft with infinite, universal, inexhaustible love."[2] Father Zossima's words explicitly draw out the connection to universal love: some form of love almost certainly is an affective attitude that may accompany the discovery of the worth of all persons and our person/person relationship to all persons without exception (about which more in the next chapter). In *The Brothers Karamazov*, then, it seems to me that we find, especially in Father Zossima's words, an allusion to a universal discovery of the worth of others (even though in these passages there may be other themes interwoven, as there may be in Donne's devotion).[3] However, even if we did not find in literature any references to a universal discovery of the worth of persons, it would remain that the real possibility of such a discovery can be shown, given the argument of the last chapter.

On the other hand, unhappily yet clearly, it is possible to come into the presence of some persons and not come into the presence of others. One may appreciate the inherent worth of those in one's immediate family, and respond to them with great love, while not entering into the presence of others outside one's family. Again, beyond a simple feeling of national identity, one may appreciate the ultimate value of one's fellow compatriots and fail to come into the presence of those outside one's country, or one may realize the inherent value of those of one's own race and yet fail to enter into the presence of those of other races. And so on. There is, that is to say, no guarantee that because we realize the inherent worth of some persons, we shall realize the inherent worth of all persons. The moral insight, to use Royce's term, need not be universal. This is so even though what gives persons their inherent worth in each instance is the same: their

2. Ibid., pt. 2, bk. 4, I, "Father Ferapont," 169–70.
3. Markel, for instance, says that each of us has "sinned against all men," and Zossima urges that each monk must confess to himself "that he is worse than others, than all men on earth" (*The Brothers Karamazov*, 301 and 169). The theme that each of us has sinned against all persons is not unrelated to relationship morality, and we shall return to it. Donne, in Devotion XVII, interweaves the theme that "*affliction* is a *treasure*," for it makes us fit for God.

personhood. Upon reflection this should not be too surprising. In general it does not follow that if I recognize an instance of a type, I shall recognize the next instance of that type. Think of identifying paintings by Picasso, or morels, or invalid arguments. Even for purely intellectual identifications, then, it does not follow from one's identifying one instance that one will identify the next. But, moreover, as I argued in the last chapter, the discovery mode by which the person/person relationship is discovered is not purely intellectual. For what prevents our realizing the inherent worth of others is not failure of enquiry but self-deception or the kind of blindness that it creates, which issues in a failure of realization. And it is perhaps understandable that we should be able to realize the inherent worth of those close to us, while being blind to the worth of those further from our ken. So it is that the scope of the discovery of the person/person relationship can vary. But this does not mean that the scope of the person/person relationship itself varies. And in fact it does not. Its scope is invariably all persons. It holds between one person and each and every person and between each and every person and each and every person. That is, it does if it obtains at all, for it is a relationship between persons as persons.

Before we turn to the action-scope of the person/person relationship, we should bring into high relief one further aspect of its person-scope, even though, strictly, it is something implied by what we have already seen. Each and every person has the person/person relationship to each and every person. If so, however, persons have this relationship not only to every *other* person but to themselves as well. The idea that one can be related to oneself may sound odd, but reflection quickly removes this initial impression. As one can like or hate another, so one can like or hate oneself—and doing so is to have a relationship to oneself. Such examples could be multiplied; self-deception is another instance. Though such relationships to oneself are substantive (in a way that the formal relationship of self-identity, which I refrain from mentioning, is not), they are not universal. It is an implication of the person/person relationship's being absolutely universal that each person has the person/person relationship to himself or herself. That this is an implication can, I think, hardly be disputed. My concern, though, is not merely to draw attention to the fact that there is this logical entailment, but to bring into relief the moral import of persons' bearing the person/person relationship to themselves. We begin to do so by raising a question: If persons bear the person/person relationship to themselves, will they always appreciate that they do? The answer to this question is that they may not. Now how can that be? Surely everyone knows that he or she is a person. In a way, of course, this is right. Everyone will count himself or herself when counting the number of persons in a room. One's appreciating that one has the person/person relationship to oneself, though, goes well beyond understanding that the designation "person" applies to oneself, just as one's appreciating that one has the person/person relationship to all persons goes beyond the glib acknowledgment of class inclusion expressed by "I am a person and so is everyone else." Appreciating that one has the person/person relationship to oneself involves an appreciation that the ends principle applies to oneself, and, as we saw in the last chapter, it is possible not to treat oneself as an end. Not doing so, degrading oneself, is an indication that one does not appreciate that one has the person/person relationship to oneself. However, this is not the full story. Failing to realize the person/person relationship to oneself is failing to come into one's own presence, in the sense we have discussed. It is to fail to recognize one's inherent worth as a person and to fail to respect, revere, or to love oneself, or to have some other attitude in the respect/love range toward oneself.

When persons do not come into their own presence, they do not realize the person/person relationship they have to themselves, and from the perspective of relationship morality, in a clear sense, they are wrongly related to themselves. To be sure, for relationship morality, they are yet in the person/person relationship to themselves: there is no getting out of that relationship short of ceasing to be a person, which no person can do. Yet they are wrongly related to themselves in that they have failed to realize that they have this relationship to themselves and so do not respect themselves as they should and do not acknowledge their intrinsic worth as they should.

The idea that persons can be wrongly related to themselves may remind some of what Søren Kierkegaard said about the nature of persons in *The Sickness unto Death*.[4] There we are told by the pseudonymous Anti-Climacus that a person, or "the human self," is "a relation that relates itself to itself and in relating itself to itself relates itself to another," and, we are told, there can be a "misrelation in that relation." Kierkegaard's idea here is that a person is a relationship—a relationship between elements in tension (the infinite and finite, the temporal and eternal, freedom and necessity), which, furthermore, relates itself to itself and thereby relates itself to another (the power that established it, or God). This interesting and charged conception

---

4. Søren Kierkegaard, *The Sickness unto Death*, trans. Howard V. Hong and Edna H. Hong (Princeton: Princeton University Press, 1980), 14–15.

of a self, or of a person, serves well the purposes of Anti-Climacus in *The Sickness unto Death*, which is to examine the various forms that the "misrelation of despair" can take. However, the point of the conception, we should note, is that a person *is* a relationship, not that persons are related to themselves in a further relationship, as they are in the person/person relationship. Kierkegaard's idea of a self, or person, may have some merit, and, in any case, I do not see that Kierkegaard's idea is at odds with our own. For our present purposes, though, it is beside the point.

Still, others have made the observation that persons can be wrongly related to themselves, even if Kierkegaard did not. George Nakhnikian in effect makes this claim.[5] For Nakhnikian, just as we are rightly related to others when we love them with what he calls "undemanding love," so we are rightly related to ourselves when we love ourselves with undemanding love. Accordingly, we fail to be rightly related to ourselves when we do not love ourselves with undemanding love. And we might fail to love ourselves with undemanding love in several ways, in Nakhnikian's view, for there are several interconnected constituent dispositions that make up the "dispositional aspect of undemanding love," such as being patient and not being possessive. In the next chapter, in considering the respect/love range of attitudes, we shall want to discuss Nakhnikian's notion of undemanding love, but here and now, beyond noting the similarity of this part of his reflections to what I have presented, I want to look at a particular claim that he makes about undemanding love as it is given to others and to oneself. Nakhnikian claims that as two species of undemanding love, "self-love and other-love are logically inseparable." The nub of his argument is that "if I love myself *as a human being*, then I love anyone *as a human being*, and if I love anyone *as a human being*, then I love myself *as a human being*."[6] Nakhnikian's claim relates specifically to "undemanding love," we should bear in mind. He fully appreciates that there are popular senses of "love" in which one might love oneself and not love others. But undemanding love is love for persons by virtue of their being persons, and as such we have equally good reason to give such love to others and to ourselves. This is Nakhnikian's point, and it is correct, I believe. Beyond this point, however, his words suggest that *if* I love myself as a person, then I will love others, and *if* I love others as persons, then I will love myself. Neither is necessarily so. Rather, as Nakhnikian sees, I will love myself as a person if I love others, and love

5. George Nakhnikian, "Love in Human Reason," *Midwest Studies in Philosophy* 3 (1978): esp. 301–5.
6. Ibid., 305 (Nakhnikian's emphasis).

others if I love myself, provided I am "(fully) rational"—fully rational, we should say (going beyond Nakhnikian), not in the sense of being logically consistent, but in the sense of not being blind, not being blind to the personhood of all persons. Here is the rub. Granted that the personhood of each and all gives us all sufficient reason to love all persons, all others and ourselves, as persons, still it is possible for us to fail to realize in the relevant way the personhood of some or even many persons. Even though one may grant the truth of the proposition that everyone is a person, still one may, in the way we have discussed (in the last chapter), fail to come into the presence of many persons—and one of those into whose presence one fails to enter may be oneself.

Now we come to the second scope of the person/person relationship, its action-scope. What actions are covered by the person/person relationship? It would appear that all actions of moral import are covered, at least indirectly. As I have argued, various particular relationships, like that between spouse and spouse, and various general relationships, like that between speakers and hearers, determine the specific form that various obligations take, as well as their type; moreover, such relationships are the source of these various obligations. But the ultimate human relationship is the person/person relationship. It underlies all other relationships in that it generates the fundamental and absolute obligation for each of us to treat all persons as persons. This is the obligation for each of us to treat not only other persons but all persons, including ourselves, as persons. Once we fully recognize the universal person-scope of this relationship, as we do by recognizing the inherent worth of all persons, we in effect recognize this fundamental obligation. However, a role for other, more limited relationships remains. While the person/person relationship creates the obligation to treat persons as persons, other relationships—such as the marital relationship and speakers' relationships to their hearers—indicate the different forms that the respect can variously take, and they remain the source of their various and more focused obligations. Thus, to take one example, given the person/person relationship I bear to all persons, including my mother, I ought to treat all persons as persons, including my mother; at the same time, the mother-son relationship determines the type of respect I owe to my mother as a mother and creates the obligation I have as a son to pay her filial respect, while my mother, being the particular person she is, clarifies the form of the filial respect I ought to give to her.[7]

7. Maclagan invites comparison on this point. He says of the "guiding rules" of morality, of

In this way, then, since the person/person relationship creates the obligation to treat all persons as persons, even though it itself is not sufficient to determine all the myriad forms that that treatment may take, it remains that all actions with moral import come under the purview of this relationship and hence, at least indirectly, are in its action-scope. What we have just seen, of course, does not imply that if I have no familiar particular relationship to another person, like the mother-son relationship, and no familiar general relationship to other persons, like the speaker-hearer relationship, then I have no definite and recognizable obligation toward them. The bare and basic person/person relationship itself generates, for instance, the obligation to treat all persons with justice. The person/person relationship is sufficient to obligate us to treat with justice strangers half a world away whom we shall never meet when our actions, or actions of our society or nation, touch them (as in the case of economic exploitation or self-interested military intervention), or when the question of the fair allocation of natural resources arises (as in the case of sharing the world's energy sources). The actions we take in pursuit of justice in these cases come directly under the purview of the person/person relationship.

So far, in looking at the action-scope of the person/person relationship we have considered what might be called overt, or exterior, action. In another dimension of its action-scope the person/person relationship also covers interior actions. And, again, it does so both indirectly and directly. The category of interior action, as I am using it here, includes intending. Forming certain intentions can violate an obligation created by a particular relationship. Clearly, if a husband violates the trust of his wife by committing adultery, he has violated his marital obligation. Moreover, if he attempts to commit adultery but is thwarted by unforeseen circumstances (he is in an automobile accident on the way to the assignation), his attempt violates his marital obligation, even if it does so in a less serious way. Also, though, if he forms the intention to commit adultery but does not proceed out of fear of the consequences to himself, he violates his obligation—for, in effect, he is a would-be attempter, and he does not act out of self-regard. So much emerges if we reflect along lines provided by Herbert Morris.[8]

---

which he allows there may be indefinitely many, "that they are the various ways in which the single formal principle of respect for persons specifies itself in the variety of human relationships." "Respect for Persons as a Moral Principle II," *Philosophy* 35 (October 1960): 298–99.

8. Herbert Morris, "Shared Guilt," in *On Guilt and Innocence: Essays in Legal Philosophy and Moral Psychology* ((Berkeley and Los Angeles: University of California Press, 1976), 121–22; reprinted from *Wisdom: Twelve Essays*, ed. Renford Bambrough (Totowa, N.J.: Rowman & Littlefield, 1974). Morris' example is different, and his focus in this passage is not on obligations as they are generated by relationships.

Morris also considers other "mental states" that are relevant to our present concern, the action-scope of the person/person relationship. His own concern, we should mention, is not our present concern or our wider concern with the nature of the person/person relationship and the morality of relationships but touches upon it, or them, at several points. Morris' concern is with the meaning of what Markel, Father Zossima's brother, says in *The Brothers Karamazov*: "Every one is really responsible to all men for all men and for everything." This is the very passage I brought forward earlier as an allusion to the universal discovery of the inherent worth of others, and Morris' concern with the meaning of Markel's saying is one point at which his concern touches our own wider concern. Morris has little trouble understanding how each person is responsible *to* all men, for, he allows, this is the familiar claim that we are responsible to all men for any wrong done to any man; and Morris has little trouble understanding how we are responsible *for* all men, for this is only to say that we have obligations to others by virtue of their humanity (or personhood, as I may as well say). But the third claim—that every one is responsible for everything—is more difficult for Morris.[9]

It is in his pursuit of the meaning of this third claim that Morris helps us understand the dimensions of the action-scope of the person/person relationship. In this pursuit, after considering how we can be morally responsible for our intentions, he goes on to consider how we can be morally responsible for our desires.[10] And here he draws closer to our concerns, for he focuses on the particular relationship of "reciprocal trust and fidelity" that a husband has with his wife. It is in this connection that he gives us the fruitful notion of "accept[ing] desires to do acts that are wrong." In Morris' conception, individuals accept desires to do what is wrong when they "form intentions to realize [such] desires or, if having [such] desires, they do not form such intentions, [but] fail to do so for reasons that are not morally creditable." This helps, I think. I would only add that accepting a desire to do what is wrong—violating trust in a marital relationship, in Morris' example—could also take the form of dwelling upon and savoring the desire in fantasy, even without any thought of actually doing the action. In any event, Morris helps us see how not only harming or intending to harm another through an overt act, but also accepting and nurturing the

---

9. Ibid., 111–12. We shall return to Markel's moral claims, and Morris' reflections on them, in the final chapter, where we shall explore and clarify the practical implications of relationship morality.

10. Ibid., 124–25.

desire to do such an act, is harmful and hurtful to persons and to our relationships to them. The reason for this, as Morris says, is that mental states like accepting a desire can themselves be destructive of a relationship like that between a husband and a wife "because [such a] relationship is partly defined in terms of feelings and thoughts."

We see, then, how forming an intention and accepting a desire can violate a marital relationship and, by extension, other close particular relationships, like friend-friend relationships, which involve respect and love in a way familiar to us all, but these relationships are distinguishable from the person/person relationship itself. These interior acts—forming intentions and accepting desires in marital and friend-friend relationships— are in the scope of the person/person relationship, though they are so only indirectly.

Are there interior acts that are directly covered by the action-scope of the person/person relationship? There are. And this is so even though it may seem eminently deniable, given the strongly felt difference between familiar and close relationships, like a marital relationship, and the person/ person relationship. Morris says that in contrast with the relationship between a husband and wife, "our relationship to others in society is only rarely that of love or friendship. It ought however to be a relationship . . . in which there is reciprocal care and trust and respect."[11] While Morris may be right about the relationship to others in society that he has in mind, for relationship morality our *fundamental* relationship to others in society, and indeed to each and every person, not only ought to be but *is* just such a relationship, a relationship in which care or respect, or a like attitude, *is* due to persons. From the perspective of relationship morality, the person/ person relationship to each and all obtains but is rarely recognized. Observe, however, that the requirements of a relationship are what they are because the relationship is what it is, not because we recognize the relationship to be what it is. A husband's intention to commit adultery, or his accepting the desire to do so, is destructive of the marital relationship precisely because the relationship is what it is. His having an attitude of respect or love is a requirement of the relationship, and such a mental state is at odds with this requirement. He ought to have an attitude of respect or love, but he may not; and he ought to recognize this obligation, but he may not. Still, though he has no feeling of respect or love, and though he does not acknowledge that he ought to—though he is unaware of the nature of the

11. Ibid., 125.

relationship and its requirements—*ceteris paribus* he is at fault. For the requirements of the relationship nevertheless remain what they are. Now, if we are all in the person/person relationship to one and all, this does not entail that we have an attitude in the respect/love range toward one and all or that we acknowledge that we should. We ought to have such an attitude, and we would if we realized that we were in the person/person relationship to each and every person, but we may not realize that we are. There is, again, a distinction between being in the person/person relationship to every person and realizing that we are. But the requirements of the person/person relationship are of the relationship, not of our realizing that we are in it. And a direct requirement of the person/person relationship is our having respect for persons, for all persons, whether of our acquaintance or not, or some attitude toward them in the respect/love range. Thus the person/person relationship itself is like a marital relationship in being "partly defined in terms of thoughts and feelings," and just as interior acts can violate the requirements of the more familiar relationship between a husband and wife, so interior acts can violate the requirements of the more rarely realized person/person relationship.

Let me make this last point in one more way, using an example provided by D. Z. Phillips, which he borrows from H. O. Mounce.[12] In the example we are invited to imagine that someone has drawn "an excellent likeness of one's mother asking one to stick a pin in the picture, taking care to aim at one of the eyes." Mounce, Phillips tells us, comments that he supposes hardly anyone would not find it hard to comply with the request. But beyond noting or postulating this response, Mounce has no comment on it. As Phillips sees it, it is a "primitive moral response." Mounce further develops the example by asking us to suppose that one does comply with the request, and then later one's mother comes to have a severe affliction in her eye. Phillips discussed this example with a class of forty students and found two different reactions. Fifteen of them saw no difficulty in sticking pins in the picture and said that they would not feel guilty if the mother later got an eye affliction. This was because they saw no causal connection between the two events. The other students did not feel that they could stick pins in the picture and said that they would feel guilty if an eye ailment developed. However, this was not because they believed there would be a causal connection at work. They did see a connection between the two events, but not a causal one. What they meant, Phillips says, is that "they

12. D. Z. Phillips, *Faith After Foundationalism* (London: Routledge, 1988), 328–29.

felt that sticking pins in the picture reduces serious possibilities to a game; it plays around with things." And, Phillips adds, "when the affliction occurs, an internal relation between the 'playing around' and the event makes the guilt understandable." But "what this elucidation shows," Phillips says, "is not that people refused to stick in the pins as a *consequence* of such beliefs, but that primitive moral responses occur and that people, if asked to reflect on them, may reply in this way."

I find this example very interesting. It is, I think, an instance of what Kierkegaard called an *Experiment*, that is, an experiment in imagination, or imaginary construction. As Kierkegaard saw, such "experiments" can have philosophical importance. Phillips, it seems to me, is pretty clearly right in his suggestion that in order to have a moral reluctance to stick pins in the picture, it is not necessary to believe that that act might in some way cause a physical ailment. However, this is not to say that I think Phillips has gotten out the significance of the example when he says that there is an "internal relation" between the playing around with pins and the affliction (by "internal relation" Phillips apparently means at least in part a relation that is not accidental). We might better remind ourselves of Morris' comment that certain relationships between persons are partly defined in terms of thoughts and feelings. The relationship between a mother and her daughter or son is just such a relationship. Accordingly, the very thought of sticking pins in a picture of one's mother, which, to put it mildly, is not an act of endearment, and the feelings it would evoke, strike at the relationship.

Now let us change the example slightly, to make it bear on our concern with the action-scope of the person/person relationship. Let us imagine that the picture is of a person unknown to us, a stranger. Do we now feel no reluctance about sticking a pin in the picture, taking care to aim for an eye? I think not. There is still a moral hesitation, even if it is less pronounced. The reason, again, is not because one faintly believes in a causal connection (whether or not there is such a belief). The reason is that we have a relationship even to strangers that does not countenance our doing to them what amounts to violence in thought. That relationship is, of course, the relationship we have to persons by virtue of their being persons, the person/person relationship. So in this way too we can see, or begin to see, that certain interior acts are directly covered by the action-scope of the person/person relationship.

There is more to see about the nature of the person/person relationship, more to its logic, as it might be put. And I shall try to bring out these further features of its logic in the next two chapters. In this chapter we have seen how the person/person relationship itself, as a relationship, morally requires an attitude of respect or love toward persons, or some like attitude in the respect/love range. A mark of our having discovered the person/person relationship to persons is our evincing an attitude in this range. As a mark of our discovering the person/person relationship to persons is our evincing an attitude in this range, so our having an attitude in this range is a requirement of the person/person relationship. In the next chapter I shall explore the dimensions of the respect/love range of attitudes and examine the character of various attitudes that seem to be included in this range. A main concern in this book is to show how relationships are foundational to morality. We have seen enough so far, though, I suspect, to be able to begin to appreciate how relationship morality, informed by the person/person relationship, requires more than what we may refer to as ordinary morality or conventional morality. Nevertheless, if relationships are foundational to morality in the way relationship morality maintains, the requirements of relationship morality, including the requirement of an attitude in the respect/love range, are in fact just the requirements of morality well understood.

5
Agape and the Respect/Love Range of Attitudes

In this chapter we want to explore the affective side of coming into the presence of persons, or, what is the same thing, the affective dimension of the discovery of the person/person relationship to persons. Our concern is to examine the possible diversity in what I have called the respect/love range of attitudes, the range of those varying but like attitudes that might form the affective side of coming into the presence of persons, the affective dimension of discovering the inherent worth of persons. Earlier, in Chapter 3, I argued that a part of the recognition or discovery of the worth of persons as persons is a positive affective response, a response of love or a like attitude. An attitude in this range is a part of the discovery of the inherent worth of persons at least in the sense that the existence of such an attitude evinces the recognition of the worth of persons as persons and the lack of such a response to persons is strong, even conclusive, evidence that no such recognition has been made. Also, as we saw in the last chapter, an attitude in this range is a requirement of the person/person relationship itself. Now, in order to get clearer on the internal nature of the discovery of the worth of persons, and on the requirements of the person/person relationship, let us look more closely at the respect/love range of attitudes and its constituents. An evident candidate for a constituent attitude is love. But if one such attitude is love, what is the character of this love (for love, it would seem, can be understood in many different ways)? And if it need not be love, what other like attitudes may play this role? We shall address both questions in what follows.

What, then, is the character of love? Or, rather, what is the character of the love that evinces a realization of the worth of persons? It is the second question that is our question. And to answer it, we should observe, we need not pronounce on the character of all love or even insist that there is a common character to the many forms that love can take. There is a wealth of reflection on the nature of love, and our sorting through some of the major perceptions of love's character will help us to approach the answer to our question.

Let us begin with Aristotle. In the *Nicomachean Ethics* Aristotle provides us with his view of love in connection with his discussion of friendship. There are, he says, three kinds of friendship, and he delineates each kind.[1] All three involve love or affection (*philia*), but each involves what amounts to a different conception of love, at least in the sense that for each there is a different reason or ground for loving. First, there is friendship based on utility. "Those who love each other on the ground of utility," Aristotle says, "do not love each other for their personal qualities, but only in so far as they derive some benefit from each other." That is, their love is "motivated by their own good" or gain. This is the kind of friendship that one sometimes finds between two business associates or colleagues in a profession. Although neither may find the other particularly pleasant, each gets something useful from the other. This kind of friendship may be real enough, even if it might be more just to term it an "association" than a "friendship." For its entire basis is this mutual usefulness. Thus, when one party leaves the particular business or concern that provided the mutual usefulness of the relationship, the friendship dissolves. Second, there is friendship based on pleasure. In this kind of friendship friends love each other "on the ground of pleasure," and their affection for the other person "is motivated by their own pleasure." Two individuals have this sort of friendship, not when each finds the other useful in gaining some end, but when each finds the other pleasant or enjoyable. Often, Aristotle suggests, friendship between young people is of this sort, for "their chief interest is in their own pleasure and the opportunity of the moment." Young people, Aristotle observes, may fall in love and then out of love in a single day. He of course has in mind that kind of erotic love that is based on a sexual desire quickly satisfied. However, we should appreciate that pleasure-related love need not be ephemeral, nor is it limited to the young. It may take the form of a more mature and extended affection between two friends who enjoy the same thing: the theater or sports or just conversation. In this case, too, the basis of the friendship is the pleasure that each gains from the other's

---

1. NE 1155b16–1157b4, from which come the quotations in this paragraph and the next.

company. In both utility-related and pleasure-related love or affection the reason for the affection is something, either some benefit or some pleasure, that one friend expects to get from the other. In each case the other is treated as a means, either to gain one's own benefit or to gain one's own pleasure. Pretty clearly, neither of these two kinds of love will do as an attitude in the respect/love range. Neither kind of love is for persons as persons. In fact, in neither case is the other person loved for what he or she is; rather, as Aristotle says, the one loved is loved just insofar as he or she is useful or pleasant.

But for Aristotle there is a third kind of friendship, that which he calls "perfect friendship." Perfect friendship is based on goodness and is the kind of friendship that exists between those who are good, or virtuous, and are similar in their goodness, or virtue. In this kind of friendship friends "each alike wish good for the other" and they "desire the good of their friends for the friends' sake." In perfect friendship friends are "most truly friends," Aristotle says, "because each loves the other for what he is, and not for any incidental quality," such as utility or pleasure. The love or affection involved in perfect friendship sounds more promising. It does so, though, only initially.

The third kind of friendship, Aristotle tells us, is between "those who are good" and is limited to the good.[2] Its affection, good-related love, like all love for Aristotle, is given in accord with merit, or what is due.[3] It is always their merit that makes individuals lovable, for Aristotle, although merit can take different forms. In utility-related love it is being useful; in pleasure-related love it is being pleasant. And in perfect friendship it is having goodness or virtue. It is ridiculous for the less meritorious, or less lovable, to demand to be loved as they love, Aristotle says.[4] They properly give more affection than they receive. Though Aristotle makes this point generally about friendship, it holds specifically for perfect friendship, where merit is a matter of virtue. Thus, in this kind of friendship it is one's virtue that makes one lovable, and in a friendship between two virtuous persons of unequal virtue, the more virtuous of the two friends merits more love. It is apparently with perfect friendship in mind that Aristotle says bad men cannot be loved and cannot love even themselves, because they have no lovable quality.[5] Also, despite what he says about perfect friendship, in

2. NE 1156b6.
3. NE 1159a35.
4. NE 1159b15–19.
5. NE 1166b25.

some places, it seems, he sees its affection as being given for the good of the individual who gives it. In his early comments on all friendship he says that "it is the good of the individual [i.e., one's own good] that is lovable for the individual."[6] And in regard to perfect friendship itself he observes that "the good [those who are friends in such a relationship] are both good absolutely and useful to each other" and that "they please one another too."[7] On the basis of such passages as these George Nakhnikian concludes that, for Aristotle, in perfect friendship "good men . . . love each other for the good qualities that each has, meaning the qualities that necessarily make their possessors a beneficent resource for those who love them."[8]

There are several reasons why Aristotle's conception of good-related love, the affection between friends in perfect friendship, will not do as an attitude in the respect/love range. For one thing, it cannot be a love of persons as persons because it is too limited in scope. Not only does friendship, including perfect friendship, require acquaintance, but one can have a perfect friendship only with others who are virtuous (assuming that one oneself is virtuous). Love of persons as persons extends to all persons. However, even if we set aside this consideration, still this conception of love will not do. It will not for two further reasons. First, as Nakhnikian points out, this kind of love, given all that Aristotle says about it, still appears to be given at least in part for one's own good. The good involved is not "incidental," is not a mere benefit; it is a good that has to do with what individuals are in themselves, the good of virtue. But still, even though such a good is a moral good, it is a good; and it remains that, for Aristotle, arguably, the affection of perfect friendship is given in part for the increase of one's own virtue. Love of persons as persons is not given for the sake of one's own increase, not even the increase of one's own virtue. Second, this kind of love is given in accord with virtue. Aristotle is quite clear about this point. This means that not all would deserve this love and not all would deserve it equally. The love of persons as persons is deserved equally by all persons simply because they are persons.

So Aristotle's thinking about love does not give us much help. There may be, and doubtless are, human relationships formed in accord with his three kinds of friendship (although I see no reason to think that all friend-friend relationships fit into one of his categories). In any case, none of his three conceptions of love provides the notion we need. Before we move on,

6. NE 1155b21–25.
7. NE 1156b12–17.
8. George Nakhnikian, "Love in Human Reason," *Midwest Studies in Philosophy* 3 (1978): 294.

though, let us consider what Aristotle says about the love of mothers for their children. "Some women," he observes, "give their children to other women to bring up, and although they love them, knowing who they are, do not seek to be loved in return, if it is impossible to have this too; they are content if they see their children getting on well, and they bestow their love upon the children even though the children, through ignorance, make no response such as is due to the mother."[9] Aristotle, in observing the delight mothers take in loving their children, means to show that friendship consists more in giving than in receiving affection. He apparently fails to notice that the mother's love for her children in his example fits none of his conceptions of love.[10] The mother described by Aristotle does not love because she expects something in return—not something useful, not pleasure, not even an increase in her virtue. (Could a mother make such a sacrifice for the sake of her own secret pleasure or for the sake of her own virtue? Yes, I suppose so. But such a mother would not be acting out of maternal love as Aristotle, and not Aristotle alone, understands it; and Aristotle does not present the mother in his example in such a light.) Also, the mother in Aristotle's case does not give her love to her children in accord with their "merit." They are not useful to her, nor do they give her pleasure (since they are absent). Thus she does not give them her love in accord with either of these two forms of merit. Nor does she give them her love in accord with the third form of merit, for she does not love them in accord with their virtue. They may be too young to have dispositions virtuous or otherwise, and if they are old enough to have wicked dispositions, she properly loves them nevertheless. Aristotle, then, in spite of himself, perhaps gives us some help, but only by pointing beyond his own conceptions of love to maternal love and caring.

Maternal love or caring deserves our further attention, and we shall return to it. At this point, though, let us look at a conception of love that is very different from Aristotle's, that of the contemporary philosopher Irving Singer. Aristotle's conceptions of love arose with his discussion of friendship. Singer's primary focus in developing his conception of love is romantic love. Not that Aristotle is unaware of sexual love or that Singer is unaware of the affection of friendship. It is just that the avenues of their concerns are different. This, however, is not the big difference between Aristotle's conception, or conceptions, and Singer's. The main difference is an internal

9. NE 1159a27–33.
10. Nakhnikian also makes this observation and argues for it. "Love in Human Reason," 293–94.

one between the conceptions themselves. Singer develops his conception as "a modern theory of love," a new "analysis" of love, that is, of sexual love between human beings.[11] He is careful to allow that even within romantic love there are different types of love, as he regards "falling in love," "being in love," and "staying in love." And while he sees no reason to "define love in essentialistic terms," he does proceed in his analysis to tell us what on his view constitutes love, or romantic love. "To love another person," he says, "is to create a relationship in which that person takes on a new and sometimes irreplaceable value." Love between human beings is, as he sees it, constituted by different "appraisals" and "bestowals" of value. Of these two the bestowal of value is more significant in that it is a "necessary condition" for love, although appraisal of value is not to be discounted.[12]

How does Singer understand these constitutive elements of his analysis of love? Both appraisal and bestowal are, as he says, "valuational categories." Beyond their shared genus, though, they importantly differ. Appraisal is a species of assessment: "In appraising another person, we assess his or her utility for the satisfaction of needs, desires, appetites, impulses, instinctual drives that affect us every moment of our lives. A woman's intelligence or a man's vigor and virility have obvious value of this sort. In the experience of love, men and women find value in each other through appraisals of an endless variety."[13] Singer identifies two main sorts of appraisal: "objective" appraisal, in which "we estimate a person's value in relation to the interests of some prior community," as in a beauty contest, to use Singer's example; and "individual" appraisal, in which we "decide what another person is worth in relation to our *own* interests or needs."[14] In matters of love objective appraisals are always "supplemented by individual appraisals." There are two features of all appraisal to be noted. First, appraisal of another person is always in relation to interests or needs. And second, appraisals are "judgments about matters of fact"; they are "probabilistic predictions" (about how well a person will meet certain needs) and also "generalizations based on empirical evidence" (regarding a person's intelligence or vigor, say); as such judgments, appraisals can be mistaken.[15]

But, for Singer, love cannot be reduced to appraisal. Love in significant

11. Irving Singer, The Modern World, vol. 3 of The Nature of Love (Chicago: University of Chicago Press, 1987), chap. 10, esp. 389–92.

12. Ibid., 390.

13. Ibid., 390.

14. Ibid., 391 (Singer's emphasis).

15. Ibid., 390–91.

part is the bestowal of value on the one who is loved. "When we love, we *create* value," Singer says.[16] "Lovers create a value in one another that exceeds the individual or objective value each may also be appraised to have."[17]

Here we see the essential difference between Aristotle and Singer. For Aristotle, love is affection *based* on something. The ground of affection varies for Aristotle: for one kind of love it is usefulness, for another it is pleasure, and for a third it is virtue. But in each case the basis of love, as a basis upon which love can be founded, is not something that love creates. In Singer's terminology, as he himself says, Aristotle makes love wholly a matter of appraisal and gives no recognition to an element of bestowal.[18] Singer does not discuss mother love in this connection, but by extrapolation he could analyze mother love so that it included the bestowal of value. Such a view of mother love would go a long way toward avoiding Aristotle's difficulty. Using it, Singer could say that in Aristotle's example the mother's love for her children creates value in them, and that is why her love for them is not in accord with (her appraisal of) their merit.

Still, for our purposes, Singer's conception of love is inadequate. The operative categories in Singer's analysis of love are appraisal and bestowal of value. Singer believes that both are involved, and the question that he seems to pursue in reaching his analysis of love concerns the relative importance of each in a romantic relationship. I think that Singer is right in maintaining that love cannot be understood only in terms of appraisal. Given that one is seeking an analysis of love in terms of the valuational categories of appraisal and bestowal, the missing element must be bestowal. But why should we accept it that love can be understood in terms of these valuational categories?

Let us look again at Singer's categories of appraisal and bestowal. One might wonder if appraisal is involved at all in love. Property is appraised for investment purposes. One appraises different makes of cars before making a purchase. But does one appraise another before falling in love or giving love? Such a notion strikes one as discordant with the idea of love, romantic or otherwise. Part of the problem is that, as it seems to me, Singer conflates appraising with finding. So it is that he says men and women "find value" in one another "through appraisals" (in the passage quoted above). Maybe

16. Ibid., 392 (Singer's emphasis).
17. Ibid., xii.
18. Ibid., 396. Singer also sees Plato, St. Augustine, Freud, and Santayana as having ignored the element of bestowal.

so, at least sometimes. But not all finding is appraisal. When we unexpectedly discover a strength in another person, it is not through an appraisal. It may be in spite of our assessment of that person's abilities that we discover his or her strength. Such a finding is a discovery of value, but it is not "valuational" in that it is not the result of an evaluative assessment, as in appraisal, or the imputation of value, as in bestowal. So, if we accept it that finding value or worth in those we love is in some way involved in loving them, as I think we should, we need not equate this finding with appraisal. And this means we need not fall back on bestowal—the creation of value in those we love, as opposed to finding value they have independently of our love—as the only alternative to appraisal.

Also, and just as important, by linking value and appraisal Singer constrains our vision regarding the nature of the value that persons may have. The value unexpectedly discovered in another may or may not be an ability or skill. Moreover, the value discovered may be a value that another has in himself or herself irrespective of one's own interests or needs. Singer considers values found by appraisal, such as the intelligence or vigor that he mentions, to be values in relation to the interests or needs of the one who finds them, a perception no doubt encouraged by his category of appraisal, since an appraisal is typically in relation to interests or needs. What emerges here is that, for Singer, the values found by appraisal are both relative and accidental. They are relative in that they exist only in relation to another's interest or need, and they are accidental in that people may or may not have them. For relationship morality there is in persons their more fundamental inherent worth as persons. This is an inherent value that persons have by virtue of being persons, irrespective of any other person's interests or needs. As I have argued, it awaits a discovery of a certain kind—which, like the unexpected discovery of another's strength, is neither an appraisal nor a bestowal.

Singer's analysis gives us a better way of understanding Aristotle's example of mother love than is provided by Aristotle's conceptions of love, but an even better alternative is available: that the mother sees and reacts to the worth of her children, not her children's worth in relation to her interests or needs, not her children's worthwhile attributes, but the inherent worth her children have independently of their particular attributes, a worth that she sees with her mother's eyes. This would be a form of the moral insight, albeit a very special form. It is a mother's discovery of the worth of her own children as persons, and it is no doubt not unimportant that she is related to them as their mother. For relationship morality such a realization-discovery is possible, since every person has inherent worth. The mother is acutely aware of that worth as embodied in her children—whether or not she is able to see that worth in any others or to respond to others with caring. This construction is better than the one we come to on Singer's analysis, I suggest. On his view, as opposed to Aristotle's, the mother may love her children though they lack appraisable merit; but also on his view, if the mother ceases caring, the children decrease in worth. Surely this is contrary to our untutored moral intuition.

In sum, then, the analysis of love that Singer offers us does not countenance the category of discovery or realization of value, as opposed to appraisal, and so it of course does not countenance the possibility of a universal realization-discovery of the inherent worth of persons and our consequent person/person relationship to persons. And related to this, his conception of love will not provide us with a concept of love that could be the affective side of the discovery of the inherent worth of persons as persons. While there may well be romantic love relationships in accord with Singer's analysis, we shall have to look further for an understanding of love that resides in the respect/love range.

George Nakhnikian's category of "undemanding love" may be of more help to us, I think. We encountered this category of love in the last chapter. Now let us take a closer look. Like all forms of love, Nakhnikian says, undemanding love is a combination of a mental state and dispositions.[19] I think that all love may have these two aspects, as Nakhnikian says. Certainly the love that forms the affective dimension of discovering the inherent worth of persons will have a feeling side (in opposition to emotional indifference) and a dispositional side (in opposition to behavioral indifference). Our question is this: Does Nakhnikian's analysis of these two aspects of undemanding love give us the notion of love that we need? In its dispositional aspect, Nakhnikian says, "undemanding love is neither blind affection nor an amiable emotion. It is a rational affair. Its defining constituents are realism and benevolence. . . . These defining elements entail five other dispositions: patience, absence of magisterial judgment, autonomy, absence of possessiveness, and absence of being controlling."[20] These seven interlocking dispositions constitute the dispositional role of undemanding love, in Nakhnikian's analysis, and apply equally to undemanding love of others and to undemanding love of oneself. Nakhnikian,

19. Nakhnikian, "Love in Human Reason," 296.
20. Ibid., 301.

we will recall from our earlier discussion, makes the same kind of point I do. In his terms, one can love oneself as well as others with undemanding love, or fail to do so. In my terms, one can enter into one's own presence as a person as well as into the presence of others—one can realize the person/person relationship to oneself as well as to others—or fail to do so. For Nakhnikian, when one fails to love oneself or others, one is wrongly related to oneself or others, and a violation of each of these seven dispositional constituents of undemanding love provides one way to be wrongly related to oneself or to others.

Notice Nakhnikian's point that undemanding love is "a rational affair." This claim is central to Nakhnikian's main concern, which is to show that undemanding love is reasonable, or even, as he says, "an essential component of human reason."[21] In the last chapter we touched upon this aspect of Nakhnikian's thinking. However, a further word or two may be in order. There is something to the idea that love is in some sense rational, I think. It is a *kind* of failure of rationality not to respond to persons with love (or with some attitude in the respect/love range). But to say that love is rational can be misleading in two ways. First, it may suggest that the irrationality is a failure to trace logical implications or to reason in a consistent way. For relationship morality, discovering the inherent worth of persons and coming into their presence may importantly involve a realization-discovery. From this perspective the irrationality of not responding to persons with love or a like attitude is not a failure of consistent reasoning but more a failure of consistent sensitivity. There is a cognitive failure, but it proceeds from a kind of blindness. It is not a matter of laxity in investigation or reasoning. It is better understood as a failure of what might be called realization-rationality than as a failure of enquiry-rationality.[22] Second, to say that love is rational may suggest that it involves a "rational" self-interest. As we shall see, Nakhnikian's view, given all that he says about "reason," does not wholly escape making this suggestion either.

Now let us look more closely at the analysis of the dispositional side of undemanding love that Nakhnikian gives us. Does this analysis capture the dispositional side of the love that is the affective side of coming into the presence of persons? I would make several comments. For one thing, there is some question about how undemanding love relates to respect for persons.

21. Ibid., 287.

22. See my *The Cognitivity of Religion: Three Perspectives* (London: Macmillan; Berkeley and Los Angeles: University of California Press, 1985), 110–11 for the contrast between enquiry-rationality and realization-rationality.

At one point Nakhnikian says that he is going to analyze "the dispositional aspect of undemanding love in terms of respect," and this makes it sound as though, for him, the dispositional side of undemanding love corresponds exactly to respect. Elsewhere he seems to regard respecting others as just one of the constitutive dispositions of undemanding love, along with being patient and other dispositions.[23] It does not seem that it can go both ways, unless Nakhnikian has in mind two forms of respect. Also, I think that respect for persons must have what Nakhnikian calls a "mental-state" aspect and cannot be wholly dispositional. But Nakhnikian is right to detect some kind of consanguinity between the love he describes and respect for persons. It seems to me that respect for persons is a strong candidate for inclusion in the range of attitudes we are examining (about which, more later).

On balance I have little or no quarrel with the idea that the dispositional aspect of such love—where such love is considered as the affective dimension of coming into the presence of persons—is composed of the seven constitutive dispositions he names. Two of the dispositions—not being controlling and not being possessive—might seem problematic as part of undemanding love of oneself. But Nakhnikian himself explains. The first is not the lack of self-control but the eschewing of such devices as scorn and ridicule directed toward oneself, and the second, on analogy with not being possessive toward others, amounts to not viewing oneself as existing solely to meet one's own needs.[24] Nakhnikian, I think, is essentially right here. His point is closely related to the point I made earlier (in Chapter 3) that one can fail to treat oneself as an end, as when one degrades oneself. However, I would propose some small emendations or elucidations to Nakhnikian's general account of undemanding love's dispositional character.

Though we might grant that Nakhnikian's seven dispositions are sufficient to capture the dispositional side of the kind of love he has in mind and the kind of love we are seeking to understand, still, we should observe, often what will count as patience, absence of control, and so on in particular relationships between persons will be importantly determined by the relationship. This is in accord with our argument in Chapter 1 that the individual form of various obligations, such as the obligation to honor one's parents, is clarified by particular relationships. Again, it may be that in some instances of this kind of love other dispositions will be constitutive.

23. Nakhnikian, "Love in Human Reason," 301 and 303.
24. Ibid., 303–4.

Perhaps in some manifestations of such love, depending on the persons in the love relationship and their particular relationship, a disposition to be encouraging or even a disposition to be strict or hard will be constitutive. In fact, I do not see that Nakhnikian has to deny this. For him, as we have noted, respect for persons is in some way closely tied to the complex disposition of undemanding love. Being respectful of persons he understands as accepting them as they are. Acceptance of persons as they are, however, he says, "does not require complacency" but "quite the opposite": accepting a person "implies wishing that [that person] change for the better because we wish [that person] well." For Nakhnikian, then, the disposition of undemanding love, which at its "core" is this respect for, or acceptance of, persons, can require actively encouraging a person to change. Otherwise, wishing that a person change for the better, with no effort to help bring about that change, would amount to complacency. In this way undemanding love, for Nakhnikian, does not require us to approve of all that the one loved does. It allows, even requires, us to work to help others change for the better, as I read him. The requirement that one not be complacent about the well-being of those loved and that one encourage that well-being is a part of love in many of its manifestations, I think, and surely it is a part of the love for persons as persons, which by its nature cannot be indifferent to persons. However, Nakhnikian is clear that this requirement does not allow us to demand of others that they change "for the reason that [they produce] in us anxiety, nostalgia, malaise, discomfort, hostility, resentment, or fear."[25]

This reflection brings us to the other aspect of undemanding love, in Nakhnikian's conception, its aspect as a "mental state." In its aspect as a mental state, Nakhnikian says, "undemanding love is experienced as felt freedom from anxiety, from insecurity, from any awareness of being in want of anything from the person loved. In the loving experience there is tenderness and affection for the person loved."[26] While it may seem that in this comment Nakhnikian has in mind only an intimate relationship between two persons, in fact he does not, as he goes on to make clear. And of course he could not, since, for him, undemanding love is due to all persons, strangers or not, by virtue of their being persons. We should note here the place that Nakhnikian gives to the "good feelings" of tenderness and affection. Undemanding love, for Nakhnikian, as we just saw, holds no

25. Ibid., 296–97.
26. Ibid., 296.

place for such negative feelings as anxiety, hostility, or resentment. So too for the love we are seeking as the kind of love that is the affective side of discovering our person/person relationship to all persons. That love, given to persons simply because they are persons, we must allow in accord with Nakhnikian's analysis, will not involve an anxiety that others be as we would have them or a resentment of them for being what they are or for doing what they do. It will not involve the nostalgic wish that they be as they were, nor will it be lessened by fear of what they might do, nor will it harbor hostility toward them. Love of persons as persons accepts human beings as they are, not for the sake of their potential to change. It is concerned for the well-being of persons and will encourage change for the sake of that well-being, but not for the sake of the relief of one's anxiety or out of resentment or from the inspiration of the other negative feelings Nakhnikian names.

Nevertheless I am not sure that the love we are seeking to understand will accommodate no "bad feelings." Once again, in accord with Nakhnikian's analysis, such love may imply the wish that those loved change for the better, and, as we have seen, this wish, if it is not complacent, may require encouraging that change. But now, we must acknowledge, encouraging such a change, as opposed to complacent approval, may be both hard to provide and hard to be followed. I do not think that Nakhnikian denies this. What follows, though, is that Nakhnikian's undemanding love, and the love we are seeking to understand, in certain of its embodiments in specific relationships will require of us applications of energy and devotion that may fail and in their constant failure exhaust us and make us feel bad, even over the long run. This may occur in the case of encouraging a friend to do the best he or she is capable of or in the case of raising children. I am not arguing that such feelings arising in the context of love and concern for another are not ultimately good morally, but I am pointing out that they are not what is generally meant by "feeling good."

Perhaps Nakhnikian would agree. In one way he seems to, but he also seems to resist this implication. And this brings me to a final comment on Nakhnikian's notion of undemanding love. At the end of his essay he observes that "the mental components of undemanding love" include peace of mind, freedom from anxiety, and other good feelings and then goes on to say that the mental states and dispositions of undemanding love "are by their very nature suffused with intrinsically good feelings. . . . The degree to which a human being is undemandingly loving is the degree to which he is joyful and unhysterically energetic. The most loving are the ones who live to the fullest. This is the ultimate reason why virtue is its own reward."[27] Earlier Nakhnikian had rightly denied that human beings can love people only insofar as they think of them as providing some benefit to themselves or as being an extension of themselves.[28] Earlier yet, though, he had observed that "reason" is in part "an unconditional, primal, passional concern for one's own well being."[29] The main thrust of his essay, as we have noted, is to show that love is rational and even a part of reason. And so it is perhaps not surprising that he ends up saying that love is "suffused with intrinsically good feelings," that those who love are joyful and energetic, and that love is in this way its own reward. It looks as though the good feelings of undemanding love make it reasonable for Nakhnikian, so that he is not that far from Aristotle, despite his own criticisms of Aristotle's views on love.

Maybe, though, Nakhnikian, by *intrinsically* good feelings, means feelings that are morally good even though they can feel burdensome, take a toll of emotional energy, exhaust us, and, in fact, not feel very good at all. If so, he must mean this in the face of his final comments lauding peace of mind and the other good feelings that may well accompany love. On balance, it seems that he means good feelings in the more generally accepted sense. Still, it is well to keep in mind Nakhnikian's insistence that when we love undemandingly, we love "a person for his own sake," and we love with "perfect good will with no thought of expected returns." Such love as this is not for the sake of the good feelings or energy or any other such "Aristotelian good" that we get in return. The complication we have noted may arise in part because Nakhnikian sees undemanding love as distinguishable from, but compatible with, "transactional" love, or love that is for the sake of "reciprocal need fulfillment," and he sees the combination of the two as better than either alone.[30] Yet it remains that Nakhnikian's notion of undemanding love is helpful to us: it is love for the sake of persons. It points toward a love for persons as persons, with no further reason for its existence. If we come to have a reason to love when we discover the personhood of others, that reason is precisely that they are to be loved because they are persons. And that reason does not reduce to "good feelings" or to any other Aristotelian good that we may or may not find accruing to ourselves.

27. Ibid., 314.
28. Ibid., 291.
29. Ibid., 288.
30. Ibid., 294.

I want now to turn to what may be the prime candidate for the kind of love we are seeking to understand, Agape. Agape may not be, and in fact is not, the only affective attitude that can mark coming into the presence of persons, but it may perhaps be the crowning attitude in the range of such attitudes. We will recall that we have already encountered the notion of Agape. In Chapter 3 we saw that W. G. Maclagan argued that it was "*in* Agape" that we recognized the inherent worth of persons. Let us begin to examine the idea of Agape by looking again at Maclagan's discussion. "Agape" of course is a term that has a strong religious association, particularly with the New Testament, but Maclagan uses it with no claim to be employing it in "an orthodox Christian manner."[31] And although he mentions three theological views on the nature of *divine* Agape, he does not enter into a discussion of their merit.[32] (Later we will have no comment on two of these views, but for now we can leave them to one side.) Maclagan's concern is to provide an analysis of *human* Agape. More exactly, he is concerned to analyze the human *experience* of Agape, the "Agape-experience," as he calls it.[33] Involved in the experience are two "conditions," or "factors": a "rational" factor and a "natural" (or, in Kant's sense, "pathological") factor. He gives each some attention.[34] The "rational factor consists in our general consciousness of obligation," while the natural condition, or factor, "is provided by our capacity for sympathy." The rational factor, which is our "living consciousness of duty," has two functions, he says, one negative and one positive. Its negative function is "to remove the psychological obstacle to Agape . . . created by our natural self-centeredness," and, more specifically, to support "detachment." (Its positive function we shall come to shortly.) The sympathy Maclagan has in mind as the natural factor of Agape is not "animal sympathy," as seen in the spreading of excitement through a crowd, but an amalgam of what he calls "passive sympathy" and "active sympathy." Passive sympathy is an "imaginative 'feeling oneself into' the experience of the other, an emotional 'identification' of oneself with the other." It remains passive in that, in itself, it has no practical, or behavioral, expression. That is reserved for active sympathy, which is psychologically generated by the feelings of passive sympathy. Such active sympathy, in the "matrix" of passive sympa-

31. W. G. Maclagan, "Respect for Persons as a Moral Principle I," *Philosophy* 35 (July 1960): 206.
32. Ibid., 208.
33. Ibid., 209.
34. Ibid., 209–12.

thy, is close to Agape, Maclagan says, but as something "purely natural" and "without principle" falls short of being Agape.

"Agape proper," for Maclagan, is "precisely the reflective, 'principled' (and therewith moralized) version of this active sympathy." Until made principled, active sympathy is not yet moral, nor is it Agape. It is the "positive function" of the living sense of obligation, the rational factor of Agape, to accomplish this "fusion of active sympathy with the general moral interest."[35] This, in summary, is Maclagan's account of Agape, or the experience of Agape, "in" which, for him, we come to recognize the worth of persons.

Does Maclagan's conception of Agape provide us with a grasp of the kind of love we are seeking to understand? To the good, Maclagan is clear that Agape has a passive (feeling) and an active (practical, behavioral) side, just as, for Nakhnikian, undemanding love has a mental-state and a dispositional side. And the love we are seeking to understand will involve both our feelings and our actions, even if the feelings and actions of love do not arise fully formed precisely with the realization of one's person/person relationship to others. But several other comments suggest themselves. For Maclagan, Agape is "integrated" with the recognition of the worth of persons, and it is a "version" of sympathy. Agape emerges when sympathy is transmuted by becoming fused with our moral concerns, that is, I think, our concerns with our obligations to others. This "fusion" is needed to get moral duty back into Agape's ambit, on Maclagan's view. I think that sympathy in itself, as a spontaneous impulse, may lack moral direction or import, as Maclagan sees. Sympathy for a person may lead us to do what is wrong on his or her behalf. So something more is needed, it appears, to make sympathy moral. But I do not see that it is a fusion with a moral consciousness *within* Agape. Rather, for us, the discovery of the worth of persons has an affective side, which may be Agape, and the discovery of the worth of persons, when it is the discovery of the worth of all persons, *is* the discovery of the universal person/person relationship to persons, upon which our obligations ultimately rest. We may have understood before that we have obligations, but now, after we have entered the presence of persons, our obligations to them are vivified by our appreciation that our obligations are an expression of our person/person relationship to all persons and that in keeping our obligations we express our sense of the inherent worth of persons. Thus, as I see it, sympathy, or that version of sympathy that is Agape as Maclagan would

---

35. Ibid., 216.

have it, comes to have a moral direction by virtue of its being a part of the discovery of the worth of persons. Consequently, we need not postulate a "fusion" of active sympathy with our moral concerns internal to Agape. In fact, one of the elements that is fused in Maclagan's account seems foreign to Agape and its cognate attitudes. For Maclagan, Agape is in part a consciousness of moral duty (so far with no sympathy for persons) that in the Agape-experience is joined to a natural, spontaneous sympathy. But it seems odd to regard a consciousness of moral duty, even if profound, as a part of Agape, when such a consciousness may be devoid of sympathy or concern for persons as persons. For us, sympathy or concern for persons, or some like attitude—even, or especially, Agape, albeit perhaps in a slightly different construction—is one side of the discovery of the worth of persons, and it is this discovery, marked by an affective response, that vivifies whatever moral consciousness we may have had.

In other ways, though, Maclagan's analysis is helpful. If, as we say, the discovery of the worth of persons has an affective side, then it must involve an emotional, or affective, experience. And Maclagan helps by stressing the *experience* of Agape in the recognition of the worth of persons, whether or not we agree with his analysis of that experience. The discovery of the worth of persons, as a realization, is experiential, and it involves an emotional experience on its affective side. This is so whether the realization of the worth of persons is made suddenly or over time. And this is so whether or not the affective response is Agape fully realized. Maclagan's analysis, in any case, is helpful in pointing to the affective *experience* in, or as a dimension of, our realization of the worth of persons.

There is more in Maclagan's discussion that merits our attention, and later, at points in our own examination, we shall have to return it. Now, however, let us look at other constructions of Agape. Maclagan is not alone in giving us a way to think about this morally significant form of love. Nakhnikian, for instance, thinks of his "definition of undemanding love as being a philosophical analysis of the love that Jesus might have had in mind, the love to which Paul later referred by giving the Greek word, 'agape,' a new meaning."[36] In effect, then, Nakhnikian gave us his construction of Agape. Let us press further toward an understanding of the nature of Agape, or the notion of Agape that will be useful to us, by examining the seminal view of Anders Nygren and his crucial distinction between Agape and Eros.

36. Nakhnikian, "Love in Human Reason," 305. Not that Nakhnikian thinks Paul was clear about Agape. See his note 16.

For Nygren, Agape and Eros are two distinctive forms of love. Both Greek words are appropriately translated as "love." Each, for him, names a significant form of love, and these forms are in fundamental opposition to one another. In one dimension Agape and Eros broaden out into two deeply opposed attitudes toward life, he says. In another dimension each is a "historical conception." In this dimension each has its own roots, its own primary locus of development. Eros, Nygren argues, is primarily developed in the dialogues of Plato, while Agape, as a historical conception, derives from Paul and the New Testament.[37]

Agape and Eros, for Nygren, are competitive forms of love, and they compete on the same ground. Both provide forms of love for one's fellow human beings and forms of love directed toward God. In fact Nygren discusses Agape and Eros in relation to four forms, or subtypes, of love: (1) God's love for humanity, (2) human beings' love for God, (3) human beings' love for their fellow human beings, and (4) human beings' self-love.[38] The conception of Agape we are seeking is of course Agape of persons for persons, and so we want to attend particularly to Nygren's third and fourth subtypes. Let us begin, though, by noting several elements of Nygren's contrast between Agape and Eros in their attitudinal dimension. In one place he lists ten points of contrast, five of which relate to our concern with human Agape for persons.[39]

1. Eros is acquisitive desire; Agape is giving.
2. Eros is egocentric love; Agape is unselfish love.
3. Eros depends on want and need; Agape does not; it is freedom in giving.
4. Eros is determined by the worth of its object; it is not spontaneous but is evoked and motivated; Agape is directed to both "the evil and the good"; it is spontaneous and unmotivated.
5. Eros recognizes value in its object; Agape creates value in its object.

As Nygren brings out, these various aspects of Eros are evident in Plato's *Symposium*.[40] One inspired by Eros seeks to acquire the vision of Absolute Beauty, for the sake of one's own completion, in order to fulfill a lack; and

---

37. Anders Nygren, *Agape and Eros*, trans. Philip S. Watson (New York: Harper & Row, 1969), 32–33 and 208.

38. Ibid., 211–18.

39. Ibid., 210.

40. Ibid., 174–75.

one's Eros is motivated by the worth of its desired object. Also we find in the *Symposium* what for Nygren is another feature of Eros: it seeks what is higher or highest, as Absolute Beauty is seen to be. This appears to be an essential feature of Nygren's conception of Eros. Regarding it we shall note only that Eros, or at least a love very like Eros, need not be so lofty. One can well imagine an acquisitive, egocentric love, for the sake of one's own need, motivated by the worth of its object, such as, say, a collector's love of fine porcelain or, in the sphere of human relationships, a seducer's love of the possession of a woman's charm or, again, the domineering and possessive but nonsexual love of one person for another (for Eros between persons need not be erotic or sexual).

Now, with these five points of contrast between Agape and Eros in mind, let us begin to focus more on Agape. For Nygren, there is Divine Agape, God's love for human beings, and also human Agape toward God and toward one's fellow human beings. He discusses both.[41] Also, as we have noted, Nygren discusses Agape, in contrast with Eros, in relation to four forms, or subtypes, of love—not that he allows that Agape and Eros manifest themselves in each subtype. Strictly there is no Eros of God for human beings, since, for Nygren, Eros is an "upward movement" toward what is highest, and "there is no way upwards for God."[42] This point we need not argue one way or the other here, since our concern is exclusively with human Agape. More exactly, our concern is with human Agape for persons, and here we mean persons as opposed to God. (This of course does not deny the possibility of human Agape for God. But this form of Agape is beside and beyond our present concern.) Also, for Nygren, there is no self-love that is Agape.[43] This point we shall have to return to shortly. In any case, in developing the notion of Agape we need, which is Agape of persons for persons, we want to concentrate on Nygren's third and fourth subtypes of love: love for one's fellow human beings and self-love. Yet, even so, it will be useful to draw upon Nygren's comments on Divine Agape. He discusses four features of Divine Agape, three of which are echoed in human Agape and correlate with several of the five features of the contrast between Agape and Eros that he gives us. Nygren's four features of Divine Agape are these:

1. Agape is spontaneous and unmotivated.
2. Agape is indifferent to value.

41. Nygren discusses Divine Agape on pages 75–81 and human Agape on pages 95–102 in ibid.
42. Ibid., 210 and 211–12.
43. Ibid., 217.

3. Agape is creative.
4. Agape is the initiator of fellowship with God.

These are the features of God's Agape for human beings, but they, or the first three, are reflected in human Agape. I shall comment on each and, as well, on the features of Nygren's contrast between Agape and Eros.

Let us take the last feature first: God's Agape is the initiator of fellowship with God. This feature we need not dwell upon or even discuss, for it is a feature of God's love that has no transference to Agape in its human manifestations (although Nygren allows that human Agape analogously "has creative power to establish a new fellowship between men").[44] The other features do have transference, and these I shall discuss in order.

Agape is spontaneous and unmotivated. There is, for Nygren, nothing about humankind that evokes or motivates God's love. There is nothing in "the personal worth of men" that motivates God's love; His love is not a judgment on what human beings are like.[45] So too for the human Agape for our neighbors that is commanded by God.[46] This human Agape for others of course cannot be for the sake of personal gain or in proportion to merit. Nor can it be for the sake of gaining God's love or even for God's sake: human Agape for other human beings must be a spontaneous love for "the concrete human being, [not] the Divine idea of him."[47] This feature of Agape correlates with the first, second, third, and fourth points of contrast between Agape and Eros that we noted: Agape is not acquisitive, is unselfish, does not depend on one's wants or needs, and is spontaneous and unmotivated. This feature of Nygren's conception of Agape helps us to formulate the notion of Agape we need, I think. In that notion Agape is not motivated by hope of gain or by the idiosyncratic worth of any individual. It is spontaneous in the presence of persons.

Agape is indifferent to value. This feature is closely related to the first. God's Agape, Nygren says, "allows no limits to be set for it by the character or conduct of man." It extends to both the evil and the good.[48] Again, so too for human Agape. It is not reserved for those deemed worthy. It includes love of one's enemies, for one's enemies are, as much as any, one's neighbors and, as much as any, receive the spontaneous and unmotivated love of

44. Ibid., 96.
45. Ibid., 76.
46. Ibid., 96–97.
47. Ibid., 215.
48. Ibid., 77–78.

Agape.[49] This feature correlates with the third and fourth points of contrast between Agape and Eros: Agape does not depend on one's wants or needs, and it is spontaneous and unmotivated. This feature also helps us. Agape in the notion we need is not in response to the value that others have in relation to our wants or needs. Such values are both relative and accidental, as we observed in our discussion of Singer's analysis of love. Also, Agape cannot be in response to various values others have that are not in relation to our wants or needs but still are idiosyncratic, such as their value as mathematicians or artists or athletes, or even their value as good and moral persons. Such values are again accidental in that they are values that persons may or may not have. However, we do need to modify Nygren's second feature slightly in order to incorporate it into the notion we need. While Agape is indifferent to all accidental value, it is not indifferent to the inherent worth that persons have as persons. It is in response to their inherent worth as persons.

Agape is creative. Divine Agape, as Nygren understands it, imparts value. Human beings in themselves have no value, but God's love for them creates value in them.[50] This feature of Divine Agape is apparently shared by all Agape, for Nygren, since it is a point of contrast between Agape and Eros that he explicitly states, the fifth that we cited: Eros recognizes value in its object, while Agape creates it. Does this feature help us? Let us divide the question and ask it of Divine Agape and human Agape separately. Integral to the perspective of relationship morality is the perception that persons as persons have inherent worth. Can it be, on such a view, that God's love creates this inherent value that persons have as persons? I think that there is a coherent religious view that allows that this is so, that God's love is the source of the inherent worth of persons, although I suspect it is not the view that Nygren holds. For such a religious, or theological, view, God's bringing into being His creation is a part of His love, and God in His love created persons with inherent worth as persons: that is what persons are by their nature, beings with inherent worth. On this view God created beings with inherent worth *by* creating persons, and if He had created beings without inherent worth He would not have created persons. This religious and theological view, of course, is radically different from the view that God created persons and *then* imparted value to them through His love. This second view, which I suspect is closer to Nygren's, asserts that human

49. Ibid., 101.
50. Ibid., 78.

beings *in themselves* have no value and hence, in opposition to the first religious and theological view, implies that persons could exist without inherent worth. Can it be, for relationship morality, that *human* Agape creates the worth persons have as persons? Here our denial can be less encumbered and is in accord with what we said earlier about Singer's analysis of love as creative of value. Relationship morality need not deny that Agape can create various values in those loved—the value of fellowship, say. But, for relationship morality, human Agape is a response to the inherent worth of persons, a worth that they would have though it were unrecognized. Nygren's third feature of Divine Agape, and of human Agape, then, is not helpful to us.

Thus, in formulating the notion of Agape we need, we can retain the first and second features of Divine and human Agape that Nygren gives us, provided the second feature is properly modified. However, we must reject Nygren's third feature, as well as the fifth point of contrast between Agape and Eros, with which it correlates. The other four points of contrast, properly qualified, again help us to formulate the concept of Agape we seek. Just here, though, an additional few words are needed regarding the second point of contrast: Agape is unselfish. As Nygren seems to understand this aspect of Agape, it entails that human Agape excludes self-love in all its forms.[51] Agape in the notion we want to identify cannot be selfish, but it must include a kind of self-love. Agape cannot be self-indulgent, cannot be centered on self, not even on the spiritual or moral development of oneself; it, in short, cannot be egocentric, and it is the egocentricity of Eros that Nygren rightly identifies as the contrast with Agape. But while Agape cannot be egocentric, it still can, and must, allow a kind of self-love. Here Nakhnikian, for whom self-love is undemanding love of oneself, is more helpful than Nygren. Agape, for relationship ethics, is an affective response that is a part of the recognition of the worth of persons as persons. All persons have such worth, including oneself. As one can come into the presence of other persons, so one can come into one's own presence. And as an appropriate affective response to others whose inherent worth one realizes is Agape, so it is Agape in response to oneself and one's own inherent worth.

Before I summarize our findings in the form of a definite notion of Agape, let me comment further on certain theological views of Divine and human Agape, which, if correct, would impinge on our notion. Maclagan, in his

51. Ibid., 130 and 117.

discussion of Agape, as I remarked, mentions three theological views on the nature of Agape. Two of these deserve our attention. The first is that God's love gives a worth to its objects; the second is that, while no inherent worth attaches to persons, it is our duty to imitate God's love for human beings as much as we are able.[52] The first, of course, is Nygren's view, and we have already discussed it. The second requires attention at this point. In one interpretation, what it comes to is that we ought to love others, not for their sake, but for God's sake. Peter Geach, I think, may hold such a view as this. It emerges in his reflections on "the virtues," one of which is charity. He of course means charity in the religious or Christian sense, not in the tepid and mitigated sense so often used in common parlance. Charity in this strong sense is nothing other than love, and Geach uses the two terms interchangeably. While he does not use the term "Agape," he pretty clearly has in mind what Nygren designated by this word. For Geach, there is a Divine charity, or love, just as for Nygren there is a Divine Agape.[53] And for Geach there is the charity that human beings must have, as for Nygren there is the Agape that human beings are commanded to have. Charity, for Geach, is love of God above all, and it is love of our neighbors "for God's sake."[54] For Geach, it seems, the ultimate reason for loving others is not their worth as persons: others are to be loved, not for their own sake, but for the sake of God. Two comments about Geach's understanding of love of our neighbors are in order. First, this notion of human love, or Agape, for others, as love for others for God's sake, is at odds with the notion of Agape that we need. In the conception needed by relationship morality, human Agape responds to persons as they are; it is not for the sake of anything beyond the persons loved, not even for God's sake. On this point relationship morality is in accord with Nygren, as we have seen; for him, love of neighbor is directed toward the neighbor himself or herself, with no further object in mind. The second comment that I would make is that, theologically, Christians are not forced to Geach's view, even though there may be a strong religious sentiment that all should be for the sake of God. Nygren, for instance, partakes of this sentiment. So it is that Nygren allows that *in a sense* human love of neighbor is "for God's sake," but only in the sense that God, "being Himself Agape," causes or brings forth Agape in the hearts of His creatures, not in the sense that God is the ultimate reason for loving others.[55]

---

52. Maclagan, "Respect for Persons as a Moral Principle I," 208.

53. Peter Geach, *The Virtues* (Cambridge: Cambridge University Press, 1977), 69.

54. Geach, *The Virtues*, 17 and 86.

55. Nygren, *Agape and Eros*, 216.

There is a long tradition here. St. Bernard of Clairvaux in the twelfth century wrote of four degrees of love, in the fourth of which one does not love even oneself except for the sake of God.[56] But such love for the sake of God is to be understood essentially in terms of doing the will of God. It is attained when our "disposition of soul" is at one with God's will and "His will is seen perfectly fulfilled in us and by us." In the fourth degree of love, for Bernard, "every human affection will . . . melt away from self and be entirely transfused into the will of God." Bernard goes on to speculate that this perfection of love may not be attainable for any in an embodied state or for any before the resurrection, embodied or not. We need not linger over these theological speculations. Our concern is wholly with Bernard's understanding of what it is to love for the sake of God. Such love can be for God, one's neighbors, or oneself, and I think we can see that, for Bernard, such love, when it is directed toward one's neighbors or oneself, being only love that is perfectly at one with God's will, can yet be for the sake of those loved. Love of neighbor, he says, must be "love in God," and this means, for him, that love of God must come first. However, this does not mean that we are to love others for the sake of God in the sense Geach seems to have in mind. For love of neighbor to "be a matter of perfect justice," Bernard says, it must "be referred to God as its cause." As for Nygren, so for Bernard: God is the cause of our love for our neighbors. And for Bernard, we must love God first and "refer" our love of our neighbors to God as its cause. But God's being the cause of our love, even when this is recognized, is not the same as God's being the reason that we love others. Thus, even when it is urged that all be for the sake of God, this need not require that love of neighbor be for the sake of God in the literal sense that the reason we love others is for the sake of God, and not for the sake of those loved. Might Geach agree? I think that he could, but unlike Nygren and Bernard, he gives no gloss that denies the literal meaning. In any case the construction of love of neighbor as love of others literally for God's sake is not the only way to understand the second commandment of love. Nor is it the best. For one thing, it goes against the parable of the good Samaritan (Luke 10.29–37), the great lesson of which, one would have thought, is that love of neighbor requires one to love and have a caring heart for those brought low and those for whom one may not initially be inclined to care. Also, we should mention, such a construction amounts to what has been called

56. Saint Bernard of Clairvaux, *On the Necessity of Loving God*, in *The Wisdom of Catholicism*, ed. Anton C. Pegis (New York: Random House, 1949), 251–57.

covenant-fidelity; this is a matter that we shall take up in the next chapter in its connection with relationship morality.

Now let me summarize the understanding of Agape that emerges from our investigation. We should bear in mind that what is to be formulated is a concept of Agape needed by relationship morality, a form of love that can be the affective element of coming into the presence of persons, which is to say the affective part of the discovery of the worth of persons, of our person/person relationship to persons. There may be other coherent conceptions of Agape. This has not been denied. I have not argued that Nygren's notion of Agape is incoherent or that Maclagan's is. Nor have I argued that Nakhnikian's notion of undemanding love, which he proposes as a way of understanding Agape, is flawed internally. However, I have not adopted any of these conceptions of Agape without amendment, for none will do as well as the notion I am about to define. At the same time, as will be evident, I have drawn upon each in formulating the definition of Agape needed by relationship morality. Also, there may be forms of love between persons that do not come to Agape in our or in any conception of Agape. This too has not been denied. Aristotle's forms of friendship, love in accord with Singer's analysis, and Nakhnikian's "transactional" love may all occur in human relationships. Perhaps some of these may even animate valuable human relationships. But it would remain that they are distinguishable from the Agape that marks coming into the presence of persons.

Here is our definition of Agape:

1. Agape is giving and not acquisitive. It is undemanding and is not conditional. It is spontaneous in the presence of persons. It seeks nothing in return. These are features importantly expressed in Agape's dispositional side.

2. Agape, as an affective attitude, also has a feeling side. There is in many cases an "Agape-experience" that appropriately invites comparison with sympathy. The Agape-experience is one form of, and even the primary form of, the affective response that is a part of the discovery of the worth of persons, of our person/person relationship to persons.

3. Agape is indifferent to the various forms of accidental value that persons may or may not have. It is a response to the inherent worth of persons as persons.[57]

57. Just as the understanding of Agape we require cuts across Nygren's conception of Eros as recognizing value and his conception of Agape as creating value, so too it cuts across Alan Soble's

4. Agape is not limited to intimate relationships. Agape can of course find expression in intimate relationships, an expression that is different from its expression in human relationships that are not intimate. In both kinds of relationships, however, Agape remains Agape. Agape as love for persons never seen is, and must be, affective. But it would be foolish and wrong to maintain that the affective tone or depth that is a part of coming into the presence of persons generally is indistinguishable from that which is a part of coming into the presence of persons face-to-face in an intimate relationship.

5. Agape, as an accompaniment of the discovery of the worth of others, encourages detachment, that is, detachment from egocentric concerns; it is the affective side, or one form of the affective side, of overcoming the "illusion of selfishness," to use Royce's expression. But this encouragement, strictly, is the product of Agape *as* the affective side of the discovery of the inherent worth of persons, for when the discovery is universal, one comes to see that all persons are equally of worth, including oneself. This detachment, then, opposes selfishness, but not that self-love that reflects the realization of one's inherent worth.

We now turn our attention to another affective attitude: caring. I have in mind caring particularly as exemplified by maternal care. Maternal care, of course, should not be distinguished sharply from love. The care mothers give to their children is, or is a part of, mother love, we should allow. Nevertheless, there is a form of caring, a form that I deem to be paradigmatically present in a mother's care for her children, that I want to examine. It is in the deeply personal caring of a mother for her children that the form of caring relevant to our concern is most evident and most strongly present. So I want to begin by focusing on maternal care, but the form of caring that finally we want to elucidate, of course, cannot be limited to the maternal relationship. What I hope to find is a conception of caring that is at once embodied in the deeply personal care a mother gives to her children and also broad enough in its nature that we can understand such caring as a possible attitude of one person toward all persons.

---

conception of Eros as love that is property-based and reason-dependent and his conception of Agape as love that is neither. Alan Soble, *The Structure of Love* (New Haven: Yale University Press, 1990), 4–6 and passim. Agape, in our understanding, is not dependent on any accidental property or value that those loved may or may not have, and is not based on reasons related to such properties; however, Agape does depend on—is in response to—a property that persons have as persons, their inherent worth, and this property does, in a sense, provide a reason for Agape.

We begin, then, with maternal care. It is the attitude of maternal care, we will recall, that confounded Aristotle's categories and that we reflected on earlier in relation to Singer's analysis of love. Nakhnikian also reflects on maternal care—or, rather, as he says, "the love of adults for infants," which he sees as one variety of undemanding love.[58] He has in mind parental love in particular, if not exclusively, and he distinguishes it from undemanding love for adults. The reason he does so is to be noted, for considering it helps us set aside a form of caring that will not be helpful to us. For Nakhnikian, love for an infant expresses itself in caring for the infant. But, he says, "one does not presume to take care of [another adult]" who is in possession of his or her faculties, for doing so is at odds with respect. This last claim seems right to me, but only if we intend a certain narrow sense of caring, a sense in which caring is "taking care of" those who cannot care for themselves. Such taking care of others resembles parental care, and in its more egregious manifestations, which I think Nakhnikian may have in mind, is sometimes called paternalistic. Taking care of others in this sense, or providing care for others, amounts to taking care of certain needs that others have, with the assumption that they cannot manage to meet these needs on their own, and without the consultation of their wishes and feelings. Pretty clearly, this kind of care can be provided without there being a caring attitude at all. In short, even though mothers do take care of their children, this kind of care, per se, is distinguishable from maternal care. It is not only presumptuous to give such care to an able adult, but such care is not the whole of maternal care or, for that matter, the whole of the care one might give to an impaired adult.

Within feminist thought the idea of an "ethic of care" has been identified and critically examined, as we saw in Chapter 2. Furthermore, the attitudes of caring, and of maternal caring in particular, have been usefully reflected upon by a number of feminist authors. Jean Grimshaw, for instance, explores the extent that relationships between mothers and children can be seen as models for other relationships. They cannot be, at least not in any simple way, she argues. For among other things, mothers are called upon to nurture and to teach their children in ways that have no parallel in many adult relationships.[59] In fact, she concludes, "insofar . . . as women give priority in their lives to the maintaining of relationships with others, and to attention and care for others, such capacities should not be seen just as

---

58. Nakhnikian, "Love in Human Reason," 308.
59. Jean Grimshaw, *Philosophy and Feminist Thinking* (Minneapolis: University of Minnesota Press, 1986), 250–51.

'maternal.' "[60] This conclusion, of course, leaves it open that caring in some form, even if not maternal caring, can properly inform relationships women have to others and, in respect to our broader concern, that caring in some form can be the affective attitude that is part of our recognizing our person/person relationship to persons.

However, Grimshaw also raises some problems with the very concept of caring.[61] For one thing, she points out, appeals to caring can be used oppressively or to disguise exploitation: women who go out to work, and in doing so deviate from a perceived social norm, may be accused of not caring for their children and husbands; a corporation may advertise itself as "caring" in order to disguise its unalloyed concern to maximize its profit. This difficulty, such as it is, of course relates not to caring itself but to misplaced appeals to caring. Also, "experts," such as doctors and psychiatrists, may dominate and reduce to passivity those under their care. This is often the case, as Grimshaw sees it, in the form of treatment male doctors provide for their women patients. In such cases, though, as Grimshaw says, the care involved is paternalistic.[62] Care need not be paternalistic, as we have noted. Not even the care provided by doctors to their patients need be paternalistic, as Grimshaw herself goes on to observe.[63] Another difficulty lies in supposing that care or caring can provide a guideline for right action. In itself, she suggests, it cannot. It cannot, for instance (to use an example she provides), resolve the question of how much time one should spend in committed political action at the expense of time spent with one's family. This, I think, is right. In fact none of the affective attitudes we are examining will operate as guidelines, much less criteria, for right action. (Relationships, as the source and determiners of obligation, come closer to doing that.) I believe that we can agree with Grimshaw on all these points and yet allow all of the following: that care or being caring is an appropriate attitude in human relationships of many kinds, that it can be the affective part of recognizing the inherent worth of persons, and that a perspicuous and signal form of caring is a mother's care for her children.

But what does caring come to when it is not paternalistic and not merely providing care for others? What notion of care is it that has as its germ the care mothers give to their children? Helpful to a consideration of these questions is an analysis of caring provided by Nel Noddings. Caring, for

60. Ibid., 252.
61. Ibid., 215–26.
62. Ibid., 218.
63. Ibid., 223.

her, is embodied in "the approach of the mother."[64] But she does not see caring as necessarily maternal. It can be expressed, for instance, in the relationship between a lover and his beloved, or in the relationship between a son and his mother.[65] And, for her, caring may not issue in direct, observable action. While there are caring acts, there may be no simple, determinate criterion of caring action. Instead, "the acts performed out of caring vary with both situational conditions and type of relationship." Also, for Noddings, caring, from the standpoint of "the one-caring," is a matter of feeling, a frame of mind[66]—that is, we may say, an affective attitude. So far, then, there is much that is promising for our own concern in Noddings' approach to caring.

Now let us look more closely at her notion of the "caring relation" as a general notion of caring. Noddings identifies three requirements of the caring relationship.[67] Two apply to "the one-caring," one to "the cared-for." The caring relation requires, first, engrossment on the part of the one-caring; second, motivational displacement on the part of the one-caring; and third, reciprocity on the part of the cared-for. Each deserves some attention.

Engrossment. In the caring relation the one-caring, for Noddings, is personally and emotionally involved. She discusses this element in terms of such relationships as that between lovers and that between a son and his mother.[68] Pretty clearly, and as the very word would suggest, engrossment of the one-caring with the cared-for is found only in intimate relationships between persons.

Motivational displacement. Invariably in caring for persons, Noddings says, there is a "displacement of interest" in the one who cares in favor of the interest of the one cared-for. This point is analogous to Nygren's point that Agape is unmotivated. While one can care for oneself, for "the *ethical* self," such care emerges from caring for others. In the "deepest sense," she observes, one who cares only for oneself does not care at all.[69] This follows, I think, from motivational displacement being a requirement of one's caring, and it is analogous to Nakhnikian's point that self-love, where it is undemanding love, is not self-indulgent. Essentially, then, the motivation of the one-caring "is directed toward the welfare, protection, or enhance-

---

64. Nel Noddings, *Caring: A Feminist Approach to Ethics and Moral Education* (Berkeley and Los Angeles: University of California Press, 1984), 2.

65. Ibid., 10 and 12.

66. Ibid., 16.

67. Ibid., 150.

68. Ibid., 10–14.

69. Ibid., 14.

ment of the cared-for." In itself the motivational displacement that Nod-dings finds fundamental to caring imposes no limit on the scope of caring, we should note; those cared for, as far as this feature goes, could be few or many or everyone. However, in accord with her focus on intimate relation-ships, Noddings goes on to specify that to act as one-caring is to act "with special regard for the particular person in a concrete situation."[70]

Reciprocity. This requirement of the caring relation must be fulfilled by the cared-for. It takes the form of responsiveness, which Noddings explores by once more reflecting on intimate relationships, especially the relationship between a mother and her children.[71] Reciprocity on the part of the cared-for need not take the form of returned care. A boy's responsiveness to his mother's care might take the form of his acknowledging and responding to his mother's concern when he is late for dinner, or his sharing his aspirations and accomplishments with her. To accept happily such responsiveness is natural on the part of the one-caring, but, Noddings is clear, "to demand such responsiveness is . . . inconsistent with caring." At the same time, it is a requirement of the caring *relation* that the one cared for be responsive.[72] However, there is some latitude in the form this required responsiveness can take. It might take the form of acknowledging the care given, but there can be reciprocity when there is no explicit acknowledgment. Reciprocity from the cared-for might take the form of a "happy growth" of the cared-for before the eyes of the one-caring. Thus, for Noddings, reciprocity need not be returned affection; it can take the form of the happy growth of a child, perceived by the mother to be a response to her caring. And here we might again recall the mother in Aristotle's example: she was happy to see her children getting on well though she received no affection from them.

While there may be merit to Noddings' analysis of caring, pretty clearly, as it stands, it is not the notion of caring we need. The notion of caring we need must include a mother's caring for her children, a son's caring for his mother, and caring in all the various intimate relationships; but it must also encompass the care one may have for strangers half a world away. In particular, her requirement of engrossment on the part of the one-caring does not fit the general notion we need—not if engrossment is an intense personal involvement with another person, as Noddings seems to understand it. This, of course, is not to deny that engrossment is a required feature of caring in intimate relationships. It may well be, as Noddings maintains. But

70. Ibid., 23 and 24.
71. Ibid., 71–73.
72. Ibid., 73–74.

I think that there is good reason to allow that caring is not limited to intimate relationships: one can care for those not seen and never met, whose needs cry for attention—a point to which another feminist thinker, Rita Manning, is very much alive (as we saw in Chapter 2). Noddings' second requirement, motivational displacement, fits better into the general notion of caring, we need. If one is not prepared to set aside or modify the pursuit of one's interests, then arguably one does not care. But I see no reason to limit such motivational displacement to intimate relationships, as Noddings does. Her third requirement is reciprocity. She says that caring does not demand reciprocity, but the caring relation requires it. Her point is clear enough: one can give care to another without any reciprocation, and hence without being in that kind of caring relationship that is marked by a response from the cared-for. This allows, we should observe, that the one-caring would yet have a *kind* of caring relation with the one to whom care is given. The mother who sees no happy growth in her children may yet care and care all the more for them, and though there be no form of reciprocity, a relationship of caring will exist between her and her children, namely the relationship defined by one's giving care to another. It seems, then, that reciprocity is not a requirement of even intimate caring relationships; a fortiori, it is not a requirement of the general notion of caring that we need.

Given her analysis of caring and its concentration on intimate relationships, Noddings has a problem locating caring in ethics, as she is concerned to do. She observes that, on her view, "the caring relation [is] ethically basic" and suggests that "our inclination toward . . . morality derives from caring"; however, for her, caring is "a natural impulse to act on behalf of the present other."[73] The one cared for must be "present" in an intimate relationship. So it is that she rejects "the notion of universal caring—that is, caring for everyone"—and allows only that we can "care about" everyone in the sense that we make ourselves ready to care for those that we may meet in a face-to-face encounter.[74] In short, for Noddings, while the inclination to be moral may "derive" from caring, caring for others cannot be involved in moral action on behalf of those we have not met. I think that Noddings is right to be suspicious of the idea that moral action *must* involve caring for others (about which more in the next chapter), but her analysis of caring excludes caring from any moral action on behalf of those not intimately known.

73. Ibid., 3 and 83.
74. Ibid., 18.

Still, I think that Noddings' analysis may be helpful to us in developing the general notion of caring we seek, a conception of caring that will indeed allow it to be basic to ethics and will allow it to be the affective part of the recognition of the inherent worth of persons, all persons. What conception is this? We can approach the conception we need by revisiting Noddings' three requirements of the caring relation. Caring in the general notion we want to identify is an attitude of the one-caring. It is characterized by these features:

Affectionate concern for those cared for. This concern is not necessarily engrossment, in Noddings' sense, but in accord with her characterization of the attitude of the one-caring, it is concern for the welfare or enhancement of those cared for. In intimate relationships this affectionate concern is engrossment with the cared-for. But in other caring relationships it is not. Yet, we should allow, engrossment is the paradigmatic expression of this aspect of caring or is the most highly potentiated form of this affectionate concern.

Motivational displacement. Caring requires that the one who cares act on behalf of those cared for, as Noddings says. And while caring in itself does not provide a criterion for caring acts, such action, we should agree with Noddings, requires a displacement of one's interests in favor of those of the one cared for. This aspect of caring at once embraces the dispositional side of the caring attitude and corresponds to the unselfishness of Agape.

Happy acceptance of a response from the cared-for. Is a reciprocation on the part of the cared-for required by caring or by every caring relation? I have argued that neither caring nor every caring relation requires reciprocity. Nevertheless the place that Noddings' analysis gives to reciprocity points to a characteristic of caring as an attitude of the one-caring that may distinguish it from Agape: the centricity of a happy acceptance of a response. In intimate caring relationships the one who cares is happy for a return of affection. This would be so in the case of a caring relationship between a mother and her child or in the case of a caring relationship between lover and beloved. In these cases the one-caring rejoices in the returned affection for its own sake and for what it means for the one returning the affection. In caring relationships that are not intimate, the happily received response, in accord with the kind of point that Noddings made, may be the perceived growth of those cared for or their recovery or their relief from suffering—as when one acts caringly for those suffering hardship or social injustice half a world away. Now, I think that something similar may be said of love and of Agape in particular: those who have Agape can be happy to see a response in the form of growth or recovery or relief; and when Agape occurs in an intimate relationship, those who have Agape can be happy for returned affection. Yet it strikes me as significant that in developing the Agape concept this feature—one's being happy for the return of affection—while hardly forbidden, is not prominent. As Noddings helps us appreciate, the conception of caring has its home, as it were, in intimate relationships. Agape, on the other hand, has its home in selfless giving in relationships that may well not be intimate. The paradigms are different for the two affective attitudes. Both paradigms are coherent; both are recognizable in human relationships and reactions. And neither paradigm reduces to the other. The mother who has care for her child or the lover who has care for the beloved may not have Agapeistic love for all persons, and the individual who responds with Agape to all persons may not be in any intimate caring relationship. Still, as caring (which is more clearly affectionate and intimate) is not limited to close relationships, so Agape (which is more clearly a response to persons as persons) is neither lifeless nor excluded from intimate relationships. Caring and Agape, we may say, start conceptually from different ends of the spectrum of human relationships, one from close and intimate relationships, the relationship between a mother and her children perhaps being exemplary, the other from the widest possible relationship, the relationship one has to neighbor. But they meet in a common area of scope.[75]

This general notion of caring identifies an attitude of caring that meets our needs. It, like Agape, can be an attitude toward all persons and can be the affective part of the realization of the inherent worth of all persons. That the attitude of caring is not limited to intimate relationships between persons is recognized by some, if not all, feminist writers, as we have observed. Grimshaw, in particular, I think, recognizes this. While she is of course aware that caring can occur in various "personal relationships," she also allows that the notion of caring may be applied to "social life."[76] And we might recall here a comment that Gilligan made on caring, quoted

75. Marilyn Friedman, in an interesting paper, argues both that justice is relevant to close personal relationships and that care can express itself in the public realm, as in foreign aid. And she allows that both the moral perspectives that Carol Gilligan calls "care" and "justice" (which we encountered in Chapter 2) "take account of relationships in some way." But, she insists, "from the standpoint of 'care,' self and the other are conceptualized in their *particularity*" (Friedman's emphasis). Marilyn Friedman, "Beyond Caring: The De-Moralization of Gender," in *An Ethic of Care: Feminist and Interdisciplinary Perspectives*, ed. Mary Jeanne Larrabee (New York: Routledge, 1993), 266 and 269.

76. Grimshaw, *Philosophy and Feminist Thinking*, 223–24.

earlier (in Chapter 2): "The moral imperative that emerges repeatedly in interviews with women is an injunction to care, a responsibility to discern and alleviate the 'real and recognizable trouble' of this world." Here, clearly, is the recognition that the attitude of caring may extend to persons beyond one's immediate acquaintance.

Now let us see where we are. We have so far seen that there are conceptions of Agape and caring that designate attitudes in the respect/love range of attitudes. Are there other attitudes that belong in this range? There are, I believe. Notable among these other attitudes is respect for persons as persons. Such respect, like Agape and caring, would have both an emotional, or passional, side and a dispositional side, and would not presuppose an intimate personal relationship or acquaintance. This attitude toward persons, like Agape and unlike caring, would have its home in our relationship to all persons as persons. Its emotional aspect may be rather unlike that of a mother caring for her children, or caring in any intimate relationship. This, however, does not mean that such respect cannot occur in intimate relationships, or that respect for persons as persons in its most general manifestation must lack feeling. There is, it seems, some tendency to think of respect as lacking feeling. Thus, we will recall, Nakhnikian tends to equate respect for persons with the dispositional side of unde-manding love, that is, with the active side to the exclusion of the feeling side. Maclagan, too, thinks of respect for persons in this way. For him, "respect for persons and Agape are identical as regards their objective significance, their practical or directive import, but they are subjectively different."[77] Respect for persons lacks the "warmth" of Agape; when we speak of respect for persons, as Maclagan sees it, we abstract the objective import from the "emotional quality" of the attitude of Agape. On the contrary, I suggest, respect for persons does have a quality of feeling, though it may not be that of Agape or caring. Respect for persons need not issue, as Maclagan suggests, in adhering to moral principles doggedly with dead feelings. To think so, to think that respect for persons involves no feelings toward persons, is to come very close to confusing respect for persons with respect for principle (something we touched upon earlier, in Chapter 3, and about which more in the next chapter). The feeling side of respect for persons is akin to *concern* for persons, a felt concern; and if it is lacking, instead of respect for persons, what is being acted upon is respect for the demands of moral principle. Such concern for persons, though, may and

---

77. Maclagan, "Respect for Persons as a Moral Principle I," 216–17.

should extend to all persons. Respect for persons is respect for persons *as persons*. It is not respect for the ability, skill, or moral character of persons, all of which, like respect for moral principle, may involve no feeling of concern for any person. Like Agape, respect for persons is indifferent to such accidental values. Further, respect for persons should be distinguished from respect for the rights of persons. Although respect for persons' rights flows from respect for persons as persons, they are distinguishable, and the former can exist without the latter (more about rights later, as well, but not until Chapter 9).

Reverence for persons is another attitude in this range. It is not to be confused with reverence for human life. Reverence for persons is precisely for persons, and while it may entail reverence for the very lives of persons, it does not entail an attitude toward human life, found among some medical practitioners, that seeks to maintain life at any cost for as many days, hours, or minutes as possible. Other attitudes that belong to this range may be sympathy or empathy for persons as persons and compassion for persons as persons, as opposed to sympathetic sentimentality for appealing persons. Let me say a few words about these attitudes taken together with those we have already identified.

All the attitudes in this range have analogues of the features we found in Agape. They are giving-attitudes: unlike Eros, they are not seeking-attitudes that look to fulfill what is felt as a lack. They are not conditional: they do not give conditionally, as one would meet a contract. They are spontaneous and unmotivated: they are natural reactions that arise spontaneously when one comes into the presence of persons. They are indifferent to accidental value. Each has both an emotional and a dispositional side. None is limited to intimate relationships. Each, as an accompaniment to the discovery of the worth of others, encourages detachment from egocentric concerns.

All the attitudes in this range are to be distinguished from various other attitudes to which they are distantly related. Each, and Agape in particular, is distinguishable from love in many of its manifestations. Agape and the other attitudes in this range are of course distinguishable from Eros toward other persons, but also from a sexual love that has no other reason for its being than shared pleasure, and from a romantic love that is transactional or based on need-related values. However, this is not to say that Agape cannot exist in a romantic love relationship. Again, each is different from various forms of friendship based on shared interest, although this is not to deny that one can share interests with those for whom one cares. Each, and caring in particular, is distinguishable from paternalistic caring-for or anxious caring-about. Each, and respect in particular, is distinguishable from respect for a person for his or her ability or accomplishments, although it is of course possible to respect the abilities of those whom one respects as persons. Each should be distinguished from liking people. When one likes a person, one finds in that person attractive personal traits and enjoys being in his or her company or in communication with him or her. Not liking a person should not be confused with having contempt or disdain for that person, but when one does not like another person, one will find little attractive about that person and not wish to be around him or her very much. Happily—and, I venture to say, often—especially in intimate relationships but also in general relationships, one who has an attitude in the respect/love range toward others will also like them. However, it is possible to like others without loving them and to love them without liking them; it is possible to respect as persons those we do not like; and it is possible to care for, with a caring attitude, those who are not likable. There are as well other attitudes related to those in the respect/love range but still distinctly different from them. For instance, while each of the attitudes in this range carries within itself unconditional acceptance of persons as they are, none involves unconditional approval of persons as they are. One expression of Agape or caring for others or oneself can be the encouragement of change for the better in others or in oneself. Also, none of the attitudes in this range is simply the tendency to be nice or agreeable or uncontroversial; although these attitudes may often be expressed by being nice or agreeable or by holding back from controversy or by respectful politeness, at times love or caring may require opposition to another's wishes and entering into controversy.

The notion of Agape we have identified may be the crowning attitude of the respect/love range of affective attitudes. On balance, though, this may be a distinctly Christian intuition. The question whether seeing Agape as the crowning attitude is a distinctly Christian perception I shall not pursue, although I shall observe that having Agape for persons is hardly limited to Christians. In any case Agape is not the only attitude in the respect/love range of attitudes, and some of the other attitudes, such as respect for persons as persons and caring for persons as persons, may be distinctly free of Christian or religious coloration. What I hope has emerged in this chapter is that Agape is in a range of cognate attitudes any one of which bespeaks a realization-discovery of the worth of persons as persons, the coming into the presence of persons, whether the presence of some or of all persons.

My concern in this chapter has been to reflect on the diversity of the respect/love range of attitudes and to identify the character of the various attitudes that might mark coming into the presence of persons. It has not been to argue that human beings have experienced such attitudes in their concrete lives. I think that some have, but I have not argued that some have. I shall end this chapter with two final observations: First, if we should encounter any individual who responds to some or all persons with an Agapeistic or caring attitude or with any other attitude in the respect/love range—bearing in mind the precise notions of these attitudes developed in this chapter—we have reason to conclude that that individual is responding to the inherent worth of those persons. Second, aside from our encountering individuals who embody an attitude in this range, the best argument for the possibility that individuals may come to embody such an attitude is the possibility of the discovery that requires some one of these attitudes as its affective dimension, the realization-discovery of our person/person relationship to persons.

6

Further Ramifications of Coming into the Presence of Persons

In the last two chapters we have pursued the logic of coming into the presence of persons by examining the two scopes of the person/person relationship and by examining the diversity in the range of attitudes that can form the affective side of coming into the presence of persons, the affective dimension of discovering the person/person relationship to persons. In this chapter we want to continue our enquiry along these lines. Our effort will be to bring into relief certain finer points of the logic of both the person/person relationship and the discovery of that relationship. I intend to address four aspects of their logic, or their interconnected logics. First, we shall review and look more closely at the contrast between acting on moral principle and acting morally in a way informed and vivified by the person/person relationship; here we shall want to consider treating persons as persons as a matter of what has been called covenant-fidelity. We shall then consider the discovery of the person/person relationship in the light of Cardinal Newman's category of "real assent" and in the light of Martin Buber's categories in *I and Thou*. Third, we shall begin to address the question of the relationship between relationship morality and religious belief in God, or at least a part of that question, by trying to identify the place in the Western religious heritage, particularly in the Christian heritage, reserved for the moral perception that a universal person/person relationship exists. And finally we shall explore the extent to which the person/person relationship not only underlies moral obligation in the way that we have seen, but also provides the basis for resolving conflicts between obligations.

First, then, the matter of principle. Here what we want to bring out is the superficially invisible but in fact deeply dividing contrast between acting morally on the basis of principle and acting morally in a way that is informed by a discovery of the person/person relationship. As we have seen, within the perspective of relationship morality, several distinguishable if related attitudes may provide the affective dimension of the realization of the inherent worth of persons. The affective component of coming into the presence of persons, that is to say, may be any of several related attitudes. Perhaps one of these attitudes is preeminent; this has not been denied, nor has it been claimed. On the other hand, it must be denied on behalf of relationship morality that fully realized moral behavior is precisely principled behavior. There is an ultimate and enduring difference between principled behavior grounded in an appreciation of the validity of a moral principle and moral behavior consciously grounded in an appreciation of the person/person relationship.

The point to be seen here should be distinguished from the point that we fail to attain fully realized moral behavior when we act on wrong principles. Of course fully realized moral behavior cannot proceed from wrong moral principles, even if such behavior may, upon occasion, fortuitously turn out to be morally right. This, I would suppose, is intuitively clear and may be taken as a moral axiom. An example we considered earlier (in Chapter 3) was the possibility of someone acting on a principle that forbade him or her to help those persons in need who are of some particular ethnic background. This is an instance of acting on a principle, and in a sense it is acting morally, for it is acting in the moral sphere, even though it almost certainly will amount to acting wrongly; and, too, the operative principle is in a sense a moral principle, for it may issue in any number of moral judgments, wrong as they may be. True as this moral axiom is—fully realized moral behavior cannot proceed from wrong moral principles—the point that I want to pursue is not the point that this axiom is true.

Nor is the point I want to pursue here the point that in order to attain fully realized moral behavior we must not only act in accord with true moral principles but must recognize the binding force of those principles. This too may be a moral axiom. To see its force we need to consider moral principles that are binding, such as the principle of justice that requires us to be fair in the comparative treatment of others, and the ends principle (Kant's "practical imperative"), which requires us to treat persons as ends in themselves and not merely as means. I do not mean to say that this is the only sort of moral principle there is. There are other sorts as well, for instance, the sort of moral principle identified by Grimshaw. For her, we will recall (from Chapter 2), a principle names something to which we are to give moral consideration. Thus, recalling her examples, "Consider whether your behavior will condone that which you think to be morally wrong" is a principle, as is "Consider whether your behavior will stand in the way of maintaining care and relationships." The first principle does not forbid an individual to do what will condone actions that that individual thinks are morally wrong, and the second principle does not forbid an individual to do what will stand in the way of maintaining care and relationships; these principles say only that consideration should be given to these elements. Such moral principles, then, are not binding on our behavior (even though, in a way, they may be binding on our reflection). Grimshaw's conception is coherent, but not the one I want to use here. Some moral principles, given their commonly acknowledged role within ethics, are best regarded as binding: for instance, the just cited principle of distributive justice or fairness. Moreover, some moral principles of this type are best regarded as absolutely binding, such as the principle that we ought never to inflict pain needlessly and, notably, the ends principle.

Now, with this clarification in mind, let me try to bring out the force of the second moral axiom: fully realized moral behavior must not only be in accord with true moral principles but must be in recognition of the binding force of those principles. There is a clear sense in which that person has a deficient, if not incoherent, moral stance who acknowledges the principle of fairness, is in general fair, but then goes on to deny that the principle of fairness creates any moral obligation for him or her. Such a person may well be fair in his or her treatment of others (out of habit or fear of retaliation, say), but then it is as though that person were to say, "I acknowledge a general obligation to be fair in my dealings with others, but I do not see that I am bound by this principle." This incoherent position of course should be distinguished from the position of one who recognizes the binding nature of the obligation to be fair but judges that in some particular case some other obligation takes precedence, a position that is coherent. Similarly, if one recognizes the ends principle as a valid moral principle, in general treats persons as ends, but then goes on to claim not to be bound by this principle, he or she will have a deficient or incoherent moral stance. And here, regarding the ends principle, since it is judged to be absolute and not prima facie[1] and so not subject to being overridden by a superior

---

1. I shall use the term "prima facie obligation," or "prima facie duty," in the sense provided by W. D. Ross in The Right and the Good (Oxford: Clarendon Press, 1930), chap. 2. Specifically, prima facie obligations are not absolute, in the sense that they can be overridden by a superior obligation.

obligation, there will be no question of another obligation taking precedence. However, this difference—that between absolute and prima facie obligations—does not affect the force of the second moral axiom. If someone recognizes the (prima facie) principle of fairness and, in accord with the second axiom, acknowledges that he or she is bound by it, even regarding strangers, that person's moral position lacks this sort of incoherence; and if one recognizes the (absolute) ends principle and acknowledges that he or she is bound by it, even regarding individuals felt to be distasteful, that person's moral position escapes such incoherence.

Still, from the standpoint of relationship morality, behavior that respects both of these moral axioms may yet not be fully realized moral behavior. It is fairly evident that action that is in accord with only the first axiom may still be morally deficient—for being in accord with the first axiom means only that action is not driven by a wrong principle. But how can action in accord with both axioms still be deficient? If action is in accord with the second axiom, it is in accord with the first. So the question comes to this: If action is in accord with the second axiom, why is it not fully realized moral action? The answer that relationship morality gives to this question, in its brief form, may be put this way: because the grounding of such principled action may still be deficient. From the standpoint of relationship morality, fully realized moral behavior is generically different from moral behavior that proceeds from, rests ultimately on, principles, even though they be true moral principles and their binding force be recognized. This is so, for relationship morality, because action that rests ultimately on principles proceeds from a form of morality that has no recognition of the person/person relationship. The nub of the difference between principled moral behavior that proceeds from the recognition of the validity of moral principles and moral behavior that rests ultimately on a recognition of the person/person relationship is just this: in the one form of morality an appreciation of the inherent worth of persons, an informing discovery of the worth of persons, is absent, and in the other form it is present. This difference has ramifications in the form of further substantial differences. Let me try to bring them out in order to support the judgment of relationship morality that moral behavior that issues from principle, without a deeper grounding in a recognition of the person/person relationship, is not fully realized.

These further differences we want to identify are differences that persist even though the binding nature of the principle is recognized as much by those acting on the principle as a matter of principle as it is by those acting in a way informed by the discovery of the inherent worth of persons. If the principle is the ends principle, we want differences that persist even though those acting on the ends principle as a matter of principle may accept, and even insist upon, the proposition that everyone is a person and the further proposition that we have a duty to all persons to treat them as ends. And we want differences that persist even though those acting on principle consistently act upon the universal application of the principle in question, the ends principle or some other, as much as those acting in a way informed by a realization of the worth of persons. In fact there are three such differences to be noted.

First, there is a difference in action. That is, there is a difference between the action-scope of a morality that proceeds from principles and the action-scope of a morality informed by a recognition of the person/person relationship, as in relationship morality. This is so even though there may be virtually no difference between them regarding overt action. Thus these two forms of morality may agree on the overt manifestations of respect for persons required by the ends principle. However, at the same time, one following the ends principle as a matter of principle may recognize no implications of that principle regarding his or her interior actions. He or she, consequently, may accept thoughts and desires at odds with the interior demands of respect for persons as persons. Such an individual may, for instance, dwell in thought on a desire sexually to brutalize another person or a desire to do great harm to an enemy, believing it consistent with the ends principle to do so as long as such desires are not acted upon. For relationship morality, on the other hand (as we saw in Chapter 4), the person/person relationship is violated by one's holding such thoughts and desires, even though there be no intention to act upon them.

Second, there is a difference in attitude. That is, there is a difference between these two forms of morality regarding what attitudes toward others may morally accompany right action. This difference, like the first, relates to the interior dimension of morality; nevertheless it is a distinguishable, second difference. It is a difference that would exist even though there were a perfect congruity between the action-scopes of the two forms of morality, so that those acting on principle, like those following a relationship morality, did not accept thoughts and desires that violate relationships. For a form of morality that sees right action as action on principle, one can act in accord with principle and yet be indifferent to persons as persons, or like C. P. Snow's Skeffington, one can even have contempt for persons, as long as one acts as the principles of morality require (as we saw in Chapter 3).

On the other hand, for relationship morality, or a morality informed by a discovery of the person/person relationship, love or care or respect for persons, or some like attitude, is morally required. It is true, I think, that those who act morally on principle have, and must have, respect for principle, respect for duty, for the moral law. However, respect for moral principle allows a lack of respect for persons as persons. Respect for persons as persons is not respect for principle, not even for the principle that persons are to be treated as persons. One can regard it as a moral duty to treat persons as persons and never merely as means and unfalteringly do so out of respect for the moral law without respect for any person as a person.

Third, there is an epistemic difference relating to the level of grounding. One who acts on principle regards principle as ultimate. For such an individual there is no grounding beyond principle. True, for those with this form of morality there may be a reason to regard some actions and not others as required by duty, and there must be some way in which they acquire their moral principles. Still, for them, moral principle once identified is seen as ultimate: principle is seen as peremptory in its demand that it be followed, though there be no basis for that demand beyond moral principle itself. So it is that those who act on principle act out of a sense of duty, out of commitment to duty or the moral law as such, without any recognition of the grounding of that duty in the worth of persons. On the other hand, those who follow relationship morality see moral principle as grounded in the inherent worth of persons. In this way, for relationship morality, there is an epistemic justification for the moral demands of duty in a way that there is not for those who act morally precisely on principle.

Both those who act on principle and those who follow relationship morality may feel bound by moral duty. However, it is as though there were two conceptions of duty, and a different conception is at work in each of the two forms of morality. Earlier (in Chapter 3) I suggested that we distinguish between two conceptions of duty as it relates to the ends principle. In one conception we act out of a sense of duty when we treat others as ends precisely because the ends principle requires it. In the second conception we act out of a sense of duty when we treat others as ends, in accord with the principle, but precisely because we recognize the inherent worth of persons, upon which the validity of the ends principle rests. While I earlier developed this distinction specifically in regard to the ends principle, it can be extended to moral principle in general.

For these reasons, then, there is a difference between acting morally on principle and acting morally in a way that is informed by a recognition of the person/person relationship. And, for relationship morality, it is a difference of great proportions: acting morally on principle fails to include the foundation upon which moral principle rests and of necessity, therefore, is not fully realized moral behavior.

Notice that I have not argued that acting morally on principle is incoherent, only that such moral action is not fully realized, given the perspective of relationship morality. A morality that sees moral behavior precisely as acting morally out of respect for principle is internally coherent and not unknown in the sphere of human morality. In fact it is a recognizable and common form of what has been called guilt morality. Guilt morality is itself a major type of morality that stands in contrast with relationship morality, and later (in Chapter 12) I shall discuss that contrast. Moreover, acting morally on principle is not altogether to be despised. As I said earlier (in Chapter 3), we must morally respect those who act out of principle, provided the principles are true. We must, I think, morally respect those individuals who are indifferent to persons as persons but nevertheless consistently treat persons as persons on principle, as we must morally respect the integrity of the Skeffingtons of the world who, despite feelings of contempt for many, insist on treating all persons justly as a matter of principle. It may be that many, by following principle and principle alone, do much good for others; it may be that they are morally courageous in the face of hard demands and against popular prejudice and that they are morally upright in denying their own desires for the sake of keeping their obligations. Such individuals as these are very different from those who cite bad moral principles as an excuse, like the individual who refuses aid to someone in need, because he or she holds a principle that forbids giving aid to anyone of that person's ethnic type. Dare we deny that if everyone were a consistent Skeffington the world would be better? Nevertheless, from the standpoint of relationship morality, it would not be as good as it could be.

At the end of Chapter 2, I allowed that relationship morality, which sees morality as involving caring or a like attitude, owed an explanation as to how there could be forms of morality that are not animated by any such affective attitude. That explanation has now begun to emerge. In fact we have found two forms of morality in which no positive affective attitude toward persons is required. In one form individuals operate morally, that is, within the moral sphere, but on the basis of bad moral principles. In the other form, which is more clearly recognizable as a form of morality and which is closer to relationship morality, individuals act rightly on the basis of moral principle. Later, in Part IV, we shall discover that there are yet other such morality forms.

Before we leave this matter of acting morally on principle let me turn the issue slightly in order to bring in a religious analogue. I have in mind covenant-fidelity. Religious persons who act out of covenant-fidelity act morally for the sake of the covenant it is believed we have with God.[2] They may well follow the commandment to love their neighbors, but to love people, for covenant-fidelity, is to regard and treat people as God prescribes in His covenant. In one form of covenant-fidelity, in Donald Evans' formulation, "to love people . . . is to look on them in the role-accepting ways which God prescribes and to live accordingly; for example, one looks on each person as a brother for whom Christ has died and acts accordingly." To love other persons is essentially a matter of seeing them in the role assigned by the covenant and treating them in accord with that role. Not only is what counts as love defined by the covenant with God, but, for covenant-fidelity in an extreme form, it provides the entire basis, or ground, for love. "In an extreme version of a covenantal approach," Evans says, "there is nothing at all in human nature as such which claims or calls forth our love."[3] For such a covenant-fidelity, then, to follow the moral law God prescribes, and even to live in a loving way, is to do so for the sake of our covenant with God—not for the sake of persons, not because persons as persons deserve and call forth our love or respect. This may well remind us of Peter Geach's view. For him, we recall, we are to love our neighbors for God's sake. For covenant-fidelity, we are to act toward our neighbors with love, in ways God prescribes, for the sake of our covenant with God. I am not suggesting that religious or Christian morality must take the form of covenant-fidelity. In fact, I would argue that this is not the case (and later, in Chapter 13, I shall bring forward such an argument). In any case, the analogy between acting morally on principle and covenant-fidelity is clear, I think: For the form of morality that views moral behavior as morally principled behavior, we act morally when we act for the sake of principle or the moral law; for covenant-fidelity, we act as we ought when we act for the sake of our covenantal relation to God. For neither do we morally act for the sake of persons themselves in response to the inherent worth of persons.

2. See Donald Evans, *Faith, Authenticity, and Morality* (Toronto: University of Toronto Press, 1980), 193–96, for his criticism of covenant-fidelity and a discussion of the issue Evans sees it presenting between himself and Paul Ramsey.
3. Ibid., 193 and 195.

Now let us turn to the second concern of this chapter. What light is shed on the discovery of the person/person relationship by Newman's category of "real assent" and by Buber's categories in *I and Thou?* Given some emendations to Newman's category, arguably the discovery of the person/person relationship to all persons or to any person requires a real assent. And, moreover, our seeing that this is so helps to bring into relief some essential features of the discovery.

Newman contrasts real assent with what he calls "notional assent." Let me provide a brief but, for our needs, serviceable sketch of these two categories. Both real assent and notional assent are species of assent to propositions; each is a way of affirming the truth of something that might be claimed or believed. Also, although Newman, in *A Grammar of Assent,* is greatly concerned with religious belief, his two categories have both religious and secular instances. Despite these similarities, however, his two forms of assent are very different. We can draw from Newman's discussion four interrelated contrasting features.[4]

First, real assent contemplates things, and notional assent contemplates notions of things, or abstractions.[5] Though a real assent can be given to a false proposition, real assent issues from the "apprehension . . . of an object," while notional assent issues from some kind of "intellectual act." We may be led to make notional assents through reading or by accepting an authority or by concurring with opinions generally taken for granted, as opposed to having personal experience of a matter. Much of our useful store of everyday knowledge is not gained through personal experience and, for Newman, is a matter of notional assent. For instance, most of us, happily enough, make a notional assent to the proposition, "Arsenic is a poison."

Second, real assent, more than notional assent, leads to action. Newman says that while no assent is "necessarily practical," nevertheless practice is led to "indirectly" when there is a real assent.[6] Newman finds it necessary to say that practice is led to "indirectly," because he feels human beings need a motive like self-love, fear, or hope before they can act. However, we need not subscribe to Newman's view on motives in order to take his point. We might then allow that a real assent to, say, "That man needs our help" can directly lead to our taking action without the existence of a motive, or at least without the sort of motive Newman mentions. Also, for Newman,

4. John Henry Newman, *A Grammar of Assent* (Notre Dame, Ind.: University of Notre Dame Press, 1979), chap. 4, "Notional and Real Assent," 49–92, esp. 76–86.

5. Ibid., 52 and 79.

6. Ibid., 81–82.

while real assents can and do affect conduct, notional assents cannot. This point, too, invites emendation, I think. He makes this claim in a context where he is equating real assent and belief.[7] But notional assent, we might think, also is, or leads to, belief. Despite our giving it only notional assent, many of us believe that arsenic is a poison, and that belief leads us to exercise some caution when we are around arsenic. Amending Newman, then, let us allow that notional assent can result in some kind of belief and that it, or the belief it leads to, can affect action. Maybe, though, Newman means only that real assent, created by contact with things themselves, invigorates action in a way that notional assent does not, even when it is a matter of reasoning. For Newman, notional assent has several different sources, one of which is reasoning; and our conscious acceptance of propositions based on reasoning is firmer than other notional assents, which may be a matter of habit or taking for granted what others believe.[8] Still—and this is how I think we might understand Newman's point—even when a notional assent is a firm assent there is a point to saying it is less affecting than personal experience and its resultant real assent. I may avoid arsenic on the basis of what I have read or heard or reasoned to, but if I have been poisoned myself and survived, I will henceforth avoid it with an unrivaled devotion.

Third, real assent depends on personal experience, while notional assent does not. Real assents "are of a personal character," deriving from the experience of the individual, which may be special and idiosyncratic, in contrast with notional assent, which draws upon commonly shared notions.[9]

Fourth, real assent provides "intellectual moorings" for notional assent, which, by itself, it would lack. These moorings are provided by the individual's personal experience, the "real apprehension" of "objects" themselves. Without this grounding we "are at the mercy of impulses, fancies, and wandering lights."[10]

For Newman, there are as well other features of real and notional assent. For instance, he has it that all general propositions get only notional assent and that real assent requires the activity of the "imagination." However, we need not incorporate these points into our amended categories, which, being thus amended, are not difficult to illustrate. For most of us, I suppose, our knowledge of the electrification of our houses, the working of our cars'

7. Ibid., 87.
8. Ibid., 52–76, esp. 75.
9. Ibid., 82.
10. Ibid., 85–86.

transmissions, the internal mechanism of the elevators we ride on, and our knowledge of much more that we daily take for granted is an amalgam of notional assents to various general propositions. At the same time, the acceptance of other propositions, such as "Arsenic is a poison," "The loss of a child is hardly bearable," or "Living alone on the desert is being utterly alone," may for some be a matter of notional assent and for others a matter of real assent.

Observe that it is possible for there to be either kind of assent to the same proposition—a point about which Newman himself was very clear. This means that within Newman's categories, "All persons deserve to be treated as ends and not merely as means" and "All persons have inherent worth" and "Each person is related to every person by virtue of their being persons" may be given either a notional or a real assent. And now I think that we are ready to apply Newman's categories to our concern. Quite in line with what we saw earlier in this chapter, it is not off the mark to say that acting morally out of a notional assent to these propositions is acting for the sake of moral principle, while acting morally with a real assent to them is engaging in moral conduct that is "moored" in personal experience, specifically one's discovery of the inherent worth of persons. Let me in more detail relate the four features of the amended category of real assent to the realization-discovery of the worth of persons, or, what is the same thing, the realization-discovery of our person/person relationship to persons.

1. The realization-discovery of the person/person relationship is a realization of something about persons, and persons must be encountered, experienced, "apprehended," and reacted to for this realization to be made. Given the nature of realization-discoveries, one does not come to make a realization-discovery that one has a person/person relationship to persons by being told about it—although one might thereby in some sense discover the person/person relationship and in so doing make a notional assent to this proposition. Nor does the realization-discovery result from reasoning to the existence of the person/person relationship from the nature of morality, although, again, a kind of discovery may be made, leading to a notional assent that, in this case, may be a very firm assent. But Newman's categories help us to see and to articulate the difference between a notional certitude of principle, gained from an a priori deduction, and a certitude of the person/person relationship, grounded in an experiential discovery of the worth of persons.

2. The realization-discovery of the person/person relationship has practical implications. It leads to action. Prima facie evidence that no discovery

has been made is the absence of any tendency to respond to persons as persons. But also, we must allow, the complete lack of moral action is prima facie evidence that moral principle is not subscribed to even at the notional level. The difference is that the experiential discovery of the worth of persons invigorates moral action more than a nominal assent to principle (thus the difference in the scope of action we have noted).

3. Within the realization-discovery of the person/person relationship is what Maclagan called the Agape-experience or an analogous experience. For Royce, the moral insight, as he called it, requires our experiencing the other as ourselves. While there may be some question as to just what about persons this experience is of, and some questions about its affective nature, the realization-discovery of the person/person relationship, like all realization-discoveries, is a matter of some individual's realization of the significance of the familiar. It is of necessity a discovery made by an individual out of his or her own experience.

4. The realization-discovery of the person/person relationship provides a "mooring" for the acceptance of moral principle, in particular for the ends principle. This point is related to the epistemic difference between acting on principle and acting morally in a way grounded in the appreciation of the worth of persons. Those who act on principle, I said, regard principle as ultimate. However, they may, or even must, have come in some way to regard as moral principles those principles they accept. How did they? They did in those ways that individuals come to make notional assents—by being taught these principles by parents or other authorities or by reading or perhaps even by inference. So they have a reason for identifying as moral principles the principles they accept, but they have no further reason for regarding them as *moral*. Once they are accepted, they are ultimate. By contrast, the realization-discovery of the worth of persons provides an epistemic grounding for the morality of moral principles, a justification in one's own experience.

So Newman, or our use of his categories, helps us see how a realization-discovery of the person/person relationship leads to a very different kind of moral assent than does the acceptance of principle. With this discovery we have a mooring for the ends principle, for the proposition that we are in the person/person relationship, and for the proposition that persons have inherent worth. The moral realization-discovery, of course, is not precisely of the truth of these propositions; it is of the inherent worth of persons and of our relationship to persons by virtue of their worth as persons; it is of these "objects," to use Newman's term, as opposed to propositions. But if a true discovery, it entails the truth of these propositions and so leads to a proper real assent to them.

The categories of another religious thinker, Martin Buber, can also be used to amplify our understanding of the logic of the person/person relationship and its discovery. Buber, in *I and Thou*, says that human beings have a "twofold attitude" toward the world.[11] On the one hand, we can approach the world and persons with an I-It attitude, and on the other hand, we can approach them with an I-You attitude. An I-It attitude is manifested when we seek to learn about others, to assess their skills, to engage them in our projects, and in general to treat them "as a thing among things."[12] The I-You attitude is very different. It is manifested when we encounter and enter into relation with another. To what extent, let us ask, does Buber's category of the I-You enhance our understanding of entering into the presence of persons?

First let us note and remove what appears to be some unclarity in Buber's thinking about whether the I-You in its manifestation is a relationship or an encounter. At times he seems to think of it as a relationship (or, to use Buber's word, or Kaufmann's, a relation) between an I and a You; at times he seems to think of it as an encounter of an I with a You.[13] And of course one might well point out that encounters are different from relationships: encounters happen, while relationships obtain. The resolution is straightforward, I believe. The I-You seems to be a relationship entered through an encounter of a certain sort, an encounter that involves "a living sense of confrontation," as Buber says in a passage where he connects encounter and relation.[14] On this reading, for Buber, when we confront another human being as a You, we thereby enter a relationship with that person.

Now, this echoes the realization-discovery of persons: for relationship morality, one encounters persons through entering their presence and realizing their worth as persons, and one thereby enters a kind of relationship with them. This relationship is not the person/person relationship itself, which exists realized or unrealized, but is the further relationship one enters upon realizing that one is related to persons according to the person/person relationship. Unlike the person/person relationship itself, which exists by virtue of the shared personhood of persons, it is an entered relationship,

11. Martin Buber, *I and Thou*, trans. Walter Kaufmann (New York: Charles Scribner's Sons, 1970), 53.
12. Ibid., 90.
13. See, for instance, ibid., 55, 109, and 129.
14. Ibid., 69–70.

created and entered by something we do: for Buber, what we do is to speak the "basic word I-You"; for relationship morality, what we do is to encounter persons as persons—we enter their presence and discover their worth as persons.

For Buber, is encountering a You the same as realizing the inherent worth of a person? He does not say so. But the contrast to the I-You is treating persons, as things among things, with an I-It attitude. In the domain of the I-It, human beings are used for our projects; that is, there is no recognition of persons as ends in themselves, we may say.[15] On the other hand, for Buber, the I-You realm is not limited to persons. He allows that one can have an I-You relationship with a tree. In fact there are three "spheres" in which the world of relation, the I-You, arises: life with nature, life with men, and life with spiritual beings.[16] For relationship morality, we enter into the presence of persons in discovering the person/person relationship. We do not enter into the presence of trees, at least not in the same sense that we enter into the presence of persons.[17]

There are some further apparent differences between Buber's thought and relationship morality. For one thing, Buber uses "object" and "thing" as distinctly negative terms, and, for him, what we designate an object or thing we perceive or react to with an I-It attitude. Here Newman is closer to relationship morality. Newman does not use "object" negatively; for him, we make real assents when we apprehend "objects." For relationship morality, in accord with Newman's categories, we make a real assent to the worth of persons when we have personal experience of that "object." But there is no real opposition between Buber and relationship morality here, I submit. Rather, there are two senses or uses of "object" at work. Buber's sense is that in which we say we should not regard or treat persons as objects; this is the sense of "object" in which to treat persons as objects is to treat them as means, as tools. And relationship morality agrees that persons are

15. See ibid., 110, where Buber portrays the individual enmeshed in the I-It as living in a world "shot through with ends and means."

16. Ibid., 56–58.

17. Buber goes on to say that in each of the three "spheres" he distinguishes, "we gaze upon the train of the eternal You" (ibid., 57). Buber, as a religious thinker, is very much alive to a religious application of the I-You category, which, though we cannot pursue it here, I would not wish to deny. In *The Cognitivity of Religion*, 104–17, I provide a discussion of coming into the presence of God through a religious realization-discovery of God's presence in all that is familiar to us (all that we gaze upon, we may say, following Buber). See Chapter 3, note 17, above. Later, in Chapter 15, we shall examine the question whether inanimate life has inherent value and the possibility of coming into the presence of plants and of natural objects.

not to be treated as objects in this sense. Newman uses "object" in that sense in which a person, or the worth of persons, can be an object of our experience, a sense that allows that persons can be objects of respect and God an object of devotion; this is the sense of "object" in which objects are objects to which a subject's experience, respect, or devotion is directed. And relationship morality agrees that persons and the worth of persons can be objects in this sense. Also, though, Buber seems to regard experience itself invidiously. In an I-You encounter the one encountered is neither experienced nor described, for Buber.[18] To have experience of another human being is to make that person an It in the I-It matrix. At the same time, however, it is possible to *behold* a person as a You: in the "act of beholding," that beheld is not a thing among things.[19] For Buber, there is no experience of persons within the I-You where experience is studious examination or curious observation. But beholding persons is not experiencing them in this or these ways: in beholding persons we are moved. As we may behold the glory of God, so we may behold the glory of persons in their personhood, we may say. So Buber's discussion does not dismiss experience of the sort that Maclagan finds in an Agape reaction or that, following Newman, we can say informs a real assent to the worth of persons as persons. But our reflecting on Buber forces us to distinguish more carefully between beholding persons and experiencing them in other ways.

At least to this extent Buber's reflections help our effort. But there is another matter. For Buber, persons "appear" by entering into relation to other persons.[20] Buber could mean by this that before there is an entered relation or an encounter there literally is no person, only a human being, capable of being either a You, a person, through encounter or an It through being treated as a thing among things; or, alternatively, he could mean that persons are ineluctably persons, but emerge—appear—as persons to others only in a relationship or encounter. I favor the latter, which fits with relationship morality: persons are discovered to be persons, are beheld as persons, just when one discovers that one is related to them as person to person.

We now take up the third concern of this chapter: What place in the Western religious heritage, particularly in the Christian heritage, is allowed

18. Buber, *I and Thou*, 59.
19. Ibid., 90; and see 61 and 61 n. 6 for Kaufmann's note on "behold" (*Schauen*).
20. Ibid., 112.

for the moral perception that a universal person/person relationship exists? This question constitutes a part, but only a part, of the larger question of the relationship between relationship morality and religion. Only later will we be in a position to deal with other parts of the larger question (in Part V).

There is, I suggest, a definite and natural place in the Western religious heritage for the moral perception of a universal person/person relationship. In fact that heritage may be said to be the home, or a home, of this moral perception. Yet, things are not so simple. Even if we limit our reflections to the Christian heritage, we find no one unified view of the inherent worth of persons. Rather, there are several different and apparently competing Christian views that impinge upon this perception. We have already encountered the view, which Nygren seems to have held, that persons are given value by being loved by God but have no value in themselves. And there is the view that human nature is "unclean" by virtue of its great distance from the wholly other nature of God, a view that we shall address in Chapter 13. Here, though, let us look at one other, more or less traditional Christian view that initially seems in open opposition to the inherent worth of persons, namely, the view that the lives of human beings in this earthly existence are worthless. This view, in the formulation of it developed by Kurt Baier, embraces three propositions: (1) since the Fall, life on earth for humankind has not been worthwhile, but instead a vale of tears; (2) a perfect afterlife awaits human beings after the death of the body; and (3) human beings can enter this perfect life only if they endure their earthly lives to the bitter end.[21] Such a view may not have been unknown in the Middle Ages. One perhaps recalls the story of St. Bernard of Clairvaux averting his eyes from the beauty of nature; deeply ascetic, he considered the Romanesque church decorations of the twelfth century as vain and distracting from prayer and contemplation. Again, we may recall that for the medieval author of *The Cloud of Unknowing* one has a "true knowledge and experience" of oneself when one knows oneself to be a "wretch, filth, far worse than nothing," this knowledge and experience being humility, he says.[22] However, the medieval view embodied in this fourteenth-century work seems to be that life is worthless, or wretched, when lived without God, in a life of unredeemed sin, outside an entered relationship to God. So it is that the author of *The Cloud* links human wretchedness with sin and

21. Kurt Baier, "The Meaning of Life," reprinted in *Meaning and Existence*, ed. William T. Blackstone (New York: Holt, Rinehart & Winston, 1971), 805.

22. *The Cloud of Unknowing*, ed. James Walsh, S.J. (New York: Paulist Press, 1981), chap. 32, 181.

allows that humility, which is "nothing else but a man's true understanding and awareness of himself as he really is," may be attained by reflection on one's sinful state.[23] On this understanding, wretchedness is not inherent in earthly existence as such, but in sinful existence. The idea that material existence as such is evil or corrupt is more Platonic than Christian. Still, let us allow that there is a Christian view like that expressed by Baier, which says that earthly life itself is worthless and that its only function is to be a necessary step on the way to a perfect afterlife. Two comments must be made on such a view.

First, this is not the only Christian view of our earthly life. Much in the Christian heritage joyfully celebrates the wonder and beauty of God's creation and joyfully accepts God's way. In the Psalms we find the Psalmist proclaiming that the heavens tell of the glory of God (Ps. 19); we find the Psalmist proclaiming that goodness and mercy will follow him all the days of his life (Ps. 23), that the hills gird themselves with joy (Ps. 65), that all the earth should make a joyful noise to God (Ps. 66); the Psalmist proclaims that his heart and flesh sing for joy to the living God (Ps. 84), that as the Lord reigns, let the earth rejoice (Ps. 97); and he calls upon all the lands to make a joyful noise to the Lord (Ps. 100). For Kierkegaard, in *Fear and Trembling*, it is joy that distinguishes a trusting faith in God from "infinite resignation," infinite resignation being a state of despair in which one gives up hope and, with a kind of tranquility, resigns oneself to the loss of "everything" in this life. Infinite resignation is attainable by a great exertion of will and brings rest but no joy. Faith, on the other hand, is joyful in its trust of God's goodness in this life.[24] For Kierkegaard, then, the kind of relationship to which God calls us, the relationship of faith, is imbued with joy for this life.

23. Ibid., chap. 13, 148. The author of *The Cloud*, however, characterizes this cause of humility as imperfect. A second cause of humility is God's superabundant love. This cause is perfect and results in perfect humility; and it is completely distinct from reflection on our wretchedness, though in this life perfect humility presupposes a movement through imperfect humility. Chaps. 13–15, 147–53.

24. Søren Kierkegaard, *Fear and Trembling* and *Repetition*, ed. and trans. Howard V. Hong and Edna H. Hong (Princeton: Princeton University Press, 1983), 34–50. In *Fear and Trembling* Kierkegaard's exemplar of faith is Abraham, who, in Kierkegaard's rendering, though he follows God's command to take Isaac to the land of Moriah, does not doubt that Isaac will not be taken from him; he has faith in God and does not doubt His promise. Though he proceeds with dread, though he is prepared to give up what is most dear to him, he is joyful in his trust of God and his certainty that he will not lose Isaac. By way of contrast, if Abraham had had only infinite resignation, in his heart he would have given up forever what is most dear, in his case Isaac, and so attained the peace of resignation, but he would not have had joy; his faith would have been lost, not to be regained even with the sacrifice of the ram.

Second, it should be commented that, strictly, saying earthly existence is in itself without value, if this means it is a vale of tears, a time of tribulation and suffering, is not to say that human beings are without inherent value. So this view does not really deny the moral perception of the inherent worth of persons. To get an incompatibility we have to add the element of the Fall (as Baier does) and understand that doctrine such that fallen human beings have no worth in themselves.

However, allowing that there is such an otherworldly Christian view, whether or not we qualify it in accord with these two comments, still with Christianity, as within Judaism, there is the contrasting central theme that human beings are created in God's image, enunciated in the Book of Genesis (Gen. 1.27). Elaine Pagels observes that "the Genesis accounts of creation introduced into Graeco-Roman culture [the idea of] the intrinsic worth of every human being, made in God's image." This idea, she further observes, was taken up in the eighteenth century by the American authors of the Declaration of Independence when they affirmed the "self-evident" truth that "all men are created equal," a notion that she says would be rejected by Aristotle, among others[25]—a point quite in accord with what we saw, in Chapter 5, of Aristotle's understanding of the character of love. And earlier, in the fifteenth century, Giovanni Pico della Mirandola embedded this religious idea in his *Oration on the Dignity of Man*, citing "David's testimony [that man is] but little lower than the angels."[26] David is of course King David, the Psalmist, and the reference is to the Psalms.[27] True, Pico finds this idea in all cultures and traditions and in his embellishment of it gives it a Platonic turn. It remains, however, that the idea of the inherent worth of human beings is an abiding theme of the Christian tradition.

Moreover, it is a central and informing theme of the Christian heritage, although this is not to say it is the only informing theme. There are of course many themes in the Christian heritage and its variants. In the sphere of human worth it is as though there were two competing themes: the theme that human beings are fallen, sinful creatures and the theme that human beings are in the image of God. These two themes ultimately can be made

25. Elaine Pagels, *Adam, Eve, and the Serpent* (New York: Random House, 1988), xix and xx.

26. Giovanni Pico della Mirandola, *Oration on the Dignity of Man*, trans. A. Robert Caponigri (Chicago: Henry Regnery, 1956), 8.

27. Ps. 8.5 in the King James Version is "For thou hast made him [man] a little lower than the angels, and has crowned him with glory and honour." In the Revised Standard Version it is "Yet thou hast made him little less than God, and dost crown him with glory and honor."

peaceably to lie down together, I submit (and later, in Chapter 13, I shall try to show how they can be reconciled). In any case, whether or not it is resolvable with other themes, there is in the Judeo-Christian heritage the theme that human beings are created in the image of God. And in addition to proclaiming that human beings are created by God, this theme, as Pagels says, proclaims that human beings, created in the image of God, have inherent worth. In short, in its germ this theme embodies, in the language of relationship morality, the moral perception of a universal person/person relationship, which is the perception that persons are related to one another as beings of inherent worth. Perhaps not all see this moral perception as a part of Christian teaching; Baier, I suppose, would not—although he consistently could, as I have suggested—and Nygren apparently does not. Be that as it may, the theme that human beings are created in the image of God provides within Christianity a natural place for the fundamental moral perception of the worth of persons, and it is this Christian understanding of human worth that issues in an understanding of the commandment to love our neighbors as the commandment to give to all persons the love that they deserve and that their nature calls forth or should call forth.

Our fourth concern in this chapter is with conflicting duties. I have argued that the person/person relationship is foundational to obligation. To what extent, however, does it determine the resolution of conflicts between obligations? It is this question that we must explore, and with its exploration we shall complete our investigation of the person/person relationship vis-à-vis moral obligation.

Notoriously, our moral obligations can come into conflict. For instance, it may be possible for an individual to save another from life-threatening danger only by not doing what he or she promised to a third individual. This is one of the stock examples of a conflict of duties. Trite though it is, it is at least a clear example of the conflict between the obligation to help those in need and the obligation to keep a promise. Other illustrations of conflict cases could be marched by, but I will take the point that obligations can and at times do conflict to be evident. As I said earlier, there is nothing incoherent in the position of a person who, in a conflict-of-duties situation, judges one duty to take precedence. Sometimes, in fact, as in our stock example, if we assume that the promised action is not a life-and-death matter, it may be quite clear what one ought to do, that is, which obligation is superior.

So far there is nothing problematic, I would think. The question is, What considerations decide which obligation takes precedence in conflict cases? Sir David Ross, in *The Right and the Good*, reflected on cases of conflict between what he called "prima facie duties" (that is, "conditional" obligations subject to being overridden by a superior obligation). As he saw it, there is no self-evident overarching principle that decides such conflicts. Rather, he said, "we come in the long run, after consideration, to think one duty more pressing than the other."[28] As A. C. Ewing says, commenting on Ross's view, "we just have to judge each case on its individual merits."[29] As far as this point reaches, it is correct, I believe; and it is in agreement with relationship ethics. In fact much of what seems to me to be unproblematic about conflict-of-duty cases is in accord with Ross's exposition, although some is not. While Ross believed that we could be certain of our prima facie obligations, he felt that we could never be certain which obligation takes precedence in a conflict case.[30] He felt that we can never be certain in conflict cases, because it is neither self-evident nor deducible from self-evident premises which duty is superior in cases of conflict. However, I see no reason to follow Ross here; in straightforward, uncomplicated cases, like the conflict case in our example, the superior duty may be evident, and we can be certain of it.

Ross provides us with a list of prima facie duties, or types of prima facie duties, which he calls a "provisional list of the divisions of duty," but he does not claim completeness for his list.[31] It includes, for instance, obligations to keep a promise, obligations to repay a good turn (obligations of gratitude), obligations to better the lot of others (obligations of beneficence), and obligations to improve ourselves (obligations of self-improvement). For Ross, different obligations "rest on" different factors. Some duties rest on one's own previous act: thus one's obligation to keep a promise rests on one's own previous act of implicitly or explicitly making a promise, and others, obligations of reparation, rest on one's previous harmful act toward another. Some, the obligations of gratitude, rest on the beneficial acts of others toward ourselves. Some, the obligations of beneficence, rest on the fact that we can better the conditions of others. And some, the obligations of self-improvement, rest on the fact that we can improve ourselves "in respect of virtue or of intelligence." Ross, correctly, I think, finds no single principle that accounts for the various types of prima facie duties; he finds no criterion

28. W. D. Ross, *The Right and the Good* (Oxford: Clarendon Press, 1930), 30–31.
29. A. C. Ewing, *Ethics* (New York: Macmillan, 1965), 73.
30. Ross, *The Right and the Good*, 20 n. 1, and 30.
31. Ibid., 21, 22, an´ 23.

for obligations in the strong sense of "criterion" used by Mill. So, for Ross, since there is no general principle that settles all conflict-of-duty cases, there is no general principle for the determination of prima facie obligations in the first place: in neither case is there a criterion in the strong sense.

As I say, I believe that Ross is correct on both these points. Moreover, both claims are in accord with relationship morality. Properly understood, the claim that there is no overarching principle that determines all prima facie duties denies that either the utilitarian's good effects or some person's prior act determines all instances of moral duty, or indeed that anything else does, in the way a criterion in the strong sense would. But it does not deny that the source of all moral duties is in relationships between persons. In the case of each type of prima facie duty Ross names, it is some relationship between persons that creates the obligation. In the case of the obligation to keep a promise, obligations of reparation and of gratitude, certain acts create relationships between persons that, certeris paribus, would be violated if the promised act were not performed or the harmful act not redeemed or the beneficent act not repaid. In the case of bettering the condition of others, any of several general relationships between an individual and other persons, or the person/person relationship itself, would be violated. Even in the case of the obligation to improve oneself, failure to do so, which would amount to a form of lack of respect for oneself, would violate a relationship, namely, the person/person relationship that one bears to oneself.

But let us remind ourselves, our concern just here is with the resolution of conflicts between obligations, and specifically with the role of the person/person relationship in such resolutions. What resolves conflicts between obligations? What resolves the conflict between, say, our obligation to our family and our obligation to relieve the hunger of strangers half a world away, when these obligations cannot both be met? As I remarked, Ross's claim that there is no single factor, no criterion in the strong sense, that can be cited to resolve all conflict-of-duty cases is in accord with relationship morality. Relationship morality has no strong criterion for the resolution of such conflicts. There probably is none, which is essentially the judgment of Ross, for whom such conflicts must be resolved on the individual merits of each case. Relationship morality can explain why no such principle, or criterion, as "Justice decides" or "Welfare decides" or "Family first" will properly decide all conflicts of duty. Morality, at bottom, does not rest on a single principle or criterion. It rests on relationships between persons, and sometimes what one relationship requires us to do will conflict with what another relationship requires us to do. In such a conflict case, for relationship morality, the ultimate resolution is a matter of comparing and weighing the demands of our different relationships (for instance, the demands of our relationship to our family as against the demands of our larger relationship to those suffering social injustice). But, for relationship morality, there is no neat principle that says, "Always favor your closest personal relationship," or one that says, "Always favor your relationship to the greater number of persons."

However, relationship morality has more to contribute than the observation that in conflict-of-duty cases the resolution, finally, is a matter of weighing the demands of our different relationships. Consider again the stock example we had before ourselves shortly before, the case in which the obligation to help those in need conflicts with the obligation to keep a promise. In such a case, if the need is for life-saving aid and the promise is to meet someone for a spot of pleasant conversation, clearly the obligation to give help is superior. And the reason it is superior is also clear: preventing danger or death, we want to say, morally outweighs keeping a promise to meet someone for conversation. This is so clear, in fact, that it is perverse, or at least misleading, to say that we have to *weigh* the effects of not giving aid against those of giving aid in order to determine what we ought to do. The probable effects are clear from common experience. It remains that, in an intuitive way, in this kind of case, effects determine the right course of action. Still, this is not the whole story. The person/person relationship also has a role to play. It enters in putting constraints on the moral consideration that is to be given to effects. It is the person/person relationship that accounts for our moral intuition that, in the absence of overriding considerations, preventing harm to one person is equally as important as preventing harm to the next person and for our moral intuition that we are not entitled simply to disregard the harm done to any person. Corollaries of the person/person relationship are that (1) each person's worth is equal to any other's and (2) each person has inherent worth. In the same way, these background constraints, generated by the person/person relationship, operate in the resolution of other conflict-of-duty cases.

Of course often we need not fall back on explicit reflection on the person/person relationship, or its constraints, in order to reach a resolution of a conflict of duties. Often, as in our stock case, our moral duty is plain enough. But in other instances, when we do have to reflect explicitly on the harm we may do in taking one course of action or the other, when we do have to weigh the effects of our choosing one action or the other, the constraints we have identified become a part of our reflection. Whether or not these constraints are a part of our explicit moral reflection, however, they are operative as constraints on how conflict cases are to be resolved (rather in the way the meanings of the words we use constrain the meaning of what we say, whether or not we reflect on the words we use). With one addition I believe that these comments are sufficient to show that the person/person relationship has a role to play in determining the resolution of conflicts of duty. The additional comment is this: neither the person/person relationship nor the constraints it generates entails that we ought to treat persons identically. For one thing, the needs of individuals vary; for another, when needs are the same, other individual relationships may morally determine the form of moral action; this is why one is under a special obligation to provide for one's own family (with whose members one has a special and particular relationship) before providing for the family of a stranger (with whose members one has no such special and particular relationship), although if the stranger's family is in danger of starving and one's own family is not, the respective demands of one's relationships may well require one to aid the stranger's family.

So far, in our effort to explore the extent to which relationships are foundational to ethics, we have addressed obligation, including the conflict of obligations. With this last section on conflicts of obligations we come to the end of our examination of obligation as a distinct part of morality. We have dealt with it at such length mainly because a necessary part of that examination was a scrutiny of the ultimate human relationship, the person/person relationship. Now we must turn to the other mansions of morality: moral principles, justice, the good, virtue, and rights. Not surprisingly, for relationship morality, the person/person relationship is not irrelevant to these parts of morality as well, but now that the character and logic of the person/person relationship have been established, we can more briefly treat these other elements of morality. However, there is one intervening matter we have to address before we take them up, a matter that might justly be deemed pressing for an ethics that sees relationships between persons as foundational. Before we proceed further we must address the question, What is a person?

7
What Is a Person?

On virtually any view of ethics, morality is an affair involving persons. Morality, on any view faintly in touch with human moral phenomena, embraces the behavior of persons toward other persons. This is true irrespective of whether we regard morality as divinely ordained, whether we regard moral behavior as extending to nonhumans, and whether we regard moral dispositions, the virtues, as basic to moral action; and it is true irrespective of the theory of obligation we adopt. For any viable view of ethics, then, it is not irrelevant what a person is. However, if on our view the foundations of obligation are relationships between persons, the person/person relationship being the ultimate relationship, or, more strongly, if on our view the foundations of all morality are, brick and mortar, relationships between persons, the person/person relationship being the ultimate relationship, then it seems we must take seriously indeed the question "What is a person?" This is the issue of personhood, and, clearly, relationship morality must address it.

The issue of personhood should not be conflated with the issue of personal identity. That is, the question "What is a person?" should be distinguished from the question "What makes a particular person that person?" It might be possible to know what a person is without knowing what makes a particular person that person. To put the point another way, there is a logical difference between recognizing persons as persons and recognizing particular persons as those persons, just as there is a difference between recognizing an object as an apple and recognizing it as the same apple we saw yesterday.[1] True, these questions can be seen as related, as I think they

---

1. Notice that this point remains unaffected even though it should turn out that an individual

were seen by John Locke. For Locke, a person is "a thinking, intelligent being, that has reason and reflection, and can consider itself as itself, the same thinking thing, in different times and places; which it does only by consciousness."[2] Persons are beings with consciousness, for Locke, but his real concern is with personal identity, and he goes on to claim that what makes a person the same person is having the same consciousness (importantly expressed in memory). Related though the two issues may be, it remains that they are distinguishable, and one may venture a criterion for what makes a person a person without venturing a criterion for what makes a particular person that person. Thus there is logical space in which to claim that having consciousness—some consciousness—makes a person a person, without claiming further that it is having the same consciousness that establishes personal identity. The first claim does not raise the question of when consciousness is the *same* consciousness; the second claim does.

The idea that persons are persons by virtue of having consciousness, suggested by Locke, has a certain intuitive appeal. It is undeniable that human persons generally exhibit this attribute, and in important ways it seems to determine the treatment of persons as persons, as opposed to things. Does consciousness provide a criterion for personhood? Many have thought so. Recently this thesis has been argued for by R. E. Cranford and D. R. Smith. They maintain that "consciousness is the most critical moral, legal, and constitutional standard, not for human life, but for human personhood" and that "consciousness is the most important characteristic that distinguishes humans from other forms of animal life."[3] This is their thesis, and their concern is to address the bioethical issue of the proper medical treatment of permanently unconscious patients. Cranford and

---

over time may be more than one person, or "self," even though it should turn out that we can, to use Derek Parfit's language, "subdivide a person's life into that of successive selves." On such a view as this, one may be one person in, say, one's adolescence and another person in one's old age. See Derek Parfit, *Reasons and Persons* (Oxford: Oxford University Press, 1986), chaps. 14 and 15, esp. 319; cited by Charles Taylor, *Sources of the Self* (Cambridge: Harvard University Press, 1989), 49. While we may have an abiding intuition that we are the same person from birth to death despite psychological and bodily changes, and while much of the way we speak of ourselves requires that this is so, some uses of the word "person" support the contrary idea, as when one says, "I am no longer the person I was." However, whether or not the latter more truly reflects "personal identity" need not detain us, for our concern is not with the issue of personal identity but with the issue of personhood.

2. John Locke, *An Essay Concerning Human Understanding* (New York: Dover, 1959), bk. 2, chap. 27, sec. 11, I, 448.

3. Ronald E. Cranford and David Randolph Smith, "Consciousness: The Most Critical Moral (Constitutional) Standard for Human Personhood," *American Journal of Law and Medicine* 13 (1987): 233.

Smith are right that moral implications flow from their proposed standard for personhood, and shortly we shall note some of these. Our main concern, though, must remain with their proposed standard itself.

There is, I think, a certain confusion regarding their proposed standard, or criterion, for personhood. It emerges both in what they say about the meaning of "consciousness" and in their elaboration of consciousness as a standard for personhood.

They say that there is "no satisfactory concept or philosophical definition of consciousness or awareness." Nor will they try to provide one, they say. They then observe that "consciousness and the capacity to experience pain and suffering are functions of the neocortex" and go on to conclude that since "permanent unconsciousness means a total loss of consciousness," "permanent unconsciousness means the loss of all neocortical functions."[4] On this view, consciousness means the presence of neocortical functions. While Cranford and Smith seem confident of their conclusion about what permanent unconsciousness "means," they should be more hesitant. Their thesis is that the most critical standard, or criterion, for personhood is consciousness. If consciousness means the presence of neocortical functions, then we can reason that when such functions are absent, consciousness is lacking, and hence, given their thesis, personhood is lacking. But for this inference to go through, it must be that consciousness means the presence of neocortical functions in the strong, semantic sense of "means," for it is only meaning in this sense that will allow us to treat one term as synonymous with the other term. It is not sufficient that consciousness means the presence of neocortical functions in the causal sense of "means," the sense we use when we say that smoke means fire or that fire means smoke. While fire causes smoke and smoke, like heat, is an indicator of fire, conceptually there can be one without the other—and in fact there sometimes is, as in the case of smokeless charcoal fires. Cranford and Smith, though, are not saying that consciousness means the presence of neocortical functions in the semantic sense; they admit this in their way, I think, when they admit there is no satisfactory philosophical definition of consciousness to which they can appeal. Their claim apparently is that consciousness causally means the presence of neocortical functions, as an effect signals its cause. But the truth of this claim does not establish that permanent unconsciousness is synonymous with, or even the same thing as, the loss of neocortical functions, and so, even assuming the truth of their thesis, does not allow us

4. Ibid., 237.

to conclude either that the presence of neocortical functions is the standard for personhood or that the loss of such functions entails the loss of personhood.[5]

It is not a part of my critique that Cranford and Smith cannot cite the concept of consciousness. It is a perfectly good, common, pretheoretical notion. However, it is not part of our pretheoretical concept of consciousness that its permanent loss equates with the loss of neocortical functions: one can have a grasp of the concept of consciousness, be able to say what the word means in a dictionary sense, and be able to apply the concept correctly, while having no notion of the brain's anatomy or functions.

Allowing that there is an adequately clear concept of consciousness available to Cranford and Smith, I detect a second confusion in their elaboration of consciousness as a standard for personhood. Their claim, as first stated, is that consciousness is "the most critical" standard for personhood. But very soon they have shifted their position to "the view that *the capacity for consciousness* is the most important moral and constitutional definition of human personhood." Later, when they are considering implications of their view for when fetal rights are to be recognized over maternal rights and for the temporal point "when human personhood begins," they suggest that personhood begins when "the fetus develops consciousness . . . and the capacity to experience pain and suffering." Since a being must have consciousness in some degree in order to experience pain and suffering, they are naming but one condition: consciousness. At this point, then, they have reverted back to the thesis that consciousness is the proper standard for personhood. At the end of their essay they speak of "consciousness, or the capacity for consciousness," as though they were the same thing.[6] But of course they are not.

What of Cranford and Smith's general thesis? It is one thing for consciousness to be the criterion for personhood; it is another for the capacity for consciousness to be. Pretty clearly consciousness is not the criterion: as Cranford and Smith, along with the rest of us, would surely insist, sleeping persons are yet persons, as are those in temporary unconscious states of other sorts. What about the capacity for consciousness? Is it the criterion

5. It of course is not necessary to hold that "consciousness" means, semantically, the presence of neocortical functions, in order to hold that consciousness and neocortical functions are identical, as might be asserted by the identity theory in some form. My critique of Cranford and Smith in this paragraph relates to their apparently confused use of "means." The identity theory has its own problems.

6. Cranford and Smith, "Consciousness: The Most Critical Moral (Constitutional) Standard for Human Personhood," 236 (my emphasis), 239, and 247.

for personhood? Cranford and Smith are interested in defining the conditions under which individuals are not persons, and so they focus on cases in which their proposed criterion is not met. Those who lack the capacity to regain consciousness are "permanently unconscious." What Cranford and Smith want to argue, it seems, is that a permanently unconscious individual is not a person. There are three types of permanently unconscious individuals, they suggest.[7] First, there are those in a persistent vegetative state (or PVS); individuals in this state have eyes-open unconsciousness with "physiologic sleep/wake cycles." Second, there are those in a state of coma, who have an eyes-closed unconsciousness. And third, there are anencephalic infants, infants with an eyes-open unconsciousness born with "essentially no cerebral hemispheres, but [with] a variable amount of functioning brain stem." Such patients or individuals are to be distinguished from those with minimal consciousness on the one hand and from the brain dead on the other hand (brain dead individuals have no brain functions, while these three types of permanently unconscious individuals have some brain functions).

Cranford and Smith offer several lines of argument for the conclusion that permanently unconscious individuals are not persons. First, they argue that "regardless of one's views on . . . human personhood, permanently unconscious patients are in an entirely separate category from all others."[8] In various court cases they have been distinguished from, for instance, the profoundly demented and those with minimal consciousness. This, however, shows nothing regarding the issue of personhood, even with the court cases cited; for even if the permanently unconscious are in a separate category from all others, they may yet be so *within* the class of persons.

Another argument that Cranford and Smith use is that permanently unconscious individuals no longer have any interests. Though by some commonly used medical standards such patients may not be dead (they are not brain dead and have cardiopulmonary functions), nevertheless, Cranford and Smith maintain, they have no interests in further medical treatment or in continued existence. Permanently unconscious patients do not have any interests, they say, because they can no longer experience anything. At the same time, they allow that society may have interests *regarding* persons. They allow that "important social goals" may be served by "showing respect and care" for the bodies of unconscious patients and also may be served by

7. Ibid., 237–38.
8. Ibid., 234.

respecting their previously stated wishes.[9] A good part of what Cranford and Smith have in mind here seems to be the retrieval of organs for the use of others in need of an organ transplant.[10] But permanently unconscious individuals themselves, they are saying, have no interests.

Also, they argue, permanently unconscious individuals cannot be said to have rights, because the "rights enumerated in the Constitution and the Bill of Rights are predicated on principle, or the capacity for principle."[11] The distinction between legal and moral rights, we should observe, does not burden Cranford and Smith's discussion. When these two lines of argument are combined, Cranford and Smith are affirming that lacking the capacity to become conscious, the permanently unconscious have neither interests nor rights. Given that persons have interests and rights, the conclusion they would draw is clear.

However, counter to Cranford and Smith, it can be argued that permanently unconscious individuals are yet persons for the very reason that they have both the interests of persons and the rights of persons—moral rights, if not legal rights. Let us take interests first. For one thing, note that if we can ask whether the interests of others outweigh the interests of the permanently unconscious in a setting of limited resources, as it appears we can, our doing so presupposes that the permanently unconscious have interests. I do not want to suggest that a consideration of the interests of the permanently unconscious necessarily points to the continued maintenance of their lives in a vegetative state. It could be argued that it is in their interest (in accord with their dignity or inherent worth as persons) to be allowed to expire. Cranford and Smith do not see this possibility, for it rejects their assumption that only individuals with consciousness can have interests. Yet, arguably, consideration can be given to a permanently unconscious person's good, considered as a function of that person's worth or dignity. And consideration of the good of permanently unconscious persons may not only allow but require the discontinuation of their physiological lives, especially, but not only, in accordance with their earlier expressed wishes.

Though there be no known wishes, we can ask regarding those who are permanently unconscious, What is in their interest, relating to their good

9. Ibid., 241. Later they come close to qualifying their claim that permanently unconscious patients have no interests, when they say that such patients "do not have any interests except for preservation of the body" (243). But, they say, this is "questionably an interest in light of the permanent loss of consciousness," which reaffirms their claim.

10. Ibid., 245.

11. Ibid., 247. They allow one exception: "the right to life itself." But this right, they say, "becomes meaningless when consciousness can never exist . . . or . . . is forever extinguished."

and worth as persons? We can ask, Is it in their interest or not to continue life support that sustains the vestiges of life? It may be that the maintenance of life is not always a good. This may be so for *conscious* persons in certain cases of suffering without the possibility of recovery; in such cases it is far from clear that maintaining a suffering existence for the maximum number of hours is in the interest of the patient. A similar argument may hold for an unconscious vegetative existence without the possibility of recovery of consciousness, where a person's life has been reduced to tissue existence. On this reasoning, permanently unconscious individuals may be allowed to expire not because they are no longer persons with interests but because they *are* persons and because a consideration of their interests may require the cessation of life support.

This much shows that we can intelligibly consider the interests of the permanently unconscious. What of the rights of the permanently unconscious? We can consider and respect the good of those who are permanently unconscious, where this good is a function of their inherent worth; and it is in their interest that we do so. But this is sufficient to make a prima facie case that the permanently unconscious have rights, at least the moral right to have their good respected.

It should be noticed that we are not reasoning that permanently unconscious individuals are persons because they have interests and rights. Such reasoning would presuppose that *only* persons have interests and rights, and this may be false (animals may have interests and may also have rights, without being persons—a matter we shall explore in Chapter 15). However, the interests and rights of permanently unconscious human beings are not just any interests and rights. They are the interests and rights of persons, of human persons: permanently unconscious human beings have an interest in having their good as human persons respected, and a corresponding right to have that good respected. And we can legitimately reason that permanently unconscious individuals are persons because they have the interests and rights of human persons.

At some points Cranford and Smith argue for their proposed criterion for personhood on the basis of social considerations (such as organ retrieval and the allocation of limited resources).[12] At most, such an argument would establish a case for adopting a legal definition of death in terms of the permanent loss of consciousness, and we should observe that the issue of what is a person, even allowing that a person ceases to be a person at death,

---

12. Ibid., 245 and 246.

is different from the issue of what is the best legal definition of death. There may be weighty social reasons for adopting a legal definition of drunkenness in terms of the amount of alcohol in the blood, but depending on the amount specified, some who meet the definition may not be intoxicated, while some who do not meet it may yet be intoxicated. So too with the issue of personhood, although in this case there is not the analogous justification for a tolerance of error. In any case, at the end of their essay Cranford and Smith become tentative and suggest that more debate is necessary before "any definitive labels" are applied to the permanently unconscious.[13]

Others too have reflected on the issue of personhood. Among them is Joseph Fletcher, who, like Cranford and Smith, sees a need in biomedical ethics for increased clarity about what it is to be a person. The "synthetic concepts" *human, man,* and *person,* he says, require "operational terms" to enable us to "get down to cases—to normative decisions." Fletcher wants to describe "the nature of man," which he sharply distinguishes in meaning from "human nature." The latter term he regards as designating a "fixed" nature that is "given in the nature of things," and he agrees with those who reject such a notion. What Fletcher proceeds to do is to propose an operational definition of "man," a "profile of man" as he says, consisting of a list of "criteria or indicators." Really, though, his concern is with "person" and personhood. While Fletcher uses "man," "person," and "truly human" interchangeably, his concern pretty clearly is with personhood. What is critical," he says, "is personal status, not merely human status." And "a 'man' . . . is not just human, he is a person." His "profile of man," then, is intended to define, at least provisionally, "personhood."[14]

Fletcher proposes fifteen positive "criteria or indicators" in his "profile."[15]

1. Minimum intelligence. He suggests that any individual "who falls below an I.Q. grade of 40 in a standard Stanford-Binet test, amplified if you like by other tests, is questionably a person; below the mark of 20, not a person."
2. Self-awareness. That is, he says, "self-consciousness," "the quality we watch developing in a baby"—as others have expressed it, aware-ness of oneself as a distinct entity.

13. Ibid., 248.
14. Joseph Fletcher, "Humanness," in *Humanhood: Essays in Biomedical Ethics* (Buffalo, N.Y.: Prometheus Books, 1979), 10–12.
15. Ibid., 12–16.

3. Self-control.
4. A sense of time. A sense "of the passage of time."
5. A sense of futurity.
6. A sense of the past. That is, "memory."
7. The capability to relate to others. The ability to form "inter-personal relationships of the sexual-romantic and friendship kind."
8. Concern for others.
9. Communication. "Completely and finally isolated individuals are subpersonal."
10. Control of existence. Not being "helplessly subject to the blind workings of physical or physiological nature."
11. Curiosity.
12. Change and changeability. This feature importantly involves creativity.
13. Balance of rationality and feeling.
14. Idiosyncracy.
15. Neocortical function. This is "the cardinal indicator"; all the others hinge on it, Fletcher says.

How are we to understand these fifteen features? For Fletcher, is it that when they occur in conjunction, these fifteen features are sufficient for personhood? Is it that all are necessary for personhood? Is it that at least some are necessary, but not all? Or is it that none is necessary, although each indicates personhood? While he says that his profile invites addition or subtraction by others, he tends to present these fifteen features, or some of them, as necessary conditions, and not as indicators. Arguably, none is necessary for personhood.

Peter Singer, reflecting on Fletcher's profile, has argued that many of its features or indicators are not necessary for an individual to be a member of Homo sapiens. He argues this in order to show that the issue of what it is to be a person, the issue of personhood, is not the same as the issue of what it is to be a member of Homo sapiens, a point that should be granted, I think. The features Singer considers are minimum intelligence, self-awareness, self-control, a sense of the future, a sense of the past, the capacity to relate to others, concern for others, communication, and curiosity (that is, Fletcher's first, second, third, fifth, sixth, seventh, eighth, ninth, and eleventh features). But, as Singer observes, "a newborn infant, an accident victim whose brain has been so damaged that he is in an irreversible coma, and an old man in a state of advanced senility are all members of the species

Homo sapiens, though none of them possesses all of Fletcher's 'indicators,' and the road-accident victim, at least, possesses none of them."[16] Singer does not argue that none of these features is necessary for personhood. But the very examples Singer provides may also be offered as examples of *persons* without one or all of the nine features from Fletcher's profile that Singer considers. The mother who takes in her arms her newborn infant has no doubt that her infant is a person. The family members who try to decide what is right for an accident victim in an irreversible coma are trying to help a person they love. One's grandfather does not cease to be a person if he becomes senile. Moreover, the accident victim in an irreversible coma is permanently unconscious and so, we may assume, lacks neocortical function, Fletcher's fifteenth indicator. The other fourteen indicators depend on the fifteenth, Fletcher says. So, if all the others depend on the presence of neocortical function and the accident victim lacks this brain function, we should conclude that he lacks the first fourteen features as well. Yet, arguably, in accord with what emerged in our discussion of Cranford and Smith's thesis, he is yet a person with the interests and rights of a person.

Aside from this consideration, various of Fletcher's features, regarded as necessary conditions for personhood, are somewhat parochial. For instance, his eleventh feature, curiosity, makes an odd concession to post-Renaissance sensibilities, as opposed to those of the medieval period. We may agree that there is something of worth in curiosity and yet be reluctant to agree with Fletcher that "indifference is inhuman," as he says in connection with his eleventh feature. In the thirteenth century Jean de Joinville, the chronicler of the Seventh Crusade, expressed no curiosity about "the Earthly paradise," said to be the source of the spices the crusaders found in Egypt. Such a lack of curiosity accords with a prevailing medieval sentiment. It is in accord with Anima's condemnation of "a craving for knowledge" in *Piers the Ploughman* and in accord with the advice in *The Imitation of Christ* that it is folly "to give our minds to things curious." Surely Jean de Joinville, even if he were consistent in this lack of curiosity, would, along with his medieval

16. Peter Singer, "Animals and the Value of Life," in *Matters of Life and Death: New Introductory Essays in Moral Philosophy,* ed. Tom Regan (New York: Random House, 1980), 235. Singer, in this essay, as elsewhere, is concerned with the ethical status of animals. In connection with that concern he wants to sort out the terms "person," "human being," and "member of the species *Homo sapiens.*" His reference to Fletcher is to a paper entitled "Indicators of Humanhood: A Tentative Profile of Man," which is an earlier version of "Humanness." In "Humanness," in spite of the essay's title, and in spite of the title of the book in which it appears, *Humanhood,* Fletcher, as we have seen, is clear that his "profile of man" contains "criteria or indicators" for "personal status," or personhood. Fletcher clarifies his concern in added material not found in the earlier paper.

contemporaries, not to mention the invincibly incurious of our time, remain human and a person. Something similar might be said about Fletcher's tenth feature, control of existence. Since the Renaissance and on into our scientific and technological age, a certain value has been found in control of our environment and physiology. But this was not always so and is not so for various of our contemporaries. Again, Fletcher's fourteenth feature, idiosyncracy, seems odd cast as a necessary condition for personhood. Human beings are "idiomorphous," Fletcher says; each human being is "distinctive." He mentions a concern with cloning in connection with this feature, but he does not mention identical twins. Would twins that were the same in behavior and feelings fail to be persons? It appears so, on Fletcher's view.

Also, we should note that Fletcher provides five "negative points," or features, regarding personhood. By "negative point" he does not mean a feature that shows an individual not to be a person, but rather a feature that is not a necessary condition for personhood. In stating them he continues to use "man" in place of "person."

1. Man is not non- or anti-artificial. Persons may be conceived and gestated outside the womb.
2. Man is not essentially parental. Individuals can be "fully personal" without having offspring.
3. Man is not essentially sexual. "Sexuality . . . is of the fullness but not of the essence of man."
4. Man is not a bundle of rights. Fletcher's concern here is with what he regards as an erroneous "notion of a human nature" that includes " 'human rights' and certain other given things, like 'original sin' and 'the sense of oughtness' and 'conscience.' "
5. Man is not a worshiper. "Faith in supernatural realities," or "mystique," is "not essential to being truly a person," although, "like sexuality, it may arguably be of the fullness of humanness."[17]

Fletcher, it seems to me, may well be right that these five features are not necessary for personhood, except perhaps for the fourth feature, depending on how it is understood. As far as Fletcher's fourth "negative point" relates to rights, his objection is to the idea of "objective, preexistent" rights that are "absolute" in the sense that they cannot be overridden. There is a large

17. Fletcher, "Humanness," 16–18.

issue here. However, I am inclined to say that there are moral rights that do not depend on legal or social arrangements and in this sense are "preexistent" to such arrangements, although they or many of them can be morally overridden and so are not "absolute." (In Chapter 9 we shall deal with the question of rights and their place in relationship morality in some depth.) Perhaps we can amend Fletcher's point thus: it is not essential to persons that they be seen as having legal or moral rights; that is, a person whose legal rights have been made forfeit by the courts, or whose moral rights are overridden by greater moral concerns or are not recognized by others, remains a person.

Like Cranford and Smith, Fletcher thinks that we need to make humans nonpersons in order to justify not maintaining life, and, like Cranford and Smith, he gives great importance to neocortical functions, his fifteenth and "cardinal" indicator. But, unlike Cranford and Smith, Fletcher refrains from defining consciousness in terms of neocortical functions. In fact, if we distinguish consciousness from self-consciousness, or self-awareness, consciousness is not on his list. Self-awareness is his second feature, and he is not alone in seeing it as an indicator of personhood. Self-awareness was important for Locke, and Peter Singer sees it as the defining feature of persons, construing it as involving a minimally rational understanding of the world and the capacity to feel pain and pleasure.[18] However, since self-consciousness presupposes consciousness, for reasons we raised in our discussion of Cranford and Smith's thesis we should conclude that self-consciousness is no more the defining feature of personhood than is consciousness. And as Singer's own example of the accident victim arguably shows, it is no more a necessary condition for personhood than the other features on Fletcher's list of criteria.

There may be other features that could be proposed as the necessary conditions of personhood. Instead of my sifting and sorting through such candidates, let me now try to propound a view of personhood that will adequately serve the needs of relationship morality. Personhood, I submit, may entail no necessary and sufficient, or even only necessary, natural features such as minimum intelligence or consciousness. In this respect it may be like a number of other concepts, concepts like *intelligence* and *jealousy*, for instance, and even more humble and commonplace concepts. In a well-known section of *Philosophical Investigations* Wittgenstein shows us

---

18. Singer, "Animals and the Value of Life," 235–36. This is not to say that, for Singer, only humans or all humans are persons (240).

that there are no necessary and sufficient conditions for all the things that are games.[19] At the same time, there are many *indicators* that someone is intelligent or that something is a game. We may come to see that some activity is a game by observing the lighthearted spirit of the participants or by noting the element of winning or by detecting the ferocity of the competition. In the same way we may come to see the intelligence of someone by discovering intelligence in one of its many manifestations. The concepts of *game* and of *intelligence,* as some would say, are "polythetic."[20] And as there are several indicators of games and intelligence, so there may be many indicators of personhood. All fifteen of the "criteria or indicators" in Fletcher's "profile" may, in this way, be indicators of personhood. Intelligence in some degree, self-awareness, self-control, a sense of the future, a sense of the past, the ability to relate to others, concern for others, and the ability to communicate may all be indicators of personhood, as may be the ability to control our environment, curiosity, creativity, a balance of rationality and feeling, idiosyncracy, and having a functioning neocortex. We can draw other indicators from Fletcher's list of "negative points," for they are "negative" only in not being necessary conditions for personhood: a parental role, sexuality, and a religious sense may all be indicators of personhood. Other indicators not touched upon by Fletcher's reflections might be a sense of humor, humility, arrogance, courage, vulnerability, and more. In a former age, when explorers expected to encounter chimeras as much as they expected to find elephants, we can imagine such explorers coming across individuals very different from themselves racially and culturally, whose humanity and personhood were not immediately apparent; and we can imagine these explorers coming to see the personhood of these encountered individuals through detecting their intelligence or sense of humor or religious sense or curiosity or their concern for one another, even if in what was to them an exotic form. These features, then, in this encounter would serve as a sufficient indication of the personhood of the individuals encountered. But this is not to say that they are generally sufficient, that they would be sufficient in other instances or that they are necessary in every instance.

On the view of personhood I am presenting, then, there is no criterion

---

19. *Philosophical Investigations,* sec. 66.

20. See Rodney Needham, "Polythetic Classification: Convergence and Consequences," *Man,* n.s., 10 (1975): 349–69. Needham, who is aware of Wittgenstein's reflections on "family resemblance" concepts, relates polythetic classification to the categories of natural science and especially to the categories of social anthropology.

for personhood in the strong sense of "criterion," the sense in which John Stuart Mill thought utilitarianism provided a criterion for right actions. That is, there is no feature or set of features that is necessary and sufficient for personhood. There are instead any number of indicators of personhood, any of which may be able to bring us to see that an individual is a person in certain circumstances, although, at the same time, in various other circumstances, each may be defeated as a positive and conclusive indicator of personhood. There may be a vast range of such indicators of personhood, well beyond what I have so far suggested. It may not be off the mark to say that philosophical ruminations on the nature of man have often brought to center stage some such indicator. Is man by nature a social being, as Aristotle and many of his day and place thought?[21] Is man by nature a rational being? These features of human beings may be indicators of personhood, even though not essential to being a person. Kierkegaard, as Anti-Climacus in *The Sickness unto Death*, saw a self, or person, as a dynamic relationship, relating itself to itself and to God. Kierkegaard, as Johannes Climacus in *Concluding Unscientific Postscript*, proclaimed that actual individuals are "existing" individuals; that is, they are in a "process of becoming."[22] For Johannes Climacus, persons are "existing" by virtue of their "subjectivity"—their striving and becoming—and a stress on the "objective" makes individuals fantastic or comical.[23] For Kierkegaard, in both works, persons are not static, though they might try to be. Like Aristotle, Kierkegaard draws to our attention indicators of personhood, albeit indicators very different from those evident to a philosopher of Athens in the fourth century before the Common Era. Kierkegaard, in the nineteenth century of the Common Era, in the midst of a Christendom settled upon an "objective" understanding of religious faith, rediscovers the "subjectivity" of individuals. Yet as the hermit monks of Christianity's early centuries remain persons, Aristotle notwithstanding, so, Kierkegaard notwithstanding, "objective" believers (and "objective" nonbelievers) remain persons. Not that either Aristotle or Kierkegaard failed to recognize that this is so, for each is arguably presenting a picture of what it is to be a *fully realized* person (or a fully realized human person). In any case, though Aristotle and Kierkegaard may draw to our attention important features of

21. NE 1097b10–12.

22. Søren Kierkegaard, *Concluding Unscientific Postscript*, trans. David F. Swenson and Walter Lowrie (Princeton: Princeton University Press, 1941), 79. See *Sickness unto Death*, 14–15, cited in Chapter 4, note 4, above.

23. Kierkegaard, *Concluding Unscientific Postscript*, 109.

personhood, these features are not necessary conditions for being a person; they are rather indicators. In the same way, others—poets, dramatists, novelists—may draw to our attention other important, perhaps culturally emergent, indicators of personhood.

To say that there is no criterion for personhood in the strong sense of "criterion" is to say that persons do not have a "fixed nature" in one sense. It is to say that the nature of persons is not fixed in the sense that it cannot be specified in terms of necessary and sufficient natural features like having intelligence, self-awareness, curiosity, and the like. Observe, however, that this is not to say that persons have no fixed nature "given in the nature of things." This question is left open. It may be that in the nature of things, in God's creation, if you will, it is given, and so in a sense "fixed," that persons are persons by virtue of a nature that is not "fixed" in the first sense.

Also, we should observe, though persons have no fixed nature in the sense we have identified, there yet can be, and is, no uncertainty in the multiplicity of straightforward, simple instances of personhood. In the last chapter we saw that in uncomplicated cases of conflict between moral duties it may be quite clear which duty is superior, even though there is no overarching principle that governs all conflict-of-duty cases. So too regarding personhood. It is, I think, just wrong to believe that unless there is an established general principle that provides certainty for every judgment that something is an X, we can never be certain that a thing is an X. Wittgenstein detected a philosophical passion for generality, but when language is working, we need not appeal to a general principle in order to be certain of our judgments about any number of matters, such as, in clear cases, our judgment that someone is intelligent or that two people are in love. (In this connection it will be recalled that in Chapter 6, when I sought to clarify the concept of the specific form of love that might be the affective side of the discovery of the worth of persons, I explicitly refrained from offering a general analysis of love. And also in this connection, it should be said again that for relationship morality relationships are foundational to moral obligation and to all morality, but this does not mean that they embody a criterion in the strong sense for obligation or moral rightness.)

Nevertheless there is a persistant sense on the part of many that there must be some underlying feature that defines our personhood. For many may want to ask how it is that we can identify persons as persons without an identifying feature. How, then, do we identify persons as persons? Normally we do not. We meet persons. We meet people at gatherings, meet new colleagues, meet old friends. Rarely do we identify persons as persons. And when we do identify persons as persons, we do so by virtue of an indicator, or what in the identification-situation operates as an indicator. The explorers we imagined earlier, who came upon persons of an appearance beyond anything they had encountered before, identified the individuals they met as persons; and they could have done so by virtue of some such indicator as intelligence or sense of humor or religious sense or curiosity or their concern for one another, perceived by the explorers through the veil of cultural difference. We can, I suppose, imagine other settings in which an individual is identified as a person. In a room filled with store mannequins we might identify what we initially took to be a mannequin as a person standing immobile in their midst. Perhaps in this case the indication that there is a person before us would be a slight movement of the eyes. This is an extraordinary situation, admittedly; but then it is only in extraordinary situations that we identify persons as persons. On the view that there is no single defining feature, no strong criterion, for personhood, we can yet be sure in such cases as these that those we identify as persons are persons. Meanwhile, in more ordinary cases, when we meet persons we know and persons we do not know, there is no issue of their personhood. Here we can be certain those we meet are persons (or, more accurately, there is no uncertainty in that the question of our certainty does not arise), not because we identify those we meet as persons, but because there simply is no real question about whether those we meet are persons.

Still, I can imagine that many will hold out for a common feature of persons by virtue of which, persons are persons. The passion for generality of which Wittgenstein spoke is both well-entrenched and coherent, and I do not suppose that my comments set to rest this inveterate philosophical concern as it applies to personhood. My effort has been to show that there is an alternative to its presupposition, a coherent alternative, which relationship morality can use. So it is, given this alternative, that it is not an embarrassment for relationship morality that there is no strong criterion for personhood that can be used to answer the question "What is a person?"

But now let us turn to another question: What gives value to personhood? This question merges with the other. In fact they are hardly distinguishable in that, for relationship morality, a person is a being with the inherent worth that persons have by virtue of being persons. This inherent worth is the value of persons we discover when we enter into the presence of persons. Coming into the presence of persons, of course, should not be conflated with meeting persons. We do not necessarily come into the presence of persons when we meet persons in a room or on the street. To put the point another way, there is a difference between coming into the presence of persons in the moral sense we have sought to clarify and coming into the *physical* presence of persons. Coming into the presence of persons in the moral sense is to be significantly affected by the realization of their worth as persons. It is to make the moral discovery of their worth as persons. All of this we have seen.

Now, however, we want to ask what it is about persons that gives them inherent worth. Though there is no single defining feature of persons that makes them persons, is there some feature shared by persons that gives them inherent worth? Some have thought so. Among those who have thought so are Immanuel Kant and Josiah Royce. Kant and Royce, as we have seen (in Chapter 3), both allow for the inherent worth of persons and even give a place to the moral discovery of the worth of persons as persons. For Kant, persons are inherently valuable because they are rational beings capable of morality, and coming to see the inherent value of persons is a matter of coming to see their rationality and, for him, their consequent capacity to participate in the moral life. For Royce, we attain the "moral insight," as he called it, when we realize that others are a "mass of states of experiences, thoughts and desires," just as real as we are. For relationship morality, there is no problem attaching to their shared insistence on the inherent worth of persons. However, there is a problem attaching to their respective construc-tions of the recognition of the worth of persons. There is a problem, that is to say, with the respective ways that Kant and Royce understand what it is about persons that gives them inherent worth.

Taking Kant first, we should be reluctant to equate the recognition of persons' intrinsic worth with the recognition of their rationality and capacity for virtue, as Kant does. Maclagan, in his reflections on respect for persons as persons, has strongly registered just this reluctance.[24] Respect for persons, I have suggested, is a personal attitude in the range of attitudes any one of which may form the affective side of the recognition of the intrinsic worth of persons. Maclagan's concern is whether respect for persons as persons is the same thing as esteem for rational wills capable of virtue. Clearly, he believes, it is not. Even if a person has a completely corrupt will, a will incapable of right moral action, he or she remains a person and is worthy of respect as a person. Similarly, even though demented and utterly irrational,

24. W. G. Maclagan, "Respect for Persons as a Moral Principle I," *Philosophy* 35 (July 1960): 199–200.

so much so that he or she is not responsible for his or her actions, a person yet remains a person and worthy of respect as a person. In the first case, which Maclagan considers, a bestial person has a corrupt will incapable of moral goodness (it of course is not relevant to the present point that in practice we may be unable to judge with any confidence that a person has such an incurably corrupt will). In the second case, which augments Maclagan's considerations, a psychotic has a will incapable of moral action or of any action for which responsibility would accrue (and here such judgments can be made and are made, and, notably, psychotics of this description, though perhaps confined, are legally and morally required to be treated as persons with the worth of persons and all the rights of persons consistent with their confinement). In each case, then, the person remains a person worthy of respect. From such considerations as these Maclagan concludes that respect for persons does not equate with esteem for rational wills capable of right moral action.

This reasoning is very forceful, for surely bestial persons and psychotics do retain their intrinsic worth as persons and remain worthy of respect as persons. (That this is so does not deny that the person with a corrupt will deserves punishment or, alternatively, requires treatment; and it does not deny that the psychotic should be committed to an institution for his or her protection and the protection of others. Rather, what this being so implies is that any proper disposition of their cases will respect their intrinsic worth as persons.) True, Kant might yet affirm that the person with a corrupt will and the psychotic conceptually are capable of morality by virtue of their yet being persons. In this way Kant could give a place to respect for them as persons that is compatible with a respect for persons construed as esteem for rational wills capable of virtue. But, of course, if Kant should say this, he would have to allow that, at least sometimes, we recognize beings as rational beings capable of virtue by seeing that they are persons and not the other way around. He would have to allow, that is to say, that we can come to see that beings are persons (and so, in his thinking, capable of rationality and virtue) independently of any manifested rationality or morality. So, even allowing that Kant might make this reply, it remains, as Maclagan suggests, that the deeper basis of the worth of persons is their being persons and not any manifested rationality or virtue.

Similar comments hold for Royce's construction of the worth of persons. For Royce, we come to appreciate the worth of others through the realization that they are experiencers like ourselves. However, at least sometimes, this is not and cannot be the way of our recognition. For we can recognize the humanity and personhood of a brain-damaged person whose brain has ceased to function at the higher levels, as we can recognize the personhood of a child who from birth has been in a persistent vegetative state, a child who is at times awake but never conscious—despite the thesis of Cranford and Smith, as we have seen. Of course, Royce could make the claim, analogous to that we conceded to Kant, that these persons conceptually are capable of having experiences, though physiologically they cannot. While this point may be correct (at least I shall not argue against it), still any who come to appreciate the intrinsic worth of such persons as persons will not do so by coming to appreciate that they have experiences like our own. Just to the extent that we are clear that such brain-damaged individuals are yet persons, we should be clear that the recognition of others' personhood, and of the worth of others as persons, is not contingent on recognizing that they too have experiences.

Just as various strong criteria can be and have been proposed for personhood, so various strong criteria can be and have been proposed for what it is about persons that gives them intrinsic worth. Not surprisingly, these criteria tend to be the same as those proposed for personhood. In each case, though, the same kinds of counterexamples that were brought forward to show that the proposed features—consciousness, minimum intelligence, and so on—are not necessary for personhood can be used to show that they are not necessary for, and so cannot be the correct construction of, the inherent worth of persons.

For relationship morality, in coming into the presence of persons we discover their inherent worth as persons. It is an essential property of persons that they have inherent worth as persons, but this does not entail that persons have inherent worth by virtue of any natural property or set of natural properties. " 'Human worth,' " says Joel Feinberg, "is best understood to name no property in the way that 'strength' names strength and 'redness' names redness." And, he suggests, "In attributing human worth to everyone we may be ascribing no property or set of qualities, but rather expressing an attitude—the attitude of respect—toward the humanity in each man's person."[25] "The inherent worth of persons" surely does not name any *natural* property, but it yet names a property of persons—just not a property that reduces to or presupposes and supervenes upon some invariable set of natural properties, like minimum intelligence, rationality,

---

25. Joel Feinberg, *Social Philosophy* (Englewood Cliffs, N.J.: Prentice-Hall, 1973), 94; quoted by Louis P. Pojman, "A Critique of Contemporary Egalitarianism: A Christian Perspective," *Faith and Philosophy* 8 (1991): 488.

consciousness, and so on. More circumspectly, it is a property *if* we can indeed enter into the presence of persons, for in doing so we *discover that persons have the property of inherent worth.* In discovering the inherent worth that persons have as persons, we not only take up an attitude of respect toward persons, although respect, or some attitude in the respect/love range, is a dimension of that discovery. If we do indeed discover the inherent worth of persons, far from baselessly taking up an attitude of respect toward them, we find ourselves respecting persons as persons precisely because that is a proper attitude to have toward beings with the property of inherent worth.

There is one other question that we should consider. It is not unrelated to the other two and, in a sense, overlaps the others. This third question asks, What gives unique value to human existence? However, this question, unlike the others, presupposes that human existence has unique value. Many, I think, would agree that this is so. One who does not is Peter Singer. Singer considers four "attempts to explain why all human life possesses unique value," all of which he finds wanting.[26]

First, he asks, is consciousness uniquely human? (He means consciousness, not self-consciousness, which is distinguishable from consciousness per se and which, as we have seen, Singer thinks defines personhood.) Consciousness, he argues, is not uniquely human. Many nonhuman animals feel pain: mammals and birds show as clearly as humans that they feel pain; and this alone requires some form of consciousness. Singer buttresses this argument with references to the anatomy of the nervous systems of humans and nonhuman animals, but the fact that we perceive the pain felt by animals by itself seems to me to be sufficient. For, clearly, many nonhuman animals—such as dogs and cats in our common acquaintance—feel pain, and, clearly, feeling pain requires some form of consciousness; thus, from this consideration alone we may conclude Singer is right that consciousness is not uniquely human. Earlier, in our examination of Cranford and Smith's thesis that consciousness is the "standard," or strong criterion, for personhood, I tried to show that neither consciousness nor the capacity for consciousness is necessary for personhood. Singer's point here, marshaled against that thesis, shows that having consciousness in some form is not sufficient for personhood—assuming that not all the various animals that undeniably have consciousness in some degree are persons. However, what

26. Singer, "Animals and the Value of Life," 222–32.

Singer intends to show is not that conscious will not do as the criterion in the strong sense for personhood, but that it will not explain the unique value of human life. I think that we can agree with him that it does not.

Second, can we say that human beings are uniquely valuable because only human beings have an immortal soul—a view that Singer associates with Descartes's thinking? Singer argues that we cannot, for the existence of immortal souls cannot be proven.

A third attempt to explain the unique value of human life appeals to what Singer calls the "Dominion Theory." The name of this theory derives from Genesis: in Gen. 1.26 God creates "man" and gives them "dominion" over "the fish of the sea, and over the birds of the air . . . and over every creeping thing." On this view, Singer suggests, God gave human beings dominion over all other creatures, to do with as they would, because animal life is "of little or no value." But this view cannot be supported, Singer argues, because the belief that there is a God cannot be justified. We should observe that the Dominion Theory is only one theological view of the relationship between human beings and the rest of nature established by God. Stewardship is another, as Singer notes, although he sees it as a variant of the Dominion Theory that does not deny that human beings are "entitled to kill individual animals if [they] wish to do so." There are, I would suggest, other ways within the Judeo-Christian tradition of understanding the relationship between human beings and the rest of His creation; however, we cannot explore this matter here.

Singer examines one more attempt to explain the unique value of human life. In this attempt it is claimed that human beings, but not other animals, have "intrinsic worth," or "intrinsic dignity," or are "ends in themselves," a view that Singer finds in Kantian thinking. He rejects this view because he finds no good reason to attribute intrinsic worth to human beings and not to animals, when animals as much as human beings can experience pain and pleasure.

Let me comment further on these four "attempts" to explain the unique value of human life, by going back to the question that elicits them: What gives unique value to human existence? The answer proposed by relationship morality is, If human beings are the only persons, it is their personhood. But, for relationship morality, whether or not human beings are the only persons, none of these four features define or explain the inherent worth persons have as persons.

Consciousness does not because persons have inherent worth even though they may be permanently unconscious and because (assuming at least some animals with rudimentary consciousness are not persons) some beings with consciousness do not have the inherent worth of persons. Having an immortal soul does not because, though human persons may be immortal, we do not discover this in discovering their inherent worth: one in the time of war may come to appreciate the personhood and inherent worth of those who are the enemy without coming to believe in the immortality of anyone.

Again, regarding the Dominion Theory, it does not define or explain the inherent worth of persons, because we do not discover its truth in discovering the inherent worth of persons: though the Dominion Theory in Singer's elaboration were false (so that it would be false that animal life is of "little or no value"), persons would yet have inherent worth, and by entering into the presence of persons, we could yet discover their inherent worth. As for the Kantian view that persons have intrinsic dignity, or intrinsic worth, or are ends in themselves, "intrinsic dignity" is an alternative expression for "intrinsic worth," and while both can be used to name the worth that persons have as persons, neither defines or explains it (except in the sense a synonym defines or explains a term); and, again, persons being ends in themselves does not define or explain their inherent worth, for either "ends in themselves" is an alternative expression for "inherent worth," or persons being ends in themselves is a fact about persons that follows from their inherent worth and is explained by their inherent worth, rather than the other way around.

For relationship morality, *are* human beings the only persons? Cranford and Smith, who tend to use "personhood" and "human personhood" interchangeably, may think that human beings are the only persons there are. But the terms "human being" and "person" are not synonymous, as Singer points out.[27] Of course, the two terms could still name just the same individuals. However, relationship morality holds no brief that the only persons are human persons.

For relationship morality, human beings have inherent value by virtue of their personhood, but relationship morality does not entail that human beings are uniquely persons. One possible nonhuman person is God, the Divine Person in whose image human persons are created, according to the Judeo-Christian tradition. Another possibility is that some nonhuman animals are persons, as Singer claims.[28] (We shall examine this claim later, but not until Chapter 15.) Another possibility is that there are

27. Ibid., 234–35.
28. Ibid., 240.

extraterrestrial creatures who are persons, though they are quite unlike human beings in appearance, or that there may in the future be persons who are artificially created beings made of a substance other than flesh.

At the same time, relationship morality allows that in our present moral experience we enter the presence of only human persons. Say that it is true we *morally* experience only human beings as persons. Still, this leaves it open that one may encounter God, enter the presence of God, in a different but analogous religious discovery experience, and it leaves it open that we may have moral obligations toward other beings who are not persons but do not lack in value.

William Blake wrote in "The Divine Image" in *Sons of Innocence,*

> For Mercy has a human heart,
> Pity a human face,

and he wrote in "A Divine Image" in *Songs of Experience,*

> Cruelty has a Human Heart,
> And Jealousy a Human Face.

Mercy, pity, cruelty, and jealousy have a moral dimension, we may say; any being that expresses them thereby enters the moral sphere. Their expression is an indicator of personhood, in the sense of "indicator" that we have been using. And in our experience, cruelty, mercy, and jealousy, fully realized, are distinctly human. So it is that we hesitate to say that lions are cruel in taking their prey or that house cats are cruel when they capture sparrows, although dogs can, in a manner, be jealous of one another. Also note the titles of Blake's poems: "The Divine Image" and "A Divine Image." The expression of these qualities marks human likeness to the Divine Person, Blake implies.

Personhood is a moral-religious category. Significantly for the concerns of relationship morality, it has a moral dimension. Perhaps it is not too far off the mark to say that the issue of personhood should be turned around: instead of seeking a property that is a strong criterion for persons that would define personhood and by which we could identify persons (or that would define or explain the inherent value of persons), we should allow that persons are all those beings into whose presence as persons we can enter and whose inherent value we can thereby discover. This allows that there may be nonhuman persons and also that in our moral experience human beings preeminently are persons.

PART III

RELATIONSHIPS
AND THE
MANSIONS OF MORALITY

8

Principles, Justice, and Goods

For relationship morality, morality rests upon relationships between persons, that is to say, in our lived moral experience, preeminently upon human relationships. For relationship morality, we act morally when we act in accord with our relationships—in accord with our intimate personal relationships, but also with our broader, general relationships, and in accord with our fundamental relationship to all persons as persons, the person/person relationship. This is not to say that it is always necessary to deliberate explicitly on our relationships in order to act morally. Often we may act morally spontaneously, without making a conscious judgment, without any process of reflection, yet with an intuitive sensitivity informed by our relationships. Other times, of course, in conflict cases that confront us as such, conscious deliberation may be necessary. However, such deliberation is not to be equated with acting on principle.[1] While, as we have seen,

---

1. Cf. Hubert I. Dreyfus and Stuart E. Dreyfus, "What Is Morality? A Phenomenological Account of the Development of Ethical Expertise," in *Universalism vs. Communitarianism*, ed. David Rasmussen (Cambridge: MIT Press, 1990), 239 and 243. The Dreyfuses point out that when those with a degree of moral experience act morally, often they do not deliberate; they act spontaneously, without reflection. Nor, a fortiori, is deliberation on a principle present. However, while this much seems right, the Dreyfuses link deliberation with decision and choice and with reasoning in ways open to some question. Though a mother may not deliberate before she stops her child from pulling the cat's tail, it is yet her decision, or choice, to do so. She does, after all, choose not to let the child continue to pull the cat's tail, if that option is open to her, as it presumably is. Also, though she does not mull over in her mind what she ought to do—and in this sense does not reason about what she ought to do—she may yet have a reason for stopping her child from pulling the cat's tail. That this is so becomes evident if we reflect on what she is able to say retrospectively when she is asked by another child why she stopped the first child from pulling the cat's tail: "It hurts the cat to have his tail pulled."

relationship morality recognizes that there can be a species of morality that is acting on principle (with or without deliberation), such a morality is distinguishable from a morality consciously grounded in an appreciation of relationships between persons. This does not deny that there are moral principles, indeed, valid moral principles, with entailed moral obligations. If relationship morality is foundational to all of ethics, then it underlies and supports such moral principles, as well as the other mansions of morality. So far I have argued that human relationships, including the person/person relationship, (1) give us the form of obligations and (2) are the source of obligation. But the mansions within morality, broadly understood, besides obligation include moral principles, justice, goods, virtue, and rights. Can relationships account for all of them? I shall treat these five overlapping subdivisions of morality in order, the first three in this chapter, the last two in the next chapter.

First, moral principles; and here I think that we can be brief. In our discussion of the contrast between acting on principle and fully realized moral action (in Chapter 6), it was brought out how those moral principles on which we can and often do act rest on relationships between persons. This is so, I argued, for the principle of fairness and for the ends principle, and, by extension, it is true for any practical principle of morality. This of course should not be surprising, for such principles are essentially rules of obligation and we saw early on that obligations have their source in relationships. Also, though, there are other kinds of moral principles. Grimshaw, as we have noted, draws to our attention what might be called "consideration principles," the sort of moral principle that says, for instance, Consider whether your behavior will condone that which you think to be morally wrong. Now, such moral principles are different from practical moral principles in that they are not morally binding on behavior. However, a modicum of reflection indicates that they too are grounded in relationships between persons, or at least that they are if the general thesis of relationship morality is correct and all of morality ultimately rests on relationships. This is so because consideration principles, if I understand Grimshaw's category, embody some *moral* consideration and not just anything constitutes a moral consideration. "Consider the effect on the chrome shine on my car" cannot be such a consideration principle, then, for without a very elaborate story, such a principle lacks moral import. Consideration principles, if they are moral principles, will, as in the case of Grimshaw's own examples, entreat us to consider some moral obligation or good or virtue or right. Thus consideration principles must finally rest upon relationships if these mansions of morality do.

And so let us turn to the other mansions of morality, starting with justice. Before we proceed further, let me emphasize a point already made in passing: the subdivisions, or mansions, of morality overlap. They may do so to such an extent, in fact, that it is misleading to call them subdivisions. The mansions of morality not only interconnect and lead into one another, but they share space. So it is that justice may be considered a distinctive part of morality (as by John Stuart Mill and others) as well as a virtue (as by Aristotle and Plato) and a good (as by Ross and Ewing). After this acknowledgment and caveat, however, in order to make the discussion manageable, we shall treat justice as a distinctive category, as we shall treat the other mansions of morality.

Our concern with justice is of course with moral justice, as opposed to legal justice. Our concern is not with the justice internal to the legal system of a state, which is defined by the laws of the land, but with the justice of morality, which can be used to judge the laws of the land. As moral justice can be considered a part of morality, so moral justice itself can be considered as having parts. Retributive justice, then, is the part of justice that has to do with just punishment for wrongdoing, while distributive justice is concerned with fairness in the comparative treatment of persons. Rights, too, belong to the realm of justice, many would say. Mill insisted on this point,[2] and I would not wish to deny it. However, without denying either that there is the right not to be punished unjustly or the right to be treated fairly in comparison with others, I will discuss rights separately.

Perhaps the best way to show that relationships are foundational to justice is to show that human relationships account for justice, whether we think of justice as universal in scope and invariable in its essence or we think of justice as not universal but determined by societal or communitarian factors. There are, we are told, "two principal orientations in contemporary ethics."[3] One, universalism, holds that justice is universally the same, and the other, communitarianism, holds that justice is pluralistic and contextual. The issue between these two "orientations" extends to other elements of morality (such as virtue) and at times beyond morality proper (to, for instance,

2. John Stuart Mill, *Utilitarianism* (Indianapolis: Hackett, 1979), chap. 5.
3. David Rasmussen, "Universalism v. Communitarianism: An Introduction," in *Universalism vs. Communitarianism*, 1–2.

rationality). Nevertheless, for our present purposes, we shall regard the issue between them as it relates to justice, to distributive justice primarily and to retributive justice secondarily. The issue, as it relates to distributive justice, may be put this way: Is there a universal form of distributive justice valid in all social contexts, or are there different cultural spheres of human inter-change in which distributive justice takes different forms?

To some this may sound rather like the old issue between ethical relativism and ethical absolutism, and in fact the terms "relativism" and "relativity" do occasionally occur in the new discussion.[4] Inveterate philosophical controversies die hard, and if they die in one form, they often recur in another. Perhaps in the instance before us, the controversy over the nature of justice, this is because there is some element of truth on each of the opposing sides: universalism and communitarianism, in the new form of the opposition.

It does seem to me that both sides may in different ways be fundamentally right, that each may be pointing to something that is true about justice. So it is that universalism explains how there can be "wicked communities," that is, communities whose practices are at odds with justice.[5] And it explains how we can meaningfully question the standards of justice in a community, including our own.

On the other hand, communitarianism may be credited with going beyond an "abstract standard of justice."[6] Allowing that distributive justice is fairness—equal treatment—still there is the question of what constitutes equal treatment. This question, as we can see, following the analysis of a communitarian like Michael Walzer, breaks down into two further ques-tions: (1) What is to be considered in giving equal treatment? (Is it need? Is it merit?) And (2) what is to be distributed in treating persons equally? (What are the goods to be distributed in a just distribution?) Walzer argues, regarding the first, that there is "no single standard" for just distributions and, regarding the second, that there is "no single set of primary or basic goods [for] all moral and material worlds."[7] Let us take the two subquestions in order.

1. Walzer, for whom there are various communitarian "spheres" of

4. Alessandro Ferrara, "Universalisms: Procedural, Contextualist, and Prudential," in *Universal-ism vs. Communitarianism*, 13; Michael Walzer, *Spheres of Justice* (New York: Basic Books, 1983), 312.

5. Cf. Ferrara, "Universalisms: Procedural, Contextualist, and Prudential," 23. Ferrara men-tions the existence of "wicked communities" as a problem for communitarians, Walzer in particular.

6. Cf. Ibid., 20, where Ferrara cites Walzer as making such a claim.

7. Walzer, *Spheres of Justice*, 10 and 8.

justice, is right, I think, that equal treatment in different settings turns on different "principles"; for instance, it turns on merit in some cases and on need in other cases. Thus, fair treatment in the area of job hiring, certainly in hiring for public employment, requires giving central attention to merit, while fair treatment in the area of welfare and social security requires giving central attention to need.[8] Here, then, are two "spheres" of justice.[9]

We can see in another way that various factors, including societal or contextual factors, must be brought to bear to determine what will count as equal treatment. Equal treatment, as William Frankena observes, is not identical treatment.[10] Those able to walk and those in wheelchairs are not treated equally if both are given an identical opportunity to climb a flight of stairs to the second story in order to apply for a job. Rather, to be treated equally, those in wheelchairs need to be provided an alternative means of reaching the second story, such as an elevator. Thus, since equal treatment is not, or may not be, same treatment in the sense of identical treatment, other considerations must come in to decide equal treatment. And these factors are importantly societal. In a society in which all who are unable to walk are regularly accompanied by young extended-family members who physically assist them up any stairs they might encounter, or in a society in which all job applicants are treated deferentially so that the application form would happily and as a matter of course be brought down the stairs upon request, equal treatment of job applicants in wheelchairs would not require the provision of some means of access other than stairs. Again, as far as distributive justice is concerned, societal or contextual factors may help to determine what counts as a need (for instance, whether having a job is a need) and the form needs take (whether having a certain sort of job is a need); and societal or contextual factors may help determine the form merit takes (given that job performance creates merit, societal factors may determine what counts as a valuable performance on the job). In these ways, then, about as communitarians hold, contextual factors determine, or help determine, what counts as equal treatment.

2. Also, communitarian considerations may decide what will count as goods to be distributed in accord with distributive justice. Walzer says that all the goods with which distributive justice is concerned are social goods.[11]

---

8. Cf. ibid., 23–26, 64 ff., and 129 ff.

9. For Walzer there are others as well. See Ferrara, "Universalisms: Procedural, Contextualist, and Prudential," 21, for some eleven that Walzer identifies.

10. William Frankena, *Ethics*, 2d ed. (Englewood Cliffs, N.J.: Prentice-Hall, 1973), 51.

11. Walzer, *Spheres of Justice*, 7.

He means that they are goods because they are socially valued. Though a beautiful sunset may be valued privately, it is "also, and more obviously," an object of "cultural assessment" and so, he implies, at bottom a good for the latter reason. "God's goods," he allows, are exempt from this rule, for when God sees that all He has made is good (Gen. 1), that goodness does not wait upon the agreement of humankind. But, Walzer says, this is the only exception he can think of. Perhaps, though, there are, besides Walzer's social goods, goods-in-themselves that are not socially determined. (We shall come back to this question later.) Also, says Walzer, "there is no single set of primary or basic goods conceivable across all moral and material worlds—or, any such set would have to be conceived in terms so abstract that they would be of little use in thinking about particular distributions."[12] In a way Walzer may be right about social goods being socially determined. Bread, he says, carries different meanings in different places: it may be valued as food or as a religious symbol or as a means of hospitality. So it is not clear its primary value is that of food, Walzer wants us to see. Of course this does not show that food in some form is not universally valued as a good. To this I suppose that Walzer would respond that the category of food is too abstract to guide any particular distribution. And this response is fair enough. Walzer's point is that it is socially determined whether bread is valued primarily as food; also, we may observe, for the purpose of distributive justice, what is to count as food is, to a great extent, socially determined. Pork in the southern United States is food, but it is not in Israel and Saudi Arabia. More exactly, a just distribution of food, of that social good, in the southern United States might include pork, but it would not in Israel or in Saudi Arabia. So too for other social goods that are necessities, such as clothing and shelter. Regarding clothing, whether a covering for the head is an essential item of clothing, as well as what type of head-covering is essential, may, irrespective of climatic conditions, be socially determined as a matter of religious observance. Besides such necessities as food and clothing, other things that are often valued as social goods—power and reputation, for instance—may be even more clearly socially determined.

In sum, communitarianism, like universalism, points to something true about the nature of distributive justice. The truths pointed to by each are, as it were, comingled in the nature of distributive justice. Moreover, it seems to me, there is another comingling, or interdigitation, of the various

12. Ibid., 8.

principles of distributive justice and the goods to be distributed that has long been appreciated.

Such an appreciation is, I think, shown by William Frankena in his treatment of distributive justice.[13] Frankena identifies three principles of justice: the meritarian, the equalitarian, and the needs/abilities view. He then argues that equality is the "basic standard of distributive justice." He allows that merit in some form may at times be a proper or reasonable basis of distribution, but when it is, it presupposes that those affected have an equal opportunity or equal access. So equality of treatment remains more basic. Again, while we may distribute goods to those in need, distributive justice requires that we make an "equal contribution to the goodness of [the] lives [of those affected]," that they be helped equally. And so once more equality of treatment is the more basic principle. Moreover, for Frankena, just as merit (so far as distributive justice is concerned) is merit earned when there is equality of opportunity, so helping according to need (so far as distributive justice is concerned) is equal help or "making the same relative contribution to the goodness of [the] lives [of those affected]." This concedes that equality and needs and merit, as well as the goodness of our lives, are related such that none (so far as distributive justice is concerned) can be understood abstractly, in isolation from the other elements in the equation.

The issue between universalism and communitarianism can also be raised regarding retributive justice. And here again it would appear that both sides have some part of the truth. One revered principle of retributive justice is that the punishment must fit the crime: no proper punishment can be disproportionate to the wrong done. But, as Mill saw, this is not the only principle that can be invoked in the determination of a just punishment for wrongdoing.[14] Other principles can be and are invoked to decide a proper punishment. A second principle is that punishment is to be decided on the basis of what is necessary to rehabilitate the wrongdoer, and a third principle is that proper punishment has a deterrent force, on the wrongdoer or on others. The universalist position here, or one possible universalist position, would be that each of these three principles has a general or universal validity as a prima facie principle. It is also from a universalist perspective that certain forms of punishment, such as torture, would be rejected as cruel and unjust regardless of the social traditions that might countenance them. The communitarian position would be that each of the three principles as it

13. Frankena, Ethics, 48–52.
14. Mill, Utilitarianism, 54.

stands is too abstract to be applied in a particular case. The universalist sees that if a proposed punishment does not fit the crime, that constitutes a prima facie case against the justice of the proposed punishment; and so too if the punishment does not rehabilitate or does not deter. The communitarian sees, regarding the first principle, that what determines whether the punishment fits the crime is, within limits, contextual or social: whether being in prison for a year is fitting punishment for car theft depends on the societal and personal import given to being at liberty and the social value attached to the ownership of automobiles. So too for the other principles: whether being taught a trade is rehabilitative depends on socioeconomic factors, and whether being in prison for a year will in fact deter a wrongdoer or others depends on various social factors.

Relationship morality, I suggested, can account for what is correct in the universalist's position on justice as well as for what is correct in the communitarian's position. Let me now try to show how this is so, starting with distributive justice. Distributive justice, both universalism and communitarianism agree, is treating persons equally. But the communitarians say that this principle is too abstract; it is an empty formula until filled in with a reference to concrete societal factors.

The strength of universalism is that it can account for the possibility of an entire society or community being "wicked," or unjust, and for the possibility of one's meaningfully questioning the justice of one's own society in certain of its practices, or even in the entirety of its social arrangement. Relationship morality in turn accounts for this strength of universalism by appealing to the universal person/person relationship. The person/person relationship implies that all persons, since they have equal inherent worth, ought to be treated equally. It is implied that persons as persons, irrespective of the practices of the society or community to which they belong, ought to be treated equally. In this way the person/person relationship is the source of, and generates, the universal principle of distributive justice that provides the basis for the judgment that communities are lacking in justice.

But also, relationship morality provides an account of the determination of just distributions in specific concrete or contextual instances in accord with what is right about communitarianism. It is a strength of communitarianism that it recognizes the role of societal factors in determining (1) the applicable principle of distributive justice in a context and (2) what will count as a social good. What, however, are these social factors? Though they vary, at bottom those critical for the determination of justice are formed by relationships between persons.

1. Consider principles of distribution. Relationships determine whether the applicable principle is merit or need. Relationships determine when merit, rather than need, is the proper basis for a just distribution. In the sphere of employment, public and public-services employment in particular, a just distribution of employment requires that all be given an equal opportunity. However, though drawing by lot would give all an equal opportunity to gain public employment, it does not qualify as the applicable principle of distributive justice in this sphere. Merit is the proper basis for the just distribution of public employment and of public-services employment (medical services, teaching, and the like) because there is a relationship between public, or public-services, employees and the public, a relationship in which such employees have certain responsibilities to members of the public. These responsibilities of course vary with the particular employment, but in general, *ceteris paribus*, they will be better met by the better qualified. (Notice, however, that this does not mean that the public at large will, or can, judge merit in every area of such employment; yet it remains that such employees have responsibilities to the public.)

In those cases where just distribution is determined by need, what constitutes relevant need, or needs-that-ought-to-be-met under justice, to a great extent is a matter of relationships. What constitutes distributive justice in these cases will be greatly determined by the relationship between the needs of those in need and the capacity of those called upon to meet those needs. That is, in these cases what greatly determines distributive justice is precisely the *relationship* between those in need qua those in need and those responsible for the distribution of the relevant resources qua distributors of resources. And this holds at all the various levels where need is the operative principle of distributive justice, at the societal level and on a smaller scale where teachers have resources to distribute to students and parents have resources to distribute to offspring. Parents, in order to be fair to their offspring, ought to encourage their abilities and development equally (though of course not necessarily identically). That is, they ought to as much as is within their power of capacity. Say that a parent has two children, one with obvious physical abilities and another with a budding artistic ability, but say that the parent is quite lacking in skills in one of these areas. As much as possible the parent, in justice, ought to encourage his or her child's development in this skill, despite the parent's own deficiency, but to some extent that deficiency will impinge on the parent's ability to provide as much example-setting encouragement to the one child as to the other. Again, the government of a state can meet the needs of its citizens only as well as they are understood and can be addressed by available resources. Distributive justice was not violated by Renaissance Venice when it did not provide prophylactic medication against malaria, though in the late twentieth century distributive justice may be violated by governments of states that do not address those diseases whose prevention and cure are understood.

The point here is not that what counts as meeting the demands of justice in such cases is always a simple matter. It may not be. For one thing, it may not be altogether clear to what extent it is within the power of those responsible for the distribution of resources to meet the needs in question. Though the parent may not be able to encourage a skill of a certain sort, perhaps he or she can acquire the skill or can find ways of encouragement that circumvent his or her own deficiency (by enrolling the child in an art class or gym class, say). Though the government may not be able to address a particular disease, perhaps it could if it rearranged its priorities. Also, of course, the extent to which parents and governments ought to make such efforts depends not only on the degree of need but on what other obligations they have and the relative stringency of these other obligations (which, in turn, is a function of relationships).

2. Again, the social factors that determine social goods, or more exactly, that determine what are social goods so far as distributive justice is concerned, are constituted by relationships between persons. Strictly, our concern here is only with social goods as far as distributive justice is concerned. Thus, we can allow that societal opinion, not relationships, determine what a society values, and we can allow, contrary to Walzer, that there are things that are privately valued. However, when the question of distributive justice arises, what will count as a good that ought to be justly distributed will be determined by relationships. In the case considered above, whether the government (in the wake of a natural disaster, say) ought to distribute pork as food, as that social good, will be determined by the relationship between the distributors qua distributors and the recipients qua recipients, and that relationship is importantly defined by the religious or traditional beliefs of the recipients.

Relationships between persons are similarly definitive for retributive justice. Relationship morality accounts for the universalist perception that torture is an unjust punishment regardless of societal approval: retributive justice in any allowable form requires that the inherent worth of the one punished not be utterly disregarded, that the person/person relationship to that individual not be violated, as most would concede it would be by torture. Again, it is relationships that decide which principle of retributive justice is most applicable in a particular case. Whether the punishment should be fashioned to fit the crime or whether it should be designed to rehabilitate or to deter the wrongdoer or others is determined by the wrongdoer's relationship to others in society and, as well, by the relationship of other potential wrongdoers to the rest of society. The extent to which the wrongdoer is a "threat" to society, for instance, is relevant, as is the likelihood of his or her rehabilitation; both are functions of his or her relationship to others in society. Moreover, relationship morality can explain how it is, in accord with communitarian views, that once it is determined which principle of retributive justice should be applied, social factors determine the particular punishment. For the social factors that make it reasonable to assign a particular punishment under each of these principles importantly involve the relationship of the wrongdoer to society. It is reasonable to judge, on the basis of the social and personal value attached to liberty and the social value attached to automobile ownership in a society, that incarceration for a year is a fitting punishment for stealing a car. Being incarcerated, the wrongdoer's relationship to society changes; and for society to judge that the punishment fits the crime, it must be that in the eyes of society the wrongdoer's losing for a year a relationship to the rest of society, a relationship marked by liberty of movement and association, is deemed a fitting compensation for car theft. And regarding the other two principles of retributive justice, it is reasonable to judge that a year's training at a trade will rehabilitate a wrongdoer, or that a year's imprisonment will deter the wrongdoer from repeating the crime, on the basis of the likelihood that a year's punishment will change the wrongdoer's past relationship and generate a new relationship to the rest of society.

Now let us turn to the next primary moral category we should consider: that of goods. To an extent this category has already entered into our discussion of distributive justice, since distributive justice is, importantly, a just distribution of goods. We have seen that Walzer puts forward a view about the character of the goods that relate to distributive justice: the only goods with which distributive justice is concerned, he says, are "social goods." And we have seen how Frankena brings out that the categories of justice, need, and the good are interconnected, this being the interconnection of the mansions of morality that I earlier noted. Still, as with justice, we shall endeavor to treat the moral category of goods as a distinguishable category, or subdivision, of morality. Our question, then, is, In what way are relationships between persons foundational to goods? Before we settle down to this question some honing is in order, however.

There are goods and there are goods, and there are different ways of thinking about the goods that there are. In a way, anything that some person values becomes a good—at least to that person; so, to use Walzer's example, a beautiful sunset may be a privately valued good, as may having a bright red car or always having at hand a sharp, or dull, pencil. Nothing is too trivial to be privately valued by some individual or other, and, parting company with Walzer, I think we can allow that any number of such privately valued goods may not be "social goods" that are culturally valued. Our concern here will not be with purely private goods. Also, as we have seen, there may be "social goods" in Walzer's sense: objects that are goods within a society precisely because they are socially valued. Having a reputation of a certain sort may be such a social good because it is valued by a society, and pork may be such a social good because it is socially valued as food. Such social values, as Walzer brings out, can be important for distributive justice. But, again, our concern here will not be with social goods, or not with them chiefly. In part this is because often such goods are goods-as-means to some further goal. Our chief concern, rather, will be with what some have called intrinsic goods or goods-in-themselves. Such goods are goods because of their intrinsic nature, not because some individual, perhaps idiosyncratically, has come to value them or because society has come to value them in some socially determined form; and such goods are not goods because they lead to the attainment of other things that are valued, whether or not they do so.

Let us ask, then, What goods are intrinsic goods or goods-in-themselves? (I shall use these closely related terms interchangeably.) In order to consider how relationship morality is foundational to intrinsic moral goods we must consider what these goods are. And here we enter a bit of a thicket. For there is not only a disagreement about what these goods are but also a disagreement about whether there are any such goods at all. Yet candidates for such goods have been proposed, and we shall perhaps gain a little light by considering the candidates.

For John Stuart Mill, if he is the hedonistic utilitarian that he is usually thought to be and that he seems to have taken pains to present himself to be, there is but one good-in-itself: pleasure. Actions are right for Mill, in his famous phrase, "in proportion as they tend to promote happiness," and by "happiness" he says he means the presence of pleasure and the absence of pain. The only positive good the promotion of which makes actions right is pleasure. Other things aimed at in human conduct are, at best, good as means to pleasure, although he allows that for some individuals virtue and music, for instance, may come to be "cherished . . . as a part of their happiness."[15] Perhaps it is not surprising that Mill, as a utilitarian, reflected on the nature of the good and came to an explicit view about its nature, since for him, as for other utilitarians, actions are made right by their promotion of the good. Mill was explicit that the only thing desirable for itself is pleasure, but other utilitarians have viewed the good rather differently.

Hastings Rashdall rejected Mill's hedonism and proceeded to develop a moral view that he called Ideal Utilitarianism. On Rashdall's view, "actions are right or wrong as they tend to produce for all mankind an ideal end or good, which includes, but is not limited to, pleasure." "Pleasure is *a* good," he allows, but it is not *"the* good."[16] It is reasonable to assume that, for animals, given what we understand of their capacities, pleasure may well be the only good they are capable of and pain their only evil.[17] But human beings are capable of other goods. Nor is pleasure the most valuable good for human beings. At the head of the list of "higher, or intrinsically more valuable" goods comes virtue. However, other goods as well are more valuable than pleasure, for Rashdall. He names "intellectual cultivation and intellectual activity, aesthetic cultivation, [and] emotion of various kinds."[18] The emotions he has in mind are those "connected with" "knowledge, culture, enjoyment of beauty, [and] intellectual activity of all kinds."[19] Also, for Rashdall, some pleasures are bad, such as the pleasure derived from watching a bullfight or from drunkenness.[20] Mill never quite said that some pleasures are bad, but he did try to distinguish more valuable from less valuable pleasures.[21] Rashdall, like others, argues that Mill cannot do so consistently as long as he retains the hedonsitic view that pleasure is the only good.[22] For Rashdall, we can and do ascribe greater value to some pleasant states for reasons other than their pleasantness or quantity of pleasure; we do so on the basis of their other content, for instance, their

15. Ibid., 7 and 35–36.
16. Hastings Rashdall, *The Theory of Good and Evil,* 2d ed. (London: Oxford University Press, 1924), 1:184, 2:37 (Rashdall's emphasis).
17. Ibid., 1:215.
18. Ibid., 2:37.
19. Ibid., 1:191.
20. Ibid., 1:99.
21. Mill, *Utilitarianism,* 8–10.
22. Rashdall, *The Theory of Good and Evil,* 1:25–27.

intellectual or esthetic content, which for him, as opposed to Mill, have their own intrinsic value.

Sir David Ross, who was not a utilitarian and explicitly argued against not only hedonistic utilitarianism but ideal utilitarianism as well,[23] also reflected on the good. Interestingly, although he rejects Rashdall's utilitarianism, he agrees to a great extent with Rashdall on their being goods, on what goods there are, and on their ranking. "Three main things are intrinsically good," Ross says. They are "virtue, knowledge, and with certain limitations, pleasure." The limitations regarding pleasure's status as a good are, first, that though we "clearly recognize a duty to produce pleasure for others, it is by no means so clear that we recognize a duty to produce pleasure for ourselves," and, second, that "one's own pleasure is a good and there is a duty to produce it, [but] only if we *think* of our own pleasure not as simply our own pleasure, but as an objective good." Beyond these three, he suggests, "there is a more complex good . . . consisting in the proportionment of happiness to virtue."[24]

He goes on to discuss each of these four goods.[25] The first intrinsic good, virtue, he further characterizes as "virtuous disposition and action, i.e. action, or disposition to act from any one of certain motives." The moral motives he names include "the desire to do one's duty" and "the desire to give pleasure or save pain to others." (Later we shall have to consider more carefully how the moral category of virtue relates to our general concern in this chapter; for the present we need only note Ross's characterization of virtue and how he, and Rashdall, count it as a good.) Knowledge, as such, Ross also regards as a good. While we sometimes judge it is better for individuals not to know some things, such as how ill they are, this is not because the knowledge itself is bad but because its consequences are judged to be bad, Ross argues. Later, in his Gifford Lectures, he amended slightly his view of knowledge and said that "knowledge, or perhaps . . . the activity of the mind which leads to knowledge, is good."[26]

Pleasure, for Ross, as we noted, is a good only "with certain limitations."

---

23. W. D. Ross, *The Right and the Good* (Oxford: Clarendon Press, 1930), 17–22.

24. Ibid., 24–27 (Ross's emphasis). Ross's claim that we have a duty to produce our own pleasure only if we think of it as an objective good can be compared to Kant's claim that we have an "indirect duty" to assure our own happiness—since those not content are more easily tempted to the transgression of duty. Immanuel Kant, *Groundwork of the Metaphysic of Morals*, Akademie edition, 339; H. J. Paton, *The Moral Law*, or Kant's *Groundwork of the Metaphysic of Morals*, 3d ed. (New York: Barnes & Noble, 1956), 67.

25. Ibid., 134–41.

26. W. D. Ross, *Foundations of Ethics* (Oxford: Clarendon Press, 1939), 270.

He further suggests that pleasure really is a prima facie good, on analogy with prima facie duties. That is, a state of pleasure is good if there is no other feature that prevents it from being good. For Ross, as for Rashdall, in animals pain is always bad and pleasure always good; for Ross, this is because there is no question of desert or moral good or evil in the case of animals. But with humans—moral beings—undeserved pleasure or pleasure that is the realization of a morally bad disposition is bad, and pleasure is good when deserved or when it is the realization of a morally good disposition (or the realization of a natural capacity, such as seeing a lovely vista). Similarly with pain: for human beings, it is bad when undeserved and good when deserved. In his Gifford Lectures Ross modifies his earlier thinking and says that "pleasures, if ever good, must be good in a different sense" from the sense in which virtuous acts are good. He came to reject the idea that they had different places on the "same scale of goodness," such that they could be compared and measured against each other.[27] The remaining good initially mentioned by Ross is the apportionment of pleasure and pain to virtue and vice. It is on the recognition of this good, he says, that the "duty of justice" rests. For Ross, justice is essentially meritarian, and such an apportionment is required by justice. These four goods, for Ross in his earlier work, are the only goods. All other candidates, such as esthetic enjoyment, are a form of one of these or a combination of two or more of them, he affirms. Later, though, he would discuss artistic creativity (as opposed to artistic enjoyment) as a distinct intrinsic good.[28]

There is, then, a consanguinity between the thinking of Ross and that of Rashdall on the good and the goods that there are. There is one further element in their thinking that we should note. For each it is not accidental that there are just the goods that there are. The goods they recognize they see as being in accord with human nature. As Ross puts it, while his list of four goods "has been arrived at on its own merits, by reflection on what we really think to be good," it is lent some support by the fact that it "harmonizes with a widely accepted classification of the elements in the life of the soul."[29] These elements are "cognition, feeling, and conation." Knowledge is the good of our cognitive side; pleasure is the good of our feeling side; virtue is the good of our conative side; and the allocation of happiness to virtue is a good deriving from the relation between the feeling and conative sides of our nature. So Ross suggests. Rashdall is similar. He

27. Ibid., 275.
28. Ibid., 270.
29. Ross, *The Right and the Good*, 140.

says that "what is moral for man depends upon his actual psychological constitution, including his sensitive, aesthetic, and emotional nature," and, he says, while it is an a priori truth "that it is right to promote the true good of all that lives and is conscious," still "what actually is for the good of man or any other creature cannot be ascertained without a knowledge of the nature and capacities of that creature."[30] Like Ross, he speaks of "the different parts of our nature represented by the trinity of thought, feeling, and will"; sometimes, he says, a course of action that will satisfy one part will not satisfy the other parts, but "the ideal good of man would include all three."[31] The main idea here, which is shared by Ross and Rashdall, is that the good for human beings is what it is by virtue of, or at least in accord with, human nature. And, for Rashdall, though not for Ross, we must know human nature in order to know what the good is for human beings. Beyond that, they seem to share the same view of the tripartite structure of the "soul" or human nature (a view found in the thinking of Aristotle and, earlier, in the thinking of Plato, although the Greek division of the soul is slightly different).

Are there other goods that might be identified or proposed? There are. A. C. Ewing, who was not unfamiliar with the thinking of Ross and Rashdall, followed them in allowing that "the mind [has] three aspects, that of feeling, that of knowledge and that of will and action." He goes on to suggest that if we are to propose but one good, the best candidate is harmony, though it would be manifested in different ways in our three aspects: on the feeling side, when we are in harmony with ourselves and our environment, it would be happiness; on the intellectual side, when we are in harmony with reality, it would be truth or knowledge; and on the side of will and action, when we are in harmony with others, it would be social virtue and love. Esthetic experience would be "enjoyment of a kind of harmony," and also, he suggests, there may be another good, or form of the one good, harmony with God, or religious peace.[32]

Ewing, plainly, is more or less in the tradition of Ross and Rashdall on the good. But others have not been. In one place Peter Singer regards, or comes close to regarding, the "interests" of individuals as their good.[33] In connection with the principle of equality he says, "The interests of every being affected by an action are to be taken into account and given the same

---

30. Rashdall, *The Theory of Good and Evil*, 1:159.
31. Ibid., 1:76.
32. A. C. Ewing, *Ethics* (New York: Free Press, 1953), 67–68.
33. Peter Singer, *Animal Liberation*, 2d ed. (New York: New York Review, 1990), 5–9.

weight as the like interests of any other being." By "being" Singer does not mean human beings alone; he means human beings and (as he, as opposed to Ross and Rashdall, would say) other animals. And by "interests" he means well-being. What considering the interests of the beings affected by our actions requires depends on their "characteristics." Thus concern for "the well-being of a child growing up in America would require that we teach him to read," while "concern for the well-being of a pig" may require only that we leave it alone with other pigs and with adequate space and food. The only defensible prerequisite for having interests, for Singer, is the capacity for suffering and enjoyment, or sentience: a mouse has an interest in not being kicked, he observes, but a stone does not. In the last chapter, in fact, I questioned whether even the capacity for consciousness was necessary for having interests; I argued that it was not and that permanently unconscious individuals may still have interests. If that argument was right, then of course consciousness (or sentience) is not necessary for having interests. *Being interested* may require sentience, but *having interests*, which is very different, does not. However, in this context Singer is more concerned to affirm that nonhuman beings with sentience have interests than he is to deny that human beings without sentience have interests. Says Singer, sentience is "the only defensible boundary of concern for the interests of others." All sentient beings have interests, for Singer, and though what is in their interest, or contributes to their well-being, may vary, interests, Singer argues, constitute a good shared by human beings and other sentient beings. (In Chapter 15 we shall explore Singer's thinking about the interests of animals, as it relates to our obligations toward animals.)

So far we have considered ethical views of the good that in some way have looked to the nature of the beings for which the good in question is a good. Now, before we take up what relationship morality has to say about the intrinsically good, let us consider two instances of a rather different approach. The first is that of Charles Taylor.

For Taylor, "the goods we recognize as moral" are those which lay "the most important demands on us," which override the demands of lesser goods. His main thesis is that there is a diversity of such moral goods. It is not merely that there are different goods: there is no single order of moral goods. "The ethical," he says, "is not a homogeneous domain, with a single kind of good, based on a single kind of consideration."[34]

---

34. Charles Taylor, "The Diversity of Goods," in *Utilitarianism and Beyond*, ed. Amartya Sen and Bernard Williams (Cambridge: Cambridge University Press, 1982), 142.

Taylor recognizes "at least three kinds of consideration which are morally relevant." The first "is captured by the notion of utility," by which Taylor means Mill's notion of utility: "what produces happiness is preferable to its opposite." The second is "the universal attribution of moral personality." It affirms that "in fundamental ethical matters, everyone ought to count, and all ought to count in the same way," which carries with it the absolute requirement "that we respect other human agents as subjects of practical reasoning on the same footing as ourselves." (Let us note without dwelling upon it how Taylor's "universal attribution of moral personality" is thoroughly Kantian in connecting respect for "human agents" with their ability to use practical reason, as opposed to the idea of the inherent worth of persons as persons that we have developed.) And third "there are the variety of goals that we express in languages of qualitative contrast." Flowing from these three principles is "a plurality of goods."[35]

There is, in accord with the first consideration, the good of social utility. In accord with the second there are the goods of just distribution and the rights of individuals.[36] But also, in accord with the third consideration, there are the diverse goals of various "languages of qualitative contrast."[37] For Taylor, the third consideration, with its variety of goals, in itself presents us with a diverse range of goods; and, he argues, contrary to utilitarian and Kantian orientations, which see the variety of qualitative contrasts as morally marginal, the third consideration is central to our moral thinking.[38] If Taylor is right, a varied range of moral goods derives from very different "languages of qualitative contrast" that are deeply embedded in our morality. It is this aspect of Taylor's view that we should particularly heed.

Taylor illustrates his notion of "languages of qualitative contrast" with four examples.[39] Each in a definite way embodies a different distinction between "actions, or feelings, or modes of life [that are] morally higher or lower, noble or base, admirable or contemptible." For the first, personal integrity is a central goal. Here "what matters is that one's life express what one truly senses as important, admirable, noble, desirable." For the second, the goal is Agape/charity, as seen, for instance, in the life of Mother Theresa, and the "aim is to associate oneself with, to become in a sense a

35. Ibid., 142; see 130 ff.
36. Ibid., 132–33.
37. Ibid., 142–43.
38. Ibid., 133.
39. Ibid., 132–34. I shall designate the goal of his second "language of qualitative contrast" as "Agape/charity." Taylor, on page 133, uses the term "agape," but then, two pages on, shifts to "charity."

channel of, God's love for men." The third centers on the goal of liberation and "sees the dignity of human beings as consisting in their directing their own lives." And the fourth has as its goal "rationality" and holds up "the model of a human being who is clairvoyant about his goals, and capable of objectifying and understanding himself and the world which surrounds him."

The goods embodied in these "languages" are incommensurable with other lesser goals such as wealth or comfort. For those who hold that integrity, charity, liberation, rationality, or some like higher goal is the good, we ought to sacrifice such lesser goods for the higher.[40] This is part of what puts such "languages" in the moral domain. Also, the diverse moral goods that these "languages" embody are incommensurable with each other: they are not all subsumable under any "single-consideration theory."[41] They, or their "languages" and the "moral outlooks" they evince, "are based on very different pictures of . . . the human condition [and] frequently lead to incompatible prescriptions in our lives."[42]

Going back a moment to the earlier-cited distinction between universalism and communitarianism, we might point out a universalist element in Taylor's thinking. He would, he says, defend the view that the second consideration, "the universal attribution of moral personality," is valid.[43] But in this thinking about the plurality of "languages of qualitative contrast" he is more a communitarian.[44] Here, in this part of his thinking, we find the idea that, though there may be moral goods that are in a sense ultimate (for the goods embodied in these "languages" are goods above lesser goods like wealth), these higher goods are not intrinsic goods for all human beings by virtue of their nature; rather, they are intrinsic goods for those with a particular "moral outlook," for those who use one or another "language."

The second instance of moral thinking that does not seek to identify what are moral goods by reflecting on the nature of the beings for whom those goods are good is found in the writings of John Kekes. As communitarians look to a community for the determination of goods, as Taylor, for instance, looks to the "community" of users of a "language of qualitative contrast," so Kekes looks to individual self-direction for a determination of goods and a good life. Good lives, he is clear, are self-directed, and there is

40. Ibid., 135.
41. Ibid., 144.
42. Ibid., 134.
43. Ibid., 132.
44. Kenneth Baynes sees Taylor as being in the communitarian camp. Baynes, "The Liberal/Communitarian Controversy and Communicative Ethics," in Universalism vs. Communitarianism, 63.

no one good life that is *the* good life for each and every individual, as there is not but one possible good life for any one individual. Good lives embody ideals, and there are numerous possible good lives because there are various ideals.[45]

Self-direction is or involves the acceptance of an ideal, for Kekes, but not the whimsical choosing of a fabricated ideal. "Self-direction essentially involves judgment, reckoning, and returning into ourselves to reflect and reason, [and] the objects upon which we concentrate are traditional ideals."[46] They may be formulated in a traditional text or they may be exemplified in the life of a person. Kekes mentions Socrates, Alexander the Great, and Jesus in this connection. Our "moral tradition," for Kekes, limits the range of ideals within which we may find an ideal that realistically can guide us and claim our commitment. However, our moral tradition does not impose any one of its ideals upon us. It does not follow, Kekes points out, that "all ideals are equally acceptable": the ideal chosen must come from our moral tradition, but also the ideal of a good life "must take account of human nature," a nature that is "partly open and partly closed."[47] But, for Kekes, there are no "ideals imprinted on human nature"; rather, "human nature restricts our possibilities, but it does not determine them."[48] Though we must take into account our "common wants and capacities,"[49] doing so yet leaves open a large number of possible ideals.

For Kekes, then, moral goods are not to be determined by reflecting on human nature. For one thing, human nature is "partly open," for him; for another, though we humans have certain undeniable wants and limitations on our capacities, that yet leaves great scope for the exercise of self-direction. "The only goods are those individuals find as such," he says.[50] In this way Kekes also rejects the idea that goods are "social goods" determined by societal attitudes. Kekes, I think, might allow that the ideals of our moral tradition may be social goods in something like Walzer's sense, but such ideals are not yet goods; they become goods and part of some individual's good life only when an individual, through self-direction, comes to value them and so finds them good.

The only exception his account seems to require is self-direction itself.

45. John Kekes, *The Examined Life* (Lewisburg, Pa.: Bucknell University Press, 1988), 183–85.
46. Ibid., 71.
47. Ibid., 184 and 186.
48. Ibid., 183–84.
49. Ibid., 171–72.
50. Ibid., 185.

For Taylor, self-direction is the central value of the third language of qualitative contrast, for which the goal or good is liberation, but it is not a central value of the others. On Kekes's account, by contrast, self-direction is required for an encountered ideal to be adopted as a good, and so emerges as not just one, but *the,* underlying intrinsic good. Regarding the other goods, however, for Kekes, one person's good may or may not be another's, and, I think he must allow, what is a good for a person may cease to be with a newly chosen direction to one's life.

What does relationship morality have to say about the good? For relationship morality, the good of persons is inextricably tied to the inherent worth that persons have as persons. The good of persons, we may say, is, in one way, determined by the inherent worth of persons, or by the person/person relationship, in the specific sense that what is a moral good for persons must be compatible with their worth; it must not violate the person/person relationship, including the person/person relationship one has to oneself. The inherent worth of persons is not itself the good of persons, for we cannot contribute to the inherent worth of persons but can contribute to their good. This understanding of the good is in accord with, or compatible with, much of the thinking of the various authors we have surveyed. In fact there is more conflict between the different views of these individual authors than between any one of their views and the understanding of the good integral to relationship morality.

One area of issue between the authors we have examined is the extent to which the moral good is determined by human nature or by the nature of the beings for whom the good is to be a good. For Rashdall, we must know the nature of human beings, and of animals, to know their good. The goods for human beings that he proposes—virtue, pleasure, knowledge, and esthetic appreciation—reflect his tripartite view of human nature. Ross and Ewing similarly regard human goods as determined by human nature, which they too see as having the three aspects of knowledge, feeling, and action. The idea that the soul has three parts goes back to Aristotle and Plato, as I remarked. But here we are interested in the other idea: that human nature determines the good of human beings. There is an identifiable tradition in moral thought, going back to Aristotle, that sees human good as determined by human nature; and Rashdall, Ross, and Ewing stand in that tradition.

Not all who have thought about the good are in this tradition, however. Charles Taylor is not, and John Kekes is not. Kekes allows that Aristotle is right "in thinking that we are made better by developing certain virtues and that what they are follows from human nature," but wrong in thinking that human nature is "fixed" or completely closed.[51] Also, for Kekes, the diametrically opposite position (exemplified perhaps by Sartre, although Kekes does not mention Sartre in this connection) is wrong in positing that human nature is completely open; yet Kekes agrees with this position that there is no fixed human nature. Kekes stands opposed to Rashdall and the Aristotelian tradition, then, in denying there is a fixed human nature that determines the good for human beings.

The view of relationship morality on the determination of the good for persons is consistent with Rashdall's perception that human nature determines the good and with Kekes's denial of such a determination. To be sure, for relationship morality, there is no set of natural properties like consciousness or being reasonable that *defines* persons or personhood (as we argued in the last chapter). We can, though, distinguish between such a criterion or defining set of conditions for persons and human nature. We can, at any rate, if we think of human nature as a fixed set of natural fulfilling proclivities that virtually all (if not absolutely all) human beings in fact have. If Rashdall is right, then there is such a human nature, which determines our good, and so it is likely that there are universal goods. If, furthermore, Rashdall is right in the way he understands human nature, then virtue, knowledge, pleasure, and so on are goods for virtually all human beings. And this may be so. Yet though this may be so, we should be clear that a human being with, say, no capacity for knowledge or its intellectual pursuit would yet be a person: we may contribute to the good of virtually all persons by contributing to their knowledge or understanding, but we cannot define personhood in terms of the capacity for knowledge (as we have seen). If, on the other hand, Kekes is right, then there is no such determining nature: human nature is at least partly open and does not, as such, determine our good, and so it is less likely there are universal goods (except perhaps for self-direction). Both constructions are consistent with the way relationship morality sees the determination of the good for persons, for whether or not there is for virtually all human beings a fixed human nature that determines their good, whatever is a good for persons will be in accord with the inherent worth persons have as persons.

Also, relationship morality can to a great extent agree with Taylor's reflections on morality and the diversity of goods. Relationship morality recognizes the kind of plurality of incommensurate forms of moral life he at least points toward. (In Part IV, drawing upon what Taylor says elsewhere,

51. Ibid., 185–86.

but also going beyond Taylor and using other categories than the good, we shall look at different moralities that contrast with each other and with relationship morality in order to bring relationship morality into high relief against the moral space they block out.) And it is sympathetic to Taylor's point that there is no "single-consideration theory" that will account for all human goods. Earlier it was brought out that though obligations have their source in human relationships, including the person/person relationship, as relationship morality maintains, this does not mean that there is a strong "criterion" for moral rightness or obligation; relationship morality proposes no such criterion. In locating the source of obligations in relationships it proposes no set of necessary and sufficient conditions that can be used to decide our moral duty (see Chapter 1). So too for moral goods. Relationship morality proposes no single consideration or strong criterion that can be used to identify human goods or goods for persons. But for relationship morality, moral goods must be compatible with the inherent worth of persons, which is their ground. Not that Taylor, strictly, denies this. He denies that all the moral goods are commensurate, and he also says they lead to incompatible prescriptions. If so, they are incompatible with one another. Yet even if this is so, it does not make them incompatible with some ground they all share—which for relationship morality is the inherent worth persons have as persons. I do not mean to say that relationship morality accepts that the goods there are *are* incompatible with one another. They may not be, although at times they may come into conflict, as prima facie duties may come into conflict. But when prima facie duties come into conflict there still can be a moral resolution. Perhaps there can be a moral resolution when goods come into conflict. Let us assume that the goals associated with the four "languages of qualitative contrast" identified by Taylor are indeed goods for persons. Let us allow, that is, that each is compatible with the inherent worth of persons. Now consider the goal associated with one of these "languages," the goal of personal integrity— doing what "one truly senses as important, admirable, noble, desirable," as Taylor expresses it; it will be in conflict with Agape/charity, the goal associated with another of the "languages" Taylor identifies, if one sees as important and admirable a way of life that rules out Agape, for instance, gaining power at all cost in the world of high finance. But these two goals or goods cease to conflict when one comes to see Agape/charity as important and admirable, that is, when one comes to an arguably better understanding of what should be admired. So there is hope that conflicts between goods can be morally resolved. However, even if this were not the case and goods were incompatible, it would remain that they still could all be grounded in the inherent worth of persons.

For relationship morality, what is intrinsically good is in accord with the inherent worth of persons, and in this limited sense at least, the inherent worth of persons determines the good or goods for persons. This means that whether or not we consciously respect persons as persons, we contribute to the good of persons only when we act in a way consistent with respect for their worth as persons. With this point in mind, let us recall the goods proposed by our authors. Virtue, knowledge, and esthetic appreciation are some of the traditional goods proposed by Rashdall, Ross, and Ewing. I think that a good part of the reason these proposed goods appeal to us intuitively is that contributing to someone's virtue, knowledge, or esthetic appreciation seems to us to be a way of contributing to that person's good, and it would not seem so if we thought that in contributing to his or her virtue, knowledge, or esthetic appreciation we were degrading that person. Something similar can be said about Kekes's central good of self-direction and the goods that Taylor draws to our attention: personal integrity, liberation (which corresponds to Kekes's self-direction), Agape/charity, and rationality. When we fail to act as respect for persons as persons requires, we violate the person/person relationship we have to them or to ourselves. This is in accord with Rashdall's thinking that the pleasure of drunkenness is not good: though a pleasure, it is, as he says, degrading; that is, pursuing it goes counter to the demands of one's inherent worth as a person and violates one's person/person relationship to oneself. We can, I think, begin to see how goods must accord with the inherent worth of persons, including one's own inherent worth, by thinking about mistakes about goods. If I think wealth or fame is a good and pursue it as though it were a moral good, I may well violate my relationships to others (if I acquire wealth or fame at the expense of friendship, say). But, moreover, I may well violate my person/person relationship to myself. I will do so if in pursuing wealth or fame I degrade myself, if I do not treat myself as an end, if I do not respect my worth. And this is the sort of thing one may come to see about one's goals and the effect that valuing them has on oneself.

Thus virtue, knowledge, and so on are goods, if they are and when they are, because they are in accord with the inherent worth of persons. So too with pleasure, another traditional good. Ross, who allows, with qualifications, that pleasure is a good, proposes another good that involves pleasure, as we saw. He, in an Aristotelian way, regards the apportioning of pleasure and pain to virtue a good. For Ross, pleasure is a good when deserved, but not when it is undeserved, and for him, it is a further good when pleasure is allocated as it is deserved. But perhaps pleasure, like love of the sort we discussed in Chapter 5, is, contrary to Aristotelian intuitions, deserved by persons as persons. However, I shall content myself with merely raising the possibility and shall not argue that this is so. In any case, whether pleasure is deserved by persons just because they are persons, so that giving pleasure to persons just because they are persons is a good, or, instead, pleasure is deserved only by those who merit it, so that giving specially deserved pleasure only to those who merit it is a good, depends on what is in accord with the worth of persons as persons. Ross would be right in his perception of what is a good if undeserved pleasure were degrading, as an unbridled life of pursuit of one's own pleasure more clearly is.

Relationship morality has no definitive list of intrinsic goods that are universal goods for persons. Relationship morality is very clear, though, that intrinsic goods are in accord with the inherent worth of persons. This being so in itself does not mean that a good for one person is a good for all persons. Nor does it mean that what is intrinsically good for one at one time will always be an intrinsic good for him or her. Nor does it mean that all intrinsic goods are equally valuable.

The point here is not about *private* values. Of course people privately value different things, and what they privately value may change, and they often privately value different things in different degrees. The point here is about intrinsic goods. Such a good as knowledge may be intrinsically valuable, that is, valuable in itself and for no further end, but if it is an intrinsic value, on the argument of relationship morality, it is by virtue of its relationship to the worth of persons. Still, what is intrinsically valuable for one, what contributes to his or her good, may not be for another. And it may be a good, an intrinsic good, for him or her at one time and not be a good at another time. This is the kind of point to which Taylor and Kekes are sympathetic, but it is not forbidden to Rashdall and Ross, I think. For this point can be right even if there should be a human nature in the specific sense we allowed, and even if it is a part of our nature that, say, acquiring knowledge is fulfilling, so that virtually all (but not absolutely all) human beings would have their good contributed to by knowledge. The special form of knowledge that is self-knowledge is most often a good, I would say, even when it is painful (as opposed to what Kekes implies when he says one must find a thing good for it to be a good). Yet there may be times when self-knowledge is crippling. Some have argued that self-deception can at times, as in the process of maturation or in times of crisis, be protective or healthy and morally permissible.[52] Ross, as we have noted, regards knowledge as always a good, although he allows that in some cases imparting knowledge may have bad consequences—as may be the case if we told a man how sick he is, to use Ross's example. Presumably Ross would agree that it is better in such a case not to inform the sick man, that is, to withhold from him the "good" of knowledge. If so, for Ross, though knowledge is a good in accord with human nature, and always a good, it at times is a "good" to which we ought not to contribute. It might be more perspicuous to allow that in this instance knowledge is not a good. Also, recall that for Rashdall pleasure is not always a good, even though, for Rashdall, pleasure is a good by virtue of our nature. There may be other goods, too, that are goods not only accord with our inherent worth as persons but also in accord with some fixed nature virtually all human beings have, yet that at times cease to be goods for some persons. Life itself may be such a good. Life may be a good in accord with the inherent worth of persons, so that we ought to contribute to the maintaining of persons' lives; yet at times it may also be that we contribute more to the good of a person by allowing that person to die (as was argued in the last chapter in connection with a different issue, that of personhood).

Before we leave the topic of the good, let me comment on two subsidiary issues that orbit around the question of the good. One has to do with whether goods require consciousness, and the other has to do with whether moral goods are prior to moral rightness.

Many assume that for beings to have a good they must have consciousness. Rashdall, for instance, regards the goods he identifies as consisting in certain states of consciousness. Thus he says that not only does "pleasure" mean "pleasant consciousness," but "virtue" means "virtuous consciousness."[53] And goods require consciousness for another reason, for Rashdall. For Rashdall, as opposed to Mill, happiness does not equal pleasure, although it involves pleasure,[54] and, says Rashdall, "pleasure is an element in every state of consciousness to which we can assign ultimate value," so that "even with regard to Virtue, it is difficult to answer the question whether I should judge Virtue to possess value, if it gave me no sort of pleasure or

52. See John King-Farlow and Richard Bosley, "Self-Formation and the Mean (Programmatic Remarks on Self-Deception)," in Self-Deception and Self-Understanding: New Essays in Philosophy and Psychology, ed. Mike W. Martin (Lawrence: University of Kansas Press, 1985). And see Mike W. Martin, Self-Deception and Morality (Lawrence: University of Kansas Press, 1986), 117 ff., for some examples congenial to the "Vital Lie Tradition."

53. Rashdall, The Theory of Good and Evil, 1:65.

54. Ibid., 2:57–58.

satisfaction."[55] For Ross, similarly, "intrinsic goods are . . . states of mind or relations between states of mind."[56] And, for Singer, as we have noted, having interests requires sentience.

I am not sure that we need agree either that goods are states of consciousness or that they involve pleasure (and so require consciousness in this way). Perhaps enjoying or appreciating a good—knowledge, say— requires consciousness, but that is a separate matter. Might it not be, as Socrates suggests in the *Crito*, that we would contribute to a person's good if we kept that person from committing an evil act? But this we might do without contributing anything to that person's consciousness—as when we remove a temptation of evil before the other becomes aware of the temptation. And, once more, let us recall that if our earlier argument is right, we may be able to contribute to the good of those who are permanently unconscious by allowing them to die. In any case, though most of the goods we can identify may indeed be goods for conscious persons, it is not necessary to conclude that all goods for persons require consciousness.

The other subsidiary issue to be commented on is whether there is in ethics a priority of the good over the right. Is the right (right action, obligation) determined by the good (through contributing to the or a good), or is it not? Those with utilitarian intuitions come down on one side of this issue, and those with opposite, nonutilitarian intuitions come down on the other side. For Rashdall, who holds a position in the utilitarian redoubt, "the idea of 'good' " is logically prior to and gives content to "the idea of 'right.' "[57] Right actions are to be understood in terms of a prior good: actions are made right by their producing the or a good. Kant and Ross, in their different ways, are opposed to utilitarianism. For Kant, good effects in themselves never make actions right or create obligations. For Ross, they do so at times (as with our general obligation to do good for others) but are not the exclusive source of right action or obligation (as with the obligation to keep a promise, where it is making the promise, not the good effects of keeping the promise, that creates the obligation and makes doing what was promised right). The undying utilitarian intuition is that right actions *must* in some way bring about more good than wrong actions and that doing so

55. Ibid., 2:37. It may be at least in part this element in Rashdall's thinking that leads him to a curious judgment about why infanticide is wrong. "We condemn infanticide," he says, "because we consider the feelings which the prohibition cultivates to be of more intrinsic worth than the good which it secures" (1:190).

56. Ross, *The Right and the Good*, 140.

57. Rashdall, *The Theory of Good and Evil*, 1:135.

defines right action. This intuition is so strong that when faced with counterexamples a utilitarian may give up consequentialism and concede that in these cases perhaps no more good consequences are created but that still the act itself, as opposed to its consequences, is a created good.[58] The undying intuition on the other side is that moral obligation is not in this way dependent upon bringing about a good and that the right is always, or often, identifiable without reference to the good.

Both sides, the utilitarian and the nonutilitarian, I suggest, are flexible enough to justify many, if not all, of the ethical judgments that most of us would recognize as right ethical judgments—and this is so even if the utilitarian remains a rigorous consequentialist. Although this does not mean that each side is equally correct or that their respective justifications for our various ethical judgments are the ones we would or should give, it does allow that whether we believe that the good is prior to the right or that the right is often or always prior to the good, we will in many cases come to the same, and the same correct, ethical judgments.

For relationship morality, both goods and duties have as their ultimate source the same thing: relationships between persons and especially the person/person relationship, which we violate when we do not act in accord with the inherent worth persons have as persons. Neither the good nor the right is finally fundamental, and neither need be seen as more fundamental than the other. Yet, neither being more fundamental, it is understandable that either might be so regarded. The fact that both goods and obligations are grounded in relationships explains why both the utilitarian and the nonutilitarian sides can justify correct ethical judgments: all that is required is that the goods and the obligations they depend on be in accord with relationships, including the person/person relationship. Also, we find near at hand an explanation why no resolution of the issue of the priority of the good is forthcoming: while the right does not rest ultimately on the good (as the nonutilitarians see), the right itself is not ultimate (as the utilitarians see). It is not, I think, to the discredit of relationship morality that it can in this way account for the persistence of this inveterate philosophical issue in ethics.

58. Cf. Ewing, *Ethics*, 76, and see Rashdall, *The Theory of Good and Evil*, 1:96–97.

9

Virtues and Rights

We turn now to virtue. Not that we have not already liberally referred to virtue. In our just-completed discussion of the good, not a little reference to virtue was necessary, since virtue is a primary moral good for Rashdall, Ross, and others. Again, as was said, the mansions of morality lead into one another. It should not be surprising, then, that the moral categories of virtue and the good overlap. In fact there is more of a connection between virtue and the moral good than we have so far seen—a point to which I shall return toward the end of our discussion of virtue. First, though, we need to consider the moral category of virtue in its own right. For we have not yet characterized virtue or noted what the particular virtues are or are said to be. Nor, of course, have we seen what connections there are between virtue, considered as a distinctive category, and relationships.

What is a virtue? A moral virtue is generally understood to be a morally desirable personal trait or characteristic or disposition. It is a feature of a person's character and not any particular thing that a person does, although there is a connection between virtue and right action that is not merely accidental. Still, allowing that actions can be virtuous, virtues themselves are features of persons, not of actions. This much is fairly straightforward and widely agreed upon.

Some, in a more rigorous fashion, have tried to state necessary, or at least plausibly necessary, conditions for being a moral virtue. Robert Merrihew Adams and Philippa Foot, among others, have indicated several such conditions:[1]

1. Robert Merrihew Adams, "Common Projects and Moral Virtue," *Midwest Studies in Philosophy*

1. Foot says that "virtues are in general beneficial characteristics, and indeed ones that a human being needs to have, for his own sake and that of his fellows." Few would disagree with this, Adams observes.
2. Another condition is suggested by James Wallace. For Wallace, virtues are human excellences, and "human excellences will be tendencies and capacities for living well the sort of life that is characteristic of human beings," which for him is a social life.[2]

In connection with this condition, however, as Adams, Foot, and Wallace appreciate, it is important to observe the distinction between virtue, understood as moral virtue, and other human excellences, such as skills and abilities of various sorts. Skills and abilities may be human excellences, and moreover they may in some sense be virtues, but they will not be virtues in the morally relevant sense. We may say of an entomologist that one of his or her virtues is having a ready knowledge of all the identified species of beetles, but such a virtue, however valuable it may be in entomology, is not a moral virtue. For that matter, nonhuman virtues may be spoken of, as when one says of a car that one of its virtues is that it handles well at high speed, meaning that this is one of its excellences or desirable qualities.

3. Moral virtue "belongs to the will," as Foot expresses this condition, construing " 'will' . . . in its widest sense, to cover what is wished for as well as what is sought." The idea that the moral virtues are in some way within our power is traditional, going back to Aristotle.[3] Even the virtue of wisdom, Foot argues, is a matter of will in the broad sense of "will."
4. Moral virtues are important for the living well of human life *in general.* Adams observes that both Foot and Wallace accept this condition as necessary. This condition explains why a splendid familiarity with the known species of beetles is not a *moral* virtue.
5. For some, morality (and so moral virtue) has to do with how one relates to others. For Foot, the moral virtues are beneficial characteristics one needs both for the sake of others and for one's own sake. The idea here in this fifth condition, though, is that the virtues, by their

13 (1988): 302–3; Philippa Foot, *Virtues and Vices and Other Essays in Moral Philosophy* (Berkeley and Los Angeles: University of California Press, 1978), 3–10.
   2. James Wallace, *Virtues and Vices* (Ithaca, N.Y.: Cornell University Press, 1978), 37; cited by Adams, "Common Projects and Moral Virtue," 302.
   3. NE 1113b5–7.

nature, involve the interaction of persons. Adams, while he does not reject this idea, declines "to commit [himself] to this exclusively social view of morality."[4]

6. Moral virtues incorporate our desires and our intentions—indeed, our "innermost desires," Foot says. The idea that moral virtue involves our feelings or passions, as well as our actions, is again Aristotelian.[5] For Ross too, virtue has this inner aspect in that for him virtuous disposition or action requires a moral motive.[6]

7. Moral virtues are "correctives." This is a thesis that Foot considers. "One may say," she observes, "that it is only because fear and the desire for pleasure often operate as temptations that courage and temperance exist as virtues at all." And so too for other virtues, such as humility and hope, she suggests.

These features help block in the concept of moral virtue (or, more simply, virtue—understanding it to be virtue in the moral sphere). They do so even if they are not jointly sufficient or all individually necessary, for I do not think that it can be ruled out that the concept of virtue, even limiting the category to the moral sphere, is polythetic. A virtue is a morally desirable disposition or, if not a disposition, a "feature of character" or a "capacity."[7] Virtues, then, are widely recognized as deeply ingrained patterns of behavior or as what are expressed in patterns of behavior. They involve both interior acts—our desires and intentions—and exterior acts, over which we are seen as having some measure of control. But a virtue does not reduce to any single virtuous act, interior or exterior, however significant and profound that single act. A single generous act does not make one a generous person. One swallow does not make a summer, as Aristotle said in a different connection.

But arising from and going beyond this common ground of understanding there are different "theories of virtue," as they may be called. Foot com-

4. Adams, "Common Projects and Moral Virtue," 307 n. 10.
5. NE 1106b24–25.
6. W. D. Ross, *The Right and the Good* (Oxford: Clarendon Press, 1930), 134.
7. Traditionally virtues are classed as dispositions. Aristotle regards them as such (NE 1106b36, J.A.K. Thomson's translation; Ross's translation uses "state of character," but a dispositional sense is understood). Others who see virtues as dispositions include Ross himself, *The Right and the Good*, 134, and G. E. Moore, *Principia Ethica* (London: Cambridge University Press, 1968), 171. G. H. von Wright regards virtues as features of character, and R. C. Roberts regards them as capacities. Both are cited by R. B. Brandt, "The Structure of Virtue," *Midwest Studies in Philosophy* 13 (1988): 68–69.

ments: "When we talk about the virtues we are not taking as our subject everything to which Aristotle gave the name *aretē* or Aquinas *virtus*. . . . 'The virtues' to us are the moral virtues whereas *aretē* and *virtus* refer also to the arts, and even to excellences of the speculative intellect. . . . And . . . the class of virtues that Aristotle calls *aretai ēthikai* and Aquinas *virtutes morales* does not exactly correspond with our class of moral virtues."[8] For one thing, they both count practical wisdom (*phronēsis* for Aristotle, *prudentia* for Aquinas) as an intellectual virtue, not a moral virtue, while traditionally it, as wisdom regarding our moral lives, is one of the four cardinal moral virtues. Aristotle and Aquinas differ with us, and with each other, about what the virtues are, but also they think of what a virtue is differently.

Alasdair MacIntyre identifies five different accounts of virtue, or theories about what a virtue is.[9] First, there is an implicit theory going back to the Homeric poems, according to which a manifested virtue "enables someone to do exactly what their well-defined social role requires." On the Homeric account, physical strength emerges as a virtue. Second, for Aristotle's theory of virtue, virtues are not determined by social roles; rather, "the *telos* of man as a species . . . determines what human qualities are virtues." For Aristotle, friendship (in the Aristotelian construction) is a virtue, and *phronēsis*, the intellectual virtue of practical wisdom, is required for the possession of other virtues. The third theory of virtue MacIntyre associates with the New Testament. A virtue, on the New Testament's account, as MacIntyre sees it, is, as for Aristotle, "a quality the exercise of which leads to the achievement of the human *telos*," but the "good for man is . . . a supernatural and not only a natural good." The New Testament recognizes "virtues of which Aristotle knows nothing—faith, hope and love"—and also counts as a virtue a "quality . . . which Aristotle seems to count as one of the vices . . . namely humility." The fourth theory belongs to Jane Austen. It synthesizes elements from the Homeric view (giving importance to social roles) with Aristotelian elements (giving a role to the virtue of "constancy" like that which Aristotle gives to *phronēsis*) and then synthesizes both these elements with elements from the New Testament (giving importance to "real affection for people"). The fifth theory of virtue MacIntyre attributes to Ben Franklin. Franklin's view is "teleological" in the sense that

8. Foot, *Virtues and Vices*, 2.
9. Alasdair MacIntyre, *After Virtue*, 2d ed. (Notre Dame, Ind.: University of Notre Dame Press, 1984), 181–85.

it is utilitarian: virtues are qualities that are useful as means to external ends. On this account, industry is a virtue.

These various theories of virtue yield "three very different conceptions of a virtue," says MacIntyre: (1) a virtue enables one to discharge one's social role, (2) a virtue enables one to work to achieve the human *telos*, and (3) a virtue is a quality with utility. But despite these different theories of virtue and these three conceptions of virtue, there is a "core concept" to virtue, MacIntyre argues.[10]

"A virtue," in the "partial and tentative definition" he goes on to present, "is an acquired human quality the possession and exercise of which tends to enable us to achieve those goods which are internal to practices and the lack of which effectively prevents us from achieving any such goods." Deeply involved with virtue, MacIntyre finds, is the notion of "practice." By "practice" MacIntyre says he is "going to mean any coherent and complex form of socially established cooperative human activity through which goods internal to that form of activity are realized in the course of trying to achieve those standards of excellence which are appropriate to, and partially definitive of, that form of activity, with the result that human powers to achieve excellence, and human conceptions of the ends and goods involved, are systematically extended."[11] Some activities are practices in MacIntyre's sense, he says, and some are not. Tic-tac-toe and bricklaying are not; chess and architecture are.

Just here there arises the issue we explored in connection with justice, that between universalism and communitarianism. Given the role practices have in MacIntyre's definition of virtue, some see him as taking a communitarian position on virtue.[12] And it does seem that MacIntyre is faced with what might be called the evil-practices criticism. Put one way, it is the criticism that, on MacIntyre's view, evil practices will make evil human qualities count as virtues. MacIntyre, in his postscript to the second edition of *After Virtue*, replies to this very criticism.[13] He considers the "practice" of exploiting the wilderness, which, in order to be done effectively or perhaps at all, may require one to be ruthless. Still, he argues, ruthlessness will not turn out to be a virtue on his view. It will not because, he says, the

10. Ibid., 185 and 186.
11. Ibid., 191 and 187.
12. Alessandro Ferrara does, for instance. Ferrara, "Universalisms: Procedural, Contextualist, and Prudential," in *Universalism vs. Communitarianism*, ed. David Rasmussen (Cambridge: MIT Press, 1990), 28 ff.
13. MacIntyre, *After Virtue*, 273–75.

above tentative definition provides only a "provisional account" and because there are two further "stages" in his full account. In the second stage, virtues are considered "as qualities contributing to the good of a whole life," and the third stage "relates [virtues] to the pursuit of a good for human beings the conception of which can only be elaborated and possessed within an ongoing social tradition." Ruthlessness fails to be a virtue because it does not meet the requirement of the second stage that it contribute to "the good of a whole life." Other qualities might meet the requirement of the second stage but not the requirement of the third, he says.

It is true, MacIntyre allows, that there might arise an issue between "incompatible and rival traditions of the virtues" (a kind of evil-traditions problem, as it might be called).[14] This issue he also discusses.[15] If the traditions are indeed rivals, he observes, then "some kind of relationship to practices, some particular conception of human goods . . . will be features of both." (An example of what MacIntyre means by a tradition, we might note, is the "Aristotelian moral tradition," which would have as a rival, say, the tradition of the New Testament; alternatively, for Kekes, who also refers to tradition, our tradition *includes* Socrates and Jesus, but these individuals embody competing "ideals.") Traditions can indeed be internally judged, for MacIntyre; they can be judged by "their own standards of flourishing and foundering," which they may possibly share with other traditions. But there could also arise a case in which we could "discover no rational way to settle the disagreements between two rival moral and epistemological traditions," MacIntyre admits. He happily accepts this, for he holds there "are no successful a priori arguments" for the kind of overarching consideration that resolutions of all disagreements between rival traditions would entail. Such an argument he sees as involving the "resuscitation of the Kantian transcendental project" (a point to which I shall return).

Without pursuing the issue of the merit of MacIntyre's particular communitarian construction of virtue, perhaps it can be acknowledged, in accord with a general communitarian perception of the virtues, that within limits some virtues may be a function of social arrangements and also that the form of various virtues may be influenced by communities. Thus chastity is a virtue in certain religious communities, and courage in a distinctly intellectual form is a virtue in scholarly communities. This allows that some virtues are virtues for all, independently of social arrangements, in accord

14. Cf. Ferrara, "Universalisms: Procedural, Contextualist, and Prudential," 30.
15. MacIntyre, *After Virtue*, 275–77.

with universalist perceptions. Perhaps not surprisingly, MacIntyre himself insists that truthfulness, justice, and courage "are virtues . . . whatever our private moral standpoint or our society's particular codes may be."[16]

On the far side of communitarianism, as it were, there is another and more radical theory of virtue, according to which individuals invent or create the virtues, at least for themselves, by their choices and their will. This is a view that Nietzsche seems at times to hold. In various works he sounds his creation-of-values theme: these include *Beyond Good and Evil*, *Thus Spoke Zarathustra*, and *The Antichrist*. It is this theme that MacIntyre, with some justification, finds central to Nietzsche's thinking about morality and the virtues.[17] However, there are other themes in Nietzsche's writings in tension with his creation-of-values theme. There is, for instance, the Nietzschean idea that there is a "noble morality" with noble virtues standing in opposition to a base "slave morality"—an idea that seems to entail that even if all values and virtues are created by our choices, not all are equally estimable.[18] Again, in Nietzsche there is the idea that power is a fundamental basis for proper values. In *The Antichrist* he answers the question "What is good?" with "Everything that heightens the feeling of power in man, the will to power, power itself."[19] While it is not abundantly clear that there is a single definitive interpretation of Nietzsche's thinking, it appears that Nietzsche urges the creation of new *forms* of certain traditional values, such as courage and generosity. So it is that he gives us *his* four cardinal virtues: "*The good four. Honest* with ourselves and with whatever is friend to us; *courageous* toward the enemy; *generous* toward the vanquished; *polite*—always: that is how the four cardinal virtues want us."[20] The "noble man" is generous, for Nietzsche, "but not—or scarcely—out of pity, but rather from an impulse generated by the super-abundance of power."[21] And while Nietzsche condemns "Christian love," which "in the

16. Ibid., 192; see 192–94, 223. Whether he can do so with coherence and justification, however, has been questioned. See Ferrara, "Universalisms: Procedural, Contextualist, and Pruden-tial," 32–33, and Richard J. Bernstein, "Nietzsche or Aristotle? Reflections on Alasdair MacIntyre's *After Virtue*," in *Philosophical Profiles* (Philadelphia: University of Pennsylvania Press, 1986), 124 ff.

17. MacIntyre, *After Virtue*, 113–14. Bernstein calls such a moral view "decisionism" and argues that though MacIntyre argues against it, MacIntyre himself does not escape it. *Philosophical Profiles*, 131.

18. Friedrich Nietzsche, *Beyond Good and Evil*, sec. 260, in *The Philosophy of Nietzsche* (New York: Modern Library, 1954), 578–82.

19. Friedrich Nietzsche, *The Antichrist*, sec. 2, in *The Portable Nietzsche* (New York: Viking, 1954), 570.

20. Friedrich Nietzsche, *The Dawn*, sec. 556, in *The Portable Nietzsche*, 91 (emphasis in the text).

21. Nietzsche, *Beyond Good and Evil*, sec. 260, in *The Philosophy of Nietzsche*, 579–80.

end wants to be *paid* well,"[22] Nietzsche's Zarathustra commends "great love," which has overcome "even forgiveness and pity."[23]

There are, then, various theories of virtue, different conceptions of virtue, different lists of the virtues, and different ways of understanding the true form of certain traditional virtues. Before I move to the way relationship morality regards virtue, let us note at least some of the human qualities that most often are mentioned as virtues. "For us," says Foot, following the Platonic tradition, "there are four cardinal moral virtues: courage, temperance, wisdom and justice."[24] Other traditional virtues are honesty, or truthfulness, generosity, tolerance, and patience. However, this may be the place to observe that even regarding the cardinal and other traditional virtues, what is a virtue in many expressions may not necessarily be a virtue in every expression. Courage, though a virtue, may not be a virtue in every expression. Someone who shows courage in pursuing evil ends has courage, but courage in that person may not be a virtue. As Foot suggests, it may be "that not every man who has a virtue has something that is a virtue in him." She suggests this regarding courage and also regarding prudence, where it amounts to, say, "an over-anxious concern for safety," and regarding temperance, where it is "connected to timidity or a grudging attitude to the acceptance of good things."[25] Something similar, clearly, might be said for tolerance and other virtues. The alternative is to allow that virtues, operating as virtues in people, may be used for evil ends or in a morally discreditable way. MacIntyre, for instance, allows that courage as a virtue may yet issue in injustice, but he allows that such an exercise of a virtue is open to moral criticism.[26] For Foot, courage may not always operate as a virtue in people, and for MacIntyre, though courage may always be a virtue, its exercise may be wrong.

There are other virtues, or candidates for being a virtue: for instance, chastity and perseverance. Industriousness, or industry, has been regarded as a virtue, as by Ben Franklin (also mentioned by Foot, and by R. B. Brandt as a possibility, although, for Brandt, industry is more clearly also a nonmoral virtue).[27] Cleanliness, too, is a virtue for Ben Franklin, as MacIntyre notes, and amiability, as he points out, is a virtue for Jane

22. Nietzsche, *The Antichrist*, sec. 45, in *The Portable Nietzsche*, 623 (emphasis in the text).

23. Friedrich Nietzsche, *Thus Spoke Zarathustra*, first part, "On the Pitying," in *The Portable Nietzsche*, 202.

24. Foot, *Virtues and Vices*, 2.

25. Ibid., 15–18.

26. MacIntyre, *After Virtue*, 200.

27. Foot, *Virtues and Vices*, 9; Brandt, "The Structure of Virtue," 78.

Austen.[28] Loyalty has had its champions; Royce gave central importance in ethics to loyalty. Other human qualities as well have had their champions; self-glorification and pride were seen as virtues by Nietzsche. Associated with the Victorian temper are the virtues of sobriety, thrift, and tidiness, and especially the virtue of respectability, which had the interesting feature, perhaps unique among candidates for the virtues, that one could not have it without appearing to have it, for in order to be respectable, one must appear to be respectable. Sympathy and compassion have been named as virtues (as by Brandt).[29] And Robert Adams argues concern for one's own moral good is a virtue.[30]

Also, of course, there are what are regarded as "intellectual virtues," following Aristotle. Notable among them is practical wisdom (or *phronēsis*). But we might add understanding, sensitivity, and rationality. As Foot suggests, wisdom, which seems "intellectual," is regarded as a moral virtue. Moreover, I would suggest, we ought to see the other intellectual virtues just mentioned as also being moral virtues. In general, I think, the intellectual virtues are more closely connected to moral virtue than many have allowed. It is easy to see that some moral virtues are in one dimension or form intellectual: honesty and courage come quickly to mind. And, again, the intellectual virtues, or some, may be continuous with moral virtue in that certain moral virtues presuppose certain intellectual virtues; thus justice in its distributive form—being fair in the comparative treatment of others—may presuppose having an understanding of others' needs and abilities, which in turn may often require sensitivity to others. In fact it has long been recognized that there is some connection between practical wisdom or reason or some other quality of the understanding and moral virtue. For Aristotle, as we have noted already, the moral virtues require or presuppose practical wisdom. Socrates was wrong, says Aristotle, in thinking that all the virtues are forms of practical wisdom (or prudence), but right in thinking that they imply practical wisdom.[31] Practical wisdom, for Aristotle, allows one to deliberate rightly about "what is conducive to the good life generally."[32] Again, the idea that reason should guide the passions and the appetites is found in Plato and is well represented in the Neoplatonic tradition. In a different form we find the same root idea of a connection

28. MacIntyre, *After Virtue*, 183.
29. Brandt, "The Structure of Virtue," 77.
30. Adams, "Common Projects and Moral Virtue," 305–7.
31. NE 1144b17–20.
32. NE 1140a26–29.

between the understanding and moral virtue in the fourteenth century in William Langland's *Piers the Ploughman*, where the intelligence is the guide to the will, and we find it in the seventeenth century in Donne's "Holy Sonnet XIV," in which reason is God's "viceroy," though Donne confesses reason is a captive "and proves weak or untrue."

However, the connection between the intellectual virtues and the moral virtues may be more intimate yet. The idea that wisdom or reason or rationality is *itself* a moral virtue connected to the will—and not just its guide—is a different idea, and one that is right. Foot suggests that what we mean by "wisdom" is slightly different from what Aristotle meant by *"phronēsis."* For Foot, wisdom has two parts: first, "the wise man knows the means to certain ends," and second, "he knows how much particular ends are worth." But wisdom, then, is connected to the will in both its parts. For one who is wise, beyond knowing how to do good things, "must also *want* to do them," and regarding wisdom's second part, in describing someone's knowing the true worth of ends, we must refer, not just to that person's "apprehension" and "judgment" but also to that person's "attachments."[33] Understanding, sensitivity, and rationality in many of its forms may also be connected to the will, so that they too are moral virtues. In fact it may be a misnomer to call all these virtues "intellectual," for doing so suggests they are disconnected from emotion and feeling. Some forms of understanding, sensitivity, and perception may have an affective side. And it may be precisely our appreciation of their affective side that helps us to understand their connection to the will. Something like this came out in our earlier discussion of realization-discoveries, and in particular the realization-discovery of the inherent worth of persons, which is so important for relationship morality. (See Chapter 3 and also Chapter 5 above.) It may be that in some cases of insensitivity or lack of understanding what is involved is a willful blindness that amounts to a kind of irrationality that involves the will.[34]

Finally, let us mention those moral virtues that are sometimes called religious virtues. Among these the three primary virtues identified within the Christian tradition are faith, hope, and love. These are the virtues named by Paul in 1 Cor. 13, the virtues of the New Testament, as MacIntyre pointed out. Another religious virtue is humility, mentioned by MacIntyre and also by Foot. Humility may be understood as the virtue that stands

33. Foot, *Virtues and Vices,* 5–7 (my emphasis).

34. See my *The Cognitivity of Religion: Three Perspectives* (London: Macmillan; Berkeley and Los Angeles: University of California Press, 1985), 104–11, esp. 110–11, for more on the category of blindness-rationality or realization-rationality.

opposite the sin of pride. Foot suggests that humility is a virtue because it is a corrective to the human tendency we have "to think too well of [ourselves]," as hope is a virtue because "despair too is a temptation."[35] Foot's comment on hope and humility draws to our attention that these religious virtues are not exclusively for the religious, let alone exclusively Christian. So too for faith and love and other virtues often regarded as religious, such as devotion and obedience, although particular religious traditions, or strains within traditions, might understand these virtues to have an idiosyncratic form. Later, in the final chapter, we shall argue for the special place that faith and hope—and one other virtue, forgiveness—have in relationship morality.

Now, however, let us turn to the general perspective of relationship morality on virtue, bearing in mind that our concern is with *moral* virtues, as opposed to various sorts of nonmoral virtues; that is, it is with features of character or capacities or dispositions that *ceteris paribus* we ought to have, so that not having one, when we ought to have it, can be a moral fault. How are relationships foundational to such moral virtues?

One way that relationships are foundational to the virtues is that they define the form of the various virtues. Allowing that honesty is a virtue, what will count as honesty will to an extent be determined by particular relations and also by general relations. Whether honesty in a close relationship between two persons requires unsolicited divulgence or, instead, allows or even requires a discreet reticence is a matter of the relationship. Again, the difference between an honest disclosure and an embarrassing, unwanted confession in a social setting is greatly determined by social expectations and general relationships. Similar comments could be made about other virtues, such as courage and temperance (on close analogy with what was said in Chapter 1 about the form of obligations).

Another way that relationships may be seen to underlie the virtues is by reflecting on moral exceptions to the exercise of a virtue. Although the moral virtues are by definition good or morally desirable, still, as we have noted, what is a virtue may, in some instances of action or in some persons, not operate as a virtue, or alternatively, there may be instances when the exercise of what is truly a virtue is nevertheless wrong. Thus, when what would be the virtue of courage in another expression is exercised by a person for evil ends, courage is not operating as the virtue of courage in that person, or alternatively, it is the virtue of courage that is exercised, but it is

35. Foot, *Virtues and Vices*, 9.

wrongly exercised. The first way of understanding such exceptions is Foot's; the alternative is MacIntyre's. Each allows, as we may put it, that there are morally required exceptions to the exercise of the virtues. Exceptions arise when the exercise of a virtue, or what in another instance or person would be a virtue, issues in a wicked act or a harm. In short, obligations are violated, perhaps grossly violated. But on our earlier argument, relationships—most fundamentally the person/person relationship—are foundational to our obligations. Thus, what constitutes an exception is ultimately a matter of relationships, so that relationships determine when courage is not a virtue in a person or, alternatively, is wrongly exercised.

Relationships are foundational to the virtues in another way, which has to do with the inner nature of virtue. Whether the virtues are features of character or capacities or dispositions, as several have observed in one way or another, they embrace our inner selves, our deepest desires and intentions and inclinations. Allowing that virtues are dispositions, they are dispositions not only to act but also to desire and to will, and this holds for those intellectual virtues that are moral virtues. It is because virtue has this inner aspect that MacIntyre can observe that one must care about courage to be courageous.[36] This of course does not mean that one must be concerned about one's reputation as a courageous person or, I suggest, even that in order to have the virtue of courage one must be concerned to be courageous precisely for the sake of being courageous. What is true and important about the inner character of virtue is, put one way, that courage and other virtues involve desires and intentions that are themselves virtuous. So it is that Foot says "a virtue such as generosity lies as much in someone's attitudes as in his actions. Pleasure in the good fortune of others is, one thinks, the sign of a generous spirit."[37] Similarly, we may say that the desire for others to share in the truth and not labor under ignorance is deeply involved in the virtue of truthfulness, or honesty; and the desire to increase one's own understanding and the intention to help understanding where one can—a mark of which is being happy when others improve their understanding—are involved in the virtue of understanding.

Granting this last point about desires and intentions, one way not to have a virtue, or not fully to have a virtue, is to lack the desires and intentions that constitute its inner aspect. Relationship morality can account for this, for relationships require the same desires and intentions as the virtues.

36. MacIntyre, *After Virtue*, 273.
37. Foot, *Virtues and Vices*, 5.

As we have noted, harboring wrong desires and intentions can violate relationships (we saw this in Chapter 4). Virtues derive from relationships in that harboring just those desires or wishes or intentions that violate relationships will also, and for this reason, vitiate virtue. Thus one's harboring the wish to deceive a friend or parent, or to mislead a stranger, in itself and without overt action, violates one's relationship to one's friend or parent or one's relationship to the stranger and thereby vitiates the virtue of honesty. And so for other virtues. Moreover, the relationship can be the person/person relationship one has to oneself. One who practices self-deception, one who in this way willfully averts one's eyes from a truth one does not want to accept, at once does not honor one's inherent worth and vitiates the virtue of honesty in oneself. (Or if self-deception in some cases is necessary and is morally allowable, then in those cases it at once does not fail to honor one's inherent worth and does not vitiate the virtue of honesty.) Turning the point around, so that it is put positively, fulfilling our various relationships to others and the person/person relationship to ourselves requires the same desires and intentions as the virtues.

It is a corollary that, in having the virtues, one has desires, intentions, and wishes that, in being virtuous, honor the inherent worth of their possessor. Foot, we noted, says that the virtues are beneficial characteristics that one needs to have for one's own sake and for the sake of one's fellows. She reflects that virtues like courage, temperance, and wisdom benefit both oneself and others, while, on the other hand, virtues like charity and justice look as though they require "sacrifice of interest on the part of the virtuous man" and so seem "deleterious to their possessor and beneficial to others." But whether this is so, Foot says, has been an issue since Plato and before.[38] Much, of course, depends on how we understand "for one's own sake" and the cognate expression "for one's own good." Our good, our good as persons, including our individual good as individual persons, I have suggested, is a function of our relationships; specifically it is a function of the person/person relationship that exists between each and each and that one has to oneself. The good is in accord with the inherent worth of persons, and our individual good is in accord with our individual inherent worth. When we are not virtuous, we do not act in accord with, are not in our way of being in accord with, our inherent worth. Our inherent worth is not thereby diminished, but we detract from our good. We hurt ourselves, we injure ourselves, not necessarily in a utilitarian or psychological sense (although

38. Ibid., 3.

this may occur too) but in a moral sense. As Foot indicates, the idea that the virtues benefit their possessors is as old as Plato. Socrates expresses it in the *Crito*. In the Judeo-Christian heritage it is expressed in Prov. 10.2: "Treasures gained by wickedness do not profit, but righteousness delivers from death." Relationship morality agrees with Socrates and Proverbs and puts in place the foundation that explains the intuition they share.

For many, virtue is a good, as we have seen; and now we see how being virtuous contributes to one's good. It seems to me, then, that Robert Adams is not off the mark in suggesting that "concern for one's own good is a moral virtue." However, it must be borne in mind that this good is the good to which being virtuous contributes, and does not necessitate any accompanying pleasure or happiness. Adams considers three rationales for regarding a concern for one's own good a virtue. First, it might be held that "a human individual can hardly flourish without it." But, second, Adams observes, this rationale might be rejected by those who see morality as "a matter of how one relates to other persons"; for one with this view—that morality is, if not exclusively, necessarily social—an adequate rationale would incorporate relations with other persons. Adams wishes not to decide between these two, and instead brings forward a third rationale that, in a way, seems to bridge the first two. It would point out that "concern for one's own good has roots in one's relations with other people—namely, insofar as one's own good is a common project that one shares with others." Adams says that "since people do find much of their good in participating in advancing the good of others, caring appropriately about one's own good is apt to be important to the good of others as well as to one's own."[39] Of these three rationales, the third, which seems to be the chief justification for Adams himself, appears to be the strongest. The first is open to a utilitarian construction, depending how one understands what it is to "flourish." And while it may well be that often those concerned with their own good (that is, their moral good) are made satisfied and happy by their concern, being concerned with their own good because it makes them satisfied or happy would make their concern ignoble (as even Mill might appreciate, since for him it is noble to resign one's own portion of happiness.)[40] The second rationale, from the standpoint of relationship morality, does not adequately appreciate the moral force of one's person/person relationship to oneself. So the first two rationales have problems. That leaves the third rationale as

---

39. Adams, "Common Projects and Moral Virtue," 305–6.
40. John Stuart Mill, *Utilitarianism* (Indianapolis: Hackett, 1979), 15.

perhaps the strongest. But it too raises a question. Would Adams allow that a person alone could virtuously care for his or her own good? He says that he does not wish to commit himself to an "exclusively social view of morality." But his not doing so still allows that morality is necessarily social, and, of course, the third rationale, with its reference to "a common project that one shares with others," requires an interaction with others. In a similar vein, MacIntyre says, "I am never able to seek for the good or exercise the virtues only *qua* individual."[41] This in a way is right, of course, for some of the traditional virtues (generosity, for instance) are exercised toward others, and a number of traditional goods (knowledge and virtue itself) have their fullest realization in our interaction with others (not that this is MacIntyre's reason: he has in mind the societal determination of the form of the virtues and the good life). Adams, for his part, sees correctly, I believe, that one's own moral good is not disconnected from the moral good of others. However, this is to say that the *set* of virtues requires other persons and that the pursuit and full realization of various goods require other persons. And granting this last point, we still may ask, Can a person alone virtuously care for his or her own good? Can a Robinson Crusoe, for whom there is no opportunity for interaction with others? On the view of relationship morality, yes, because for the isolated individual the person/person relationship to oneself still exists and is operative. If it is a virtue to be concerned for one's own good, it is a virtue for the isolated individual; and it would yet be conducive to the good of the isolated individual to pursue the virtues of wisdom, to avoid gluttony, and in other ways honor his or her inherent worth as a person.

The virtues, on my understanding, and on the understanding to which I have addressed relationship morality, are both public and private: they have a public expression in our overt actions and a private expression in our feelings and interior acts, our intentions and our desires; virtues thrive in community with our fellows, but some virtues can also exist in a person alone. In either case, though, the virtues in their exterior and interior aspects are grounded in the person/person relationship one has to others and to oneself. Nevertheless there may be a way that individuals can have various virtues without a consciousness of the worth of persons and even without a vivid presence of the virtues in their interior aspect. One may, for instance, be generous and consistently act generously for the sake of being generous, for the sake of having the virtue—but without concern for

41. MacIntyre, *After Virtue*, 220.

those one's generosity helps. Such an individual may not be generous for evil purposes and may do much good; so neither evil intent nor harm done is a reason to say that in such a person generosity is not a virtue or that he or she is exercising the virtue of generosity wrongly. Such an individual is generous for the sake of the virtue, and is analogous to the person who acts on moral principle precisely for the sake of moral principle (see Chapter 6). But *fully* having the virtue of generosity is more than this. Fully having the virtue of generosity involves having something of that generosity of spirit of which Foot speaks; it involves having generous desires and intentions because we are concerned for persons (rather than being concerned to be generous). In this way fully having the virtue of generosity is more than being generous for the sake of virtue, as it is more than doing what is generous out of a sense of moral commitment to the duties of generosity. Something similar might be said about being courageous for the sake of having the virtue of courage and about other virtues as well. And regarding some virtues, such as love (especially if it is Agape or very like Agape), there is some reason to say that one cannot have the virtue at all if one tries to have it merely for the sake of the virtue.

What we have just seen is that fully having a virtue is *more* than having some virtue for the sake of having that virtue and *more* than acting out of a sense of commitment to the duties associated with that virtue. Brandt, however, suggests otherwise. He suggests that "to say that someone has a certain virtue is to say *less* than that the corresponding principle is part of his moral code." For Brandt, a virtue is a "relatively unchanging disposition to desire an action of a certain sort . . . for its own sake." And, he wants to argue, virtues are "*purely* motivational," so that "one can have the virtue of sympathy without necessarily having a disposition to feel guilty" when one is not sympathetic, which in Brandt's language is to say that it is not part of the person's moral code to be sympathetic. Part of what Brandt's point allows is that someone might develop the habit of being honest or generous or sympathetic and never see that failing to be so is a moral failure for which guilt is appropriate. This, I think, is right. But Brandt also wants to say that one can have the virtue of honesty or generosity or sympathy without any tendency to feel guilty in the breach; and this I think is not right—not if these are moral virtues and if they are fully possessed. Brandt distinguishes between moral and nonmoral virtues: a nonmoral virtue is a "relatively permanent aversion or desire which is normally beneficial for any agent (or those dear to him—or for some special group, or in his job) for him to have, which adds to his (their) 'flourishing.' "[42] Some virtues, like industry, for Brandt, may be both moral and nonmoral. Also, one may have a nonmoral virtue, like curiosity or ambition, and have no disposition to feel guilty, Brandt observes; though a person might feel shame when lacking in ambition or feel pity for others who lack ambition, still that person might not feel remorse for his or her lack of ambition, or indignation when others lack ambition.[43] In effect Brandt is allowing that one might have *either* a moral or a nonmoral virtue and not have a disposition to feel guilty in the breach. And, again, I think that this is a possibility, even for the moral virtues (the possibility of a pure shame morality shows this; about shame morality, more in Chapter 11). But having a moral virtue in this way is not to have it in the full sense: a dimension of moral experience is lacking.

In general, I think, one's failing to have a moral virtue, if it is a moral virtue, is failing to have a right disposition or characteristic, that is, one that one *ceteris paribus* ought to have; and this is so even if virtues are dispositions to desire certain actions, as Brandt suggests. With a qualification, William Frankena is closer to it than Brandt when he proposes that a "morality of duty" and a "morality of virtue" be seen as "two complementary aspects of the same morality."[44] The qualification is that one *in a sense* may have, say, the moral virtue of generosity or sympathy and yet see nothing wrong, nothing for which guilt is appropriate, in not being generous or sympathetic toward someone. In such persons, though, some of the links between virtue and moral wrongdoing have been severed. More of the links are in place when a person is virtuous on principle (for such a person sees that he or she ought to be as the virtue in question requires). But, as we have seen, the ultimate and foundational link is not in place, or at least is not appreciated when one is virtuous on principle.

Is there a definitive list of the moral virtues? Certainly we can compose a list of the moral virtues traditionally so regarded, some of which are more central and some more marginal. But, moreover, I think that it must be allowed that what may be a virtue in one instance may not be in another. Courage, prudence, or good judgment may often be, and also sometimes not be, a virtue in a person. Self-knowledge may most often be a virtue and yet not be a virtue in some instances, as when self-knowledge could not be borne. With certain exceptions to be noted in the final chapter, relationship morality has no definitive list of dispositions or characteristics that are

42. Brandt, "The Structure of Virtue," 77 (my emphasis), 64, 77 (Brandt's emphasis), and 78.
43. Ibid., 78.
44. William Frankena, *Ethics*, 2d ed. (Englewood Cliffs, N.J.: Prentice-Hall, 1973), 65.

universally (for every person) and invariably (for a person in every instance) moral virtues. In short, for relationship morality, the virtues are like moral goods in this respect. And the reason is the same. A disposition or characteristic may often be, and at times not be, or cease to be, a virtue in a person because of the way it relates, ultimately, to the person/person relationship. The person/person relationship provides the kind of overarching consideration that MacIntyre was dubious of. MacIntyre is right to the extent that we can provide no a priori argument for such an overarching consideration. But this is just as it should be. The person/person relationship, if relationship morality is correct, exists, but its existence is not established by argumentation, a priori or otherwise. If there is the person/person relationship between each and each, that relationship can be recognized, seen, realized; however, its recognition arises from and is a part of our moral experience. The recognition is itself experiential, the experience of a discovery of the inherent worth of persons, which relates and binds each person to each.

Finally, regarding virtue, let me comment on an issue that we need not pursue. Which is prior, which must be apprehended first, moral rules or the virtues? As MacIntyre sees it, modernity regards the justification of moral rules as prior to the identification of the virtues; so it is with Hume, Diderot, Kant, and Mill, he suggests, while Aristotle in antiquity and Nietzsche in opposition to his age agree in having the opposite perception of priority.[45] For relationship morality, this issue, like the issue of the priority of the right (moral duty) and the good, is otiose, for, again, neither comes first in that both rest on relationships, ultimately on the person/person relationship.

Finally we turn to the last department of morality that we shall consider: the mansion of rights. Our concern here is with the rights of persons as opposed to the right (moral duty or obligation), and our concern is with moral rights as opposed to legal rights (the rights that citizens or residents have by virtue of a state's constitution or by law). Roughly our concern is with human rights, or the natural rights of humankind—I say "roughly" because, first, there are some moral rights that individual persons have and others do not have and, second, there may be nonhumans that have rights (a matter to be taken up in Chapter 15). Still, to an important extent, our concern is with what have been called human rights, or natural rights.

Some, it should be pointed out, doubt whether persons have natural

45. MacIntyre, *After Virtue*, 119.

rights at all; they doubt whether there are any rights that persons have by virtue of being persons. The notion of rights, it has been held, is a moral notion that came into its own in the eighteenth century, a child of the Enlightenment. And it may well be that it was in the eighteenth century that the notion was articulated for the first time with any care, or thrust into prominence, as it was in the American Declaration of Independence and the French Declaration of Rights and in the works of the *philosophes.* But others hold the much stronger view that persons have no natural rights, and they see as evidence for this view the apparent linguistic fact that for many centuries there was no expression for "a right" in any language. Alasdair MacIntyre observes that "there is no expression in any ancient or medieval language correctly translated by our expression 'a right' until near the close of the middle ages: the concept lacks any means of expression in Hebrew, Greek, Latin or Arabic, classical or medieval, until around 1400, let alone in Old English, or in Japanese even as late as the mid-nineteenth century."[46] There are two questions to raise here: (1) Is this claim about these various languages correct? And (2) even if it is correct, what does it entail about the existence of rights?

There is some reason to doubt that the claim is correct. In Ps. 37.6 in the Revised Standard Version we are told that the Lord "will bring forth . . . your right as the noonday," although in the Authorized King James Version the word used is "judgment." Less equivocally, in Deut. 21.17 the "right of the first born" is spoken of, and here both translations agree. In short there is some indication that there is an "expression" in the languages of antiquity for "a right." But say that the claim is correct. What does its correctness entail regarding the existence of rights? Pretty clearly it does not entail that no persons had rights before the late Middle Ages, when the claim has it that expressions translatable as "a right" appeared. To think otherwise, to think that from there being no expression for a right it follows that no one had rights is like thinking that from there being no names for informal fallacies in reasoning in a certain century it follows that no one committed such fallacies in that century, or like thinking that from there being no definite designation for venereal disease in some cultural era it follows that no one had venereal disease in that era. In fact MacIntyre acknowledges that "it does not . . . follow [from his claim] that there are no natural or human rights." "It only follows," he says, "that no one could have known that there were." But does even this follow? I think not. What

46. Ibid., 69.

follows, judiciously stated, is that what was known about rights could not have been stated with some "expression"—some word or phrase—that can be translated as "a right." Peter Singer, as we noted in Chapter 7, discusses the Dominion Theory, according to which "man" has been given "dominion" over all other creatures of the earth. The Dominion Theory, Singer says, "is not so much a view about the *value* of animal life as about the *right* of humans to take animal life when it suits them to do so."[47] This seems to be a fair statement about the theory (our concern here is not with the correctness of the Dominion Theory or even with whether it is correctly said to be embodied in the Bible, but only with Singer's statement about the theory). Now, one defender of the Dominion Theory, cited by Singer, is Aquinas. Aquinas does not use any term that is translated "a right"; he uses other language and says, for instance, citing Psalm 8, "It matters not how man behaves to animals because God has subjected all things to man's power."[48] The point to note is that, as Singer sees, Aquinas is affirming a certain kind of right without using any expression we can translate as "a right."

So persons may have had rights before their language had an expression for rights, and they may have asserted certain rights, albeit indirectly and in a circumlocutory manner, before a term for rights was coined. However, though we can assume that persons do have rights, as many have assumed, there are further questions about the character of those rights and about who has which rights, as well as a question about what rights there are.

There are, it turns out, different kinds of rights and, indeed, different ways of classifying rights. While various classifications of rights can be applied to either legal or moral rights, our concern is to note how moral rights may be differently classified. Happily these classifications, and their classes of rights, are fairly straightforward. There are, in the first place, rights to do something; drawing upon the spectrum of commonly acknowledged rights, we might give as examples the right to express one's opinions and the right to move to another country. Such rights James P. Sterba calls

47. Peter Singer, "Animals and the Value of Life," in *Matters of Life and Death: New Introductory Essays in Moral Philosophy*, ed. Tom Regan (New York: Random House, 1980), 230 (Singer's emphasis).

48. *Summa Theologica* I-II, q. 102, a. 6; quoted by Singer, "Animals and the Value of Life," 230. Singer cites as well *Summa Theologica* II-II, q. 64, a. 1, in which Aquinas also espouses "the Dominion Theory," as it is called, but again without using any Latin expression that can be translated "a right."

"action rights."[49] There are also rights to receive something; the right to receive a fair share of tax relief or to the repayment of a loan would be such a right. Sterba calls such rights "recipient rights." There are rights that, as Sterba puts it, "hold against some specific, nameable person or persons," such as the right to have a promise kept or a loan repaid. He calls these rights "*in personam* rights." Fourth, there are rights that, as Sterba says, "hold against 'the world at large,' that is, against everyone who will ever be in a position to act upon the rights in question." Examples here might include the right to liberty, as it is usually understood, Sterba suggests. Also, many of the other human rights that are often proclaimed may fall into this category; they are general in that such rights, as they are often understood, create or correlate with obligations in all others to protect or not to interfere with what one has a right to. Sterba calls such rights "*in rem* rights."

Rights may be classified differently, along other lines of division, as well. Another typology of rights is proposed by Lance K. Stell.[50] In one sense of "right," he observes, we say that we have a right to do something when it is not forbidden. In this sense of "right" we have a legal right to do something when it is not forbidden by the law and a moral right to do something when it is not morally forbidden. A possible example of such a right, provided by Stell, is our right to park on a public street. (Generally this is neither legally nor morally forbidden, and so generally we have both a legal and moral right to park on a public street. But, again, our concern is with moral rights.) Some such rights, however, allow others to interfere with or to prevent what we are doing or attempting to do; and our right to park on a public street is of this sort, Stell points out. My right to park on a public street is not violated when another driver takes the last parking place before I do. Rights of this qualified kind may be called liberty-rights, or they may be called liberties, and so they are designated by Stell. There is another class of rights that are liberties in that one is not forbidden to do the thing permitted by the right, but that, moreover, require that others do not

49. James P. Sterba, *The Demands of Justice* (Notre Dame, Ind.: University of Notre Dame Press, 1980), 127–28. The classification of rights discussed in this paragraph is Sterba's.

50. Lance K. Stell, "The Just Society and Lifeline" (address delivered to a conference sponsored by the North Carolina Utilities Commission, June 28, 1978). The classification of rights discussed in this paragraph and the next is Stell's. His categories of rights are similar to those of Carl Wellman, who in turn drew upon the legal distinctions of Wesley Newcomb Hohfeld. Wellman's categories are found in his *A Theory of Rights* (Totowa, N.J.: Rowman & Allanheld, 1985); Hohfeld's book is *Fundamental Legal Conceptions* (New Haven: Yale University Press, 1919).

interfere with the permitted action, although no one is morally required to help, at least so far as the right is concerned. Examples of this sort of right are our right to move about as we please and our right to enjoy the peaceful use of our property. Stell calls such rights "negative-claim rights."[51]

Also in Stell's classification are rights that, again, are liberties but that require not only the noninterference of others but also the active assistance of certain others; here an example is the right that one to whom a promise is made has to see the promise kept by the person who made the promise. Stell calls such rights as these "positive-claim rights." They are, he says, "paradigmatically acquired by promising or contracting with second parties."

Pretty clearly, a particular right may be placed in more than one category. If the proximate source of a positive-claim right is a promise made by someone, the right created is, using Sterba's categories, an *in personam* right. If no such agreement with a second party is required, a positive-claim right could be an *in rem* right. Using both Stell's and Sterba's categories, we may observe that a recipient right may also be both a positive-claim right and an *in personam* right (the right to have a promise kept); or a right may be an action right that is also both a negative-claim right and an *in rem* right (the right to move about freely).

These categories help us to characterize the various rights that persons may have. Now let us focus on human rights, those rights human persons may have by virtue of being persons. What is the character of the human rights that persons have? Many of the main, general human rights affirmed by advocates of human rights are regarded as action rights that are *in rem* negative-claim rights (the right to express our opinion, the right to associate

---

51. Examples used to illustrate these two categories of rights must be carefully chosen. Arguably, my right to park on a public street is only a liberty; no one is under an obligation not to take the last parking place before I do. But perhaps others are under an obligation not to interfere with my taking the last parking place by, say, maliciously standing in it so that I cannot park my car in that space. My right to park on a public street may generate the obligation that others not interfere in *this* way. Again, it may be important to characterize the property right in question as "the right to enjoy my property in a peaceful way," as opposed to "the right to use my property as I please." Perhaps others are under an obligation not to prevent my peaceful enjoyment of my property. But arguably, others are under no obligation not to prevent an angry person intent on mayhem from retrieving a sword or gun. If we extend our consideration of the ways one might prevent a person from parking on a public street and readjust the formulation of the property right so that it is unqualified, these examples of rights both seem to come under a new category of rights: rights that affirm a generally permitted action with which we sometimes—often or rarely, under various conditions and in certain ways—have an obligation not to interfere. However, it remains that Stell's first two categories can be set forth in a clear fashion: a liberty is a right to do what is not morally forbidden, and a negative-claim right is a liberty with which others are obligated not to interfere—whatever examples may illustrate these categories.

with whom we please), although many others are recipient rights, which may be understood by advocates of human rights as either *in rem* positive-claim rights or *in personam* positive-claim rights (the right to work, the right to an education).

But now we come to another question. Who has whatever human rights there are? Or, as I would put the question, who has the natural rights that human persons have as persons? The answer, at one level, clearly is persons, all persons. But this answer, clearly right as far as it goes, is unsatisfactory in that it does not go far enough. It leaves open two further questions. One question (closely related to the connected questions we examined in Chapter 7, What is a person? and What gives value to personhood?) is, Are all human individuals equally persons, so that all of humankind shares and shares equally whatever rights there are? The other question is, Do persons who do not yet exist have the rights of persons? Let us take the second first.

Sterba addresses it in connection with his consideration of the rights of future generations.[52] Future generations have "welfare rights," he argues, even though they do not yet exist. Future generations of course cannot present the demands of their rights, but in order for future generations to have rights it is not necessary that they be able to present the demands of their rights. If they have rights, then those rights have demands, whether or not those with the rights are able to present them—as with the rights of very young children. And future generations do have rights, as Sterba sees it, because they may suffer or benefit from the actions of presently existing generations. It is, he argues, sufficient for future generations "to have rights against existing generations" that there are "enforceable requirements upon existing generations that would benefit or prevent harm to future generations." Specific rights that might be appealed to, Sterba suggests, are a right to life or a right to fair treatment. At issue, regarding the rights of future generations to life and to fair treatment, might be present practices that contaminate the environment and the consumption of natural resources by existing generations. If Sterba's argument is correct, some of the persons who have rights are persons who have yet to come into existence.

The other secondary question is whether all human beings are equally persons. At different times many have perceived the need to proclaim that some group of human beings share equally with others the rights of human persons. This need was recognized in the not too distant past in the United States and elsewhere when slavery was a legal institution, and more recently

52. Sterba, *The Demands of Justice*, 137-43.

it has been recognized in a time of racial and gender discrimination. One who recognized a need to proclaim the equal human rights of women as well as of slaves was the nineteenth-century abolitionist and advocate of women's rights Angelina Grimke. She wrote in a letter to Catherine Beecher, a proponent of liberal education for women and the sister of Harriet Beecher Stowe:

> The investigation of the rights of the slave has led me to a better understanding of my own. I have found the Anti-Slavery cause to be the high school of morals in our land—the school in which *human rights* are more fully investigated, and better understood and taught, than in any other. . . . Human beings have *rights*, because they are *moral* beings: the rights of *all* men grow out of their moral nature; and as all men have the same moral nature, they have essentially the same rights. These rights may be wrested from the slave, but they cannot be alienated: his title to himself is perfect *now*, as is that of Lyman Beecher [a liberal Presbyterian clergyman and father of Harriet Beecher Stowe and Catherine Beecher]: it is stamped on his moral being, and is, like it, imperishable.

And she continues:

> I recognize no rights but *human* rights—I know nothing of men's rights and women's rights; for in Christ Jesus there is neither male nor female. . . . I believe it is woman's right to have a voice in all the laws and regulations by which she is to be *governed*, whether in Church or State; and that the present arrangements of society, on these points, are *a violation of human rights, a rank usurpation of power*, a violent seizure and confiscation of what is sacredly and inalienably hers.[53]

Grimke affirms the universal and equal rights of all human beings, and more besides. She says, for instance, that our human rights "grow out of [our] moral nature." This may remind us of Kant, although Grimke does not seem to be thinking of our "moral nature" as Kant did. (For one thing, for her, our moral nature is "imperishable" and so not tied to rationality, as it

---

53. Alice S. Rossi, ed., *The Feminist Papers: From Adams to de Beauvoir* (New York: Columbia University Press, 1973), 320 and 322 (emphasis in the text).

was for Kant.) Also, for her, there is a connection between human rights and the Divine, in a Christian conception. Many, of course, have affirmed universal and equal human rights without a Christian or any religious affirmation. Shortly, when we take up what relationship morality has to say about rights, we shall return to the equality-of-rights issue.

Before we turn to relationship morality's view of rights, we should address one further question. What are the rights of persons? Not surprisingly there is no more a universally accepted list of moral rights than there is a universally accepted list of moral goods or moral virtues. However, there are a number of rights traditionally affirmed by advocates of human rights. The American Declaration of Independence proclaims that "all men . . . are endowed by their Creator with certain unalienable Rights, that among these are Life, Liberty and the pursuit of Happiness." The French Declaration of the Rights of Man, also drafted in the eighteenth century, recognized as "the natural and inalienable rights of man liberty, property, security, and resistance to oppression." For Mill, who argued that all of justice, including the rights it embodies, rests upon "utility," a chief right of persons is the right to equality of treatment.[54] Grimke, who like Mill wrote in the nineteenth century, also regarded equality of treatment as a chief right. Although Mill and Grimke did not think about the source or foundation of rights in the same way, they agreed in their opposition to slavery and in their concern for the status and rights of women—causes that came to the fore in the nineteenth century. At the midpoint of the twentieth century an extensive and detailed statement of human rights was adopted by the United Nations in the form of its Universal Declaration of Human Rights. In its thirty articles all human beings are proclaimed to have a number of specific moral rights, including the right to life, liberty, and security of person, the right to recognition as a person before the law, the right to an effective remedy by a national tribunal when one's legal rights granted by the constitution or law of a nation are violated, the right to freedom of movement and residence, the right to a nationality, the right to marry and to found a family, the right to own property, the right to freedom of religious expression, the right to freedom of opinion and expression of opinion, the right to peaceful assembly and association, the right to take part in the government of one's country, the right to social security, the right to work, the right to rest and leisure, the right to a standard of living adequate for the health and well-being of one's family, the right to

54. Mill, *Utilitarianism*, 60–61.

education, the right freely to participate in the cultural life of the community, and also the right to be free from slavery and servitude, the right to be free from torture, the right to be free from arbitrary arrest, detention, or exile, and the right to be free from arbitrary interference with one's privacy.

What, then, does relationship morality have to tell us about moral rights? For relationship morality, those moral rights that are often referred to as "human rights" are the general rights that human persons have by virtue of being persons, and under the assumption that human beings are the only persons, but only under that assumption, such rights are exclusively human rights. In any case, since human beings are persons, for relationship morality human rights are the rights human beings have as persons. What rights do human beings have, for relationship morality? The paramount right human beings have is the right to be treated as persons, that is, as beings with inherent worth. There may be, and are, other rights that flow from this right, but it is paramount. This right is, among rights, foundational, and an important aspect of its paramountcy is that it is literally inalienable. As we have seen, the framers of various proclamations of the natural rights of human beings, such as the American Declaration of Independence and the French Declaration of the Rights of Man, have regarded the rights they proclaim as inalienable. One such right, named in these documents, is the right to liberty. However, if the imprisonment of felons or the institutional confinement of those with mental disorders who are dangerous to themselves and to others is ever morally justified, then the right to liberty can be forfeited or abridged or morally overridden. Also, it would seem to be possible to surrender certain rights that are often affirmed as human rights. If, say, in time of war I give myself up for internment, I thereby give up my right to liberty, at least for a period of time. And by freely renouncing my claim of ownership regarding some or all of my property, I thereby surrender my right to own that property. When I give up my liberty for a period of time, I give up my status as a free person for that period of time; and when I renounce ownership of my property, I give up my status as an owner of that property. But the right to be treated as a person is different. That fundamental right cannot be given up by word or deed. I can give up my status as a free person and my status as an owner, as I do by giving up my right to liberty and my right to own my property, but I cannot give up my right to be treated as a person, since that would be tantamount to giving up my status as a person. Nor is my status as a person, and my right to be treated as a person, taken away by my imprisonment, even when morally justified: though I would lose my right to liberty and cease to be a free person when properly imprisoned, I would not cease to be a person. The right to be treated as a person is, for persons, truly inalienable.

Beyond this basic and fundamental right, what other moral rights are there? As with goods and virtues, relationship morality has no definitive list of moral rights or even of human rights, those general moral rights that all human beings are said to share. But it does have a test of sorts for human rights. The test of human rights claims is whether what is claimed as a right is in accord with and required by the inherent worth of persons, or, to put the same point in the language of relationships, the test of whether something is a right of persons as persons is whether not respecting the alleged right will or will not violate the person/person relationship. For relationship morality, when we do not act in accord with the inherent worth of a person, we violate the right of that person to be treated as a person; and, furthermore, if, when we deny a person liberty or an education, we do not treat that person as a being with inherent worth, then he or she as a person has the further rights to liberty and to an education. And so on for the other human rights that have been claimed for human beings. Is there not only a right to life but a right to die? Is there not only a right to liberty and security but a right to work and a right to leisure, as the United Nations' Universal Declaration of Human Rights asserts? Is there also a right to watch television for eight hours a day? If a person has a right to die, it is because being allowed to die is in accord with the inherent worth of that person. And if there is a general moral right to leisure that persons have as persons, but no such right to watch eight hours of television each day, it is because the former, but not the latter, is in accord with and required by the inherent worth of persons.

Also, this same test—the test of inherent worth or the violation of the person/person relationship—tells us when a right is lost or morally overridden; for one's moral right to, say, liberty to be properly taken away, as in a morally justified instance of imprisonment, the forfeiture of the right must be in accord with respect for the individual's inherent worth. In general, punishment imposed by the state or any authority, in order to be morally justified, must not violate the personhood of the individual punished. It is for this reason that persons are proclaimed to have a right to be free from cruel and degrading treatment. There is, I think, an implication here for capital punishment. I earlier allowed that euthanasia may, in certain cases, be in accord with respect for a person's inherent worth or dignity (Chapter 7). Given the correctness of that point, it is not true that respect for persons never allows bringing about the death of a person. Thus relationship morality does not rule out capital punishment on these grounds. However, capital punishment is not euthanasia, and it surely is not euthanasia done in accord with and for the sake of an individual's inherent worth. If the only justification for capital punishment is the protection of the welfare of others or the heinous nature of the act committed, and if the inherent worth of the one to be punished is simply discounted, then capital punishment by its nature cannot be justified.

Again, for relationship morality, this test is a test for the *kind* of right that various human rights are. That is, adverting to Stell's categories, it is a test of whether some right is only a liberty or, instead, a negative-claim right or even a positive-claim right. Whether the right to pursue happiness is only a liberty (so that it only is not forbidden to pursue happiness) or a negative-claim right (so that others must not interfere) or a positive-claim right (so that others must help) is decided by what respecting the inherent worth of persons requires of other persons in regard to the pursuit of happiness.

What emerges here is that the foundation of moral rights, specifically human rights, is the fundamental relationship that binds each person to each by virtue of shared personhood. This is the person/person relationship, which each person has to every other person and to himself or herself. It is because the person/person relationship is foundational to rights that the measure of its violation operates as a test for rights in the several ways we have seen. Now, generally, rights are against other persons in that they generate obligations in others, and so it is our person/person relationship *to others* that is foundational to rights and operates as the test. However, there is one right that generates a claim against oneself: the right fundamental among rights, the inalienable right to be treated as a person. It is violated when others do not treat one as a person, but it is also violated when one does not treat oneself as a person. And here the person/person relationship *to oneself* is foundational. The person/person relationship, then, underlies all our human rights, even the primary human right to be treated as a person.

At this juncture let me return to the contention of Alasdair MacIntyre that there are no natural or human rights. Earlier we noted it in conjunction with his claim that the languages of antiquity lacked any expression for "a right." Now I want to draw attention to another aspect of his defense of his denial of human rights. That denial he states strongly: "There are no such rights, and belief in them is one with belief in witches and in unicorns."[55]

55. MacIntyre, *After Virtue*, 69.

He believes that just as there is no good reason to believe in witches or unicorns, so there is no good reason to believe in human rights. Even Ronald Dworkin, who takes rights much more seriously, concedes that the existence of rights cannot be demonstrated, MacIntyre observes. Dworkin, in the passage MacIntyre cites, in a part not quoted by MacIntyre, says that it is not a part of his view "that any mechanical procedure exists for demonstrating the rights of parties in hard cases."[56] Dworkin then makes the point that from its being true that a statement cannot be demonstrated, it does not follow that it is false. MacIntyre agrees that this is so but comments that this point could be used equally well to defend claims about the existence of witches and unicorns.[57] MacIntyre is right, I believe, that Dworkin's formal point does not provide much support for claims about rights. And, moreover, there may be no "demonstration" of the truth of rights claims. MacIntyre, as we saw earlier, insists that there is no "a priori argument" for a principle that will settle issues between rival traditions on the virtues. Yet, I pointed out, even so, there can be a basis in our moral experience for an overarching principle that will tell us what dispositions are virtues and when they are. So too, though there may be no demonstration of the truth of rights claims, there can be good reasons for accepting a rights claim, good experiential reasons.

For relationship morality, there is in fact an experiential basis for claims about moral rights—the same experiential basis that MacIntyre overlooked regarding virtue. The fundamental basis of our rights claims, whether we are claiming our rights or the rights of others, is our moral experience of the inherent worth of persons, our realization, in our moral experience, of our person/person relationship to persons, a relationship that we violate when we violate the rights of persons. Given the kind of realization-discovery of the person/person relationship that we have discussed, the source of human rights is in a concrete way discoverable in our moral experience. And, moreover, if our realization is the *universal* discovery of person/person relationship—so that we realize that each person is universally related to each person by virtue of being a person—then we have in our moral experience a basis for the claim that all persons have natural or human rights simply by virtue of being persons. This is not to say that everyone has made this discovery. Perhaps many have not. Perhaps many respect the rights of others on principle, without a consciousness of the person/person relationship on which those rights rest.

56. Ronald Dworkin, *Taking Rights Seriously* (Cambridge: Harvard University Press, 1977), 81.
57. MacIntyre, *After Virtue*, 69–70.

Nevertheless, if relationship morality is correct, moral rights rest on relationships and ultimately on the person/person relationship. This holds for moral rights of all sorts; it certainly holds for the basic right to be treated as a person, and it holds for other human rights, as I have tried to show. Now, though, let me try to bring out in more detail how it holds for those human rights that are *in rem* rights, and then go on to bring out how it holds for *in personam* moral rights, even when such a right is a right of one individual against another individual and hence not a general human right, though a moral right. Many or all of the general human rights proclaimed by advocates have been regarded as *in rem* rights. They may be action rights or recipient rights, negative-claim rights or positive-claim rights, but many or all appear to be *in rem* rights. They appear to be rights that each person as a person has, to use Sterba's language, "against 'the world at large' "; that is, they are rights that each person has as a person, which generate obligations of one sort or another for all other persons, or at least for all those in a position to act upon those rights. Examples of human rights that seem to be *in rem* rights are the right to life, the right to liberty, the right to free expression, the right to freedom of movement and residence, the right to associate with whom one pleases, and the right to religious expression. All of these are action rights, but recipient rights also are or may be *in rem* rights, including the right to work and the right to an education. But some proclaimed human rights that are recipient rights may be *in personam* rights. The right to an education may be, at least in part, an *in personam* right if Socrates, in the *Crito*, is correct in the way he understands the tacit moral agreement between the state and its citizens and residents. If Socrates is correct, then those who live in a state have moral rights against the state arising from this agreement. These rights, embraced by the general right to the protection of the laws, include the right to security and the right to an education and, as rights that flow from an entered agreement between individuals and their state, are *in personam* rights. Perhaps, though, the best way to think of such rights is to see them as at once *in personam* rights and *in rem* rights. They are *in personam* rights against certain persons or the state on grounds such as those Socrates advances and also, independently of any such grounds, they are *in rem* rights against the world at large. So, if one is a citizen or resident of a state and abides by the laws of that state, one has a right against that state to an education; and, at the same time, refugees without a state also have a right against the world at large to an education. It remains, then, that many, if not all, human rights are *in rem* rights. *In rem* rights, in a way going beyond what we have so far seen, are explained by relationship morality and the person/person relationship. To have an *in rem* right is to have a right against all other persons able to act on the right. Clearly, to say that a person has such a right is to say that he or she is in a relationship with every other person who can act on that right. That relationship is at least the relationship between an individual claimant and everyone who is in a position to act on the right in question. How better to think of such a relationship than as a function of a moral relationship that each person who has such a right (everyone, if it is a human right) has to everyone else (for it is a right against everyone and anyone once one is in a position to act on the right)? But this is the person/person relationship. And of course, as we have seen, it is easy to understand a violation of such a right, or of any true moral right, as a violation of the person/person relationship: when I do not respect the right of a person, I fail to treat him or her as a person, that is, a being with inherent worth.

But what of purely *in personam* moral rights, especially those against a limited number of persons? Let us take as a prime example of such an *in personam* right the right created when one individual makes a promise to another individual. Such *in personam* rights, and this one in particular, arise from special relationships between persons. When one individual makes a promise to another individual, a relationship between the two is created by the making of the promise, and, for relationship morality, that relationship is the source of the right the one individual has to have the promise kept. Moral rights in general, if they are not mere liberties, create or correlate with obligations; thus, in the case of one individual made a promise by another, the right of the one individual to have the other keep the promise made correlates with the other's obligation to keep that promise. Rights and obligations are, as it were, mirror images of one another, a point that is widely recognized. Relationship morality can explain why this is so. What relationship morality sees is that, in regard to promises, as the special relationship created by the making of a promise is the source of the particular obligation to keep the promise, so it is the source of the *in personam* right to have the promise kept. The right and the obligation are mirror images of one another because each is an aspect of the same moral fact; the special relationship created by the making of the promise. If we violate our obligation by failing to keep the promise we made to an individual, we do so because we violate the special relationship we have with that person; and now we see that our violating the *in personam* right that that person has is also a matter of violating the same special relationship we have to that person. However, this relationship is the proximate source of the right, the ultimate source or foundation being the person/person relationship, just as it is the ultimate source of obligation (as we saw in

Chapters 4 and 6). When we create an *in personam* right in another person against us, as when we enter into an agreement with that person or make a promise to that person, it is relevant that the other is a person, a being with whom we stand in the person/person relationship. This is why one cannot enter into a morally binding agreement with one's car that it will start on cold days and why promises are made to persons, as opposed to, say, a stone (although one perhaps can make a promise to persons who do not yet exist, as one may be able to make a promise to one's offspring-to-be to be a worthy parent). As we saw in our earlier discussion of obligations and relationships, in violating a special relationship we violate the fundamental person/person relationship we have to that person. Now we see that in violating the *in personam* right of a person, which we do by violating our obligation to that person, we violate the same special relationship and thereby the fundamental person/person relationship we have to that person. In this way the person/person relationship is ultimately foundational to even *in personam* rights against single individuals.

Relationship morality can also shed light on other questions about rights, some of which we have encountered. Do persons who do not yet exist have rights? If Sterba's argument is correct, some of the persons who have rights are persons who have yet to come into existence. Can we come into the presence of not yet born persons? If so, they are persons and we can discover the person/person relationship to them and thereby come to see they have the right to be treated as persons and the other rights this generates. Another question we encountered is whether all human beings equally have rights? Are they equally persons with rights? Many of us, like Angelina Grimke, share the intuition that they are. If there is in our moral experience the possible discovery of the person/person relationship between oneself and another human being, then there is the discovery of an inherent worth equally shared by oneself and the other. And if there is in our moral experience the possible universal discovery of the person/person relationship between all human beings, then there is the discovery of an inherent worth equally shared by all human persons. To make this discovery is to realize that all human persons are equally persons and so equally share inherent worth. For while various attributes of persons admit of degrees, being a person, the attribute of personhood, does not.

The fundamental moral right of persons, I have suggested, is the right to be treated as a person. From this right all other rights flow. Is it a moral right of persons that they be respected as persons? It is a right of persons that their *rights* be respected: this is bound up in treating person as persons.

But, as I tried to show earlier (in Chapter 5), respecting the rights of persons is distinguishable from respecting persons as persons. It is possible to respect the rights of persons merely as a matter of principle, with no affective attitude toward persons as persons, but respect for persons as persons—that attitude toward *persons*—like Agape and the other attitudes in the respect/love range of attitudes, *is* an affective attitude. Do persons as persons have a right to be respected or to be loved? Some blanch at the suggestion that persons, all persons, have a *right* to be loved. Might persons, though, have a right to be respected as persons or to have *some* attitude toward them in the respect/love range, if not to be loved? For relationship morality, persons do have such a right, for we fail to treat persons fully as persons without some such attitude toward them. Persons deserve to be treated as persons, and we ought to love or to respect persons, or to have toward them some other attitude in the respect/love range. And if we have come into the presence of persons, some or all, we shall have some such affective attitude toward them.

So, summing up what I hope we have seen in this chapter and the last, the person/person relationship is ultimately foundational not only to obligation but to the various other mansions of morality as well. It is the source, we may say, of all of ethics. But this is not to say that it is a criterion in the strong sense for obligations, goods, virtues, or rights. Even though the inherent worth of persons, or the person/person relationship, provides a kind of test for the elements of those various mansions, still there can be a large question and much disagreement about what is in accord with the inherent worth of persons, what does or does not violate the person/person relationship. And, besides, more than an appreciation of the person/person relationship is needed to determine the content of specific obligations, the good for individual persons, and some of the rights of particular persons in concrete situations. We cannot in a simple way deduce obligations, goods, virtues, and rights from the truth that persons as persons have inherent worth; yet all these are in accord with the inherent worth of persons. The person/person relationship is the fundamental ground on which these mansions rest in that violating an obligation, not respecting a person's good, departing from the virtues, or violating the rights of persons is to violate one's person/person relationship to some or all persons.

PART IV

DIFFERENT
MORALITIES

10

The Varieties of Moralities and Guilt Morality

Enquiries, like explorations of a terrain, follow a path or a line of sight; and if the enquiry is into a phenomenon as structured as a city, it may follow an avenue or several avenues. At this point we have come to the end of the first main avenue of our enquiry: we have examined how relationships, and preeminently the person/person relationship, underlie all the mansions of morality. Now we turn to a second main avenue of enquiry. Following it we shall discover that there are various moralities. In following this second avenue we shall be doing something very different. And also, we shall be viewing morality—the phenomenon of morality—quite differently. The second avenue approaches and enters the city from a different direction, as it were, presenting us with perhaps unexpected vistas into new quarters. It is almost as though there were two cities; it is almost as though there were two different complexes of phenomena called morality. In order to bring out the severity of this difference let me redirect the analogy. One may enter into an understanding of a large city by exploring its architecture or by a study of the social and cultural groups that constitute the city's current population, two quite different avenues. Here, more severely, we may want to say that there *are* two cities. Our two avenues of enquiry into morality are as radically different as the architectural and sociocultural avenues of enquiry into the phenomenon of a city. And just as one may think it better to view a metropolitan city as on the one hand an architectural presence and on the other a farrago of sociocultural classes, so one may think it better to view morality as on the one hand an architectonic arrangement of the mansions we have discussed and on the other a series of disparate, seemingly incommensurate, bodies of human experience. But also, morality, like a large multifarious city with its various aspects, remains hugely one thing. So shall I view morality. Though morality does not merely consist of different parts but also of different aspects that are not related as parts, the human phenomenon of morality can be seen as one whole. Yet I recognize that before proceeding we should distinguish two senses of "morality," both of which in different ways refer to the same human pheomenon. The first sense is the sense we have used so far in our discussion. In this sense of "morality," morality has the mansions we have explored in the preceding chapters: obligation, virtue, and the rest. In the second sense of "morality," a morality is any of a number of bipolar systems of concepts that can deeply affect the emotions and general behavior of human beings. In this sense of "morality" there can be and are various moralities. These senses are related, but they cover different ground within the phenomenon of morality. They focus on different dimensions of morality, following different perspectives on the complex human affair of morality.

When Herbert Morris speaks of "guilt morality" and "shame morality" he is using "morality" in the second sense, or something close to it. He speaks of "the world of guilt," thus allowing that shame and shame morality constitute a different "world."[1] Each of these moral worlds is a closed and internally coherent system that provides a moral vocabulary for the guidance of behavior and for the way we think and feel about our actions. Each is a bipolar conceptual scheme with its own logic and with its own pair of negative and positive categories for moral failure and moral success. Morris baptizes each of the two moralities he identifies with the negative term from their respective bipolar systems.

Our central concern in this chapter and in the two that follow is to understand three different moralities and how they contrast with one another. Two of the three are the two identified by Morris: guilt morality and shame morality. The third is what I shall call sin morality. Sin morality, however, as we shall see, is in fact nothing other than what I have so far called relationship morality, viewed from the perspective of the second sense of "morality." Beyond presenting and examining the structures of these three moralities, I want also, as a part of showing how they contrast, to show how sin morality (or relationship morality) compares favorably with the other two. Before we compare these three moralities, though, we must see how each in itself is a coherent moral system in the second sense of

1. Herbert Morris, "Persons and Punishment," in On Guilt and Innocence: Essays in Legal Philosophy and Moral Psychology (Berkeley and Los Angeles: University of California Press, 1976), 60 and 59.

"morality." The first, guilt morality, we shall examine in this chapter; the second, shame morality, we shall examine in the next chapter; and then in Chapter 12 we shall see why relationship morality may appropriately be called sin morality and why it compares favorably with the other two moralities. However, these three are not the only moralities to be found, and before we turn our attention to the first of these three, let us gain some acquaintance with the varieties of morality forms that can be discovered.

Such distinct morality forms are different ways of conceptually arranging the opposition between behavioral failure and behavioral success in the serious aspect of our lives. As conceptual systems they reflect more than psychological differences, but the conceptual differences that distinguish different moralities are significantly embodied in psychological reactions, including the way we feel toward others and toward ourselves. Consequently, in order to appreciate these differences, we must be alive to certain psychological subtleties as they touch upon morality; we need, in other words, to do psychology in the sense that moral thinkers like Kierkegaard, Nietzsche, Dostoyevsky, and, among contemporary philosophers, Herbert Morris and Charles Taylor have done psychology.[2] Not that we need to start with raw reflection on moral experience. We can with profit draw upon the thinking of others, including those just mentioned, all of whom in some manner have delineated one or more different moralities or motioned toward the moral space they occupy. Such moralities embody the opposition between moral success and moral failure in some deep form. In each case it is a form in which moral failure can be wrenching and success something to be sought. Each such morality is a closed, coherent system. Each is complete in itself as a system of interconnected categories. To say this, of course, is not to say that each equally well embraces and accommodates our moral experience. Nor is it to deny that more than one such morality might inform the life of a single individual. While any one of these moralities could be embodied in a human life to the exclusion of the others, it is another question whether any human psyche is in fact so purely formed.

What, besides guilt morality and shame morality, are examples of such

2. The psychological dimension of the thinking of these writers is, I would suppose, evident to those familiar with their work. Kierkegaard, in various works, used psychological *"Experiments,"* or "imaginary constructs," to present in concrete form human possibilities in the ethical-religious range (see Howard V. Hong and Edna H. Hong's historical introduction to Kierkegaard's *Fear and Trembling* and *Repetition* [Princeton: Princeton University Press, 1983], xxi–xxvi). Nietzsche's work is filled with psychological reflections, such as, on the "motive" of Christian faith; Walter Kaufmann gave his biography of Nietzsche the title *Nietzsche: Philosopher, Psychologist, Antichrist*. The subtitle of Herbert Morris' *On Guilt and Innocence* is *Essays in Legal Philosophy and Moral Pyschology*.

different moralities? Several have been identified or proposed. I shall present some of these as candidates, with no decisive argument that they succeed as coherent conceptual systems, although I suspect that they are practically coherent in the sense that they are capable of being internalized in a human life so that human beings can strive to follow any one of them.

Nietzsche in his writings, as we had occasion to notice in the last chapter, explicitly distinguishes between slave morality and noble morality, or aristocratic morality. Here is Nietzsche's partial characterization of a noble morality in *Beyond Good and Evil*:

> A morality of the ruling class, however, is more especially foreign and irritating to present-day taste in the sternness of its principle that one has duties only to one's equals; that one may act towards beings of a lower rank, towards all that is foreign, just as seems good to one, or "as the heart desires," and in any case "beyond good and evil": it is here that sympathy and similar emotions can have a place. The ability and obligation to exercise prolonged gratitude and prolonged revenge—both only within the circle of equals— artfulness in retaliation, *refinement* of the idea in friendship, a certain necessity to have enemies (as outlets for the emotions of envy, quarrelsomeness, arrogance—in fact, in order to be a good *friend*): all these are typical characteristics of the noble morality.

Such a morality he contrasts with slave morality:

> It is otherwise with the second type of morality, *slave-morality*. . . . The slave has an unfavourable eye for the virtues of the powerful; he has a scepticism and distrust, a *refinement* of distrust for everything "good" that is there honoured—he would fain persuade himself that the very happiness there is not genuine. . . . On the other hand, *those* qualities which serve to alleviate the existence of suffering are brought into prominence and flooded with light; it is here that sympathy, the kind, helping hand, the warm heart, patience, dilligence, humility and friendliness attain to honour; for here these are the most useful qualities, and almost the only means of supporting the burden of existence. Slave-morality is essentially the morality of utility.[3]

---

3. Friedrich Nietzsche, *Beyond Good and Evil*, sec. 260 in *The Philosophy of Nietzsche* (New York: Modern Library, 1954), 580–81 (emphasis in the text).

In *The Genealogy of Morals* he brings out the contrast differently:

> While every aristocratic morality springs from a triumphant affirmation of its own demands, the slave morality says "no" from the very outset to what is "outside itself," "different from itself," and "not itself." . . . The contrary is the case when we come to the aristocrat's system of values: it acts and grows spontaneously, it merely seeks the antithesis in order to pronounce a more grateful and exultant "yes" to its own self;—its negative conception, "low," "vulgar," "bad," is merely a pale late-born foil in comparison with its positive and fundamental conception (saturated as it is with life and passion), of "we aristocrats, we good ones, we beautiful ones, we happy ones."[4]

"The revolt of the slaves," Nietzsche says, "begins in the very principle of *resentment.*"[5] The theme of resentment, or *ressentiment*,[6] in connection with slave morality is important for Nietzsche. Slave morality belongs to the weak, and they and it are imbued with vindicative hatred and revengefulness (elements of *ressentiment*). Those with this morality are passive, their happiness being a "deadening, a quietude." To this morality belongs that insincere prudence that seeks to avoid open confrontation. Aristocratic morality and the noble, to whom it belongs, embody openness with oneself. To aristocratic morality belongs the sincerity of an immediate reaction to what is held in contempt.[7] The "noble type of man regards *himself* as a determiner of values"; self-glorification, faith in oneself, pride in oneself, and an attitude of irony toward "selflessness" belong to noble morality.[8]

For Nietzsche, these two moralities embody very different negative and positive concepts, which hover around different poles. Within slave morality the bipolar concepts are good and evil. Evil is associated with power and dangerousness and the other noble virtues, while goodness is associated with their opposite. Within noble morality the bipolar concepts are good

---

4. Friedrich Nietzsche, *The Genealogy of Morals*, "First Essay: 'Good and Evil,' 'Good and Bad,' " sec. 10, in *The Philosophy of Nietzsche*, 647.

5. Ibid. (emphasis in the text).

6. On *ressentiment*, see Walter Kaufmann, *Nietzsche: Philosopher, Psychologist, Antichrist*, 4th ed. (Princeton: Princeton University Press, 1974), 371 ff.

7. Nietzsche, *The Genealogy of Morals*, " 'Good and Evil,' 'Good and Bad,' " sec. 10, in *The Philosophy of Nietzsche*, 648–49.

8. Nietzsche, *Beyond Good and Evil*, sec. 260, in *The Philosophy of Nietzsche*, 579 and 580 (emphasis in the text).

and bad, where the good is precisely the noble and bad is the base or despicable. As slave morality sees the noble as evil, so noble morality sees the vulgar, the timid, the cowardly, the oppressed, and the self-abasing as the bad or despicable.[9]

To an extent, as Walter Kaufmann observes,[10] Nietzsche is talking about types of persons as well as different moralities. In addition, Nietzsche has views about the origin of these two moralities. Our concern, however, is with the anatomy of the moralities that he lays out before us. Of course his characterization of slave morality is from the outside and is tendentious. The very name is polemical. Also, he goes beyond identifying slave morality as a morality when he attributes to those who have such a morality the motive of resentment, or *ressentiment*. If he is right in this contention, there may be something false, hypocritical, or even self-deceptive in the nature of slave morality. Still it is possible that it is a system by which some may live, even if they would not identify their values in the terms Nietzsche uses. It cannot be ruled out a priori that the closed system of values by which one lives, as evidenced by actions and evinced attitudes, is more keenly appreciated by and more perceptively set forth by another. If Nietzsche is right, many live by such a morality. In any case, we can discern as a possible morality the morality form he rhetorically bodies forth.

Dostoyevsky, Nietzsche said, "was the only psychologist . . . from whom I had something to learn."[11] In more than one novel Dostoyevsky gives us a psychological portrait of an individual who in some manner rejects ordinary or conventional morality and struggles to live in accord with an alternative morality. Dostoyevsky provides a literary evocation of one such alternative morality in *The Brothers Karamazov*. It is the morality of Ivan Karamazov. More exactly it is his intellectual creation: Ivan is at best ambivalent about living his created morality. Although it is Ivan's creation, it is articulated by another character, Miusov. Miusov presents it from memory as something astounding, even repulsive, that Ivan said at a social gathering. Ivan declared, Miusov says, that

> there was no law of nature that men should love mankind, and
> that, if there had been any love on earth hitherto, it was not

9. Ibid., 579–81, and *The Genealogy of Morals,* " 'Good and Evil,' 'Good and Bad,' " sec. 11, in *The Philosophy of Nietzsche,* 651.

10. Kaufmann, *Nietzsche: Philosopher, Psychologist, Antichrist,* 297.

11. He made this comment, which André Gide would take for the epigraph of his *Dostoevsky,* in *Twilight of the Idols,* "Skirmishes of an Untimely Man," sec. 45, in *The Portable Nietzsche* (New York: Viking Press, 1954), 549.

owing to a natural law, but simply because men have believed in immortality. Ivan Fyodorovitch added in parenthesis that the whole natural law lies in that faith, and that if you were to destroy in mankind the belief in immortality, not only love but every living force maintaining the life of the world would at once be dried up. Moreover, nothing then would be immoral, everything would be lawful, even cannibalism. That's not all. He ended by asserting that for every individual, like ourselves, who does not believe in God or immortality, the moral law of nature must immediately be changed into the exact contrary of the former religious law, and that egoism, even to crime, must become, not only lawful but even recognized as the inevitable, the most rational, even honourable outcome of his position.[12]

Ivan does not deny that this is his contention and later, in conversation with Alyosha, just after he has recounted to him his prose poem "The Grand Inquisitor," Ivan concedes again that "everything is lawful," "everything is permitted."[13] Ivan does not live by his morality, but his half brother Smerdyakov does, or tries to. Smerdyakov has heard Miusov's statement of Ivan's idea, and he believes that he is like Ivan in not believing in God. He takes up Ivan's theoretical formulation as his own morality and acts on it when he murders their father Fyodor Karamazov, thinking that Ivan is his silent conspirator. Smerdyakov is mistaken in thinking that Ivan has agreed to the murder, and Ivan goes mad, or nearly mad, when he comes to understand what Smerdyakov has done and why, while Smerdyakov ends by hanging himself. Similarly, in *Crime and Punishment* Raskolnikov convinces himself that he is not bound by the ordinary rules of morality. As comes out in an article he has anonymously written, he believes that there are two classes of men: the inferior or ordinary, who are bound by ordinary morality, and the "great," like Napoleon, who have a "right to crime," a right to transgress the morality that serves to control ordinary men.[14] Raskolnikov wishes to place himself among the "great," and accordingly he does not consider his murder of Alyona Ivanovna, the old pawnbroker, and her

12. Fyodor Dostoyevsky, *The Brothers Karamazov*, trans. Constance Garnett (New York: Modern Library, n.d.), 69.
13. "Everything is lawful" is the Garnett translation; "everything is permitted" is the Magarshack translation.
14. Fyodor Dostoyevsky, *Crime and Punishment*, trans. Constance Garnett (New York: Modern Library, 1950), 254–56.

sister, Lizaveta, to be a moral crime, and he does not repent. However he confesses to the authorities, apparently out of some sense of need, and at the end of the novel Dostoyevsky holds out the hope of Raskolnikov's gradual renewal of life.

Dostoyevsky presents these moralities not so much as coherent moralities but as perversions of morality born of prideful overintellectualization; but they are coherent morality forms at least in the sense that his characters act on them. It is true, to be sure, that Dostoyevsky's characters cannot psychologically escape the guilt that they intellectually deny: this is Dostoyevsky's comment on the viablity of their created moralities. By contrast, Jean-Paul Sartre in his play *The Flies* presents his hero Orestes as free of guilt. Orestes in Sartre's treatment of the Greek legend, as in Aeschylus', avenges his father's death by killing his mother, Queen Clytemnestra, and her lover-become-king, Aegistheus. However, Sartre's Orestes pronounces his act right and feels no remorse: at the end of the play he strides off the stage a hero. So there is a psychological issue between Dostoyevsky and Sartre. Say that Dostoyevsky is right. Still, that does not deny that the alternative moralities he portrays are conceptually or practically coherent. Raskolnikov confesses, and Smerdyakov takes his own life, while Ivan goes mad. But Raskolnikov and Smerdyakov have acted on the moralities that Dostoyevsky evokes. Whether Dostoyevsky or Sartre is right in the issue between them, Dostoyevsky, then, succeeds in portraying possible morality forms, forms that conceptually cohere and on which it is psychologically possible for at least some persons to act—whatever repercussions may follow.

To what extent are the morality forms in Dostoyevsky's two novels new and distinct moralities? The morality of Ivan Karamazov is certainly not the ordinary or conventional morality, for in it nothing is forbidden; but it is parasitic on conventional morality in that it speaks to the moral rules of conventional morality and affirms itself by negating them. To say that "all is lawful" or that "all is permitted" is to deny every rule of morality that proclaims some action is forbidden. Ivan's form of morality is in a way the same type as conventional morality: the central categories of both are the same. Both operate with the categories of the permissible and the forbidden, and by extention with the categories of obligation and moral rule. However, for Ivan's morality, all the conventional moral rules that forbid are annulled—at least for those who do not believe in God and immortality. At a deeper level, though, Ivan's created morality and that of Raskolnikov may be forms of shame morality. This may be true also of Nietzsche's noble morality. Whether and how Ivan Karamazov's morality, Raskolnikov's morality, and Nietzsche's noble morality might come under the rubric of shame morality we shall see in the next chapter.

Nietzsche and Dostoyevsky are moral thinkers who are concerned to reform our moral values or to deepen our morality. Nietzsche, who spoke of a "revaluation of all values" in *Ecce Homo*, is concerned with the former; Dostoyevsky is concerned with the latter. Others who have identified morality forms have had more analytic concerns and have sought simply to enhance our understanding of morality and its various attendant issues. Among those with this more analytic approach is Charles Taylor. Taylor, as we have seen (in Chapter 8), finds within the broad phenomenon of morality different "languages of qualitative contrast," each of which makes central a different moral goal. The four examples he draws to our attention, we will recall, respectively make central to moral evaluation personal integrity, Agape/charity, liberation, and rationality. Each of these "languages" makes a fair promise of being a morality in our second sense. Each embodies a different distinction between the morally positive and the morally negative. Each constitutes a closed bipolar moral system. Perhaps no one of these will comprise all of any individual's moral outlook, but that is not necessary. While Taylor calls these closed systems "languages," rather than "moralities," in another place he uses the term "ethic" to refer to such a bipolar system. In *Sources of the Self* he speaks of "an ethic of general principles" and also identifies an "honour ethic."[15] He distinguishes three "axes" in "what can be called, in the most general sense, moral thinking." All three axes, he suggests, are probably present in every culture, but there can be a great difference in the importance given to them. The first axis has to do with our sense of respect for the rights of others and obligations to others. It is this axis of morality that gives rise to or connects to "an ethic of general principles" and that, he suggests, enjoys a paramountcy in the modern world. The second axis has to do with the way we understand what makes a full life. And the third has to do with "dignity." Dignity concerns "the characteristics by which we think of ourselves as commanding (or failing to command) the respect of those around us." "Respect" in this connection, he points out, is distinguishable from respect for the rights of others; rather, he says, it is that sort of respect we express when we say of someone that he has our respect. (Such respect presumably might be given to someone in the light of his or her accomplishments or moral character;

---

15. Charles Taylor, *Sources of the Self* (Cambridge: Harvard University Press, 1989), 14–16. Cf. John Kekes on "honor shame" in "Shame and Moral Progress," *Midwest Studies in Philosophy* 13 (1988): 287–88.

as such, we should observe, it is to be distinguished from respect for persons as persons.) When the third axis is given paramount importance there emerges an "honour ethic" or a "warrior and honour ethic." Such an honour ethic, Taylor says, was "dominant among the ruling strata of archaic Greece, whose deeds were celebrated by Homer." In that culture the third axis "seems even to have incorporated the second axis without remainder," says Taylor. That is, a full life was conceived of in terms of commanding the respect of those around us.

The highest attainment for those with an honour ethic is glory. Thus Taylor writes, "For those who espouse the honour ethic, the issue concerns their place in the space of fame and infamy. The aspiration is to glory, or at least to avoid shame and dishonour, which would make life unbearable and non-existence preferable." Not that an honour ethnic is limited to archaic Greece or to warriors. If Taylor is right, it persists today as the ethic of the gentleman. It is a feature of an honour ethic that it resists a theoretical articulation of what determines the honourable and the dishonouring. One with this ethic has "a 'sense' of a qualitative distinction," for Taylor. "It has often been remarked," he observes, "that to be a gentleman is to know how to behave without ever being told the rules. (And the 'gentlemen' here are the heirs of the former warrior nobility)."[16]

Taylor, then, in different writings, points toward several morality forms. But he also explicitly identifies two "ethics" that I suggest are strong candidates for being "moralities" in our second sense. The first, an ethic of general principles, I think amounts to a form of guilt morality. The second, an honour ethic, may well be a form of shame morality, but, for reasons to be made clear in the next chapter, if so, it is a special form.

Herbert Morris draws to our attention, besides guilt morality and shame morality, what may be another morality form, a "path morality," as we may call it. Morris invites us to "imagine set before us a description of a path to be followed." Such a description of a path might take several forms. We might be told what "the thing that is done is." Alternatively, we might be given a description "employing the concept of a model man, actual or imagined, [who] manifests in his life attachment to the path." Thus we may have set before us the path of Buddhism by having its requirements described or, alternatively, by having put before us the model of the Buddha. Again, we may be presented with the path of a life devoted to medical research by being given a description of its rigors or by being made acquainted with the

16. Taylor, *Sources of the Self,* 44 and 21.

biography of one who devoted his or her life to medical research. So too for other possible paths. As far as I can see, in principle this model might hold for any number of paths, not all of which need be as elevated as those mentioned. Although Morris does not explicitly propose that following a path is a morality, he says that this "way of thinking about and responding to individuals . . . comes closer to what we understand by morality than the world of health and sickness." (Other things being equal, when one falls ill, it is something that happens to one and so not a moral failure, and so too the "good luck" or "blessing" of good health does not constitute moral success.) Still, Morris is hesitant to call the following of a path a morality, for it is "a world devoid of moral criticism and punishment and associated moral emotions of indignation and resentment and guilt." Morris may be right that punishment, indignation, and, notably, guilt are lacking, but if so, this shows only that a path morality is not a guilt morality. Following a path can still come to a form of morality in our broad conception. For one thing, it allows judgments of success when one is on the path, and judgments of failure when one has strayed from the path. For another thing, failure is negative in a distinctly moral sense. As Morris himself observes, there may be "invoked . . . the concepts of blindness, ignorance, stupidity, forgetfulness, [and] weakness."[17] In the setting of one's trying to follow a path, the judgment that one is blind, ignorant, stupid, or forgetful about what the path demands or weak in steeling oneself to meet the demands of the path would be a judgment of that kind of deep behavioral failure that is moral in the broad sense.

The logic of the path-morality form allows that a path may be for everyone or for only a certain few. Individuals may be given an opportunity to take up a path by, for instance, a teacher inviting those able and inclined to follow his or her approach to a subject matter. Such an invitation may allow that the path is not for everyone. If this is understood, then those who choose to follow are welcome, while those who cannot follow the path, or choose not to, will not be negatively judged. For such a path, it is not that those who do not take up the path fail to follow the path. So it may be with various "paths" in the disciplines of life: poetry writing, medicine, philosophy, bodybuilding, crime. But once such a path is taken, then the one following the path has entered a moral domain where he or she, and others, can judge the extent to which the path is being followed.

Also, there may be an "esthetic morality," as we might designate it, using

17. Morris, "Persons and Punishment," in *On Guilt and Innocence*, 59.

Kierkegaard's notion of the esthetic. For Kierkegaard, the esthetic is not limited to the appreciation of beauty, nor need it even involve such an appreciation, although it may. More or less in accord with the term's etymology, what Kierkegaard means by "the esthetic" embraces what we sense. In his language the esthetic relates to "the immediate," what we immediately perceive, what is immediately presented to us. For Kierkegaard, there are different "stages" in spiritual development, one of which is the esthetic. The esthetic individual is preoccupied with his or her sensations and is greatly concerned with variation of sensations and an enjoyment of the nuances of different experiences. Kiekegaard, of course, saw the ethical and, finally, the religious as further possible stages of spiritual development beyond the esthetic. For him, then, the esthetic is distinguishable from, and even opposed to, the ethical. Admittedly, the fact that he opposed the esthetic to the ethical presents my exposition of an esthetic morality with a mild embarrassment. However, given what he means by "the ethical," it is understandable that he would see an opposition between it and the esthetic. (To anticipate what will emerge shortly, what Kierkegaard means by "the ethical" can be understood as a species of guilt morality.) If, on the other hand, we allow that there are various morality forms, then I think that it is perfectly understandable that there can be an esthetic morality. For there is in the realm of what Kierkegaard means by "the esthetic" a closed bipolar system with a deep place for behavioral failure and success. Within such an esthetic morality, failure is boredom, and success is excitement or being entertained or some other more refined opposite of boredom, such as an engagement of the attention. To the extent that one lives by such a morality one will seek to escape from boredom by whatever means are available. Granted, Kierkegaard does not apply the category of morality to one following such a way of life, but he nevertheless provides us with portraits of such esthetic individuals, individuals who, in our terms, are following an esthetic morality. He does so most notably in "The Seducer's Diary" in Either/Or.[18] "The Seducer's Diary" is that of Johannes, and in it Johannes relates his elaborate seduction of Cordelia. As Johannes makes clear, his intention is not to complete the seduction as quickly as he can. More than the final triumph he enjoys the erotic process of the seduction. He is a "reflective seducer," occupied with "the subtlety, the cunning, whereby he knows how to steal into a girl's heart, the dominion he knows how to gain

18. Søren Kierkegaard, Either/Or, I, trans. Howard V. Hong and Edna H. Hong (Princeton: Princeton University Press, 1987), 301–445.

over it, the enthralling, deliberate, progressive seduction. How many has he seduced is of no importance here; what occupies us is the artistry, the meticulousness, the profound cunning with which he seduces."[19] Part of Johannes' enjoyment comes from his control of Cordelia's emotions, but part comes from his manipulation of his own moods. Unmitigated pleasure can be boring; the thrill of a possible failure is to be appreciated. Johannes has a first enjoyment in the actuality of the seduction, but also a "second enjoyment" gained through "poetic reflection."[20]

To be sure, one need not be a seducer to follow an esthetic morality. Nor need one be "reflective" in Kierkegaard's sense. And, of course, one who follows an esthetic morality might not follow it exclusively. The case of Johannes, the author of "The Seducer's Diary," is instructive, however, because it is a case of an individual who is single-mindedly pursuing an esthetic morality and for whom significant decisions about how to treat others is determined by such a morality.

There may be, and are, other morality forms. There is, for instance, an ethic of care, the morality form developed by such feminist thinkers as Carol Gilligan and Nel Noddings, as we have seen (in Chapters 2 and 5). I have not endeavored to present an exhaustive catalogue in the preceding. In fact, as I have had occasion to suggest, there may be, not one, but several forms of guilt morality. Also, there are different forms of shame morality and different forms of sin morality, as we shall see (in succeeding chapters). Now, though, it is time that we turned our attention to the first of the major morality forms we want to get before ourselves: guilt morality.

In presenting Ivan Karamazov's morality I remarked that it was an alternative to ordinary or conventional morality and also that it was parasitic on it. What is this conventional morality? It is the public morality of familiar "moral rules" that confronts us in many of our everyday encounters and as such corresponds to what Charles Taylor called "an ethic of general principles." But beyond being this it is a morality form with a complex conceptual structure, or logic. Conventional morality, or an ethic of general principles, is, I suggest, usefully understood as essentially a form of what Herbert Morris calls guilt morality.

19. Ibid., 108. This comment is made by A, the pseudonymous source of the esthetic part of *Either/Or*. Strictly speaking, his comment is made regarding "the reflective Don Juan," who is to be distinguished from "the musical Don Juan" (who, by contrast, is concerned with "how many he has seduced" and the satisfaction of the triumph). However, A's comment applies to Johannes as well.
20. Ibid., 305.

Morris elaborates his notion of guilt morality in a series of essays in which he exhibits guilt morality's structure of conceptual connections, a structure of moral connections that involve our social interactions with others and our own moral feelings. He is not concerned to put forward a traditional theory of obligation, that is, a theory about what standard or criterion in the strong sense establishes the moral rightness of actions or the rules of morality. (Happily he is not, given what we have seen in previous chapters about the poor prospects of there being such a criterion.) Rather, he presents us with an examination of the connections between moral rules (however they are ethically derived and whatever their source) and other central ethical concepts integral to a guilt morality, such as guilt and wrongdoing, forgiveness, resentment, and making amends.[21]

Important for a guilt morality, in Morris' analysis, is the concept of a limit on conduct. Often such limits are expressed in the form of moral precepts, or rules, that exclude certain behavior (such as stealing, not caring for one's children, cheating, and so on). When a limit takes the form of a moral rule, it imposes on us a duty or obligation to comply with the rule. In many instances we recognize the imperative force of these moral rules and allow that others have a right to demand our compliance. Rights and certain obligations are correlated in a way that we have noted (in Chapter 9), as Morris appreciates. Guilt enters the picture in connection with wrongdoing. In a guilt morality one is guilty of wrongdoing when one violates one of these moral rules knowingly and intentionally, without the excuse of having made a reasonable mistake or having violated the rule accidentally. As long as one does not wrongfully violate a moral rule—does not cheat, say—one remains innocent, at least so far as that moral rule is concerned. The polar opposite of being guilty is being not guilty, or innocent.

However, when one violates a moral rule knowingly and intentionally one not only is guilty, but it is appropriate for one to feel guilty for one's wrongdoing. In such cases of wrongdoing, it is not enough for the wrongdoer merely to feel regret for what has happened, which in itself implies no sense of responsibility for any wrongdoing; it is required or appropriate for the wrongdoer to feel guilty, the pain of guilt, for what he or she has done, which does imply a sense of responsibility. Guilt morality is a fault morality.

---

21. Morris develops his notion of guilt morality in the essays collected in *On Guilt and Innocence*. The exposition of guilt morality that follows is drawn primarily from sections 2 and 3 of Morris, "Guilt and Suffering," in *On Guilt and Innocence*, 93–98. Much of my discussion in the paragraphs that follow is adapted from my earlier discussion in *God-Relationships With and Without God* (London: Macmillan; New York: St. Martin's, 1989), 52–57.

One is at fault when one is guilty of wrongdoing, and from this follow both the appropriateness of indignation or complaint on the part of those one has wronged and the appropriateness of one's asking forgiveness and making amends. Making amends, like being contrite and unlike regret or forgetting, is a restorative response that reestablishes one as a member of a community.

Essential to guilt morality, we should note, is the existence of a body of public moral rules that are understood as imposing obligations on us. These moral rules are a given in guilt morality and form that morality's bedrock. Perhaps these rules would be hard to state in any definitive list, but all that is necessary is that in concrete situations the pertinent ones come to mind or at least register in their normative force.

In sum, a guilt morality, then, is one in which one sees oneself as living in a community of persons who are bound by commonly understood moral rules. When one breaks, or wrongfully breaks, a moral rule, one is guilty of an infraction. One is at fault, and it is appropriate to make amends and to seek forgiveness, which restores one's place in the moral community. In guilt morality moral success consists in living in accord with the moral community by not violating in a knowing and intentional way any of the public moral rules; and moral failure occurs when one wrongly breaks a moral rule, which makes one guilty and creates the attendant appropriateness of one's feeling guilty.

This in outline is the conception of guilt morality that we find in Morris' book. He does not present it for its own sake, but in order to address certain questions.[22] Given our concerns we need not pursue these issues. We should, however, appreciate the extent to which Morris' picture of guilt morality mirrors ordinary, or conventional, morality in its presentation of the connection between moral rules and obligation, the connection between being guilty of breaking moral rules and the appropriateness of making amends, the distinction between feeling regret and feeling guilty, and so on. The view of morality before us, Morris' conception of guilt morality, is, I submit, a fair construction of conventional morality. Kierkegaard might well agree with this point, for Morris' conception of guilt morality is quite compatible with Kierkegaard's conception of our common morality, which for him is "the ethical" or "the universal."[23] For Kierkegaard, or for Johannes

22. For example, whether feeling the pain of guilt is in any way valuable. It is, Morris concludes, in its connection to restorative responses.

23. Søren Kierkegaard, *Fear and Trembling* and *Repetition*, trans. Howard V. Hong and Edna H. Hong (Princeton: Princeton University Press, 1983), 54–81; henceforth cited as Kierkegaard, *Fear and Trembling*. See my *God-Relationships With and Without God*, 17–23, for a discussion of Kierkegaard's category.

de Silentio, the pseudonymous author of *Fear and Trembling*, the ethical is "universal" in that, first, it applies to everyone and, second, the obligations it imposes, along with their order of importance and what will fufill them, is generally or commonly—universally—understood or understandable. The ethical, or "the universal,"—conventional morality—in Kierkegaard's conception, then, may be seen as consisting in an acceptance of a corpus of public moral rules, along with the rest of the logic of a guilt morality, plus the recognition that some obligations can overrule others (which Morris allows), plus the provision that not only these rules but what meets the obligations imposed by them is open to and decided by a "universal" common sense (which Morris also allows). As I see it, Morris' category of guilt morality, with some of its implicit features amplified by Kierkegaard's reflections, applies with little remainder, not to all morality, but to ordinary, or conventional, morality.

If my suggestion is right that conventional morality is guilt morality, then we should not have to search very far to find examples of individuals following such a morality. And, in fact, commonplace moral experience seems to be replete with illustrations. We follow a guilt morality when we keep our obligations in obedience to commonly recognized moral rules against, for instance, stealing, lying, and adultery; when we recognize our guilt and feel the pain of guilt after an infraction of such a rule; and when we sense the appropriateness of apologizing and making amends for the infraction.

Also, it appears that there are various noteworthy examples of moral success that are accountable within the categories of guilt morality. Moral success in a guilt morality is a matter of being obedient to the moral rules that constrain our conduct. Sometimes, though, it is hard to obey every moral rule, hard to rise to the demands of our moral duty. In demanding cases an individual may be called to fulfill a high moral duty at the cost of sacrifice, and when this happens, the approval of those who appreciate his or her moral sacrifice is understandable within the categories of guilt morality. Kierkegaard provides us with several examples of such ethical heroes: Agamemnon, who in Euripides' *Iphigenia in Aulis* sacrificed his daughter to the irate goddess Artemis in order that the becalmed ships of the Greek expedition might sail to Troy; Jephthah, who in accord with his promise sacrificed his daughter after a great victory over the Ammonites (Judg. 11.30–40); and Lucius Junius Brutus, the founder of the Roman republic, who executed his sons for plotting a Tarquinian restoration.[24] In

24. Kierkegaard, *Fear and Trembling*, 57–59.

each case, in Kierkegaard's presentation, or that of Johannes de Silentio, a father's duty to his son or daughter is overridden by a higher duty to the state. In each case, though the people of the nation may mourn with the father his loss, they admire him for his moral courage. They sympathize, but they also understand and approve, for each, it is appreciated, has seen and met his greater moral duty. Kierkegaard's examples are all of the same type, all involving a father's sacrifice of his child for a higher obligation to the state, because, for reasons that need not detain us, he wants to contrast such ethical heroes, or "tragic heroes," with Abraham and his intended sacrifice of Isaac.[25] Also, though, we may find a slightly curious aspect to Kierkegaard's dramatic and biblical examples of Agamemnon and Jephthah in that each makes a human sacrifice of his daughter to a deity in accord with beliefs that now seem merely to be superstitions. Kierkegaard deliberately chose examples with the element of human sacrifice to a deity because he wanted these tragic heroes to parallel Abraham in this respect. However, this element is not essential to his category of tragic hero or to his examples being understandable as ethical heroes by virtue of guilt morality. We do not have this element in the case of Brutus. Also, to introduce a further example, we do not have it in the case of a rescue leader who in the midst of a perilous rescue attempt chooses his own son, the ablest of those under him, to execute a particularly dangerous operation that is necessary to save those in need of rescue. In this case, but really in Kierkegaard's too, we can identify and admire the ethical heroism of the father, within the categories of a guilt morality. For, we may say, these men did not shirk their moral duty, did not fail to do what the rules of morality required of them, even when many would have.

So guilt morality gives us a way of understanding our reactions to everyday moral failure and success, as well as a way of understanding our reactions to certain instances of heroic success. In addition, there are noteworthy examples of individuals acting in accord with apparently different moralities that, at bottom, are species of guilt morality. I have already suggested that Ivan Karamazov's morality and Raskolnikov's may be understood as forms of guilt morality. Their moralities operate with the guilt-morality categories of the forbidden and its opposite, the permissible. When Ivan proclaims all to be permitted and Raskolnikov claims that his murders are not moral crimes, they are addressing and denying the public moral rules of the conventional

25. The contrast is that Abraham's sacrifice of Isaac has no ethical justification within the "universal." For a discussion of these "tragic heroes" and Abraham, see my *God-Relationships With and Without God*, 16–27.

guilt morality. In effect they are promulgating new moral rules. Raskolnikov does not repent, as he insists he does not, because he holds that he has broken no moral rule that binds him. So runs his thinking. As we noted, in Dostoyevsky's novel he does not, despite his intellectual efforts, escape feelings of guilt. Nor, aguably, does Ivan. The reason that they do not, offered from the standpoint of guilt morality, is that neither has freed himself from the moral rules of conventional guilt morality.

We can also draw upon guilt morality to amplify our understanding of those who act morally but do so for the sake of principle, for those who act morally for the sake of principle may be seen as following a form of guilt morality, albeit in a particular manner. In Chapter 3, it will be recalled, we acquainted ourselves with examples of individuals acting morally for the sake of principle, and I suggested that this type of morality was nicely illustrated by Skeffington in C. P. Snow's novel *The Affair*. The principles for whose sake the man or woman of principle acts are, of course, normative principles; that is, they are or operate as moral rules. And this is so whether they are lesser principles embodying rules against, for instance, stealing and lying or more embracive principles, such as the ends principle itself. Skeffington, as we saw, could be understood as acting for the sake of the ends principle. Later, in Chapter 6, I argued that one who acts morally for the sake of principle may still be acting in accord with two central moral axioms. These two axioms are, first, that fully realized moral behavior cannot proceed from wrong moral principles and, second, that fully realized moral behavior must be in recognition of the binding force of the correct moral principles. Now, in order for those who act morally for the sake of principle to be following a guilt morality, it must be that guilt morality can accommodate both of these axioms. This I believe it can do. Regarding the first axiom, I see no reason to deny the proposition that the rules of guilt morality in its conventional form are, or may well be, right rules of obligation. Even if they need not be, the rules of conventional guilt morality may well be rules that are generated by our relationships, including the person/person relationship. This of course is not to say that guilt morality accounts for the source of our obligations. Guilt morality is, as I noted, silent on that matter. Nor is it to say, we should observe, that conventional guilt morality embraces *all* of the rules of obligation that relationships between persons generate. And, again, the point I am making does not deny that our particular relationships inform many of our obligations by giving them their particular form. Still, as far as I can see, guilt morality need not run afoul of the first axiom.

What about the second axiom? This axiom also is accommodated by guilt morality, it seems. In order to follow a guilt morality, it is, of course, not necessary to have an understanding of the source or justification of the moral rules one obeys. The rules of morality may simply be taken as basic, and though they have been learned and internalized, one may not have reflected on them at all. But the character of a guilt morality is such that when one wrongfully breaks or violates a moral rule, one incurs guilt and appropriately feels guilty. One has done what one ought not to have done, and one is at fault. In order for these features—accepting that one is guilty, feeling guilty, and acknowledging that one is at fault—to be in place, one following a guilt morality must feel that the public moral rules are binding. At least in this way there must be the acknowledgment that the rules of morality are binding, but this acknowledgment may be indicated primarily or even solely in one's actions and moral feelings. I do not think that one following a guilt morality must explictly see intellectually that they are binding, so that the binding nature is explicitly acknowledged. On the other hand, one may, consistent with a guilt morality, explicitly acknowledge that the principles of morality bind us morally, and, furthermore, explicitly act for their sake. This is the position of the person who, like Skeffington, acts morally for the sake of principle. Such a person may be seen as a particularly reflective follower of conventional guilt morality, but we need not go beyond the categories of guilt morality to understand the type of morality that he or she is following. In this way, then, those who act morally for the sake of principle can be understood as acting within a guilt morality.

It appears to me that guilt morality not only is a coherent conceptual system of moral concepts but also is incarnated in much practical moral behavior. Certainly we can understand much in moral phenomenology in terms of guilt morality. Yet there is another morality, also reflected in much moral behavior, that stands in graphic contrast to guilt morality. This is shame morality, and to its examination we turn in the next chapter.

11
Shame Morality

In this chapter our primary concern is to gain an understanding of shame morality. Shame morality, like guilt morality, and like other moralities we have touched upon, is a closed, internally coherent bipolar system of moral concepts. Like guilt morality, shame morality has an internal logic that binds together its distinctive elements, and, in various ways, the logic of shame morality contrasts with that of guilt morality. Most notably these two moralities contrast in their central conceptions of moral failure and the feelings appropriate for moral failure: guilt for the one, shame for the other. Correlated with this main contrast, however, are a number of more finely detailed contrasts. Consequently, given that we have the logic of guilt morality before us, as we have, we shall be able to clarify not only the nature of shame by contrasting it with guilt, but also certain finer points of the logic of shame morality by comparing them to their counterparts in the logic of guilt morality. Also, we shall want to get before ourselves examples of individuals who in their lives and actions follow a shame morality. For our doing so will help us to understand both the conceptual and practical coherence of shame morality. Last in this chapter, we shall consider different kinds of conceptions of shame, for, as we shall see, the shame at the heart of shame morality contrasts not only with guilt but with other species of shame as well.

As our exposition of guilt morality in the last chapter was greatly indebted to Herbert Morris' account of that morality form, so our present exposition of shame morality will draw heavily upon Morris' account of the morality informed by shame.[1] Shame morality, in Morris' account, on the face of it

---

1. The exposition of shame morality that follows is drawn in great part from Morris' analysis,

has very little to do with the moral surroundings that operate when a society or group shames an individual into doing something. His concern begins with that shame felt by persons when they do not live up to an internalized ideal that, imperatively, they strive to approach. In a morality that has such shame as its hallmark, the basis of the evaluation of an individual's conduct is not the violation of moral rules or the keeping of obligations, as in a guilt morality, but a comparison of the individual's conduct with his or her ideal, or "model identity." An example (a variant of one offered by Morris) is a boy, or a man, taking his older brother as a model identity in some or all aspects of his behavior. Moral failure is failure to live up to the model, as when the child unlike the older brother, cannot refrain from crying, or as when the man does not achieve professional recognition, as his older brother has. In the face of such failure one who is guided by a shame morality, to a greater or lesser extent, feels ashamed. Moral success, what is valued in a shame morality, namely achieving or living up to one's ideal, is essentially a matter of one's living up to what in one's own eyes is one's ideal identity. By way of contrast, moral success in a guilt morality is a matter of meeting public obligations, which allows one to continue as a member of the moral community. In a guilt morality, when one does not transgress any moral rule, one is not guilty of wrongdoing: the polar opposite of being guilty is being not guilty, or innocent. In a shame morality the polar opposite of being ashamed is not being unashamed, but being proud.[2] Shame contrasts with several states and feelings, but its polar opposite is pride. To the extent that one lives up to one's model identity, one is proud of doing so.

Morris recognizes that shame and guilt moralities may "overlap": the child who hits his playmate may be told both "It's wrong to hit others" and "Your big brother would never do that," and he may in time, in similar circumstances, if other conditions are met, come to feel both guilty of violating a moral rule and ashamed of not being like his brother. But still, even though an individual may be subject to or guided by both moralities, the two are "distinct," as Morris says. To the extent that one follows a guilt morality, one does not follow a shame morality, and vice versa. Several features irrevocably separate the two moralities. In addition to those we have seen, several others must be noted.

primarily from "Persons and Punishment," the section titled "Guilt and Shame," in *On Guilt and Innocence: Essays in Legal Philosophy and Moral Psychology* (Berkeley and Los Angeles: University of California Press, 1976), 59–63. Much of my discussion in the paragraphs that follow is adapted from my earlier discussion in *God-Relationships With and Without God* (London: Macmillan; New York: St. Martin's, 1989), 57–63.

2. Cf. Gabriele Taylor, *Pride, Shame, and Guilt* (Oxford: Clarendon Press, 1985), 53.

A shame morality is, as Morris puts it, a "scale morality," while a guilt morality is a "threshold morality." In a shame morality one's actions may be far from or closer to or yet closer to one's ideal: there is a scale or continuum of possible achievement and failure. In a guilt morality either one has done wrong or one has not: there are no degrees of guilt for a wrongful act.[3]

Also, importantly, a shame morality, unlike a guilt morality, is not a fault morality. Shame is not essentially tied to fault in that failing to live up to one's ideal may not entail violating any obligation and may not make one blameworthy. This is so in part because one's ideal may call upon one to do what is extraordinary and well beyond the call of conventional moral duty. As Morris puts it, "We may feel either guilt or shame in behaving as a coward; we may feel shame and not guilt in failing to behave as a hero."[4] Although Morris does not say so, we should observe that the reverse may also be true. One's internalized ideal may call upon one to do what is forbidden by conventional morality. And this leads us to another feature that distinguishes the two moralities, one that relates to the individual's determination of a model identity. While Morris does not make it explicit, I take it to be an implication of shame morality that any ideal can serve. In a shame morality one's model identity is one's own chosen or adopted ideal. While it may be implanted by others—by parents, say, or by peers— ultimately it is one's conscious or unconscious adoption of an ideal that makes it one's model identity. And within the logic of shame morality, there is no moral reason to choose one private ideal over another, as opposed to guilt morality, where the moral rules are public and given and, indeed, open to the community's common sense. True, another may say to one, "You ought not to be ashamed." But this judgment amounts to saying, "Your ideal is silly or too high or wrong," which is a judgment based on considerations external to shame morality, such as the obligations imposed by the moral rules of conventional guilt morality.

It is a corollary of there being no internally imposed limit on what may function as a model identity in a shame morality that, while one following a shame morality may have "principles" in a sense, such principles may or may not be moral principles. That is, they may or may not embody any of the moral rules of conventional guilt morality, and—what turns out to be a

---

3. Morris does of course appreciate that one who has done a flagrant and intentional wrong is, other things being equal, more guilty than one who does a wrong through negligence. But this means that *being a guilty person* admits of degrees; it does not mean that *being guilty of a specific wrong* admits of degrees. "Shared Guilt," in *On Guilt and Innocence,* 119.

4. Morris, "Persons and Punishment," in *On Guilt and Innocence,* 61.

slightly different matter—they may or may not embody the moral obligations that are determined by and have their source in our relationships to persons. Thus it is possible for one following a shame morality, for whom the visual appearance of what is served at table has become important, to have the principle that "tea cakes should always be served on pure white china." In violating this principle, through, for instance, having to serve tea cakes on off-white china because of some oversight, he or she would not be living up to a aspect of an internalized model identity and would be ashamed of what would be seen as a faux pas. However, no moral principle would have been violated.[5] Again, one following a shame morality may practice virtues that may or may not be moral virtues. R. B. Brandt suggests that curiosity and ambition may be nonmoral virtues (as we saw in Chapter 9). Let us allow that they are, or often are. Nevertheless, they could form part of an individual's model identity, so that that individual would feel ashamed when he or she experienced a waning of curiosity or ambition. But, let us ask, could one have as part of one's model identity following *moral* principles or practicing *moral* virtues? The answer, I submit, is that (with a qualification regarding virtue to be noted later) this is possible. One who has as part of his or her model identity practicing, say, the virtue of truthfulness will feel ashamed when he or she departs from veracity. And if that individual is following only a shame morality, so that there is no "overlap" with a guilt morality, that individual will feel only ashamed. Similarly, it is possible for one to abide by moral principles, and even go beyond the call of conventional moral duty, in the service of one's internalized ideal. And, again, if there is no "overlap" with guilt morality, when one fails to do what one ought to do, one will feel only ashamed. Shortly we shall look at an illustration of just such a pure shame morality in practice, which is what I think we find in Joseph Conrad's story of Lord Jim.

A further distinguishing feature of shame morality, as I understand it, although it is not made explicit in Morris' exposition, is that the individual is the definitive judge of whether he or she has lived up to his or her ideal. This, I think, explains why there is no distinction between feeling ashamed and being ashamed: as soon as one feels ashamed one is ashamed. The contrast with guilt is evident: in a guilt morality, where one's judgment of

---

5. Robert Merrihew Adams makes essentially this point in "Divine Commands and the Social Nature of Obligation," *Faith and Philosophy* 4 (1987): 269; and see his endnote 8. Adams, it seems to me, rightly criticizes John Rawls's notion of "principle guilt" on the grounds that one who violates a "personally valued principle," which may not be a moral principle, may be doing nothing for which there is a reason to feel guilty, although there may be a reason to feel ashamed.

one's own guilt or innocence is not definitive, one may feel guilty and not be guilty, or, in what may be the more frequent case, be guilty and not feel guilty.[6]

With one or two points of my own elaboration this is Morris' analysis of shame morality. A shame morality, as Morris sees it, has a certain strength over a guilt morality. "Shame," he says, "will arise when our concern is . . . that individuals realize to the fullest what they have within them," as opposed to a concern with maintaining, by the observance of moral rules, "a nice balance in relations with others" in the moral community.[7] However, as I have suggested, within the logic of shame morality there is no reason to adopt one model identity over another, and hence no reason to adopt one that is morally elevated over one that is not. For different individuals, a model identity may be provided by an elder sibling, a military hero, a sports figure, or a particularly ruthless and effective member of the underworld; or—in a religious version of shame morality (for, with qualifications, there can be such)—by a saint, a Pope, or Christ Himself; or, for that matter—since, strictly, a model identity need not be patterned after a person—by any abstract amalgam of qualities that are deemed attractive. To put the point the other way around, one can be ashamed or proud of nearly anything that in some way relates to oneself. It was perhaps this latitude in pride that Mill had in mind when he said that pride is "a name which is given indiscriminately to some of the most and some of the least estimable feelings of which mankind are capable."[8] One can be ashamed of one's lack

6. Cf. Richard Swinburne, *Responsibility and Atonement* (Oxford: Clarendon Press,1989), 79–80. Swinburne says, "The only point which might be made by talking of someone 'feeling' ashamed rather than 'being' ashamed that I can see is that the regret of the man who 'feels' ashamed is accompanied by sensations such as palpitations of the heart which are not necessarily present in the man who merely 'is' ashamed." Swinburne's observation would have been better put, I think, if he had said that the only point to talking of someone *intensely* feeling ashamed, rather than merely being ashamed, is to draw attention to the depth of the feeling of shame. This revised point more clearly leaves it in place that if one feels ashamed, one is ashamed.

Reflecting on feeling guilty and being guilty, Swinburne says, "To say that a man felt guilty might be just to say that he did what he believed wrong." This seems about right. Notice that one who means this leaves it open whether the person who feels guilty really is guilty, for it is left open whether the belief is mistaken. Also, though, Swinburne says, "To say that a man felt guilty might be to say that he was ashamed of his action." I suppose that it cannot be ruled out that someone might, in saying that another felt guilty, mean that the other was ashamed. But one who meant this, I suggest, would not be as clear as he or she might be on guilt and shame. Similarly, many might indiscriminately speak of someone deliberately spilling ink, intentionally spilling ink, or spilling ink on purpose. However, as J. L. Austin helped us see, they do not all come to the same thing; see Austin's "Three Ways of Spilling Ink," *The Philosophical Review* 75 (1966): 427–40.

7. Morris, "Persons and Punishment," in *On Guilt and Innocence*, 63.

8. John Stuart Mill, *Utilitarianism* (Indianapolis: Hackett, 1979), 9.

of courage or one's lack of charity, but also of one's tendency to show tender feelings or one's not being the brightest or handsomest in a social circle, of one's tennis game or of one's parents' social standing; and, correspondingly, one can be proud of one's courage, charity, tender feelings, brightness, tennis game, or one's parents' social standing.

It is not hard to illustrate shame morality with examples drawn from literature. André Gide's Lafcadio is a noteworthy example of someone who lives within, if not wholly within, a shame morality.[9] That he does comes out fairly early in the novel, much earlier than his "adventure" in pushing Fleuissoire from the train on the way to Naples. We see his shame morality, the rough outline of the ideal he has set himself, and his aspiration toward it in his secretly punishing himself (with small, undetectable knife-stabs in his thigh) for such failures as having allowed himself to win at chess, having shown that he speaks Italian, having had the last word, and his crying at the death of a friend of his mother's who was dear to him. We also detect his shame morality in the episode with Fleuissoire. Lafcadio finds himself sharing a train compartment with Fleuissoire, a man of middle age, an "old dromedary," whom he has never seen before—and he imagines himself pushing him out the door and off the train to his death. It will be "a crime without a motive" and a puzzle for the police, he reflects. The circumstances are favorable, and he does it, not as a whim, but to test himself against his ideal: "There's many a man thinks he's capable of anything, who draws back when it comes to the point [of action]," he observes to himself. Later, as he reads a newspaper account of the "crime," he mentally rejects such a characterization.[10] He is not a "criminal" but an "adventurer." His act of course is a crime, a moral crime, under a guilt morality; but under a shame morality, with its nonfault categories, it is tolerable to characterize it as an adventure.

However, Lafcadio's shame morality, with its elevation of folly, need not be taken as representative. A more penetrating, more sympathetic portrait of one who lives within a shame morality, and perhaps wholly within a shame morality, is provided by Joseph Conrad in his *Lord Jim*. It is arguable that Jim, guided by his shame morality, seeks, as Morris says, to "realize to the fullest what [he has] within [him]."[11]

In Conrad's novel the central fact in Jim's life, we will recall, is that he

9. André Gide, *Les Caves du Vatican*, published in English as *Lafcadio's Adventures*, trans. Dorothy Bussy (New York: Random House, 1953).

10. Ibid., 186, 192.

11. Morris, "Persons and Punishment," in *On Guilt and Innocence*, 63.

jumped, jumped from the *Patna* when it was in imminent danger of sinking, leaving it without command and abandoning its eight hundred Muslim pilgrims, who filled the ship to overflowing. As a consequence he loses his certificate, but more than that he loses his self-esteem. For Jim has set for himself a high, if somewhat romanticized, ideal, which Conrad puts in place within five pages of the novel's opening. Jim sees himself "saving people from sinking ships, cutting away masts in a hurricane," "confront[ing] savages on tropical shores, quell[ing] mutinies," "always an example of devotion to duty, and as unflinching as a hero in a book."[12] The role of duty in Jim's ideal requires a comment: his devotion to duty is a part of his model identity; thus, whether or not he feels guilty in failing to perform his duty on the *Patna*, he clearly and abidingly is ashamed of failing in his duty. In fact he is not concerned to reestablish his place in the moral community by making amends. As Conrad, speaking through Marlow, says at one point, "of all mankind Jim had no dealings but with himself."[13] Ultimately one in a shame morality is answerable only to oneself in seeking to meet one's ideal. So it is with Jim's doing his duty. In Jim's case it is not so much that his shame morality coexists with a guilt morality; it is rather that his sense of the importance of doing his moral duty is a part of his shame morality. And, of course, his ideal, or model identity, embraces much more than merely doing his moral duty, as events prove.

Jim moves from one Eastern port to another, working as a "water clerk," always moving further east when his past catches up with him. But, again, he is not so much running from others as he is running from himself. His retreat illustrates a psychological, but not therefore disreputable, difference between guilt and shame that Morris identifies: with guilt the urge is to confess; with shame we want to disappear—we cannot stand the sight of ourselves.[14] So it is with Jim in his retreat ever further east.

What he rues is "a chance missed," a chance missed to be unflinching in the face of peril. And what he seeks is "another chance." He gets it in Patusan—to which he is posted as the manager of Stein & Co.'s trading outpost. This is no mercantile sinecure. Patusan is the chief settlement in a native-ruled state occupying a remote area in the Malay Archipelago. Sprawled along a river thirty miles inland, in the late nineteenth century it is a cockpit of danger and tension between armed native factions. Jim begins by defying the cowardly but cruel Rajah. And then, in league with Doramin,

---

12. Joseph Conrad, *Lord Jim* (New York, Penguin Books, 1949), 11.
13. Ibid., 255.
14. Morris, "Persons and Punishment," in *On Guilt and Innocence*, 62.

a Malay leader, and with the help of Dain Waris, Doramin's son, with whom Jim forms a bond of friendship, he heroically captains the Malays in storming the fortress of a brigand who has terrorized the Patusan environs and holds the balance of power. Once the brigand is defeated, the Rajah is cowed and Jim emerges as a popular hero and "virtual ruler of the land." Made quickly a legend, deemed invulnerable as a god, a hero to all, he is called "Tuan Jim"—Lord Jim. He has, it seems, "mastered his fate." And, as he tells Marlow, he is satisfied, "satisfied . . . nearly."[15] He has drawn near to his heroic ideal, but he can draw nearer.

He comes by the opportunity to be the hero he would be (not to others—he has that—but in his own eyes) as a result of the incursion of that interesting Conradian character Gentleman Brown. Brown, whom Marlow describes as "a latter-day buccaneer," has stolen a ship and is fleeing in it before the law. Seeking to extort provisions, he leads an armed raiding party up the river to Patusan, of which he has somehow heard. But Brown has underestimated the defenses of the settlement, and Dain Waris, acting in Jim's absence, forces Brown and his men to retreat to a knoll. When he is reached by runners, Jim quickly returns to Patusan. He meets with Brown and, for mysterious reasons not of our concern, determines to arrange a "clear road" for him back down the river. The sentiment of Doramin and of many is otherwise, but Jim proclaims that he is "ready to answer with his life for any harm that should come to them if the white men with beards [are] allowed to retire."[16] Jim has his way. Brown departs unhindered and then, in a last act of gratuitous cruelty, ambushes a party of Patusan warriors, killing a number of them, including Dain Waris, Doramin's son. When he hears what has occurred, Jim knows what it means. Ready to keep his pledge, composedly, almost joyfully, he presents himself to Doramin, who in his father's grief, without a word, shoots Jim dead. After the shot, Marlow reports, "they say the white man sent right and left at all those faces a proud and unflinching glance."[17] Finally, in Patusan, Jim has "another chance" and does not jump.

On my reading, Jim's deepest motivation is in accord with shame morality, and we have seen enough to appreciate that Jim's pursuit of his ideal elicits from him acts of courage in a way that lends support to Morris' claim about those in a shame morality realizing to the fullest what they have within them. Other examples, with other colorations, help to provide a

15. Conrad, *Lord Jim*, 244.
16. Ibid., 295.
17. Ibid., 312.

fuller illustration of shame morality. We might, for instance, imagine someone rather like J. Alfred Prufrock, with that bald spot in the middle of his hair, of which he is ashamed. The model identity that operates as a shame ideal can have various sources, and the masculine ideal of the popular culture surely is one. This example illustrates a further element of shame morality that bears emphasizing: what falls short of one's model identity and so elicits shame may be a failure in one's actions, but it may also be something over which one has no control, such as one's family history or a physical feature like baldness.[18] Indeed, as I remarked, one can be ashamed, or proud, of nearly anything that in some way relates to oneself.

We have seen how Lord Jim's model identity inspires him to acts of courage. Other moral virtues may be exercised within a shame morality by an individual aspiring toward a model identity, as may nonmoral virtues. However, this is not to say that those following a shame morality will always *fully* have the moral virtue in question—not if fully having a virtue requires having the desires and intentions that constitute its inner aspect (as I suggested in Chapter 9). For a moral virtue, in the service of a shame morality, may be exercised precisely as a means to attaining one's ideal. We find an example of this in a characterization of Ludwig Wittgenstein offered by Colin McGinn.[19] McGinn says, regarding what he concedes were Wittgenstein's "acts of military valour in the First World War," that "it was not a matter of patriotism or comradely solidarity—in fact he detested the other soldiers; it was rather an exercise in self-purification, a proof to himself that he could live in the right spirit." And McGinn goes on to say about Wittgenstein's giving away his vast family inheritance that it "had nothing to do with a sense of economic injustice or compassion for the poor; it was purely a matter of expelling from his life anything that might compromise the integrity of his spirit—an act more of pride than of generosity." McGinn's characterization pretty clearly presents Wittgenstein as following a shame morality, even down to the detail of identifying the role of pride. What we should note, though, is how McGinn is led to deny that Wittgenstein's heroism in the war was really patriotism or that his giving away his wealth was unmitigated generosity. Given the correctness of his

18. Swinburne says, "Pride and shame, I suggest, ought to be greater in respect of the actions which we do than of the things which unavoidably happen to us, although some of the latter are important." *Responsibility and Atonement*, 79. In a footnote to this comment he expresses his gratitude to Gabriele Taylor for drawing to his attention "the fact that pride and shame may be concerned not merely with one's status as the performer of intentional actions, but may be focused on quite unavoidable aspects of oneself."

19. Colin McGinn, "My Wicked Heart," *London Review of Books* 12, no. 22 (1990): 8.

characterization, I think that McGinn is right. If Wittgenstein gave away his wealth in service to his internalized ideal, then, though his act is generous, there is a sense in which he did not fully have the virtue of generosity. (By the way, this is not to say that McGinn's characterization of Wittgenstein is right. McGinn observes that Wittenstein gave away his wealth to already rich members of his family. But Norman Malcolm, in his memoire of Wittgenstein, points out that before the war Wittgenstein gave a large amount of money for the promotion of literature. And Malcolm tells us that Wittgenstein once said "that he thought that he could understand the conception of God, in so far as it is involved in one's awareness of one's own sin and guilt"—a comment that points to moral feelings other than pride and shame.)[20] Wittgenstein, in McGinn's characterization, is strikingly generous, giving away the entirety of his fortune, and yet does not fully have the virtue of generosity, just as Lord Jim is greatly courageous and in the same way does not fully have the virtue of courage.

Another illustration of shame morality might be provided by Johannes the Seducer in *Either/Or*, or by a suitably modified variant of the Johannes character. We used Kierkegaard's portrait of Johannes earlier to present an esthetic morality. Still, at the same time, Johannes could be following a shame morality. He would be if he were not merely savoring the immediate in the experiences and emotions he was creating, but were also following an internalized ideal of reflective seduction. The two moralities could coexist or, to use Morris' term, "overlap," and, in this case, with very little tension. Of course, the details of Johannes' character and actions that exhibit an esthetic morality do not in themselves make manifest a shame morality. What would? It would be a mark of the presence of a shame morality if Johannes were proud of his seductive manipulations and ashamed of his failures. At one point he does in fact speak of his pride. He mentions his pride, along with his defiance, his cold ridicule, and his callous irony as being tempting to Cordelia.[21] But by his "pride" he seems to be referring to his manner, his proud bearing, and while one with a shame morality may have a proud bearing, it is distinguishable from the pride that one has in meeting one's ideal, which, like the shame of failure, may be open to no other's view. The Kierkegaardian portrait of Johannes, then, as it stands, may not strongly exhibit the presence of a shame morality. Nevertheless,

20. Norman Malcolm, *Wittgenstein: A Memoire* (London: Oxford University Press, 1958), 10n and 70–71.

21. Søren Kierkegaard, *Either/Or*, trans. Howard V. Hong and Edna H. Hong (Princeton: Princeton University Press, 1987), 363.

we can see what details to add to make Johannes a follower of a shame morality. He is already a darkly interior character following a secret motivation. We need only add to his motivation the pursuit of a reflective Don Juan model identity, with its attendant moral forces of pride and shame.

Now let us return to the created moralities of Dostoyevsky's characters, Ivan Karamazov and Raskolnikov. Their created moralities, I said in the last chapter, are parasitic on guilt morality. Even so, Ivan and Raskolnikov could be following a shame morality. They could be because a shame morality can coexist with and internalize a guilt morality. A shame morality can coexist with and make internal to itself the extraordinary variants of guilt morality created by Ivan and Raskolnikov, just as, alternatively, as with Lord Jim, a shame morality can coexist with and take within itself the moral duties of the conventional guilt morality. At any rate, Raskolnikov could be following a shame morality, as could Smerdyakov, who acts on Ivan's moral thinking, although, we should recall, Ivan does not himself act on his theoretically devised morality. One indication that a shame morality may be present in Dostoyevsky's two novels is that in each case a morality is created—created, it is true, through the negation of conventional morality, but created nevertheless. And one source of the ideal that guides a shame morality is such individual creation. This, however, is not sufficient to show the presence of a shame morality. What would show the presence of a shame morality is these characters feeling pride at flouting conventional morality and at overcoming any feelings of guilt and, conversely, feeling ashamed of not overcoming such feelings of guilt. And I do not believe that Dostoyevsky portrays his characters with these feelings. Raskolnikov refuses to repent—and then confesses to the police. Smerdyakov is happy to be in complicity with Ivan, as he believes he is. But it is not clear that he is proud of his doing what is forbidden by conventional morality. He is guided more by Ivan than by an internalized model identity. He seems to need Ivan's approval, and when he discovers that he does not have it, he hangs himself. Ivan and Raskolnikov, we can say, are depicted as using their prideful intellects in creating their elite moralities, but that is a different matter. So perhaps we do not find shame morality behind the scenes in Dostoyevsky's two novels. On the other hand, we can appreciate how his characters could be redrawn so that they would follow a shame morality at a deeper level. As with Kierkegaard's Johannes, the required addition is not great. We need only put Ivan or Raskolnikov or Smerdyakov in service to an internalized model identity that requires him to deny the constraints of conventional morality.

Finally, in the way of illustrations of shame morality, let us reconsider Nietzsche and his category of noble morality. As we saw in the last chapter, for Nietzsche there is a noble or aristocratic morality that belongs to the noble. One attribute of the noble individual that Nietzsche emphasizes is that he "regards *himself* as a determiner of values." In places Nietzsche insists that all values are created, as we have also had occasion to observe (in Chapter 9), but this is not to say that for Nietzsche all those who create their values are conscious of doing so. It is a part of noble morality that those following it *consciously* regard it as their own creation. Here, then, is some indication that the morality of the noble individual is a form of shame morality, since it is at least compatible with a shame morality that one should consciously create one's own ideal identity. But, moreover, as we saw, Nietzsche is explicit that "pride in oneself" belongs to noble morality. And this is a further indication that his noble morality is a form of shame morality.

It is too much to say that Nietzsche explicitly presented noble morality as a shame morality, or even that we find in Nietzsche's thought elaborations of guilt morality and shame morality. We do, however, find reflections on the effects and power of the moral emotions of guilt and shame, some of which strongly suggest Nietzsche's tacit awareness of the moral space that guilt morality and shame morality would occupy. At one point in *Thus Spoke Zarathustra*, Zarathustra, Nietzsche's prophet of the overman, says of the "pale criminal," the one suffering under a burden of guilt, that he may have been equal to the deed when it was done, but after the deed he could not bear its "image": the "lead of guilt lies upon him" and paralyzes his reason.[22] In his notes on this section of *Thus Spoke Zarathustra* Kaufmann observes that Nietzsche almost seems to be reflecting on Dostoyevsky's psychological treatment of Raskolnikov, although Nietzsche had not yet read Dostoyevsky.[23]

Nietzsche also reflected on shame. For instance, Zarathustra says, "If you have an enemy, do not requite him evil with good, for that would put him to shame," and "rather be angry than put to shame."[24] Putting to shame is something that one person does to another. As such, it seems to be distinguishable from the shame one feels when one does not live up to one's

22. Friedrich Nietzsche, *Thus Spoke Zarathustra*, first part, "On the Pale Criminal," in *The Portable Nietzsche* (New York: Viking, 1954), 150 and 151.

23. *The Portable Nietzsche*, 118.

24. Nietzsche, *Thus Spoke Zarathustra*, first part, "On the Adder's Bite," in *The Portable Nietzsche*, 180.

model identity. Again, when one puts another to shame, it does not seem that it is necessarily done in relation to the model identity of the one who is put to shame. When it is done, the one who is put to shame is made to feel wretched and unworthy, but not necessarily by virtue of his or her failing to meet an internalized ideal. Nietzsche's condemnation of putting others to shame, consequently, need not be understood against the background of shame morality. At the same time, Nietzsche recognizes the value of a sense of shame. "The danger of those who always give," Zarathustra says, "is that they lose their sense of shame." They "become callous from always meting out."[25] For Nietzsche, one of the noble virtues is generosity from strength. But if one always gives, gives indiscriminantly, not from strength but indifferently, Nietzsche seems to be saying, one will cease to be ashamed of a breach of what is a noble virtue. Here what Zarathustra proclaims is in accord with shame morality.

A further indication that Nietzsche conceives of a noble morality as a form of what would come to be called "shame morality" is found in the fourth part of Thus Spoke Zarathustra, in the section titled "The Ugliest Man."[26] The ugliest man is the murderer of God. However, it is not his being the murderer of God that makes him ugly. (For Nietzsche, we all, or many in our modern world, have "killed" God, and it is a "great deed" of which we must strive to be worthy.)[27] Rather, it is his being "full of hidden shame" that makes him ugly. The ugliest man is ashamed of his dirty nooks and ashamed that God has seen his "dirtiest nooks" and ashamed even of his "great deed." But, says the ugliest man to Zarathustra, "Your shame, Zarathustra, honored me!" While from others he received only pity, from which he flees, Zarathustra is ashamed for him—and Zarathustra's shame honors him. As one author says, commenting on this episode, "Shame honors the Ugliest Man, whereas pity shames him."[28] How might we understand this curious constellation of moral emotions? I think that the categories of shame morality are of some help. First, note that it is specifically Zarathustra's shame that honors the ugliest man. Zarathustra's shame—Zarathustra's being ashamed for the ugliest man—honors him in the light of Zarathustra's ideal, his model identity. In being ashamed for the ugliest man, Zarathustra in effect holds up for him his own higher internal-

25. Ibid., second part, "The Night Song," in The Portable Nietzsche, 218.

26. The Portable Nietzsche, 375–79.

27. Friedrich Nietzsche, The Gay Science, trans. Walter Kaufmann (New York: Random House, 1974), aphorism 125, p. 181; The Portable Nietzsche, 95–96.

28. Laurence Lampert, Nietzsche's Teaching (New Haven: Yale University Press, 1986), 297.

ized ideal and so honors him, while the pity of others only shames the ugliest man in the sense that it puts him to shame and so makes him feel wretched. And we can understand the ugliest man's being made ugly by his own shame as a comment by Nietzsche on the lowly status of his own model identity, which causes him to be "full of hidden shame." In short, though we need more than the categories of shame morality to explicate the ugliest-man episode, those categories are crucial.

Arguably, then, Nietzsche was tacitly assuming the logic of shame morality. Did he present his noble morality as a shame morality? On the assumption that Zarathusra's own morality is a noble morality, we have found some indication that he did. But if what Nietzsche means by noble morality is a form of shame morality, it is a very special form. It embodies a certain kind of model identity, a model identity composed of the noble virtues. Nietzsche, to the extent that he is recommending a noble morality, as his honorific language suggests, is recommending a shame morality with a higher, or even the highest, ideal. And, of course, he would have to go beyond the logic of shame morality to make a judgment that one model identity is better than another.

Aside from whatever illustrations of shame morality we might be able to find in literature, biographical speculation, or philosophical reflection, we should appreciate that shame morality may be a very common affair in our ordinary lives. It may gain entrance in ways we hardly notice, as when a child is told again and again to be more like an older sibling. Shame morality may be a moral force to a greater or lesser extent when we pursue some ideal of behavior in any of the various departments of our lives. The model identity that marks a shame morality can be quite limited: the one thing a person is ashamed of may be losing at tennis. For many, in this way, it may be that shame morality is not the dominant morality in their lives, as it was for Lord Jim, though it is still present. When these points are borne in mind, we can appreciate the practical significance of this morality form.

What we have seen so far is, I think, sufficient to give us an understanding of the general logic of shame morality and an appreciation of its various applications. However, in order fully to elucidate the character of shame morality, we must go further into one other matter: the character of shame itself. Shame morality turns on and essentially involves shame, but it is a distinctive species of shame, a kind of private shame, a point to which I alluded early in this chapter's exposition. Shame can take several forms, such as the form it takes when one person puts another to shame. While this form of shame was of concern to Nietzsche, it has little to do with shame morality. What we need to do, then, to complete our presentation of shame morality is to disentangle the different forms that shame can take and to distinguish them and other cognate states from private shame.

In a primary dimension, of course, shame contrasts with guilt, and we have used that contrast to bring out the logic of shame morality. Also, though, shame is different from various other states to which it seemingly bears a resemblance. Léon Wurmser, in *The Mask of Shame*, identifies several such "cognate feelings."[29] One that Wurmser names, embarrassment, seems particularly easy to confuse with shame. However, as Gabriele Taylor points out, while embarrassment is like shame in that "its concern is always with the agent himself," embarrassment, unlike shame, is "relative to the given situation." Also, embarrassment, unlike the kind of shame important for shame morality, requires an audience. In embarrassment, as Taylor says, the "concern is always with one's own position *vis-à-vis* others."[30] The situation-dependence of embarrassment and its requirement of an audience are easy to illustrate. What people are in no way ashamed of doing may become embarrassing when an audience presents itself: stepping from the tub naked is not something people are normally ashamed of doing, nor, in private, is it embarrassing, but one may well be embarrassed if one's house guest blunders in at just that moment. Again, change the situation so that one's social relationship to the audience is changed, and the embarrassment may disappear. Thus one who disrobes for a medical examination may feel no embarrassment. In the same way, men and women today feel no embarrassment wearing walking shorts that would have been embarrassingly revealing for a Victorian. Shame is different: it is not dependent on the situation. If I am ashamed of my physique, my shame will not be removed by a change in the social situation. And if my shame is the kind that is involved in shame morality, it does not depend on the reaction of an audience.

Among the other "cognate feelings" mentioned by Wurmser are bashfulness and shyness. These two feelings or states are different from shame in that they do not oppose pride, as does shame. A person who is shy about his or her accomplishments and never speaks of them may be secretly proud of those very accomplishments. Modesty, also mentioned by Wurmser, on

29. Léon Wurmser, *The Mask of Shame* (Baltimore: The Johns Hopkins University Press, 1981), 17.
30. Taylor, *Pride, Shame, and Guilt*, 75.

the other hand, does oppose pride (as well as other feelings and states, such as arrogance and lewdness). Being modest, then, like being ashamed, is one way of not being proud. Thus it provides a second contrast to pride, although the pride with which it contrasts may be public pride, for modesty may or may often be a reaction before others. Modesty is different from shame in that it is not, or need not be, a negative feeling under which one suffers; and modesty, in contrast with shame, can be felt regarding what one may be tempted to be proud of. Close to modesty is another feeling or state not mentioned by Wurmser: humility. It too opposes pride, but in the case of humility it more clearly opposes private pride. Perhaps, though, both modesty and humility have a public form and a private, or inner, form, with the public form not necessitating the inner form. I think that for one use of "modest," the person who does not brag or talk about his or her accomplishments may be modest. What if we learned that this person was in fact secretly proud of those accomplishments? Perhaps we would say, "She seems so modest, but really she isn't," although we might equally well say, "In one way she is quite modest, but in her heart she lacks modesty." Humility may be slightly different. If a person is humble in outward demeanor but turns out to be secretly proud of his or her accomplishments, I think that there is a greater inclination to say that he or she lacks true humility. Humility, after all, is counted a virtue, and so should have an inner dimension (as should modesty, if it is a virtue). Another feeling cognate to shame that is mentioned by Wurmser is anxiety. Anxiety, like shame, is a negative feeling, but unlike shame, it is focused on the future. Anxiety may be felt about one's uncertain future or about what one fears or knows will happen. While one can be ashamed of what is future, as of, say, one's poor prospects, in central cases of shame one is ashamed of what one did or failed to do. Shame, then, can be distinguished from these cognate feelings, even if at times they should accompany shame, as they surely do.

Shame is also like various other cognate but contrasting states and feelings, such as agony and regret, which might accompany shame. It remains, however, that shame is just the thing it is and not another thing. In order fully to grasp the concept of shame morality it is important to distinguish shame from what it is not. At the same time, it is important not to slight the complexity of shame. Because shame is complex, it is possible to identify different kinds or modes of shame. There is, as we have noted, that shame which is operative when one person puts another to shame. This shame is public in the sense that it arises from the interaction between persons: before I am put to shame, I may feel no shame. There is also a kind of public shame involved when a person is shamed by others into doing something. There are, or may be, times, I think, when one is put to shame or shamed into doing something without any address to that person's model identity. However, beyond these instances, there is to be noted what appears to be a distinction between public shame, or shame before others, and private shame, or shame before oneself. Shame morality involves and turns on private shame. This is not to say, however, that shame we feel before others has little or no influence in human affairs.

Shame before others is the category of shame important for Aristotle and Plato. The Greek word for shame is *aidōs*, which can also be translated as modesty. In the *Nicomachaen Ethics* Aristotle says that though modesty (*aidōs*) is not a virtue (since it is a feeling, he says, and not a disposition or state), still, since modesty is like a virtue in lying along a mean, "the modest man . . . is praised."[31] At the one extreme is the Shy man; at the other extreme "the man who feels too little shame or none at all is Shameless"; but, at the mean, "the intermediate man is Modest."[32] At the same time, though, says Aristotle, "shame is not the emotion of a good man, if it is felt for doing bad actions because such actions ought not to be done (and it makes no difference whether the things done are really shameful or are only thought to be so; they should not be done in either case); so the emotion ought not to be felt."[33] For Aristotle, then, on the one hand, modesty, as intermediate shame, is to be praised; but on the other hand, not even intermediate shame is the emotion of a good man. This tension in Aristotle's account arises, I suspect, in part because *aidōs* can be either modesty or shame, and, as we have seen, modesty and shame are different (while shyness is different from both). However, what we are interested in here is the public character of shame in Aristotle's understanding of shame.

In the *Rhetoric* Aristotle investigates "the kinds of things in regard to which men are ashamed, or unashamed, with reference to what people [that is, before what people] they have these feelings, and under what conditions they have them."[34] "Shame," he says, "must be defined as a pain or disturbance regarding that class of evils, in the present, past, or future, which we think will tend to our discredit."[35] These evils, Aristotle tell us,

31. NE 1108a30.
32. NE 1108a30–35.
33. NE 1128b20–25.
34. *Rhetoric* 1383b11–14.
35. *Rhetoric* 1383b14–15.

have among them, first, "all acts that proceed from any of the vices" and, second, not having "any part in the honourable things in which all men, or all or most persons like ourselves, participate."[36] He is clear that individuals feel ashamed or unashamed before others, but not before just any others. He says that "the people before whom we feel shame are those whose opinion of us matters to us. Such persons are: those who admire us, those whom we admire, those by whom we wish to be admired, those with whom we are competing, and those whose opinion we respect."[37] So for Aristotle, shame is public in that it is felt before others—certain others—and in that it is felt regarding what tends to our discredit in the eyes of others.

Plato, in the *Laws*, seems to have a similar notion of shame as shame before others. There the Athenian says, "We are often afraid for our reputation, when we apprehend we are getting a bad reputation from some unworthy act or speech; it is fear of this sort to which we, and I fancy the rest of the world too, give the name of shame."[38]

A not unimportant question here is whether public shame reduces to private shame. A concern for honor, or a concern for reputation, is preeminently a concern for what is public. However, there is no reason why having the honor one deems one's due, or a good reputation, cannot be part of one's model identity. If this were so, then just when one is dishonored by the community, one will be dishonored in one's own eyes and feel shame.

Concern with honorable things, with being discredited, and with one's reputation are marks of a species of public shame, although, nevertheless, public shame may come down to private shame with a model identity that requires honor before others. Also, it may be that Plato, characterizing shame as fear of bad reputation, would allow that shame can be felt for more than what Aristotle countenanced, but perhaps not. In any case, we should appreciate that shame, public or not, can be felt for nearly anything that relates to oneself. It may be a recognition of this that has led some to speak of "true shame." Richard of St. Victor says this: "Learn first to hate sin, and then you will begin truly to feel ashamed of it. If you truly hate, you quickly feel ashamed of it. That shame is known to be true when hatred of vices precedes and accompanies it. Otherwise, if you are caught in sin and confounded with shame when you are caught, I do not believe that you feel ashamed of the fault, but of the infamy. For such shamefacedness descends

36. *Rhetoric* 1383b19–1384a20.
37. *Rhetoric* 1384a26–29.
38. *Laws* 646e–647a.

not so much from sin itself as from the damage to our reputation."[39] For Richard of St. Victor, who was aware that individuals might be ashamed of their poverty or even of mispronouncing a word, what makes shame "true shame," or proper shame, is something beyond shame itself, namely, hating sin and the vices. Others, wishing to distinguish between proper shame and improper shame might follow the direction of Aristotle, or that of Nietzsche, or the perspective of guilt morality. In some way, though, it would be necessary to appeal to something—vice, virtue, honor among one's fellows, obligation—that is beyond shame itself and in respect to which proper shame will be said to be felt.

In connection with the idea of "true shame" it is useful to reflect on what is meant when it is said that someone is shameless (for Aristotle, shamelessness, as one extreme, would be, if strictly not a vice, at least not praised). Pretty clearly, to say literally that someone is shameless, or that someone has no shame, is to say that that person ought to be ashamed of some action or behavior of which he or she is not ashamed. Again, to say that what someone did was shameful is to say that it is something of which that person ought to be ashamed. Alternatively, to say that someone is shameless is to say that that person has done what is morally wrong without compunction, and to say that what someone did was shameful is to say that it was morally wrong. On either construction, though, there is an appeal to moral considerations beyond shame.

Public shame, or shame before others, is incontestable in the sense that it is real and identifiable—whether or not it ultimately is a form of private shame. Moreover, Aristotle may well be right that there is a significant species of public shame that is felt when we have done what is contrary to virtue or have failed to attain honor, and that we feel this shame particularly before those we admire and those who admire us—again, whether or not, finally, it is a matter of our model identity that we are virtuous and attain honor. Also, though, as Plato and Richard of St. Victor see, we may be ashamed when we start to get a bad reputation; and, as Richard of St. Victor sees, we can be ashamed of trivial matters and, when ashamed of our lowliness, can be "ashamed to feel shame for that which the heavenly teacher was not ashamed to descend from heaven to teach."[40] Public shame

---

39. Richard of St. Victor, *The Twelve Patriarchs*, in *Richard of St. Victor: The Twelve Patriarchs, The Mystical Ark, Book Three of the Trinity*, trans. and intro. Grover A. Zinn (New York: Paulist Press, 1979), 102.

40. Ibid., 103.

may be as wide in latitude as private shame, but by its nature it is shame that is felt before others.

As there is a public shame that contrasts with private shame, so there is a kind of public pride that contrasts with private pride, the pride that is involved in shame morality. There is some sort of distinction here even though, again, as with shame, it may be that pride before others is ultimately a matter of private pride. Pride in the first place, though, should be distinguished from certain cognate public attitudes to which it may bear some resemblance. While haughtiness and arrogance may in some forms involve pride, pride is not the haughtiness that is a kind of scornful intolerance of others, nor is it the arrogance that does not give due or considerate attention to the opinions or abilities of others. Nor is pride having a proud bearing, the proverbial bearing of an aristocrat. The person who is proud need not be scornful or inattentive to others, nor need he or she be aloof in bearing.

Public pride is different from pride before oneself at least in this: while pride before oneself can, as one approaches one's model identity, be felt in secret in a wholly satisfactory way, public pride depends on the reaction of others or arises from an interaction between persons, and it forms itself in relation to some public or moral ideal. We can distinguish between the two in this way even if finally the reason one is proud before others is that it is part of one's model identity that one have honor in the eyes of others. Here it is useful to recall Charles Taylor's category of "honour ethic," discussed in the last chapter. Such an ethic, or morality form, Taylor finds in warrior societies, as in archaic Greece, where courageous deeds were celebrated by Homer. Those who participate in such an ethic seek glory and honor and wish to avoid dishonor and shame at all costs. Cultures that embody such an honour ethic have been called "shame-cultures." The "distinguishing mark" of such a culture, Gabriele Taylor says, is that "public esteem is the greatest good, and to be ill spoken of the greatest evil." Such a "greatest good" may not be an intrinsic good but what we earlier, with Michael Walzer, called a social good (in Chapter 8). But still it could be the thing most valued by those in a society. Gabriele Taylor continues, "Public esteem for the individual, or the lack of it, depends on that individual's success or failure judged on the basis of some code which embodies that society's values. Whoever fails to meet the categoric demands engendered by that code ruins his reputation and loses the esteem of the other members of that group. He loses his honour."[41] Important, even crucial, in such a culture is

41. Taylor, *Pride, Shame, and Guilt*, 54.

the role of what Gabriele Taylor calls an "honour-group." When one loses honor in the eyes of those persons who constitute the honour-group, as opposed to others, one loses honor in one's own eyes and feels shame.[42] On the other hand, when one attains honor in the eyes of others, one has the right to be proud before them and before oneself.

As Charles Taylor appreciates, there might be various manifestations of an honour ethic. The morality of the gentleman, he allows, is a variant. There the honour-group consists of gentlemen alone, with no members from lower social strata (thus only a gentleman can insult a gentleman). Again, it is not hard to understand Aristotle's reflections about shame, and those before whom we feel shame, in similar terms. For Aristotle, those whom we admire and who admire us are members of the all-important honour-group in whose eyes we must attain honor in order to have it in our own estimation of ourselves, in order to have the right to be proud. The honor that Taylor and Taylor have in mind is of course public, or social: there is no private honor, as there can be private pride or shame. Even so, honor may be a matter of pride, and dishonor a matter of shame, precisely because in one's model identity attaining honor is given value. If so, any honour ethic, including Aristotle's form, will be a special form of shame morality.

The shame involved in shame morality is private shame. Such shame should of course be distinguished from various other "cognate feelings," such as embarrassment. But it should also be distinguished conceptually from shame felt before others. The conceptual distinction remains even though we can see that shame before others may be possible precisely because one is ashamed (before oneself) to be shamed before others when one fails in certain ways. The shame involved in shame morality is a private shame in that it is a shame one feels for oneself, whether others detect it or not and whether or not there is anything in the eyes of others that is to our discredit. This is an old distinction. Wurmser cites Werner Jaeger as attributing to Democritus the substitution of a new sense for *aidōs*, so that it becomes a private shame that one feels, not before others, as for Aristotle, but for oneself.[43] In a morality that has such shame as its hallmark the ultimate basis of the evaluation of an individual's conduct is not the violation of moral rules or the keeping of obligations, as in a guilt morality. Nor is it failing to gain honor in the eyes of one's fellows, as it seems to be

42. Ibid., 54–57.
43. Wurmser, *The Mask of Shame*, 17. See Werner Jaeger, *Paideia: The Ideals of Greek Culture*, trans. G. Highet, 2d ed. (New York: Oxford University Press, 1962), 1:330.

in an honour ethic, but a comparison of the individual's conduct with his or her internalized ideal. And this is so even though, as we have seen, attaining honor, like keeping our obligations and not violating moral rules, can be a part of an internalized ideal. This ideal is an ideal identity, what Morris calls a model identity and what others have called an ego ideal. Wurmser and Gerhart Piers, for instance, are two psychoanalysts who see shame in relation to one's ego ideal,[44] and henceforth I shall use either term to designate the internalized ideal that informs a shame morality.

The power of such a model identity, or ego ideal, and the private and often secret shame one's not living up to it can generate may be hard to overestimate. Lord Jim's shame before himself and his desire to draw near to his ideal lead him to actions of heroic proportions. On the other hand, this shame may cause an individual great pain. Dimmesdale in *The Scarlet Letter* says, "Happy are you, Hester, that wear the scarlet letter openly upon your bosom! Mine burns in secret!"[45] In connection with this passage, Helen Merrell Lynd observes that "the deepest shame is not shame in the eyes of others, but weakness in one's own eyes. Public exposure may even be a protection against this more painful inner shame."[46] Be that as it may, we should appreciate that there is this category of shame and that it is operative within a morality form that has a definite and describable logic. Not that one who follows a shame morality must be as heroic as Lord Jim or as tortured as Dimmesdale. As I pointed out, shame and pride may affect only certain limited areas in one's life. In such a case shame morality will not be the dominant morality in one's life, but still present, coexisting with other morality forms.

44. Ibid., 72–73, and Gerhart Piers and Milton B. Singer, *Shame and Guilt* (Springfield, Ill.: Charles C. Thomas, 1953), 11. Wurmser and Piers agree that shame arises when expectations associated with the ego ideal are not fulfilled, although they disagree on matters of psychoanalytic theory (e.g., about the role of the superego).

45. Nathaniel Hawthorne, *The Scarlet Letter*, in *The Portable Hawthorne*, ed. Malcolm Cowley (New York: Viking, 1948), chap. 17, 477.

46. Helen Merrell Lynd, *On Shame and the Search for Identity* (New York: Harcourt, Brace & Company, 1958), 31.

12

Sin Morality and a Comparison of Sin Morality with Guilt Morality and Shame Morality

We turn now to sin morality. Sin morality is relationship morality. It emerges as sin morality when it is presented as a morality form in accord with our second meaning of "morality." When we think of relationship morality as a bipolar moral system, we discover that moral failure in relationship morality is essentially sin in one definite meaning of "sin." And we also discover that in the dimension of the second meaning of "morality," sin morality contrasts with both guilt morality and shame morality, although there are similarities to both as well. In this chapter we shall first set forth sin morality as a morality form, and then we shall critically compare it with guilt morality and with shame morality. Our initial concern is to get before ourselves the logic of sin morality. As our contrasting shame morality with guilt morality helped us to make clear the logic of shame morality, so our contrasting sin morality with the other two morality forms will help us to make clear the logic of sin morality. But also, in connection with our second concern, we shall want to identify the deep differences that separate sin morality from the other two morality forms. For they will be particularly important for any critical comparison of sin morality with the other two moralities. We begin with an exposition of the logic of sin morality.

In order to fill in the logic of sin morality we must first clarify the notion of sin that informs that logic. Sin may be sin against a human person, just as, religiously, sin is sin against God. And just as one sins against God, in one definite meaning of "sin," when one violates one's relationship to God, so one sins against a human person when one violates one's relationship to that person. When the prodigal son returns to his father's house, in his confession he says, "Father, I have sinned against heaven and against you."[1] If we understand sin as the violation of a relationship, then we can understand both parts of the prodigal son's confession. He is confessing that he has violated both his relationship with God and his relationship with his father. That one can sin against a person as well as against God is recognized in more than one place in the Bible. Such a recognition is found in I Samuel when Jonathan entreats his father, King Saul, "Let not the king sin against his servant David; because he has not sinned against you."[2] And such a recognition is found in Genesis in the story of Abimelech, Abraham, and Sarah. Abraham comes to be a sojourner in the land of Gerar, and he tells Abimelech, the king of Gerar, that Sarah is his sister. With this understanding Abimelech has Sarah brought to him. But before he approaches her, Abimelech has a dream in which God reveals to him that Sarah is Abraham's wife. God tells Abimelech that He knows what he has done he has done in all innocence and that therefore he has not sinned against Him. What is to be noted, though, is what Abimelech says to Abraham. He restores Sarah to Abraham and asks Abraham, "What have you done to us? And how have I sinned against you that you have brought upon me and my kingdom a great sin?"[3] Abimelech's question is rhetorical. He does not believe that he has sinned against Abraham. Yet the point of his question requires that possibility.

In these cases sin is a violation of a particular relationship between two persons. Especially when the relationship is intimate, like the relationship between a father and son or the relationship between husband and wife, it is palpable that the relationship can be violated. And when such a relationship is violated, the violation is, with no sense of conceptual stress, spoken of as a sin. So it is that in Giuseppe di Lampedusa's novel *The Leopard* Don Fabrizio, as he makes his way to the door of Mariannina, a woman he sometimes visits, reflects that he is sinning against his wife. To himself he acknowledges, "I'm a sinner, I know, doubly a sinner, by Divine Law and by Stella's human love."[4] (Not that he is deterred, for he rationalizes that though he is sinning, he is sinning so as not to sin worse.)

1. Luke 15.21, the Jerusalem Bible. The Living Bible is similar, although the RSV reads, "Father, I have sinned against heaven and before you," which echoes the King James Version.
2. 1 Sam. 19.4, RSV; the Jerusalem Bible is similar.
3. Gen. 20.9, RSV. Here the Jerusalem Bible reads, "What wrong have I done you. . . ?" But of course, for relationship morality, or sin morality, to wrong a person is to sin against that person.
4. Giuseppe di Lampedusa, *The Leopard*, trans. Archibald Colquhoun (New York: Pantheon, 1960), 36.

In his adulterous act Don Fabrizio sins against his wife, but he need not go that far to sin against her. One reason it is so clear that intimate personal relationships can be violated is that such relationships are, in a way not hard to appreciate, defined to a significant degree in terms of our thoughts and feelings. This is a point that we saw Morris make (rather a long way back, in Chapter 4). However, this being so, Don Fabrizio would sin against his wife by accepting his lustful desire or dwelling on it, even though he did not act on it.

We should not think that we can speak of sinning against a person only when an intimate relationship or a particular relationship has been violated. W. K. Clifford, in "The Ethics of Belief," speaks of "sin against mankind." He means an epistemic sin, one deriving from one's not obeying the "duty" never to believe anything on insufficient evidence. We need not agree with Clifford that there is just such an epistemic duty in order to allow that there are some general obligations to others in the area of veracity and intellectual responsibility. When such a general obligation is violated, we may, as Clifford does, speak of a sin being committed against all those to whom we have that obligation. In the same way, those who practice injustice toward others in this world may be said to be sinning against them. In the sense of "sin" before us, it is possible to sin against those we have never seen. Indeed, Dostoyevsky suggests, it is possible to sin against every other person. In *The Brothers Karamazov*, very near a passage I cited in Chapter 4, Father Zossima recounts how his brother Markel said to their mother, "Mother, darling . . . there must be servants and masters, but if so I will be the servant of my servants, the same as they are to me. And another thing, mother, every one of us has sinned against all men, and I more than any."[5] These words embody two themes that are relevant to relationship morality. For our present purposes it is sufficient to observe that Markel says every one of us has *sinned* against all men. (Later, but not until the last chapter, we shall return to the other theme, that every one of us has sinned against *all* men, all persons.)

Sin against persons, violating a relationship we have with persons, is not so much something we do as it is something we do to persons. Sometimes this realization can come home to us. It is, I think, intimated at one point in Shusaku Endo's *Silence*. The protagonist of the novel is Sebastian Rodrigues, a Jesuit missionary in seventeenth-century Japan after the edict

5. Fyodor Dostoyevsky, *The Brothers Karamazov*, trans. Constance Garnett (New York: Modern Library, n.d.), 301.

of explusion. Christianity is illegal and punishable by death unless recanted. Father Rodrigues is caught and imprisoned. Finally he will apostatize, but at this point in the novel, while in captivity, he finds himself thinking about sin. "Sin, he reflected, is not what it is usually thought to be; it is not to steal and tell lies. Sin is for one man to walk brutally over the life of another and to be quite oblivious of the wounds he has left behind."[6] Father Rodrigues may mean sin against God, but even so, he points to the further character of sin as a violation of human relationships and, consequently, something done to persons. Stealing per se is not a sin, but being brutal to another human being is, he reflects. Of course, stealing and lying too violate relationships, I have argued, so they too are sins. When we steal from others or lie to them, we treat them brutally in the sense that we disrespect some aspect of their personhood—we in some measure treat them as nonpersons, as brutes. But stealing and lying considered in themselves as seemingly impersonal acts, without attention to the relationships with persons that they violate, the "wounds" inflicted, do not so far seem to be sins. They are, though, even if one is oblivious of the wounds caused, or, more in accord with Father Rodrigues' reflection, especially if one is oblivious of the wounds caused, since one then is further from a sense of the hurtful nature of what one has done to another person.

We must not think, however, that sin is necessarily against another person. In accord with our earlier discussion, one can sin against oneself. One does when one fails to treat oneself as a person, when one violates the person/person relationship to oneself.

Now, with this much of the character of sin before us, let us put in place with some specificity the logic of sin morality by comparing it with the logics of guilt morality and shame morality. Sin morality and guilt morality are similar in several respects. Both recognize obligations, and both give a place to guilt, although it is not exactly the same place. Both are fault moralities. Both distinguish feeling guilty from, say, feeling regret, and both recognize and can account for the appropriateness of making amends. Sin morality is also significantly different from guilt morality, and some, though not all, of these differences are reflected in the similarities between sin morality and shame morality. Sin morality and shame morality are alike in that neither is rule determined: neither *at bottom* is a matter of observing obligations imposed by moral rules. And since morality for neither is

6. Shusaku Endo, *Silence*, trans. William Johnston (New York: Toplinger Publishing Company, 1960), 132.

most fundamentally a matter of following rules, neither, in contrast to conventional guilt morality, must diligently heed the public's "universal" common sense in its function as arbiter of moral rules and their demands. For neither is moral success a simple matter of *not* transgressing rules. Both are what Morris calls "scale" moralities.

These points of difference and similarity are fairly straightforward, and I have presentented them just here merely to bring into relief the logic of sin morality. Shortly I shall want to compare these moralities more rigorously and critically. Next, though, let us compare them by applying each to particular moral situations. Two examples will be sufficient for illustrative purposes. The first will put in relief differences in moral emotion or reaction; the second will highlight differences in reasons for action.

1. One's country is committing some horrendous act. It is, let us say, bombing the civilian population of a country toward which it is belligerently disposed.

One shame reaction is to be ashamed because one's country has not lived up to one's ideal image of one's country; that is, it has not met a part of one's own model identity, or ego ideal, which, as we have noted, can include very much over which an individual has relatively little or no control. At the same time, another shame reaction might be to be proud. An individual with a different, more bellicose image of his or her country, internalized as a part his or her ego ideal, might be proud of such decisive, no-holds-barred action.

The guilt reaction is indignation if one feels that one oneself is not partially morally responsible. If one feels in part morally responsible, the guilt reaction is remorse.

The sin reaction can, in a way, embrace the guilt reaction of remorse but goes beyond it in a response of concern, sadness, and compassion because, whatever moral obligations were violated, the underlying person/person relationship that binds one to others, and others to others, has been violated.

2. A second example can be constructed from the myth of Prometheus if we allow ourselves certain liberties. There are several forms of the myth of Prometheus. In one, used by Mary Shelley in her *Frankenstein,* Prometheus is the creator of humankind. In another he brings fire to humankind by stealing it from the gods. The latter provides the theme on which we shall construct our variations.

The shame-morality Prometheus defies the gods for the sake of the individual he sees himself ideally to be. Though he may take pity on suffering humankind, he does so because it is a part of his model identity that he should do so. He perhaps sees himself as a savior and a hero or as a defier of authority. He is proud of his rebellion, rather in accord with the treatment of Prometheus by such Romantics as Lord Byron.[7]

The guilt-morality Prometheus defies the immoral gods because, if he did not, he would fail to abide by the moral rules that bind him. He might act explicitly for the sake of moral principle, perhaps for the sake of justice. If he steals fire from the gods, he does because he judges that his duty to humankind overrides his obligation not to steal. Unlike the shame-morality Prometheus, to the extent that he is guided by guilt morality, he will not savor with pride his defiance of the gods: he will see it as a moral duty. Such a guilt-morality Prometheus would be understandable in terms of conventional guilt morality. There might, however, be a rather different guilt-morality Prometheus who is guided by a guilt morality, but not the conventional guilt morality. Although I think conventional morality must be a form of guilt morality, there can also be, as we have seen, other variants of guilt morality. Some human beings may follow a more rigorous guilt morality, appealing to moral duty but not necessarily to "universal" duty as sanctioned by common sense. I think that some moral reformers and others of high moral dedication may have such a morality. In Albert Camus's *The Plague* Rieux and Tarrou, unlike most in Oran, see it as a duty to form and participate in the "sanitation squads," to fight against the plague in this way. They act out of a sense of high moral principle, but their actions are beyond anything called for by conventional morality. A guilt-morality Prometheus formed after this pattern will steal fire from the gods whether or not conventional morality approves of his judgment that justice requires that he do so.

The sin-morality Prometheus will act out of concern or compassion for humankind, grounded in a recognition of the inherent worth of persons. He will not act for the sake of an internalized ego ideal. In this way he is different from the shame-morality Prometheus, even though the shame-morality Prometheus should have as a part of his model identity the requirement that he be concerned or compassionate. More like the guilt-morality Prometheus, the sin-morality Prometheus will perhaps appeal to justice. However, justice is not the ultimate ground of his appeal.

These differences are real, although we should of course bear in mind

7. In Lord Byron's poem "Prometheus," Prometheus' "Godlike crime was to be kind." Chained to a rock, where a vulture continuously eats at his liver (his punishment in the myth), he feels, Byron writes, "All that the proud can feel of pain."

that shame and guilt moralities can overlap or coexist with a sin morality: elements of all three may appear in the moral life of one individual. Thus, when one's country bombs civilians, a person could feel ashamed of his or her country, indignant or remorseful because moral rules have been broken, and also, with a sense of the violation of our relationships to others, feel compassion for those made to suffer through humanity's inhumanity. When the three moralities coexist in an individual, or when a sin morality is combined with only a guilt morality or only a shame morality, tensions of various sorts may ensue, tensions deriving from the differences that divide these moralities. But the human breast has been known to harbor tensions.

Note also that beyond the differences in affective response, the concrete action taken under the guidance of each of these three moralities may be much the same: each Prometheus may steal fire from the gods. Of course, the actions indicated by the three moralities might, even must, differ greatly too. For one thing, the operative shame morality may or may not have bound itself to commitment to moral duty, while guilt morality of necessity is so bound. For another, as we shall see, the demands of sin morality finally must radically exceed those of both conventional guilt morality and shame morality in its various manifestations.

Now let us turn to a more detailed and critical elaboration of the differences that separate sin morality from guilt morality and the differences that separate sin morality from shame morality. In this part of our discussion we want to identify those deep differences that will provide a basis for a critical evaluation of sin morality in comparison to the other two morality forms. We begin with the differences between sin morality and guilt morality.[8]

First, while both sin morality and guilt morality are fault moralities, the ultimate source of fault in sin morality is not what it is in guilt morality. In guilt morality the source of fault is violating a rule or precept. In sin morality the ultimate source of fault is violating a relationship, which is sin. Of course, in sin morality there are moral rules, or obligations, and in violating such a rule one will be at fault, but this is because in violating a moral rule one violates a relationship to persons. It remains, then, that relationships are foundational in sin morality in a way that they are not in guilt morality.

Second, in sin morality one may not be at fault in violating a moral rule

8. Much of the discussion in the following paragraphs is adapted from my *God-Relationships With and Without God* (London: Macmillan; New York: St. Martin's, 1989), 54–57.

that is countenanced by guilt morality. Recall that the logic of guilt morality provides no grounding for its moral rules. They are, as it were, a given. Now, as things are, I think that the moral rules of conventional guilt morality for the most part correspond to what most of us intuitively take to be our obligations. At least, I see no reason to deny that this is so. However, there can be different variants of guilt morality, as we have seen. And there is no reason internal to the logic of guilt morality why the moral rules accepted conventionally should not be different from those that obtain. Nothing in the logic of guilt morality excludes the moral rule that one ought to return escaped slaves to their masters—and arguably this was a moral rule of the conventional morality at one time in some places in the United States. For sin morality, following such a moral rule would be wrong even if it were accepted in popular, "universal" understanding. Such a judgment is open to sin morality, though not to guilt morality, because sin morality looks beyond moral principles to their grounding in relationships, including the person/person relationship.

Another closely related difference between sin morality and guilt morality is that guilt morality carries no necessary reference to the inherent worth of persons, while sin morality, with its recognition of the person/person relationship, does. True, guilt morality can allow that persons have inherent worth. However, if an individual following a guilt morality came to judge that acting in accord with a moral rule violated the worth of persons, he or she would not thereby have found any reason, so far as guilt morality is concerned, to judge the moral rule to be wrong or deficient. Could guilt morality in one form countenance the moral rule, or principle, that the inherent worth of persons ought to be respected in our actions? There could be such a form of guilt morality. Those following such a guilt morality would feel guilty when they failed to treat persons as persons; however, their treating persons as persons, as conscientious as it might be, could still be done precisely as a matter of principle. And it would remain that internal to guilt morality, even in that form, there would be no reason to regard this moral rule as correct: it would simply be a given.

A fourth difference relates to what counts as moral success in these two moralities. Those who follow a guilt morality live in accord with their morality so long as they do not inexcusably violate any moral rules. Moral success in a guilt morality is remaining innocent of any wrongdoing, and one remains innocent as long as one does *not* do what is forbidden by the rules of morality. Those who follow a guilt morality, then, are free to do as they will in all those interstitial areas of behavior not covered by the rules of morality. Not so for those trying to live by sin morality. Success in sin morality is a matter of respecting and living up to all the relationships with persons that one has. Our relationships not only give substance to our obligations but may give rise to obligations not recognized by conventional guilt morality. But, moreover, living up to a relationship, such as the marriage relationship, is not just a matter of not violating obligations that exist—not if "obligation" means what it means in a guilt morality. Living up to a marriage relationship requires, not merely keeping the obligation to be faithful, but attention to needs and desires, the exercise of sensitivity, and more. As opposed to not breaking a moral rule, living up to a relationship is something one can draw near to and draw nearer to.

Fifth, sin morality and guilt morality have different requirements regarding what we may call their person-scopes. Earlier (in Chapter 4) I discussed the person-scope and action-scope of the person/person relationship. Morality forms can also be said to have each kind of scope in a different but related sense of these terms. The person-scope of a morality form consists of all those persons whose actions and attitudes are governed by or are open to judgment under the categories of that morality and, as well, all those persons toward whom one has obligations under the categories of that morality. In this way a morality form has a person-scope in two aspects or dimensions: (1) all those who are responsible or accountable under that morality form and (2) all those toward whom one has obligations under that morality form. Let us call the first a morality's responsibility-scope and the second a morality's obligation-scope. For an honour ethic, its person-scope in the first aspect, its responsibility-scope, consists of the honour-group, although its person-scope in the second aspect, its obligation-scope, may be wider. The responsibility-scope of an honour ethic consists of only those by whom one can be shamed (the honour-group), although, since one may be denied honor for actions toward those outside the honour-group, the obligation-scope may be wider. For shame morality, the person-scope in the first aspect consists of a single person, for a person's model identity, or ego ideal, determines only what he or she will be ashamed of or proud of, while its second aspect, depending on the ego ideal, may be limited or very wide, even universal. Now, clearly, the person-scope of guilt morality in some variants can consist of all persons: the person-scope in both aspects will be universal. In such a variant the moral community governed by the moral rules of the guilt morality is all persons. In such a variant all persons could do wrong and all persons could be wronged. Also, though, in other variants a guilt morality might have a limited person-scope in both aspects. In a society that allowed the owning of slaves, the moral community might exclude slaves: slaves might be regarded as chattel (as historically they were). Slaves being so regarded, it would be denied both that slaves had *moral* responsibilities and that those within the moral community had obligations toward them. In other variants women or foreigners or people of certain ethnic types might be wholly or partially excluded from at least the morality's obligation-scope, as they would be if it were understood that some recognized obligations did not extend to them. The contrast with sin morality is this: sin morality of necessity has a universal person-scope in both aspects. The reason it does is that the fundamental relationship that binds person to person, the person/person relationship, is universal. True, it may be that many do not recognize the universal nature of this relationship, but it is universal nevertheless. In short, sin morality structurally requires, as a part of its internal logic, that its person-scope be universal in both aspects, while guilt morality has no such requirement.

Three further differences require our attention. They are differences that our discussion prefigured some chapters ago (back in Chapter 6), when we drew out three differences between acting on moral principle and acting morally in a way informed by a recognition of the person/person relationship. We have since then seen that we can understand those who act on moral principle as following a guilt morality, and so it should not be surprising that those differences apply to our present concern. With very little recasting they become differences between guilt morality and sin morality. The first of these three final differences has to do with the action-scopes of the two morality forms.

As sin morality and guilt morality have person-scopes, so they have action-scopes, where an action-scope consists of all those actions covered by the categories of the morality. The sixth difference between sin morality and guilt morality is that sin morality covers a realm of action that guilt morality does not address; at least, conventional guilt morality does not address this realm. This difference relates specifically to interior actions or behavior. In conventional guilt morality moral rules define the limits of morally acceptable behavior, but that behavior is almost exclusively overt behavior: stealing, as opposed to fantasizing about stealing, and so on. In a guilt morality the participants are members of a moral community and so in a kind of relationship with others in society, but it is a relationship defined by the mutual obligations imposed by the commonly accepted moral rules. It is not a human relationship of love or friendship. It is not that relationship we have to our neighbors when we endeavor to love them as ourselves. It is, as Morris says at one point, a relationship "between individuals [the members of the moral community] who do not ordinarily have close ties that would, apart from obligations or a sense of obligation, provide strong motives for satisfying the interests of others."[9] In short, it is a relationship among human beings, but not the sort that is violated by our harboring desires and intentions.

Morris is aware that there are relationships that carry demands regarding our interior states. At points, as we have had occasion to observe (in Chapter 4), Morris turns his attention to relationships that are more properly regarded as close human relationships, relationships of love or friendship; and when he does he brings out the importance that states of mind bear for such relationships. For Morris, as we saw earlier, if a person in, say, a marriage relationship forms an intention to harm the other or merely dwells on the thought but does not form the intention out of fear of reprisal (and in this sense "accepts the desire"), then that person allows himself or herself a state of mind incompatible with the requirements of the relationship. But, for Morris, "normally"—that is, in the prevailing conventional guilt morality—such considerations do not bear on the issue of the wrongfulness of an act.[10] For sin morality, however, interior behavior is as important as exterior behavior. Sin morality appreciates the New Testament lesson that looking at a woman lustfully is already to commit adultery in one's heart (Matt. 5.28). So does Morris, but as his exposition of guilt morality, or conventional guilt morality, makes clear, guilt morality addresses only overt or exterior behavior. Or, if it covers some interior acts, such as trying to resist the temptation to do what is wrong, it still does not cover such interior acts as forming an intention or accepting a desire to do what is wrong. Sin morality does. For sin morality, we all have obligations toward others and toward ourselves regarding such interior acts. We do because the person/person relationship has such a requirement: it is a relationship that we damage when in our hearts we harbor hate toward another, or toward ourselves, even though we do not act on it.

The seventh difference between sin morality and guilt morality that we should note has to do with what may be called concern or motive or attitude. It is essentially this: a guilt morality allows one to follow moral rules for the sake of moral principle or even for reasons of self-interest, while sin morality requires one to act for, to strive to act for, the sake of persons.

9. Herbert Morris, "Persons and Punishment," in *On Guilt and Innocence: Essays in Legal Philosophy and Moral Psychology* (Berkeley and Los Angeles: University of California Press, 1976), 63.

10. Herbert Morris, "Guilt and Suffering," in *On Guilt and Innocence,* 97.

This point of difference between sin morality and guilt morality holds even for that possible variant of guilt morality that would cover interior acts in its action-scope. And it holds in regard to those who follow a guilt morality out of principle as well as for those who follow a guilt morality for reasons of self-interest. Let us consider separately those who follow a guilt morality out of self-interest and those who do so as a matter of principle. Earlier, in presenting the logic of guilt morality (back in Chapter 10), I brought out how guilt morality recognizes the two moral axioms that fully realized moral behavior must be in accord with right moral principles and that it must be in recognition of the binding force of those principles. Now, there may be among those who abide by all moral rules purely for selfish reasons some who do not recognize the morally binding force of those rules. They would refrain from breaking any moral rules (including those that cover interior acts, if there are any), but they would do so precisely in order to avoid public disapproval or private discomfort. Such prudential followers as these in a way, but only in a way, would be following a guilt morality. For one thing, in them the moral feeling of guilt and the desire to make amends would be atrophied, if present at all. In its full acquisition guilt morality requires some acknowledgment of the binding force of its moral rules. So perhaps we should say that such prudential followers are not really following a guilt morality. Still, while guilt morality requires the recognition in some way of the binding nature of moral rules—so that the second axiom is met—it allows that one might take up a guilt morality as a whole, including the obligatoriness of its moral rules and the moral necessity or appropriateness of feeling guilty for wrongdoing, for prudential reasons. Morris, I think, may recognize that this is allowed. He says of a system of just punishment that it "is one in which the rules establish a mutuality of benefit and burden and in which the benefits of noninterference are conditional upon the assumption of burdens."[11] Such a system of just punishment would seem to be continuous with guilt morality. It is, assuming that the "rules" are the moral rules of guilt morality and that the "burdens" are the obligations imposed by those rules. In any case, a similar claim of mutual benefit can be made regarding guilt morality as a whole. Given that such a claim can be made, or only that prudential calculators come to believe it, a guilt morality might be adopted for the sake of a share in that mutual benefit.

The individual who acts morally on principle is different. He or she

11. Morris, "Persons and Punishment," in *On Guilt and Innocence*, 33.

would follow a guilt morality for the sake of principle, for the sake of the moral law, not for reasons of self-interest, certainly not merely for reasons of self-interest. A guilt morality, so far as its internal requirements go, can be followed from either of these motives, it would seem. For within a guilt morality one who scrupulously inspects each and every public moral rule and limits his or her conduct to the demands of the imposed obligations will enjoy an earned reputation for an exemplary moral life, regardless of the admixture of enlightened self-interest or whether one acts precisely on principle. On the other hand, if an individual respects the main require- ments of his or her relationships but does so purely out of self-concern or for the sake of principle, this in itself violates any number of relationships. To take an evident case: the father who cares for his children merely for the sake of his reputation as a father, or just in order to meet his obligation as a father, and not for the sake of his children, has failed in that relationship.

Finally, in close relation to several of these differences, there is an epistemic difference between sin morality and guilt morality. Essential to guilt morality is a body of moral rules embedded in the understanding of the moral community. Yet there is no reason internal to guilt morality to believe that the moral rules embodied in a guilt morality are correct. They are simply given or basic. Though we may believe that they are correct, we can find no reason in support of this belief inside guilt morality itself. Sin morality, as we have seen, does not deny that there are moral rules that relate to the obligations that bind us. It, however, does not regard them as basic. Whatever true and correct moral rules there are rest upon relation- ships. Accordingly, sin morality provides a justifying reason for our believing that the rules of conventional morality are correct. In the same way, and on the same basis, it provides a means for evaluating moral rules as to their correctness.

These points of difference give us an adequate basis for a critical evalua- tion of sin morality in comparison with guilt morality. Next let us bring into relief those differences between sin morality and shame morality that will provide us with a basis for a critical evaluation of sin morality in comparison with that morality. Then we shall be in a position to say whether sin morality is superior to both guilt morality and shame morality and, if it is, why it is.

Shame morality significantly differs from sin morality in the following ways:
First, though each is a scale morality, the *terminus ad quem*, the end-goal, of the one is different from that of the other. The end-goal in a shame

morality, that which may be approached to a greater or lesser degree, is of course the model identity, the ego ideal, of some particular individual. Since the end-goal in a shame morality is always only that of some particular individual, there is no one end-goal for shame morality. It is a matter of the internal logic of shame morality that one will be ashamed to the extent that one fails to live up to one's model identity and proud to the extend that one succeeds in doing so. But the logic of shame morality says nothing about what any individual's model identity will be. It can be nearly anything, as we have seen. Accordingly, the end-goal of a shame morality followed by one individual can be very different from the end-goal of a shame morality followed by another individual. The end-goal of a shame morality, as a consequence, may extend to much of our lives and dominate our actions, as for a Lord Jim, or be quite limited, as for a Prufrock, ashamed only of his bald spot, or as for someone ashamed only of his or her tennis game. The contrast with sin morality is hard to overestimate.

For sin morality, the end-goal is living up to one's relationships. This is the one end of sin morality, and it is a matter of the logic of sin morality that it is. To be sure, different people have different particular relationships to others, although also, for sin morality, we all have one fundamental relationship each to each, namely, the person/person relationship. Whatever our relationships, the one end-goal of sin morality, toward which we can in greater or lesser degree draw near, is living up to our relationships. The end-goal of sin morality, then, is anything but limited. It ramifies throughout our moral lives, for we all are in any number of relationships with other persons. But even if we were not, and instead were in only the person/person relationship to others, that would be sufficient to make the end-goal of sin morality cover much of our exterior and interior actions.

A second difference is that shame morality and sin morality are opposed regarding the place of pride.[12] Failure in a shame morality results in shame, but moral success, drawing nearer to one's model identity, is something to be proud of. Thus Lord Jim's "proud and unflinching glance" when he does not balk at receiving Doramin's bullet, and thus, fittingly, given Jim's demanding ideal and his devoted pursuit of it, Marlow refers to Jim's "exalted egoism."[13] For sin morality, however, moral success is not tied to pride. As one draws nearer to living up to one's relationships, or some particular relationship, one may feel any number of emotions. One may feel

12. Some of the discussion in the following paragraphs is adapted from my God-Relationships With and Without God, 64–68.

13. Joseph Conrad, Lord Jim (New York: Penguin Books, 1949), 313.

good about the way that relationship is growing and deepening; one may feel pleased; or one may feel thankful to the other for inviting a nourishing response, or thankful to God for being granted some semblance of sensitivity. And, yes, one may feel pride. But if one is proud, it will be because it has become part of one's ego ideal to live up to one's relationships. That is, it will be because in this individual a shame morality coexists with sin morality.

For sin morality, pride is not necessarily a good thing. To the extent that it can work against respecting relationships, it is a bad thing. And given at least some ego ideals, pride may keep many of us from moving toward a fuller realization of our relationships to others. The man whose model identity forbids him to confess or to express his hurt may, for just these reasons, find it hard to deepen his relationship to a cherished other person.

Yet some have seen pride, or measured pride, as a good thing. Gabriele Taylor, for instance, suggests that pride in one form is a virtue, and it behooves us to consider her thinking. Taylor is aware that pride need not be accompanied by arrogance or conceit, in accord with what we noted earlier (in the last chapter). Also, for Taylor, pride need not be vicious. Excessive pride may sometimes be vicious, she allows, but, she says, "There is . . . one form of pride . . . which it is hard to see as being excessive in any way at all. In that sense a person [is] proud in that she [has] her pride, she [is] too proud to do this or accept that. This sort of pride has by itself nothing to do with feeling superior or with experiencing self-satisfaction; far from having even a hint of viciousness about it, it would seem to be a virtue." Such pride she characterizes "in terms of standards which, in the agent's view, it [is] necessary for her to adhere to if she [is] to keep her self-respect."[14] This pride, then, is tied to self-respect, and Taylor, not surprisingly, sees a connection between this sort of pride and shame.

> If someone has self-respect then under certain specifiable conditions he will be feeling shame. A person has no self-respect if he regards no circumstances as shame-producing. Loss of self-respect and loss of the capacity for shame go hand in hand. The close connection between these two makes it clear why shame is often thought to be valuable. It is, firstly, that a sense of value is necessary for self-respect and so for shame, so that whatever else may be wrong about the person feeling shame he will at least have retained a sense of

14. Gabriele Taylor, *Pride, Shame, and Guilt* (Oxford: Clarendon Press, 1985), 50; and see 45.

value. And, secondly, it is a sense of value which protects the self from what in the agent's own eyes is corruption and ultimately extinction.[15]

Several comments should be made about the connections that Taylor suggests obtain between self-respect and pride and between self-respect and shame. Let us take the connections between self-respect and shame first. Shame seems to be valuable because, first, feeling shame indicates that one has a sense of value and, second, this sense of value, which relates to one's self-respect, protects one from "corruption and ultimately extinction." One thing to observe is that, though shame does indicate a sense of value, what is valued in a shame morality may be nearly anything that relates to a person: it need not be valuable in any sense except the sense that it is valued as a part of the ego ideal of some individual. Taylor is, in a way, clear on this. The "standards" she refers to are standards in "the agent's view," and the "corruption" from not meeting these standards is again in "the agent's own eyes." Let us allow, though, that the standards are morally worthy, perhaps elevated, rather like Lord Jim's. Still we might question Taylor's two reasons for thinking shame is valuable. Even with this assumption in place, John Kekes provides grounds for challenging both of these reasons.[16] For one thing, he observes, "shame is not the only possible reaction to our violation of moral commitments." Instead, we might be angry with ourselves or desire to make amends, and these reactions too indicate we have a sense of value. Regarding the second reason, Kekes points out that, strictly, it is not shame but *fear* of shame that will protect us from doing what is wrong in the future. But if the concern is with not doing what is wrong, we can be deterred by much besides fear, such as by our understanding of the hurtful consequences of our contemplated wrong action or by kindness or even by self-respect itself. And, Kekes says, even if fear is a deterrent, it need not be fear of shame: fear of loss of love or fear of punishment will do as well. If, on the other hand, shame is for wrongs done in the past, Kekes points out that it is hard to see how it will protect against "corruption," since the actions that corrupt oneself in one's own eyes have already been committed.

Kekes's criticisms, or some of them, assume that what is valued is keeping

15. Ibid., 80–81.
16. John Kekes, "Shame and Moral Progress," *Midwest Studies in Philosophy* 13 (1988): 292. Kekes quotes the passage from Taylor (80–81) that I quoted above.

our moral commitments and avoiding wrongdoing. Since keeping our moral commitments and avoiding wrongdoing have moral value irrespective of inclusion in any individual's model identity, Kekes can quite correctly appeal to moral considerations that go beyond the logic of shame morality. Taylor, however, seems to have in mind a "sense of value" and an understanding of self-respect that are accommodated by shame morality (although she does not appeal to the category of shame morality). We have already seen an indication of this. A further indication of this is the way she understands "false shame." What she means by "false shame" is not the antithesis of what Richard of St. Victor means by "true shame." True shame, for Richard, is shame for that for which we ought to be ashamed, which would make false shame, shame for that for which we ought not to be ashamed. What Taylor means by "false shame" is the shame felt when "an alien standard" is imposed on one. One is perhaps shamed by others and made to feel ashamed, but not in the light of one's own standards, not because one has violated one's own model identity. Such false shame, like trying to avoid shame by denying one's standards, is corrupting for Taylor and is a way of losing self-respect.[17] Keeping one's self-respect, for Taylor, is importantly a matter of keeping up one's commitment to one's standards, that is, the standards embodied within one's model identity, whatever they may be.

Now let me comment on the connection Taylor posits between pride and self-respect. Given the way Taylor understands self-respect, it is not surprising that she sees one form of pride as a virtue. But is her way the only way, or the best way, of understanding self-respect? Self-respect may also be understood as the respect one has for oneself in regard to one's abilities or capacities. On this understanding of self-respect, one keeps one's self-respect if one does not dismiss one's abilities and if one has a realistic confidence about one's abilities. Having self-respect in this sense, we should note, does not necessarily connect to pride. One can respect and have confidence in one's abilities in a realistic way without being proud of one's abilities or of oneself.

One's respecting oneself in this way, one's respecting oneself by respecting one's abilities in a realistic way, is coherent and possible. As a part of self-knowledge, it may even be a virture. But there is another way of understanding self-respect, or another form of self-respect, that is more significant both in itself and for our present purposes. This signal form of self-respect is

17. Taylor, *Pride, Shame, and Guilt*, 82–83.

respect for oneself as a person. It is respect for oneself as a being with inherent worth. It is, in other words, just that respect that one should have for persons as persons—as it is directed toward oneself. More exactly, it is among those attitudes in the respect/love range, at least some one of which we should have toward persons as persons, including ourselves. Accordingly (and as I argued in Chapter 5), it is among those attitudes that mark or constitute the affective dimension of our coming into the presence of persons, or, what is the same thing, our realizing that we are in the person/person relationship to persons. To have this kind of self-respect is to have an attitude toward ourselves that we ought to have (in the absence of any cognate attitude). It is an attitude that is appropriate and is justified by one's worth as a person. However, it has nothing to do with pride. For it has nothing to do with meeting the "standards," in Taylor's sense, that are embodied in an ego ideal. From the standpoint of sin morality, then, we can agree with Taylor that self-respect is valuable, but argue that the forms of it that are valuable do not connect to pride. Self-respect, as respect for oneself as a person, or some like attitude is a moral requirement for sin morality. But this self-respect is not and does not require pride. It remains, then, that there is a difference between shame morality and sin morality regarding the place of pride. For shame morality, it is a good thing, marking moral success. Not so for sin morality.

A third difference between sin morality and shame morality has to do with the place sin morality gives to acting for the sake of others, with concern or love or respect for others, born from a sense of the worth of others. For sin morality, our relationships are the source of our obligations and help to define our obligations in our various relationships. But the fundamental relationship between persons is one involving us all as persons, and the basis of this relationship is the shared inherent worth that persons have as persons. This relationship underlies all other relationships between persons. Ultimately, for relationship morality, in living up to our various relationships, we must act in accord with the inherent worth of others and with a sense of their worth. Morally we are never justified in dismissing the inherent worth of any person. And while it is possible to act morally on principle, fully realized moral behavior requires that we act for the sake of others. The contrast with shame morality should be evident. A shame morality need give no place to acting for the sake of others. Lord Jim, in pursuit of his ideal in Patusan, gives up the love of the woman he has come to love and who loves him, as he must do to present himself to Doramin and to pursue his model identity. He is not meeting his pledge to Doramin for the sake of offering a purified love or for the sake of the one he loves or even with her in mind. For Jim, meeting his ideal is all. As Marlow says, "He goes away from a living woman to celebrate his pitiless wedding with a shadowy ideal of conduct"[18]—shadowy in its subjectivity, but steel in the rigor of its demands. Though Jim cherishes the one he loves, his relationship to her and whatever concern he may have for her do not carry any moral weight.

While there can be versions of a shame morality in which it is a part of one's model identity that one should honor one's relationships and act for the sake of others, even then acting for the sake of others, out of concern or respect or love for others, is not ultimate, but exists only by virtue of the demands of one's model identity. With a change in the model identity, so far as shame morality goes, the moral importance of acting for the sake of others would evaporate. Even before such a change, though, there would be a tension. One with a shame morality ultimately serves one's ideal. One with a sin morality seeks to live in accord with one's relationships, including the person/person relationship, and fully doing so requires that one act for the sake of others—not for the sake of fulfilling one's model identity.

A fourth difference that divides the two moralities is that shame morality is not a fault morality, while a sin morality essentially is a fault morality. This is not to say that shame morality cannot enhance virtue. Of course it can, with qualifications, especially where the ideal to which one aspires is a noble ideal, as we have conceded Jim's is. Jim's ideal elicits from him great courage and, in the indirect way we have noted, attention to duty and fairness beyond what is commonplace. For that matter, a less-than-alto-gether-noble ideal, such as Lafcadio's, can still inspire one to a virtue or two, as Lafcadio is inspired to at least self-discipline. It remains, though, that shame morality is not essentially tied to fault, not even in Jim's case. A sin morality is quite otherwise: when one violates one's relationships to persons, one ipso facto sins and is at fault.

Now, finally in this chapter, let us critically evaluate sin morality against guilt morality and shame morality. The needed points of comparison are before us, and on their basis a strong case for the superiority of sin morality can be made. The argument is straightforward.

It is a fact of our moral experience that we have obligations of various sorts. Our moral discourse is replete with expressions of what we ought to

18. Conrad, Lord Jim, 313.

do, what is all right for us to do, what others ought not to have done, and so on. Sometimes when we use the word "ought" or some cognate we do not mean the moral "ought," it must be allowed. But in those contexts of moral discourse where we speak of wrongdoing, the moral "ought" is being used and a moral obligation is being cited or alleged. Moral obligation is a given in our moral experience.

Only guilt morality and sin morality give a place to obligation as a matter of their internal logics. They do because they are fault moralities. Shame morality does not give a place to obligation as a matter of its internal logic, because it is not a fault morality. Shame morality allows a place for obligation only indirectly and contingently, not as a matter of its internal logic. It may be that a form of shame morality gives a place to keeping obligations, as did Lord Jim's, but this being so is contingent upon the composition of the particular ego ideal. And as far as shame morality goes, there is no moral necessity to keeping obligations per se: it is morally necessary to do so just because a particular ego ideal requires it.

Similarly, although perhaps for some less evidently, moral virtues, goods, and rights are a part of our moral experience. Clearly, the terminology of virtues, goods, and rights is embedded in our moral discourse.

Only guilt morality and sin morality can give a place to moral virtues, goods, and rights as a matter of their internal logics. For virtues (which are dispositions that one ought to have) and goods (which ought to be pursued) and rights (which ought to be respected) are conceptually tied to fault. As with obligations, shame morality can give only an indirect and contingent place to virtues, goods, and rights.

Moreover, while we can understand a Lord Jim's being ashamed of not keeping his obligations or not having the virtue of courage, in order to understand that there is such a thing as moral obligation or virtue we must look to a morality form other than shame morality.

Again, if we can meaningfully judge, as it seems we can, that a person ought not to be ashamed of what he or she is ashamed of, then we must be able to appeal to a moral basis beyond that person's shame morality. And if such a judgment is that that person's ego ideal requires of him or her actions that amount to wrongdoing, as it may be, then our appeal must be not just beyond *that* person's shame morality but beyond shame morality in any form, to some form of fault morality.

In short, being at fault is a necessary moral concept, indigenous to our moral experience and lives. And shame morality, which cannot as a matter of its internal logic accommodate fault, cannot adequately account for this aspect of our moral lives.

On the other hand, both sin morality and guilt morality are fault moralities, and both can account for this aspect of our moral lives. Both give a place to obligation. And, let us allow, both give a place to virtues, goods, and rights. (Sin morality surely does, and, with little effort, guilt morality can be extended to accommodate, in its way, virtues, goods, and rights. Extended in this way, conventional guilt morality will see virtues, goods, and rights as determined by the moral rules of the community.)

However, sin morality and guilt morality do not account for the fault aspect of our moral experience in the same way. And they do not account for obligation, virtues, goods, and rights in the same way. Guilt morality can account for obligations in terms of the moral rules that obtain in a community (and, we are allowing, can account for virtues, goods, and rights along the same lines). But it cannot account for the moral rules being what they are. Sin morality, however, goes beyond guilt morality in that it can account for our moral rules; that is, it can explain why our belief that something is morally forbidden or required is correct when it is correct. Unlike guilt morality, it provides grounds for testing the moral rules of a community. And, similarly, sin morality can explain why a disposition is a virtue, or why something is a good, or why we have the rights we do, as guilt morality cannot.

Moreover, on the assumption that sin morality has captured the foundational nature of morality, so that relationships are foundational to obligation and the other mansions of morality, we can explain conventional guilt morality as the morality form that emerges when the foundational function of relationships is lost sight of. In a guilt morality the rules are basic because no place has been given to the informing nature of relationships.

We find, then, that sin morality can account for guilt morality, but not the other way around.

Summing up the argument so far, sin morality and guilt morality are superior to shame morality because they can account for fault, while shame morality cannot; and sin morality is superior to guilt morality because whatever guilt morality can account for sin morality can account for better.

Ancillary to this reasoning, we can argue that sin morality is superior to both guilt morality and shame morality in that it recognizes the person/person relationship and its fundamental place in morality, while the other two morality forms do not. This movement in the argument presupposes that there is this relationship between persons as persons, or, what is the same thing, that we can come into the presence of persons. For reasons we have discussed (in Chapter 3), it cannot be proven that there is this relationship. Nevertheless, we can be clear that if a realization-discovery of the inherent worth of persons has ever taken place, in regard to some persons or universally, then the person/person relationship, to some or to all persons, exists. If our moral experience, or the moral experience of some, includes the realization of the person/person relationship, then that moral experience validates the claim that sin fundamentally reflects the deep nature of morality.

PART V

TWO FORMS
OF
SIN MORALITY

13

Human Sin Morality and Religious Sin Morality

Sin morality, or relationship morality, views all of morality—all the various mansions of morality in the first sense of "morality"—as resting upon relationships between persons. In our moral experience human beings are preeminently persons. We may then speak of a human sin morality in which relationships between human persons are foundational. However, as we can sin against persons, and do so when we violate our relationships to them, so, at least for religious believers in theistic traditions, we can sin against God, and do so when we violate our relationship to God. And this allows us to speak of a religious sin morality, at least within theistic traditions. (There may be conceptual room for a religious sin morality within nontheistic religions, but I cannot take up that question here.) In fact, since "sin," as most often understood, is a theological or religious term, there is a sense in which religious sin morality is conceptually prior to human sin morality.

My main concern in this chapter is to explore the connections between these two analogous forms of sin morality. Regarding these two forms of sin morality, what I hope to bring out is that, while in one way human sin morality is independent of religious sin morality, in another way it is not in that the two forms are "continuous." If I succeed in bringing out this complex relationship between human sin morality and religious sin morality, I will have accomplished the chapter's main task. Also, though, I want to consider the possibility that there are, besides a religious sin morality, a religious guilt morality and a religious shame morality. What I hope to show here is that, while such forms of religious morality are indeed possible, they would either be inadequate or in tension with religious commitment. Before I take up these concerns I need, first, to say a few words about religious sin morality and, second, at greater length, to defend the concept of sin integral to sin morality against various theological conceptions of sin that are distinguishable from it.

Human sin morality should be clear enough, but a brief exposition of religious sin morality, as I understand it, is in order. Sin—that is, religious sin, in the sense we have before ourselves—is a violation of one's relationship to God. On this understanding of sin, when we do not keep God's commandments, we sin against God, but this is just because it is a requirement of our relationship to God that we be obedient to His commandments and to His will. God is related to all of His children, all of humankind, in a general way through His loving creation, it is believed; and this general relationship between God and his human creatures is violable by human beings. But also, He has an individual relationship to each person; from the side of the believer, if one is a believer, this relationship takes the form of a faith relationship. Faith in God is the appropriate way for individuals to be related to God in the theistic traditions of the West, in the traditions of Judaism, Christianity, and Islam. Faith in God internally involves trust and traditionally calls for love and obedience on the part of the believer. These are general requirements of all faith relationships, we may say. But more may be called for. The faith relationship that an individual has to God is an individual relationship, and it may generate individual obligations.

If we turn to the stories of the Bible, examples of such individual God-relationships are not difficult to find; within a number of biblical stories it is quite explicit that God makes particular, even unique, demands of some individuals. Abraham is called upon to take Isaac to the land of Moriah. Moses is called upon to bring God's Law to the people of Israel, as later the prophets are called upon to convey to Israel the word of the Lord. In the New Testament Saul of Tarsus, become Paul, is required by God to reverse the direction of his life, to cease being a persecutor of Christians and to become a proselytizer. In these stories the one called upon cannot simply disregard God's command. Jonah, who seeks to flee to Tarshish in order to escape carrying out the mission to Nineveh that God has given him, discovers that he cannot escape. In each of these cases God makes a particular demand of a particular individual, one that holds for that individual but no other.

In these biblical stories the word of the Lord comes to the individuals involved and issues in a particular command. In the same way, contemporary religious individuals who look to God and what they have come to know of

God, may find that they are called upon to do what others are not called upon to do. As Paul says in his first letter to the Corinthians, "there are varieties of gifts and varieties of service."[1] Some may be called to be healers, some may be called to be teachers, and so on. Moreover, at any time the requirements of their individual God-relationships may put religious individuals at odds with conventional morality and banish them from the understanding of their societies, their families, and their coreligionists. One might think here of Luther, Albert Schweitzer, Dietrich Bonhoeffer, and Martin Luther King Jr. Not that an individual God-relationship necessarily requires one to be dramatically at odds with the norms of one's society. In *Fear and Trembling* Kierkegaard's contemporary "knight of faith" is portrayed as assiduously commonplace and bourgeois.[2] Yet, as much as Abraham, he is in an individual faith relationship to God that may at any time come to present him with absolute duties that are very far from commonplace.

More could be said about the nature of religious sin morality, and elsewhere I have discussed it at greater length.[3] However, these comments bring into relief the nature of religious sin morality to an extent sufficient for our present purpose, which, just here, is merely to see that both forms of sin morality turn on relationships.

Now let me say something in defense of the concept of sin required by sin morality. In the last chapter I used the story of the prodigal son to illustrate the idea that a person may sin against another person. The story of the prodigal son provides such an illustration because in it the prodigal son confesses to his father that he has sinned against him as his father. But also, as we saw, he confesses that he has sinned against heaven, against God. He sins against the one by virtue of his involvement in a human sin morality, and he sins against the Other by virtue of his involvement in a religious sin morality. As he sins against his father in violating his relationship to his father, so he sins against God in violating his relationship to God. In this chapter, as in the previous one, I am using the same very definite notion of sin—sin is sin against a person, and we sin against a person when we violate

1. Cor. 12.4–5.
2. Søren Kierkegaard, *Fear and Trembling* and *Repetition*, trans. Howard V. Hong and Edna H. Hong (Princeton: Princeton University Press, 1983), 38–41.
3. See chap. 2 of my *God-Relationships With and Without God* (London: Macmillan; New York: St. Martin's, 1989) for a discussion of religious sin morality, or what I there call "the ethics of God-relationships." And see Keith Ward, *Ethics and Christianity* (London: George Allen & Unwin; New York: Humanities Press, 1970), chap. 9, "Vocation," for a discussion of "individual vocation."

a relationship we have with that person. This concept of sin applies in human sin morality, where sin is sin against a human person or persons, and it applies in religious sin morality, where sin is sin against a personal God. But the general theological concept of sin covers a multitude. There are, in fact, a number of theological concepts of sin, a number of ways of thinking of sin, and not all that is counted as sin under these various concepts fits clearly and neatly under our conception. Still, as I shall try to show, the notion of sin that is integral to sin morality either underlies or in some other way compares well to these other conceptions of sin. I shall consider five different theological views of sin:

1. Sin is a violation of God's commands.
2. Sin is being out of harmony with God's will and purpose for humankind.
3. Sin is just another name for moral wrongdoing.
4. Sin is anything inherently blameworthy, voluntary or involuntary.
5. Sin is uncleanness.

1. *Sin is a violation of God's commands.* This view of sin, the command view, it seems to me, captures a significant part of the religious idea of sin. On nearly any traditional understanding of religious belief in God, if one breaks a Divine commandment, one sins. And if we understand God's commands to include His implicit commands and what He wills, then whenever one sins, one breaks a commandment. As far as it goes, then, this view may be unobjectionable, even correct. Notice, though, that this account of sin leaves it open that a violation of God's command is sin *because* it violates our relationship to God, a relationship that requires obedience. Not only does this view of sin not contradict the notion of sin that relationship morality relies upon; it is complemented and buttressed by that notion in that its being a sin not to obey God's commands is explained by its being a violation of our relationship to God not to obey God's commands.

Notice also that accepting this account of sin is not to endorse the Divine Command Theory, the view that what *makes* right actions right is God's commanding them. Why this is so is fairly easy to see. The Divine Command Theory says that right actions are right just because God commands them; it is the view that God's commanding is a strong criterion for right action (in the sense of "strong criterion" that we identified early on, back in Chapter 1). Now, given the command view of sin, sin is always breaking God's command, and, conversely, breaking God's command is always to sin. Let us accept it, or at least assume for the purpose of discussion, that this much is correct. Let us assume, furthermore, as the command view of sin allows, that when we keep God's commands, we do what is morally right, and that when we break God's commands, we do what is morally wrong. However, even so, it is not entailed that what *makes* morally right actions morally right is God's commanding them. It may be, instead, that God's commanding something is a "right-indicating" characteristic of what is commanded (as opposed to a "right-making" characteristic).[4] If God's commanding an action is a right-indicating characteristic, then one way to come to see that the action in question is right is to see that God commands it, but there may be other ways as well; and this is so even though—given the correctness of the command view of sin, in conjunction with the truth of the claim we admitted, that what God commands perfectly correlates with what is morally right—it would follow that in coming to see that an action is right, we would know enough to conclude that God commands or wills it.

Thus, even given the command view of sin, it is allowed that there are ways of seeing that an action is right that do not cite God or God's commands, such as reflecting on the requirements of our relationships to other human persons. Also, this view of sin allows that once we know it is right, for instance, to honor our parents, even if we come to know this because God commands it, still the specific form of that honor must be determined by individual relationships between parents and offspring.

2. *Sin is being out of harmony with God's will and purpose for humankind.* This view, like the first, is a traditional view of sin.[5] It is not opposed to the first view, unless that view is taken to be a complete account of sin. For the second view, there are two aspects of sin. Sin is a prideful state of revolt against God, a rejection of God's will and purpose for human beings, and, second, sin includes those specific sinful actions that human beings commit because they are in this sinful state. These sinful actions are morally wrong actions, which violate God's commands. However, on this view, the underlying sin is the sinful state of revolt or rejection, which leads to sinful behavior. So, for this second view of sin, there are two kinds, or spheres, of sin, one primary and one secondary. We sin in the secondary way when we

---

4. Cf. Richard J. Mouw, *The God Who Commands* (Notre Dame, Ind.: University of Notre Dame Press, 1990), 28–30.

5. See, e.g., *A Dictionary of Christian Theology*, ed. Alan Richardson (Philadelphia: Westminster Press, 1969), 204–5.

do what is morally wrong and commit individual sins, which we do when we violate God's commands. On this much the second view of sin is in accord with the command view of sin, and we have seen how sin as violating God's commands can be understood as being sin precisely because it violates our relationship to God.

In the other sphere, for this second view, sin is the state human beings are in, their state as sinners, which they are in by virtue of their revolting against God. This underlying form of sin is sin in its most serious form, for it is the father of all particular sinful actions. It is a revolt against God's will for the sake of one's own will and desire, a rejection of God's purpose for one's own purpose, a turning away from God in one's heart. The idea that a movement of one's heart is the fundamental sin recurs regularly in religious reflection. For the Psalmist, "the wicked renounce God" when they "say in [their] heart[s], 'Thou wilt not call to account' " (Ps. 10.13). Again, for Aquinas, certain sins of the affections are more fundamental than other sins. For him, covetousness is "the root of all sins," while pride is "the beginning of every sin."[6] This more fundamental aspect or form of sin is spoken of as a state, or as a movement of the heart or affections, or as a disposition. However, whichever way it is spoken of, it involves a "doing." When spoken of as a prideful state of revolt against God, it involves one's in some way revolting against God. When spoken of as rejecting God or renouncing God, it involves one's in some way rejecting or renouncing God. For Aquinas, covetousness and pride can take different forms. In some forms they are active desires—an inordinate desire for riches or temporal goods in the case of covetousness, an inordinate desire to excel in the case of pride. Pride may also take the form of contempt for God. And both covetousness and pride may take the form of an "inclination" or disposition—an inclination to desire corruptible goods inordinately in the case of covetousness, and an inclination to contempt of God in the case of pride. Now, even if Aquinas does not say so, when such desires are actual felt desires, we are allowing ourselves to have the desires, whether we act on them or not. (Compare our earlier discussion of "accepting a desire," in Chapter 4.) In the same way, feeling contempt for God involves our letting ourselves feel this contempt. Similarly, in the case of the two inclinations, if they are not opposed and no effort to root them out is made, there is involved a harboring of these inclinations. In short, in every case, however we speak of sin in its fundamental aspect, there is involved an interior action of some

6. *Summa Theologica* I–II, q. 84, a. 1 and 2.

sort. In fact in the case of the Psalms this is made explicit: the wicked renounce God *by* saying in their heart that God will not hold them to account. As I argued earlier (in Chapter 4), interior actions can violate human relationships. This is most evident in close personal relationships, like the marriage relationship or the relationship between friends, but, I argued, it also holds for other relationships between persons, notably the person/person relationship. Should we be surprised that interior actions can also violate the relationship between human persons and God? Not at all. The God against whom we can sin, in the various traditions of religious belief in God, is a God who asks of us uprightness in our hearts and minds as well as in our outward actions.

Some who hold the second view of sin also subscribe to the doctrine of original sin. Does what I have just said apply to them? I believe that it does. For Calvin and others, the underlying movement of revolt was made originally by Adam, and his descendants are the inheritors of his sin. That is, as it may be put, all human beings have sinned in Adam. The underlying idea is that all human beings are accountable for Adam's sin and that his sin is as well our own sin. How this can be is a theological issue among those who hold that human beings are accountable for an inherited original sin. For some holding this view, it is because God's covenant with Adam entails this universal accountability; for others, like Jonathan Edwards, it is because we have "a real participation in the first sin," so that it is in this way our sin too.[7] Adam, to use Edwards' image, was "the root of the whole tree," and his posterity "all the branches," so that Adam's guilt "came upon Adam's posterity just as [it] came upon him, as much as if he and they had all coexisted, like a tree with many branches."[8] We need not get into the theological issue of how, under the doctrine of original sin, all human beings can be accountable for Adam's first sin, or even whether it finally can be made out that they are accountable. We need only appreciate that for those who hold the doctrine of original sin, Adam's voluntary sin is our sin as well. It is—in some way—as well our doing, for which we are accountable. So, for those who hold the second view of sin in conjunction with accepting the doctrine of original sin, as for others who hold the second view of sin, the movement of revolt against God is a matter of our own doing. And so for all who hold the second view of sin, it remains that

---

7. Augustus Strong, *Systematic Theology* (Valley Forge, Pa.: Judson Press, 1907), 613.

8. Jonathan Edwards, *Original Sin*, ed. Clyde A. Holbrook, vol. 3 of *Works of Jonathan Edwards*, ed. John E. Smith (New Haven: Yale University Press, 1970), 389.

they can see this action, this revolting against God, as sinful just because it violates our relationship with God.

Thus sin conceived as a violation of our relationship to God may be seen to underlie both forms of sin postulated by this view of sin. It emerges, then, that the second view of sin, as much as the first, is not only compatible with the concept of sin integral to sin morality, but is buttressed by it.

3. *Sin is just another name for moral wrongdoing.* On this view, sin and wrongdoing are coterminous, or perfectly correlated. In fact, on this third view of sin, "sin" and "wrongdoing" name the same things. The difference between the two words is that "sin" connotes a reference to God, while "wrongdoing" does not. The command view of sin, as we observed, allows that there is a perfect correlation between breaking a Divine command and doing what is morally wrong. This means that the command view also allows that there is a perfect correlation between sin and moral wrongdoing. The third view of sin now before us coincides with the latter proposition allowed by the first view: that there is a perfect correlation between sin and moral wrongdoing. However, for the third view of sin, there is this perfect correlation because sin is to be identified with wrongdoing. This view of sin, I believe, may be right when properly qualified.

This third view of sin is or is very close to what Basil Mitchell calls the position of "the plain moralist." The plain moralist holds that sin "is whatever it is in man that is unacceptable to God, and violations of morality are the things, or among the things, that are unacceptable to God. So let moralists determine, in whatever way they consider appropriate, what is morally wrong, and that, whatever it is, will be sin."[9] This is the third view, with two emendations: first, we should delete the qualifying phrase "or among the things," which seems to admit that some sins are not violations of morality, though in fact this possibility is not admitted by the third view or by Mitchell's plain moralist; and, second, what will be sin for this view is what moralists *correctly* determine to be morally wrong.

Mitchell is not a plain moralist. As he sees it, while it is the case that when we do what is morally wrong, we sin, and do so in a clear way, still sin embraces much besides moral wrongdoing. He identifies three alternative ways of dealing with this apparent lack of fit; each addresses the proposed "link" between sin and moral wrongdoing whereby they are coterminous:

9. Basil Mitchell, "How Is the Concept of Sin Related to the Concept of Moral Wrongdoing?" *Religious Studies* 20 (1984): 165.

(i)   We may maintain the link between sin and moral responsibility [for wrongdoing] by limiting sin to what we can be said to be, unproblematically, responsible for.

(ii) We may extend the scope of responsibility [for wrongdoing] so as to be coterminous with that of sin.

(iii) We can sever the link between them.[10]

Given the apparent lack of fit between sin and wrongdoing identified by Mitchell, one who holds the third view might adopt either the first or second alternative. The plain moralist has chosen the first alternative, Mitchell says. Mitchell himself, however, rejects this alternative and the second, in favor of the third.

Now, as I said, it seems to me that the third view of sin, if properly qualified, may be right. In fact, I suggest, understood in one way, it is right; and understood in another way, it is wrong. First let me try to bring out the sense in which it is wrong.

On the understanding that makes the third view wrong, the religious and nonreligious determine what is morally wrong in accord with conventional morality, which they both can apply, and then the religious curiously call it "sin." True, for the religious, on the third view of sin, there is a reference to God and to God's will. But God's will on this view, or the understanding of it that we are not pursuing, is perfectly expressed in the rules of morality. The rules of morality become sufficient for the determination of sin, and any reference to God becomes otiose.

In short, the understanding of the third view that makes the third view wrong construes morality and moral wrongdoing in accord with conventional morality, the prevailing form of guilt morality. Those who reject the third view of sin do so because they identify morality with conventional guilt morality, and they correctly perceive that much of sin is beyond the scope of conventional guilt morality. It is pretty clear that Mitchell has this understanding of morality, even though he does not explicitly use the category of guilt morality. For instance, in arguing against the second alternative, he says that "from a moral point of view . . . [it] is of central importance that people do what we believe to be right and refrain from doing what we believe to be wrong." Much that is sinful, Mitchell appreciates, may not be "what we believe to be wrong": for many, much that is sin may be regarded as morally permissible. Mitchell, then, thinks of morality as

10. Ibid., 167.

essentially embodying clear moral rules, which is just the case with conventional guilt morality. On his view, as he says, we should restrict " 'moral wrongdoing' to breaches of the principles and the rules of conduct which are needed for people to live together harmoniously."[11] Here it is in two ways clear that he has in mind conventional guilt morality. First, there is the reference to commonly understood principles and rules, in accord with guilt morality; and, second, he allows that morality can be taken up for the prudential reason of living together harmoniously. As we saw in the last chapter, one of the differences between guilt morality and sin morality is that guilt morality as a whole can be followed for prudential reasons. Another philosopher and religious thinker who rejects the third view of sin is Marilyn McCord Adams. She too thinks of morality as conventional guilt morality. For her, morality is a "network of moral considerations, rights and obligations," and, as such, "morality is a human institution, roughly the best framework humans generally can master and/or apply on a large scale to promote friendly and curtail anti-social behavior and attitudes."[12] Again, morality is understood as a matter of convention, involving burdens and benefits, adopted for reasons of prudence. Mitchell and Adams are right that sin should not be identified with wrongdoing, where wrongdoing is understood as breaking a moral rule or not respecting a moral right, and moral rules and rights are just those countenanced by conventional guilt morality.

But there is another way of understanding the third view of sin, one that will make the third view correct. If moral wrongdoing is understood as violating relationships, which are the source of correct moral rules and true moral rights, as opposed to violating the rules and rights of conventional morality, then wrongdoing and sin may indeed be identical. Let us consider some of Mitchell's further concerns in the light of this second understanding of the third view. Mitchell, as I remarked, favors the third of his three alternatives: the link between wrongdoing and sin should be severed, so that the two are no longer regarded as coterminous. Part of the reason he thinks that wrongdoing and sin are not coterminous is that he finds more involved in "a loving response to the love of God" than in meeting our moral obligations. He seeks to illustrate his point with an analogy from "family relationships." He considers a husband who has "done nothing, or left undone nothing for which he could be reasonably blamed," but yet has

11. Ibid., 172.
12. Marilyn McCord Adams, "Sin as Uncleanness," *Philosophical Perspectives* 5 (1991): 2.

"failed his wife and family," as he discovers in "finding his wife increasingly estranged." "If he asked for her forgiveness," Mitchell says, "it would not be for particular offences—there were none—nor for disregarding his conscience, but for a failure of love manifested as a failure of insight."[13] It of course is no accident that Mitchell chooses such an analogy, but it illustrates more than Mitchell allows. The husband has kept all his obligations, we are to understand. Which obligations? Those commonly recognized, and so there is nothing for which he can be reasonably blamed by other participants in conventional morality. He has committed no particular offenses, we are told. One is not guilty in a guilt morality, we should recall, when one has not done what one ought not to do: moral success is negatively defined. But consider the husband in the light of sin morality. Now his failure regarding his wife becomes understandable. His failure of love tears at the marriage relationship.

For Mitchell, "a lack of sensitivity" may be a sin, for which we ought to ask God's forgiveness, but not a moral failure.[14] However, in Mitchell's own analogy, might not the husband ask his wife for forgiveness for his lack of sensivitity? I would think so, and this is precisely because being insensitive can violate a marriage relationship. Mitchell is right that a lack of sensitivity may be a sin. What he fails to bring out—even though he has all the data he needs—is that it can be a sin against a person as well as against God.

Part of the reason that Mitchell does not see insensitivity as a moral failure has to do with blame and its place in morality. He says, "To extend the rigour of moral demand, together with the sanction of moral blame, to everything of this sort [failure of insight or sensitivity], would be inappropriate and, indeed, intolerable."[15] For people may be wanting in sensitivity due to upbringing or cultural factors. Mitchell's concern is understandable. However, it provides no reason for denying that insensitivity is a moral failure. In the first place, given the principal that *ought* implies *can*, if a person's insensitivity is *wholly* due to factors beyond his or her control, then that person is not blameworthy. Mitchell does not distinguish between this case and cases where people have failed to exercise and develop their attention in ways that, though distasteful to them, are within their power. Second, the recognition that at times persons can be blamed for a lack of sensitivity does not mean that we ought to presume to judge that a particular person in, say, a marriage relationship has a lack of sensitivity. And, third,

13. Mitchell, "How Is the Concept of Sin Related to the Concept of Moral Wrongdoing?" 170.
14. Ibid., 169.
15. Ibid., 172.

even if it is somehow clear to us that a person has a blameworthy lack of sensitivity, this does not mean that we ought to or may blame that person. Depending on our relationship to that person, it may or may not be our place to blame him or her. In fact, recognizing that people can be blameworthy for a lack of sensitivity is compatible with never using "the sanction of moral blame."[16]

Another reason that Mitchell rejects the third view of sin is that he perceives that "sin does not simply denote wrongdoing . . . it operates as some sort of explanation of wrongdoing."[17] Mitchell is right, but only if "wrongdoing" is understood in terms of conventional guilt morality. So understood, the point becomes the point we examined in the last chapter: sin morality underlies guilt morality in that it can explain why there are the moral rules there are and why they are correct when they are.

For Mitchell and others, I suppose that regarding morality as sin morality represents an extension of morality beyond its present bounds. However, I do not think that this is so. Morality, with its roots and sources brought to light, just is sin morality—human sin morality and religious sin morality. For Mitchell, we are "answerable to other men . . . for [our] failure to fulfil [our] duties and obligations towards them," but we are "answerable to God for [our] failure to love [our] neighbour as [ourselves]." Yes, we are answerable to God, at least in the eyes of religious believers, for our failure in love, but we are also answerable to other persons, for our having wrong attitudes toward persons violates our relationships to them as well as our relationship to God. Violating the obligations of human sin morality is to sin against persons and at the same time to sin against God (as when we steal or fail to be just to others). Mitchell very nearly says as much when he indicates that he is thinking of sin "as a breach in man's relationship with God, and hence with other men, through failure to love him and them in him."[18] This is not quite the idea of sin in sin morality, for sin morality allows that one can sin against a person directly by a failure of love, but at least Mitchell sees that sin can be a breach in a relationship to other persons. Also, for sin morality in its religious form, violating a particular obligation to God, arising from an individual relationship to God, may be sin against God alone (as when Jonah flees to Tarshish). If wrongdoing is understood in this

16. Cf. Matt. 7.1, which can be construed as saying that we should not presume to blame others for actions we recognize we ought not to commit. I shall return to blame, in connection with forgiveness, in Chapter 16.

17. Mitchell, "How Is the Concept of Sin Related to the Concept of Moral Wrongdoing?" 166.

18. Ibid., 169 and 170.

way, as arising from a violation of a relationship to a person or to God, and sin is understood as just such a violation, then the third view of sin may be seen as essentially correct in identifying wrongdoing and sin. Certainly the third view of sin, in this construction, may be regarded as correct from the standpoint of sin morality, with which it shares the concept of sin as a violation of a relationship.

4. *Sin is anything inherently blameworthy, voluntary or involuntary.* This view of sin is very much like the last, though there is one noteworthy difference. It explicitly includes, in the category of sin, involuntary actions and omissions. Allowing that there are involuntary sins seems necessary to Robert Merrihew Adams, who holds this fourth view of sin, because, for one thing, it seems to be required by Jesus' teaching that not only those who commit murder but those who are angry with their brother without cause will be liable to judgment (Matt. 5.21–22). Anger, however, is in general involuntary, Adams observes. Often the way we express our anger is under our control, but the anger that we feel and cannot help feeling is not voluntary. And this brings the biblical teaching into conflict with the widely supported ethical thesis that we are accountable only for voluntary actions and omissions. The resolution of the conflict proposed by Adams is to reject the thesis that we are accountable only for what is voluntary. Our anger, or our unjustified disproportionate anger at least, is blameworthy even though it is involuntary.[19] Adams does not deny that many sins are voluntary, but, for Adams, there are involuntary sins as well. Among them, in addition to anger, are "jealousy, hatred, and other sorts of malice, contempt for other people, and the lack of a hearty concern for their welfare; or in more general terms, morally objectionable states of mind, including corrupt beliefs as well as wrong desires."[20]

Our involuntary sins, then, may include certain of our feelings, desires, and beliefs. Such states are involuntary because, as Adams argues, they are not under our control. Sin, for Adams, is "any action, omission, or state that is inherently blameworthy,"[21] and this includes blameworthy "states of mind," though they are not chosen and not under our control. Yet, though these sins are involuntary, they are ours, and we are responsible for them in

19. Robert Merrihew Adams, "Involuntary Sins," *The Philosopher's Annual* 8 (1985): 1. The translation of Matt. 5.21–22 that Adams uses reads, "[E]veryone who is angry with his brother *without cause* shall be liable to judgment" (my emphasis). The RSV omits this qualification. Adams does not deny that all anger is sinful, but he does not want to go into that issue and so chooses to "focus on the weaker, more qualified claim" (1 n. 1).

20. Ibid., 2.

21. Ibid., 1 n. 2

the sense that we are accountable and blameworthy. Furthermore, Adams wants us to appreciate, we ought to "take responsibility" for them.[22] Repentance requires that we take responsibility for them in the sense that we take responsibility for having them and doing something about them in the future, which we can try to do. The responsibility that Adams disallows, of course, is responsibility for willfully bringing about or controlling the creation of these involuntary but sinful states of mind.

How does Adams' view of sin relate to the notion of sin integral to sin morality? Essentially they are compatible, I believe. Let me bring out two points of agreement, the second of which establishes their compatibility. First notice that Adams appreciates that sin is not limited to exterior action. His view, as he elaborates it, recognizes that we are blameworthy for much in our mental lives. In the same way, sin morality includes in its action-scope many of our feelings and desires (as we saw in Chapter 4). For both Adams' view of sin and sin morality, feelings, desires, and beliefs, can be sinful. For Adams, though, the sin is the mental state of anger or desire or belief, each of which he regards as involuntary, while for relationship morality, in our discussion to this point, the sin is the interior action of allowing ourselves to be angry or accepting the desire. That is, the interior sin identified in our earlier discussion of sin morality is the interior action of accepting or harboring a mental state, as opposed to the mental state itself. The sin is something that in some way we willfully do. Might sin morality allow that mental states, in addition to harboring mental states, can be sins against persons or God? Strictly, in identifying as sinful, interior acts that allow or encourage corrupt mental states, we do not deny that the mental states themselves are sinful. Second, the fourth view of sin, as Adams develops it, and sin morality agree on the importance of relationships in the determination of sin. Self-righteousness and ingratitude, in Adams' discussion, emerge as sinful just because they violate a person's relationship with another person. Adams explicitly acknowledges this when he says that unless we recognize that a person can be to blame for "his self-righteous attitude," we will have an inadequate "view of the guilt in human relationships."[23] Adams' view of sin is compatible with the concept of sin integral to sin morality, for it in fact relies upon that very concept of sin.

22. Ibid., 13–14 and 13 n. 9. Adams also offers a tentative theory regarding the conditions under which states of mind must "arise in us" in order for us to be responsible, that is, accountable, for them. See 24.

23. Ibid., 4. See 2–4 and 10–11 for his discussion of self-righteousness and ingratitude. And cf. sec. 2 of his "Divine Commands and the Social Nature of Obligation," *Faith and Philosophy* 4 (1987).

So Adams and sin morality are to a great extent in agreement. For both, sins are faults and are blameworthy, and sin is a violation of a relationship. Furthermore, if it should turn out that what is involuntary violates a relationship, then for sin morality it would be a sin. Sin morality as a matter of its internal logic is not committed to the principle that we are blameworthy only for what is voluntary. Also, sin morality is not debarred from agreeing with Adams that feelings, beliefs, and mental states in general are involuntary. Accordingly, if such mental states are involuntary and violate relationships, sin morality would conclude with Adams that they are blameworthy as involuntary sins. Still, I think that it is better to see such mental states as voluntary, as in some significant way open to our control when they are blameworthy. If we do so we keep in place the principle that only what is voluntary is blameworthy. Sin morality, as we have seen, challenges the understanding of morality as conventional morality and so challenges popular understanding. But to deny the principle that we are morally responsible only for what is voluntary comes close to denying that *ought* implies *can,* which hits at the heart of our intuitive moral understanding.

It seems to me that Adams underestimates the extent to which our willfulness may play a role in those sins he argues are involuntary. Perhaps at the moment the feeling of anger descends upon us or the lustful desire occupies our heart we cannot control it, but still such mental states in a significant way may be open to our control. Adams wants to deny that those mental states that are on his view involuntary sins are under our "direct" voluntary control, and he also wants to deny that they are under our "indirect" voluntary control. In advancing his argument he divides the issue in this way, and in answering his argument I shall do the same. For Adams, "To say that something is (directly) within my voluntary control is to say that I would do it (right away) if and only if I (fully) tried or chose or meant to do so, and hence that if I did it I would do it *because* I tried or chose or meant to do it, and in that sense voluntarily."[24] This definition he accepts "provisionally" as "roughly right." We may do the same and, doing so, agree with Adams that our anger and desires and so on are not under our direct control: we cannot change them right away by an effort of will, as we can normally change our bodily position if we choose to.

Still, though, our mental states that are sinful could be *indirectly* under our voluntary control. Adams is aware that we can try to improve such

24. Adams, "Involuntary Sins," 6 (Adams' emphasis).

mental states as our motives, and he does not deny that such voluntary efforts, over time, might be successful. And, he affirms, we ought to try to "have good motives and other good states of mind" and so we are blameworthy if we do not through our voluntary actions try to have good motives and good states of mind. But, beyond this, Adams argues, we are blameworthy for a mental state even if we did not cause it or let it arise within ourselves by our voluntary actions or omissions. Ultimately, for Adams, there is something involuntary for which we are blameworthy. He considers the mental state of ingratitude:

> How . . . can you be blamed for not having fought against your ingratitude [if you did not realize you have this state and did not voluntarily consent to it]? You should have known of your ingratitude. Why didn't you? Presumably because you did not want to recognize any shameful truths about yourself—because at some level you cared more about having a good opinion of yourself than about knowing the truth about yourself. And that's a sin too, though not a voluntary one. Thus the search for voluntary actions and omissions by which you may have caused your ingratitude keeps leading to other *in*voluntary sins that lie behind your past voluntary behavior.

Although Adams does not say so, this pretty clearly is a case of self-deception. Later, in trying to show that there are involuntary mental states that are or involve involuntary cognitive sins, he presents another instance of self-deception: "The typically or consummately self-righteous person is not merely pretending to others, but has persuaded himself, that he is better than he really is. His self-righteousness includes a blindness to faults such as self-righteouness in himself."[25]

Earlier (in Chapter 3) we discussed the logic of self-deception; if we recall and draw upon that logic, we can see that Adams may not be giving due credit to the voluntary. What he fails to see, I think, is the voluntary element in the blindness to which he refers. Blindness, where it is that caused by self-deception, is motivated and intentional, we will recall. It is motivated by, for instance, our wanting to keep intact our cherished image of ourselves, as in Adams' ingratitude case. But also, it is intentional. The individual who is self-deceived deceives himself or herself. Self-deception is

25. Ibid., 10, 11 (Adams' emphasis), and 15.

not something that happens to us. Nor is it something we do by oversight. It is something we do intentionally. When we deceive ourselves, we intentionally turn our eyes away and refuse to see or to acknowledge even to ourselves the significance of what we would not see—such as the sure signs of our ingratitude or self-righteousness. We afflict ourselves with blindness, as it were, and this is something we do willfully, intentionally. It is voluntary.

Adams insists that "if one does something voluntarily one knows that one is doing it."[26] This seems to be wrong. I voluntarily risk people's lives when I drive too fast, though I may not realize I am doing so; I do not set out to risk lives or intend to, and it may be I do not even realize that I am; yet I do risk people's lives, and my action, which is under my control, is voluntary. But say that Adams is right on this point. Still, the point I am making about self-deception remains, for self-deception is intentional. In cases of self-deception self-deceivers do know, at one level, what they are doing in deceiving themselves, in turning away their awareness.

It can be argued, then, that Adams' "involuntary sins" arise from what is voluntary after all. However, we should be clear, the compatibility of the fourth view of sin and the concept of sin integral to sin morality does not depend on our rejecting Adams' contention that various mental states are involuntary sins. Since it is allowed by the fourth view of sin that whatever sins there are will be sins by virtue of violating relationships, and since the idea that sin is a violation of a relationship does not in itself rule out involuntary sins, there is no essential incompatibility between the fourth view and the concept of sin internal to sin morality.

5. *Sin is uncleanness.* And so we come to the fifth view of sin, the last that we shall consider. I have saved it for last because it is most divergent from the notion of sin integral to sin morality. The root idea embodied in the fifth view of sin is that sin is a matter of our human state, which is unclean, or profane. This means that sin is not a matter of what we do or fail to do, or even a matter of our involuntary mental states. Often those who hold this view of sin quote Isa. 6.5: "I am a man of unclean lips, and I dwell in the midst of a people of unclean lips." Rudolf Otto, who held this view, quotes this passage, as does Marilyn McCord Adams, a contemporary exponent of this view of sin.[27] Isaiah uttered these words before the Lord;

---

26. Ibid., 15, and cf. 11.
27. Rudolf Otto, *The Idea of the Holy*, trans. John W. Harvey, 2d ed. (London: Oxford University Press, 1950), 50; Adams, "Sin as Uncleanness," 6. Mitchell, for whom, we will recall, sin is a broader category than moral wrongdoing (but still essentially a matter of behavior for which we are

the lesson drawn is that our sense of sin lies in our experience of our uncleanness before the Divine. For Adams, "God and creatures are ontologically incommensurate," and "creatures are to be characterized as sinful or unclean, because the radical incommensuration of Divine and created natures obstructs relations between God and creatures."[28] We might note here Adams' reference to "relations between God and creatures," that is, His human creatures. " 'Sin,' " she says, signifies "some sort of impropriety in the relation between created persons and God."[29] Adam shares with sin morality the perception that sin is to be understood in terms of relationships. But for her, sin is an obstruction in the relationship between persons and God arising from the radical difference between God's nature and the nature of human persons, while for sin morality, (religious) sin is a matter of our violating our relationship to God, through our doing or not doing, or having mental states for which we are at fault.

Adams uses Otto's reflections on the "numinous" and the numinous experience in its various aspects to remind us of the religious sense of God's otherness.[30] The experience, or "feeling," that Otto identifies he calls the feeling of *mysterium tremendum*, and in *The Idea of the Holy* he offers an analysis of its elements.[31] Adams, following Otto's analysis, draws to our attention the various elements that Otto found in the numinous experience. There are, for instance, the feeling of dread or awe before God as the Aweful, the feeling of mystery before God as the Wholly Other, and the feeling of attraction to God or longing for God felt before God as *Facinans* (Adams illustrates this aspect with Ps. 42.1–2: "As a deer longs for the water-brooks, so longs my soul for you, O God"). Also, not unimportantly for Adams, given her thesis, there is the feeling of being profane, or unclean, before God as the August or Holy. This is not the place to criticize Otto's analysis of the numinous experience or Adams' rendering of it. But let us note that the feeling of dread before God—approaching God with fear and trembling—and the sense of mystery before God as the Wholly Other seem to be distinguishable from feeling unclean before God as the Holy. Of course, these different religious sensibilities can combine, as Otto has it they do in the numinous experience, but they need not. For Adams,

---

28. Adams, "Sin as Uncleanness," 3 and 7.

29. Ibid., 2.

30. Ibid., 3–7.

31. Otto, *The Idea of the Holy*, chaps. 3–8.

though, they are definitely interconnected. As we have noted, for her, creatures, human persons, are sinful, or unclean, *because of* "the radical incommensuration of Divine and created natures."

Both Adams and Otto reject a moralistic understanding of uncleanness and, hence, a moralistic understanding of sin, since for them sin is ontological uncleanness. For Adams, as for Otto, this uncleanness is not a matter of our individual failures, of our sinful acts and omissions in thought, word, or action—of our violating our relationship to God. It is a matter of the ontological distance from God that we as a kind of being suffer given our human nature. This sense of uncleanness is the sense of being *unworthy* before the Holy, which is supremely worthy of praise.[32] Let us admit that uncleanness, or unworthiness, before God is religiously felt. And let us admit, and even insist, that there is among the religious the prayer to be allowed to come into God's presence, though we are unworthy. Otto suggests that the unworthiness, or uncleanness, that arises from the distance between human, creaturely nature and the Divine nature is sin,[33] and it is Adams' central claim that it is. But there are three crucial questions to be asked of the fifth view of sin: (1) Can this unworthiness, or uncleanness, arising from our ontological distance from God, if it is sin, be *all* of sin? (2) Is this ontologically based uncleanness *itself* sin? (3) Is there an offending uncleanness that we have *because* we have sinned?

It would seem to be an implication of the fifth view that sin as uncleanness is not something to be forgiven by God and that it is not something of which we are guilty. Adams does not deny this. She says, "If sin is fundamentally a consequence of what God and creatures are, and the normative priority lies with God, then the logically appropriate feeling response for creatures is not guilt (which befits a rebellious use of free agency) but a sense of taint and shame." Before I address directly the three questions that I take to be crucial for the fifth view of sin, let me comment on this claim about the appropriateness of shame. In advancing this claim Adams, going beyond Otto, draws upon the *Revelations of Divine Love* (or *Showings*) of Julian of Norwich. Our failure to live by the two command-ments of love (Matt. 22.37–39), Adams says, "Julian of Norwich analyses . . . not as rebellion that results in guilt, but as incompetence issuing in uncleanness, requiring a Divine Mother's loving care."[34] To use an image shared by Adams and Julian, we are like little children, and like little

---

32. Ibid., 51.
33. Ibid., 53.
34. Adams, "Sin as Uncleanness," 21 and 12.

children we know not what we do and are not to blame. Given our natures and our incapacities we, like little children or babies, soil ourselves. Given our natures we are "incompetent," and though this brings us to shame, there is no guilt, Adams suggests. Several comments must be made on the category of shame being employed by Adams and Julian of Norwich.

The first thing to notice is that sometimes when Julian mentions shame, it is not shame alone that she mentions. One is led by the Holy Spirit to reveal one's sins, she says, "with great sorrow and great shame."[35] To the extent that shame is something we feel, shame is not all of the bad feeling we have.

Second, the kind of shame that Julian means is a kind of shame that can be taken from us. It can be "turned into honour and joy," as it will be by God.[36] As Adams puts it, shame will be canceled by honor.[37] Here the notion of shame is not public shame felt before an honour-group (discussed in Chapter 11), nor is the notion here that of private shame, the shame we feel because of our ego ideal (the shame involved in shame morality, also discussed in Chapter 11). Here, to the extent that our shame can be taken away or transmuted (which amounts to its being taken away), it seems that our uncleanness and its wretchedness may *be* our shame. It is in this sense of shame that one who, say, publicly wears the red badge of adultery, as Hester Prynne does in *The Scarlet Letter*, wears her shame. But note that one who publicly wears the scarlet letter may or may not be privately ashamed (that depends on her ego ideal), although she is made wretched. In the sense of shame used by Julian and Adams, when the scarlet letter is taken away, the shame, which is just the wretchedness of the one publicly wearing the letter, is taken away.

Both Julian and Adams, as I remarked, use the image and analogy of the baby who has fouled itself, who is filthy and unclean. Julian says (in a passage quoted by Adams) that "our heavenly Mother Jesus" "does not wish us to flee away . . . but he . . . wants us to behave like a child. For when it is distressed and frightened, it runs quickly to its mother; and if it can do no more, it calls to the mother for help with all its might. So he wants us to act as a meek child, saying: My kind Mother, my gracious Mother, my beloved Mother, have mercy on me. I have made myself filthy and unlike you, and I may not and cannot make it right except with your help and

35. Julian of Norwich, *Showings*, in *Julian of Norwich: Showings*, trans. and ed. Edmund Colledge and James Walsh (New York: Paulist Press, 1978), chap. 39, 244.

36. Ibid., 245.

37. Adams, "Sin as Uncleanness," 19.

grace."[38] Julian's image is of God or Christ as Loving Mother, and it seems to me that this is a powerful and informative image of God, as powerful and informative as the image of God as a Merciful Father. However, when the loving mother cleans the child, does she remove his shame? Is the child ashamed? I think not, surely not necessarily. What is clear is that she removes the source of the child's wretchedness. She removes the child's shame only if his uncleanness and discomfort *is* his shame. A good bit of what Julian says about shame, then, indicates that what she means by shame is not something we feel in relation to an ego ideal, but something that is distressing and can be taken from us.

Let me expand this point by bringing out that what Julian and Adams mean by "shame" is not related to pride as shame felt in relation to an ego ideal is related to pride. What cancels or transmutes shame is honor. Sometimes, though, Julian speaks of "honours" in the plural. When the sinful soul is healed, "his wounds are not seen by God as wounds but as honours."[39] Note that, in general, honor, when it is something bestowed upon one, and especially honors (in the plural) given to one, need not be the occasion of pride. Whether one takes public pride in the honors given to one, as one will if one is following an honour ethic, depends on the values of the honour-group. And whether one takes private pride in the honors given to one depends on one's ego ideal. (As we saw in Chapter 11, however, those who follow an honour ethic and receive honor from an honour-group may be proud of the honor they are given in the eyes of others just because they have the internalized ideal they do; if so, public pride is at bottom private pride.) Honor and honors, as something given to one, in general *need not* result in pride, public or private, and, for Julian, in the special instance of God's grace, they surely do not. Honor, as the cancellation of shame, brings us, not pride, but bliss and joy. Our shame—our wretchedness at our uncleanness—will be taken from us; our sins will be made honors by God's courtesy or mercy. And, for Julian, we will come to joy in the cancellation of sin: the opposite of sin is peacefully possessing God in the fullness of joy; sin is pain.[40]

But Julian does speak of our being ashamed and even has in place our wanting to go and hide or disappear, both of which relate to the shame we

38. *Showings*, chap. 61, 301. Adams quotes the same passage, but from a different translation ("Sin as Uncleanness," 17).

39. *Showings*, chap. 39, 245.

40. Ibid., chap. 72, 320.

feel.[41] This brings me to a third comment on Julian's category of shame. Adams observes that, for Julian, human beings respond to sin with grief and fear as well as shame (in accord with my first comment), and when we respond with shame, it is because sin "prevents us from doing what we, in our essential nature, want."[42] In *Showings* Julian says that the soul who confesses and reveals his sin does so "with great sorrow and great shame that he has so befouled God's fair image."[43] What Julian means by shame, the shame that we feel, arises, not because we have failed to live up to our ego ideal, but because we have made unclean "God's fair image" in ourselves; because we have made ourselves "filthy and unlike you [our Mother]," as Julian says in the passage I quoted above; because, using Adams' term, our sin turns us from our "essential nature." The idea that we would be ashamed because we have failed to meet our own ego ideal is foreign to both Julian and Adams.

What seems to emerge from these reflections is that, for much of what Julian and Adams want to maintain, it is not necessary to posit shame as something we feel *in addition* to sorrow or a sense of unworthiness or wretchedness or pain; and if they do require a felt shame, it is not shame felt in relation to an ego ideal. These comments on the category of shame used by Julian and by Adams following Julian were necessary in order to distinguish what Julian means by "shame" from the kind of ego-ideal-dependent shame involved in shame morality. Getting in place this distinction was necessary for two reasons. For one thing, for the sake of our earlier discussion of shame morality, it behooved us to distinguish what Julian means by "shame" from the kind of shame involved in shame morality. But we also needed to distinguish the two for the sake of the concern we shall be turning to shortly regarding the possibility of a religious shame morality.

Now let us return to the three crucial questions that we addressed to the view of sin as uncleanness. In addressing these questions we will do well not to deny the elements of religious sensibility that Adams, following Otto, draws to our attention: the otherness of God, the mystery of the Godhead, the dread, the fear and trembling, with which God is approached, and, to be sure, the sense of uncleanness, or unworthiness, before God. At the same time, we should appreciate that God in religious sensibility is also conceived to be, and felt to be, merciful and loving—as by Julian of Norwich: and in some forms of religious sensibility there is the felt sense of God as friend.

41. Ibid., chap. 61, 301.
42. Adams, "Sin as Uncleanness," 17.
43. *Showings*, chap. 39, 244.

Still, as I say, we do well not to deny the religious sense of uncleanness of which Adams reminds us.

But should we call this uncleanness, or unworthiness, sin? If we do, I think that we must admit that it cannot be the whole story of sin. The first of our three questions is, Can this unworthiness, or uncleanness, arising from our ontological distance from God, if it is sin, be *all* of sin? It is clear that not all sin can be uncleanness in this sense. For what shall we call the sins we commit, our individual willful sins against God? Adams, in fact, does not deny that there are such sins, but they are "second-level" sins, and for her it remains that "*fundamentally*, sin is uncleanness arising from the incommensuration of Divine and created natures."[44] And Julian too speaks of and allows that there are sins that are of our doing, as when she speaks of our confessing and revealing our sin (as we have noted she does) and when she speaks of our turning from God through sin,[45] which is something we do through our sinful actions.

Moreover, it emerges that for Julian it is not that sin *is* uncleanness, but that sin causes—the sins we commit cause—our uncleanness. If I am right, Julian would answer the third question—Is there an offending uncleanness that we have *because* we have sinned?—affirmatively. Recall the passage from *Showings*, quoted above, in which Julian says that God wants us, like children calling to their mother, to call to our "beloved Mother" that "[we] have made [ourselves] filthy" and need her help. Adams recognizes that for Julian what we do makes us unclean. But Adams sees this as "incompetence" for which we are not blameworthy. For Julian, however, this doing is not, or not always, a matter of our incompetence, of our incapacity: it is sometimes our chosen sin, our willful sin, for which we are to blame. Julian, in a way that Adams does not bring out, recognizes that "sinners sometimes deserve blame and wrath." Though, to be sure, Julian also has the sense that God will "assign no blame." How both "judgments" can be true is perplexing to Julian, and she says at one point in *Showings*, it "was my desire, that I might see in God in what way [these two judgments] might both be reconciled."[46] She is allowed to "see in God" the resolution through a vision of a lord and servant that expresses a parable. In the parable, part of which Adams quotes,[47] a servant speedily and lovingly doing the will of his lord "falls into a dell and is greatly injured." The lord imputes no fault

---

44. Adams, "Sin as Uncleanness," 22 and 21 (Adams' emphasis).
45. *Showings*, chap 76, 328.
46. Ibid., chap 45, 257.
47. Adams, "Sin as Uncleanness," 16.

to his good and beloved servant for his injury and rewards him above what he would have been had he not fallen.[48] But for Julian, as comes out in her discussion of the parable, the lesson is not that we are without blame but that "our good Lord Jesus [has] taken upon him all our blame; and therefore our Father may not, does not wish to assign more blame to us than to his own beloved Son Jesus Christ."[49] For Julian, then, we are accountable, but God will not hold us to account. Our "sins are forgiven by grace and mercy," and "we are all mercifully enclosed in God's mildness and in his meekness."[50]

Nor for Julian is our blameworthy sinning the exception and our incompetent behavior more the norm. For Julian, we are blameworthy for constant sinning. She says, "I know truly that we sin grievously all day and are very blameworthy."[51] To return to her image of the child who has soiled itself, if we are like children, we are like willful children. We befoul ourselves through doing what we ought not to do: we are not like babies who have no control and lack competence. A child crying for help could be either; but given what she says about our blameworthiness and our being forgiven, it is clear that for Julian we as sinners turn to our loving mother for help and mercy that will both make us clean and give us loving forgiveness. Adams is right, I believe, to emphasize that Julian's vision is of a loving God, a Loving Mother, who will not hold His children to account. But this does not mean, and it does not mean for Julian, that we are not blameworthy. Her vision of God is of a loving Mother who renounces blaming Her children and takes them to herself tenderly and lovingly, removing their distress and pain. A Mother's love and mercy given to innocent children is great, but it is all the greater, perhaps we may say, when it is given freely to Her wayward children.

So, for Julian of Norwich, our uncleanness is caused by our sins, for which we are blameworthy. The idea that we cause our uncleanness, or

48. *Showings*, chap 51, 267–69.

49. Ibid., 275.

50. Ibid., chap. 40, 246, and chap. 49, 264. Also in chapter 49 Julian says, "[O]ur Lord God cannot in his own judgment forgive because he cannot be angry." That is, God does not forgive with that forgiveness that presupposes anger. Compare Adams, "Sin as Uncleanness," 17, where she says, regarding Julian's not finding anger in God, "[A]s angerless, God cannot strictly speaking forgive us, if 'forgiveness' signifies the removal of anger; if it means that sin is not held against us, our forgiveness is guaranteed." While an angry person may relieve his or her anger by forgiving, forgiveness as such does not presuppose anger. (We shall have occasion to reflect on the character of forgiveness in Chapter 16.)

51. *Showings*, chap. 59, 266.

unworthiness, by our sins is not unheard-of in the Judeo-Christian tradition. Catherine of Genoa spoke of sin, "either original or acutal," as "rust," a corrupting rust of our will to sin that can stain the soul in its "pure and simple" creation—though in purgation and purgatory, the rust of sin is worn away daily by the love of God.[52] And, it turns out, this is the idea of uncleanness in Isaiah. As I remarked, often those who hold the fifth view of sin quote Isa. 6.5—"I am a man of unclean lips." Otto and Adams quote this passage. But they do not quote more from Isaiah 6, where Isaiah before the Lord has a sense of his own uncleanness. In the vision recounted in Isaiah 6 the prophet beholds God sitting upon a throne, while the seraphim stand above him (Isa. 6.1), and in his vision one of these seraphim flies to him with "a burning coal which he had taken with tongs from the altar," and, says Isaiah, "he tounched my mouth, and said: 'Behold, this has touched your lips: your guilt is taken away, and your sin forgiven' " (Isa. 6.6–7). Often, then, in religious reflection, uncleanness is not a matter of ontological difference between the Divine and created natures: it is an effect of sin.

To appreciate this point, however, is not to deny the sense of ontological difference identified by Adams. And this bring us to the remaining question, our second question: Is this ontologically based uncleanness *itself* sin? It cannot be all of sin, as we have seen Adams admit. Also, it is not the uncleanness that we find confessed and lamented by Julian in *Showings* or in the Book of Isaiah. So, is uncleanness as ontological difference itself sin? An alternative is to see sin as a product of our uncleanness in this sense, a product of our broken nature, of that which makes us unlike God. For this view, though, once again sin is committed and is different from uncleanness itself. This alternative can be illustrated with an analogy. Though Michelangelo was reluctant to fresco the ceiling of the Sistine Chapel and suffered from his years of labor on the ceiling, he was supremely confident of his ability to do artistic justice to the great undertaking. Let us say, though, that there was no Michelangelo, and that Julius II called to Rome an artist of lesser abilities. This artist, let us allow, has his artistic strengths, but also, he has limitations. And we will give him a realistic and humble appreciation of both. Called by Julius, he might feel and confess himself to be unworthy of such an undertaking. And so he would be: it is beyond his

---

52. Catherine of Genoa, *Purgation and Purgatory*, in *Catherine of Genoa: Purgation and Purgatory, The Spiritual Dialogue*, trans. Serge Hughes (New York: Paulist Press, 1979), 72–75. Although Catherine speaks of original sin, she also conceives of the soul "close to its first creation" as "pure and unstained" (*Purgation and Purgatory*, 73) and "free from sin" (*The Spiritual Dialogue*, 94).

abilities. But so far there is no sin, it would seem. He will sin only if he presumes to undertake what he is not worthy to do and out of his unworthiness does what he ought not to do. His unworthiness is a given, and may lead to his sinning, but his sin is not his unworthiness. By analogy, on this view, our ontologically based uncleanness is not itself sin, though it may lead us to sin in our actions and omissions. This alternative view seems just as viable as that of Adams and Otto, although I am not suggesting that the mere existence of such an alternative view shows that their nonmoralistic understanding of sin is wrong.

In the light of these reflections, it seems that there are two quite different ways to understand uncleanness and sin:

Construction I. On this construction, which corresponds to the fifth view of sin, sin fundamentally is what distances us from God or "obstructs," as Adams says, our relations with God. Our state of creaturely unworthiness, or innate uncleanness, arising from the ontological incommensuration of the Divine and creaturely natures, is a part of sin, though not by virtue of what we do or think or say or of any other failure on our part. But also, on this construction, our various willful violations of our relationship to God are part of sin. On this construction there are two forms, or parts, of sin. The first form of sin is not sufficient to give us a full understanding of sin, and both forms are sin because they deleteriously affect our relationship to God by distancing us from God—either as obstruction caused by our natures or alienation caused by our violation of the relationship. On this construction there are two species of sin, both in the same genus. The notion of sin integral to sin morality, on this construction, would relate to and underlie the second form of sin.

Construction II. Uncleanness arises from our sins, which we commit and for which we are blameworthy, which seems to be the understanding of Julian of Norwich, Catherine of Genoa, and Isaiah; or, alternatively, our uncleanness, as our broken and inadequate nature, disposes us to sin, which again is a matter of our blameworthy doing and not doing. On this construction, finally, there is just one species of sin, and the notion of sin integral to sin morality underlies all sin.

If Construction II is correct, then the notion of sin internal to sin morality underlies all sin. If Construction I, or the fifth view of sin, is correct, then the notion of sin internal to sin morality underlies the species of sin important to behavior in the broadest sense. At least in this way, the notion of sin internal to sin morality underlies the fifth view of sin.

Let me now sum up our discussion of the relationship between the concept of sin in sin morality and the five views of sin. The five views, again, are these:

1. Sin is a violation of God's commands.
2. Sin is being out of harmony with God's will and purpose for humankind.
3. Sin is just another name for moral wrongdoing.
4. Sin is anything inherently blameworthy, voluntary or involuntary.
5. Sin is uncleanness.

The sin-morality concept of sin, we have seen, is consistent with and underlies the first and second views. It is consistent with the third view if morality is sin morality, but not if morality is equated with conventional morality. It is consistent with the fourth view, whether or not there are involuntary sins. And it underlies or accords with the fifth view's understanding of that part of sin that is committed willfully.

We may now return to what I earlier said was the main concern of this chapter: to explore the connections between human sin morality and religious sin morality. Now, then, let me try to bring out how human sin morality and religious sin morality are related. I want to focus on the relationship between these two forms of sin morality, not on the relationship between God and human sin morality. Regarding the latter, under the assumption that there is a God, human sin morality—which, given the argument of this book, is or underlies human morality properly understood—would be God's moral order, a part of His creation; and assuming the usual view of God's commands, the obligations we have, which arise from our relationships to persons, would be expressions of God's commands. My concern here, however, is to look at the relationship between these two distinguishable forms of sin morality when each is considered in its own right. They are surely different, for the one presupposes that there is a God, and the other does not. Still, though religious sin morality requires that there is a God and human sin morality does not, this point of difference does not put them at odds, for human sin morality does not deny that there is a God.

Nor are they at odds with each other in regard to the demands of morality, our obligations and the moral demands of the other mansions of morality. This is so even if, as religious sin morality has it, there are individual faith relationships with individual obligations. For religious sin morality, Jonah alone is required by God to journey to Ninevah. However, there is the same thing in human sin morality, where a particular husband alone has that husband's obligations to his wife. Moreover, this phenomenon of morality—that a particular individual, and not others, may have certain obligations—was generally recognized prior to the identification of morality as sin morality. As Ross saw, and as our untutored ethical sense can appreciate, if one person promises another, he or she takes on a special obligation to that other person that he or she and no other has incurred. Religious sin morality, however, may be at odds with conventional morality in the moral demands it recognizes; but then so is human sin morality.

Human sin morality and religious sin morality may be said to be not only consistent but "continuous." This continuity has more than one aspect or dimension. One of its dimensions I shall try to bring out by using, once again, the story of the prodigal son. As we have seen, the prodigal son sins against his father, and he sins against God. He sins against his father directly: he does not sin against his father only in and through his sinning against God. He has violated his relationship to his father, which is real and, in the relevant moral sense, exists independently of his relationship to God: he could come to understand that he has violated his relationship to his father without understanding that he has violated his relationship to God. This is so even though he has also violated his relationship to God in his disobedience. But it is not just that the prodigal son sins against his father in violating his relationship to his father *and* sins against God in violating his relationship to God. There is a tighter connection than mere consistency. For the prodigal son *in* sinning against his father sins against God, given what God requires him to do and be in his relationship to his father. And this continuity exists, given that there is a God, whether the prodigal son does or does not acknowledge God and his relationship to God.

This dimension of the continuity between human sin morality and religious sin morality is, I believe, not greatly distant from Vincent Brümmer's meaning when he says that "the relation between the prayers and the moral life of the believer is an *internal* one."[53] Agreeing with Calvin, Brümmer defines prayer as an "exercise in faith," and, he says, "we can . . . say the same about the moral life of the believer"; for Brümmer, "in his moral life the believer relates to the world in fellowship with God, and in his prayer he seeks the fellowship with God in which he relates to the

---

53. Vincent Brümmer, *What Are We Doing When We Pray?* (London: SCM Press, 1984), 113 (Brümmer's emphasis).

world."[54] Brümmer is not using the category of sin morality; nor does he speak of faith relationships to God as such, although he does speak of fellowship with God. There are two points in what Brümmer says about the believer's fellowship with God that we should note. One is that it is pursued in prayer, and the other is that it is in fellowship with God that the believer lives the moral life. "It would be absurd," he says, "to think that we could enter through prayer into fellowship with God, if this is not manifested in the life we lead."[55]

I do not see here the implication that every moral life requires a conscious sense of fellowship with God, an entered faith relationship with God. Rather, Brümmer's comments are directed to the moral life *of believers*, and his claim is that, for believers, there is a necessary connection between prayer and their moral lives. We can extend Brümmer's comments to sin morality in the following way. *For believers*, prayer can deepen an individual faith relationship, and through prayer, with help, believers may come to a better understanding of their individual relationships' requirements; if they do, this same understanding will also help to deepen believers' understanding of the requirements of their moral lives. For sin morality, this is so because, at least for believers, understanding more deeply the requirements of their relationship to God will help them to understand more deeply the requirements of their relationships to persons. And this is wholly in accord with the first dimension of the continuity between human sin morality and religious sin morality.

In a second dimension of their continuity the two forms of sin morality are continuous by virtue of the place in the logics of each that is reserved for a fundamental, informing realization-discovery. In Chapter 3, I tried to show how the moral discovery of the inherent worth of persons as persons is a discovery of a certain type, a realization-discovery. When this discovery is made, one's person/person relationship to persons is realized, and as a part of this discovery there is an affective response in the respect/love range. It is the person/person relationship, I have argued, that is foundational to morality. It exists independently of our discovering it, but one who realizes it discovers the fundamental relationship that binds persons to persons as persons. One enters into the presence of persons in the sense that I elaborated.

For religious sin morality, there is an analogous realization-discovery of

54. Ibid., 111.
55. Ibid., 113.

the presence of God. This is the "religious discovery," and, in content, it is analogous to the moral discovery of the presence of persons.[56] Just as coming into the presence of persons is not coming into their physical presence, so coming into the presence of God is not coming to see that there is a God. It is not realizing that there is a God but coming into the presence of God, as one who already believes in God may do and as the Psalmist does in the Psalms (although anyone who did not believe in God but came into God's living presence would thereby come to see that there is indeed a God). Coming into the presence of God banishes indifference toward God, just as coming into the presence of persons banishes indifference toward persons. And, as another point of structural analogy, the religious discovery involves coming to realize that one stands in a personal relationship to the living God. Human sin morality and religious sin morality are continuous in this dimension because, for one reason, there is a close relationship in content between coming into the presence of persons and coming into the presence of God. However, they are continuous in this dimension for another reason as well: what prevents us from making the moral realization-discovery of the presence of persons prevents us from making the religious realization-discovery of the presence of God. If there is a moral discovery of the presence of persons to be made, what prevents us from making it, as I argued in Chapter 3, is a kind of blindness, the kind of blindness caused by self-deception. And that self-deception, in the case of the moral discovery, is caused by our selfishness or self-centeredness, which leads us to close our eyes to the inherent worth of persons—a recognition of which would entail for our emotions and actions toward persons much that we do not want to accept. If there is a religious discovery of the presence of God to be made, it is the same selfishness or self-centeredness that prevents that discovery. The fool of the Psalms is not saying that God does not exist, but that He does not matter—and if he did allow that God supremely matters, as he would have to allow if he overcame his self-deception and realized the presence of the living God, then he too would have to turn around his life. Notice that though what prevents the one discovery prevents the other, it does not follow that if we make the one discovery, we shall make the other.

56. I have discussed the "religious discovery" and its logic in *The Cognitivity of Religion*. See note 17 to Chapter 3 above. Also, for a more detailed discussion of the structural similarity between the discovery of the presence of persons and the discovery of the presence of God, see my "The Death of God and the Death of Persons," *Religious Studies* 16 (1980). There I try to show that the four elements of coming into the presence of persons (discussed above in Chapter 3) are analogous to elements of coming into the presence of God.

Self-deception is too subtle for that. Though we may discover that we have been deceiving ourselves regarding one matter, we may still fail to realize that we are deceiving ourselves regarding a related matter, even though the cause of the self-deception is the same in the two cases. It remains, however, that human sin morality and religious sin morality are continuous in that what prevents us from making the moral discovery is just what prevents us from making the religious discovery.

None of this, of course, is an argument that either of these discoveries has in fact been made. As I urged in Chapter 3, the only proof that the moral discovery has been made lies in our moral experience. The analogous point holds for the religious discovery. Still, we can be clear on this much: if anyone has discovered the presence of God, then there is a Divine presence to be discovered, and if anyone has discovered the presence of persons, then there is that presence to be discovered. In the latter case, discovering the presence of persons is discovering the inherent worth of persons. And this may be the place to raise the issue of how the affirmation of the inherent value of persons relates to the religious sense of our unworthiness. For if the religious sense of our unworthiness is incompatible with the affirmation of our inherent worth, and if the first is religiously necessary, then religious sin morality would end up being incompatible with human sin morality after all.

Within the Christian tradition there are, it seems, two related but competing religious intuitions: (1) in accord with Gen. 1.27, human beings are in the image of God, and (2) we human beings are fallen, wretched, broken, and distant from and unlike God. Not every Christian believer may be attracted by or have both of these intuitions; however, I suspect that each intuition seems right to many Christians. And the two intuitions together may appeal to not a few believers (I leave aside the question whether these or an analogous pair of intuitions might have an appeal in other religious traditions, such as Buddhism). These two religious intuitions appear to be in tension, but ultimately they are complementary and compatible, I suggest. What informs (2) is the sense that we human beings are in need of grace, that our faculties are limited, even corrupted, that we are broken or compromised in our understanding and will and can do nothing of worth by ourselves but need grace to understand and to begin to do as God wills. On the other hand, what informs (1) is the sense that persons, just as they are, as persons, have inherent worth. This sense corresponds with what is discovered when we enter the presence of persons and thereby discover the inherent worth of persons. As I have emphasized (and dwelt upon in Chapter 5), this inherent worth is the worth persons have as persons, which does not entail that persons have worth by virtue of ability or accomplishment, let alone moral accomplishment. Nor does it entail that there is no ontological distance between God and His creatures; it does not rule out the kind of uncleanness, caused by the ontological incommensuration of our nature and God's nature, that Marilyn Adams identifies as sin.

Julian of Norwich, who, as we have seen, is very much aware of our fallen and unclean state (although, for her, its cause is not our ontological distance from God, but our willful sins), says this: "We shall truly see in heaven without end that we have sinned grievously in this life; and notwithstanding this, we shall truly see that we were never hurt in his love, nor were we ever of less value in his sight."[57] That is, she is clear that the unworthiness we have because we are distant from God does not affect the value we have in God's sight as persons. In this connection we might once again recall the mother in Aristotle's *Nichomachean Ethics*, discussed in Chapter 5. Her love for her children, in opposition to Aristotle's categories of love and to their consternation, is not contingent on the merit of her children or proportionate to their earned value. As a mother loves her children, and as her children are not of less value in her sight even though they are uncaring or ungrateful, so, for Julian, "our heavenly Mother Jesus" is loving toward us, and we are not of less value in His sight even though we "have sinned grievously."

By way of contrast, Adams says that "finite creatures are not naturally or intrinsically valuable enough . . . to command God's love."[58] Now, it may well be that while we are commanded by God to love, neither God's love, nor any love, can be commanded by what we are. Would Adams allow that human beings as persons *deserve* to be loved? She seems, rather, to hold the view that God's love confers value.[59] This is the view that Anders Nygren seems to have held (for him, we will recall from Chapter 5, human beings have no value in themselves, but Divine Agape creates value in them). It is one of several theological views of Divine love that might be maintained.[60]

57. *Showings*, chap. 61, 300.
58. Adams, "Sin as Uncleanness," 21.
59. Ibid. And cf. her "Forgiveness: A Christian Model," *Faith and Philosophy* 8 (1991): 291.
60. W. G. Maclagan identifies three views of Divine love that "do not rely on any claim that persons as such have and can be seen to have an *intrinsic* worth" (Maclagan's emphasis). "First, and most obscurely," he says, "it might be maintained that the divine love *gives* a worth to its objects. . . . Or, secondly, it might be maintained that it is our bounden duty to be imitators of God, to assimilate our attitudes to the divine attitude so far as in us lies. . . . Or, thirdly, it might be

It is not, however, a view to which we are forced theologically. Rejecting it in favor of the view that persons do have intrinsic worth, we can allow that human persons are unworthy in the way or ways we have discussed and yet allow that they have inherent worth as persons. The two perceptions are compatible, and both together are compatible with human sin morality and religious sin morality individually and in conjunction.

These two forms of sin morality, then, may be said to be both compatible and continuous. Yet there can be a human sin morality divorced from a religious sin morality. So, although they are consistent and continuous, they are also independent, or at least human sin morality is independent of religious sin morality. Let me clarify this point by distinguishing it from a point made earlier. As I have suggested, the prodigal son directly violates his relationship to his father without his doing so being contingent upon his violating his relationship to God (even though he also violates his relationship to God): in this way the prodigal son violates his relationship to his father independently of his violating his relationship to God. The point that I want to bring out now, which is an epistemological point, is related but different. There is a sense in which human sin morality itself, as a morality form, is epistemologically independent of religious sin morality. And this is so even if there is a God.

Many have claimed that ethics is autonomous. While this claim can mean many things, a good part of what it means, in relation to religion, is that morality, as Henry Hazlitt says, "is not dependent upon any specific religious doctrine." "The great body of ethical rules," as he puts it, "have no necessary connection with any religious premises."[61] Extended to sin morality, the point becomes, moral rules, which have their source in human relationships, are discernible without reflection on our relationship with God. At least to this extent, I think, morality—that is, human sin morality—is independent of religion. Let me expand this point. Given that in order not to violate our relationship to God, we must not violate our relationships to persons, it follows that in coming to better appreciate our relationships to others, including the person/person relationship, we draw nearer to a better understanding of the requirements of our relationship to God. If this is so, however, it is so whether or not the person coming to a better appreciation of his or her relationships to other persons acknowledges

---

maintained that we ought, in simple gratitude to God, to show towards others the love He shows towards us" (Maclagan's emphasis). "Respect for Persons as Moral Principle I," *Philosophy* 35 (July 1960): 208. The first two we discussed in Chapter 5.

61. Henry Hazlitt, *The Foundations of Morality* (Princeton: D. Van Nostrand, 1964), 351.

that there is a God or a Divine will. An individual who enters into the presence of persons and realizes his or her universal person/person relationship to persons will strive to act with what is or is very close to love of neighbor, in accord with one of the great commandments. Such an individual will be acting in accord with God's will, but not necessarily consciously following God's will. For such an individual may not acknowledge that there is a God. As I pointed out, one may make the moral discovery of the inherent worth of persons without making the religious discovery: one may enter into the presence of persons without entering into the presence of God. Say that one acts with love toward others, but denies that there is a God. Though an individual in this position will not have entered a faith relationship to God, as religious believers do, one in this position will still be in a relationship to God, if there is a God, in that such an individual would yet be God's created being. And what we have just seen is that such a nonbeliever, in gaining a better understanding of the requirements of his or her relationships with other persons, gains a better understanding of the requirements of his or her relationship to God, even though that relationship is not acknowledged.[62] So, even if increased knowledge of the requirements of our relationships to persons is tied to increased knowledge of the requirements of our relationship to God, human sin morality remains epistemologically independent in the sense that we can follow it with no conscious reflection on the requirements of whatever relationship to God that we may have.

Hazlitt accepts the quasi-Freudian claim that religious belief, especially "belief in a God who sees and knows our every action, our every impulse and our every thought," helps "to secure observance of the moral code." For Hazlitt, though, religion "cannot tell us anything about what the specific moral rules ought to be."[63] This is a greater claim than the claim that we can identify moral rules without reference to or reflection on our relationship to God, and I think that it is not quite right. Given that there is a God, our coming to a deeper understanding of God's will could do wonders for our understanding of how we ought to behave toward others in our overt and interior actions. I remarked earlier, following Brümmer, that it is a part of the continuity between human sin morality and religious sin morality that in coming to better appreciate the requirements of our relationship to

62. We might say that such an individual has an *abiding relationship* to God, not by virtue of his or her faith, but by virtue of his or her practice. See *God-Relationships With and Without God,* 81–93, for an elaboration of this category of God-relationship.

63. Hazlitt, *The Foundations of Morality,* 352-53.

God—which involves doing God's will—we may come to better appreciate the requirements of our relationships to persons. If we come to understand better the love of our neighbor that God wills us to have, then we will come to understand better the requirements of our relationship to our neighbor. It remains, however, that we can come to an appreciation of the requirements of our relationships to persons without reflecting on our relationship to God, and that human sin morality is epistemologically independent in this way.

If I am right, human sin morality and religious sin morality are continuous. But could there as well be a religious guilt morality or a religious shame morality? In a sense there can be both. Let us take guilt morality first.

Perhaps the first thing to observe is that we may be said to be *guilty* of our sins. This by itself does not indicate a guilt morality, though. What it indicates is the presence of a fault morality, a morality form that accommodates blameworthiness. And sin morality, of course, is a fault morality as much as guilt morality. Where it differs from guilt morality is in its understanding of the basis of the fault. For guilt morality, as we have seen, we are at fault when we wrongfully violate a moral rule. For sin morality, we are at fault when we violate a relationship, and if we are at fault in breaking a moral rule, we are at fault precisely because in doing so we violate a relationship. In this way, as I argued in the last chapter, sin morality underlies guilt morality.

In the Judeo-Christian tradition, and in other religious traditions, it is ackowledged that God has given certain commandments to human beings. These commandments, let us allow, amount to moral rules. Also, it may be that, for some, God's commandments are equated with the moral rules of conventional guilt morality. Now, if this were done, one following such a morality would be following a religious guilt morality. But the notion of sin would have been reduced to the notion of violating a conventional moral rule—a rule taken to be given by God. "Sin" would become another word for "morally wrong," and moral wrongness would be determined as it is in conventional guilt morality. Such a religious guilt morality would correspond to the third view of sin, discussed above, according to which sin is just another name for moral wrongdoing. More accurately, it would correspond to that construction of the third view which equates sin with wrongdoing and equates wrongdoing with breaking the moral rules of conventional guilt morality.

But there is another form of religious guilt morality. In this other form of religious guilt morality, God's commands would not be equated with the moral rules of conventional guilt morality, but sin would still be seen precisely as violating one of the moral rules established by God's commands. That is, for this morality form, it would not be a sin to transgress one of God's commands *because* in so doing we violate our relationship to God: the sin would lie just in breaking the rule. This form of religious guilt morality is superficially like the second view of sin that we discussed, the command view, although finally the two are at odds. The command view of sin, we recall, understands sin to be a violation of God's commands. The difference between this view of sin and the form of religious guilt morality before us has to do with the place that can be given to a relationship to God. The command view of sin can welcome the buttressing explanation that violating God's commandments is a sin against God just because in violating a commandment we in our disobedience violate our relationship to God. But a religious guilt morality cannot accept this. If a religious guilt morality accepts such an understanding of *why* violating God's commands is sinful, it ceases to be a guilt morality, properly understood, and becomes a sin morality.

Also, for the second form of religious guilt morality, as for the first, the commitment of religious practice is seen negatively, as a matter of *not* breaking a rule. Unlike a religious sin morality, neither is a scale morality. In short, the differences between a human sin morality and guilt morality identified in the last chapter apply here. And here too it can be argued that a religious sin morality explains a religious guilt morality, but not the other way around.

Can religious morality also take the form of a shame morality? I think that it can. And, as with religious guilt morality, there can be different forms of a religious shame morality. Of course, we should not think that every time shame is mentioned in a religious work a shame morality is in the background. We have seen that Julian of Norwich, who speaks of shame and our being ashamed, is not to be understood as speaking of that shame which is internal to shame morality. Nevertheless, as I pointed out in Chapter 11, there can be a religious shame morality, for there is no reason internal to shame morality why a religious figure or ideal could not serve as an individual's model identity, or ego ideal. But, as I also noted, there can be a religious shame morality only in a qualified sense.

Let us imagine someone who sets before himself or herself an ego ideal of a saintly life. Perhaps a particular saint will be used as the ideal that informs this person's shame morality, although it might also be that the ideal is an amalgam of saintly virtues, religious maxims, teachings, and story-lessons.

Such a religious shame morality, however, is ultimately irreconcilable with religious devotion as it is understood in Christianity and other theistic traditions. One with a religious shame morality, irrespective of the content of the ego ideal that informs it, serves that ego ideal. Within a shame morality, to the extent that one fails to attain one's ego ideal, one will be ashamed; and to the extent that one does attain one's ego ideal, one will be proud. In *The Brothers Karamazov* Dostoyevsky gives us a portrait of such spiritual pride in the Macarius-like ascetic, Father Ferapont. Father Ferapont's religious ideal is to subsist on next to no nourishment. However, what brings his underlying shame morality into tension with his religious tradition is not the content of his ego ideal, or not that alone. What inescapably does so is that his primary dedication is to attaining his ideal—something he is proud of doing, in accord with his shame morality. There are two related reasons why a religious shame morality is at odds with religious commitment to God and to doing the will of God. First, in a shame morality one's primary dedication is to one's ego ideal, not to God's will. Second, one's moral success is something of which one is proud. But pride, to put it most forcefully, is a sin. Within the tradition in which Father Ferapont stands, Christianity, one's primary devotion is to the will of God, which one should humbly follow. Notice what would happen if one following a religious shame morality made it a part of one's ego ideal that one be humble. If one sought to live in accordance with a religious shame morality with this requirement as a part of one's ideal, one in effect would be aspiring to the confused, even contradictory, state of attaining a humility of which one should be proud—a state not impossible to aspire to, even if impossible to attain.

We find an appreciation of the tension between seeking to avoid shame and acting for the sake of God in devotional writing. We find it, for instance, in the spiritual writings of Richard of St. Victor. Richard of St. Victor, as we have seen (in Chapter 11), distinguished between improper shame—shame for the wrong things— and "good and ordered" shame, or "true shame," which is preceded and accompanied by hatred of the vices. However, this is not to say that he urged shame as our moral guide, not even true shame. In *The Twelve Patriarchs* Richard uses each patriarch as a symbol for a religious virtue (Judah represents love of God, Zabulon represents hatred of vices, and so on). In the same way, "the love of Dina" represents true shame in Richard's symbolism. Richard keenly appreciated

that one might do for the love of Dina—out of a concern with shamefacedness—what one might do "for God." And he saw that those who act for the
love of Dina rather than for God—and so out of concern with shamefacedness, even though the shame is good and ordered—embody "love of one's
own excellence and love of vainglory."[64] In short, in our terms, he perceived
an incompatibility between pursuing an ego ideal and having a primary
dedication to God.

What all this shows is not that a religious shame morality is impossible.
In fact, as Dostoyevsky and Richard of St. Victor appreciated in their
respective ways, such a morality is quite possible. But it is possible only in a
qualified sense in that it must be in tension with religious devotion to God.
That tension I have brought out, so far, with no reference to religious sin
morality. If we allow that religious sin morality incorporates a correct
understanding of the nature of sin and that doing the will of God is a
requirement of our relationship to God, then we can express the above
tension with an explicit reference to religious sin morality. One who lives
within a shame morality seeks to attain one's ego ideal: that is one's primary
dedication. One who lives within a religious sin morality seeks to live in
accord with one's God-relationship: that is one's primary dedication. Again
a difference between the two has to do with pride. In the former case one
will be proud of one's spiritual accomplishments quite independently of any
relationship to God. In the latter one must live according to one's God-
relationship for God's sake, not the sake of one's ego ideal, and pride as it
relates to one's own ideal marks a turning away from one's God-relationship.

This much, I think, is correct. Some, however, have suggested that
religious morality, Christian ethics in particular, importantly involves a
religious ideal. Can this be right? In a fairly clear way different religious
traditions involve moral "values"—rules regarding right action, but also
proposed virtues. Considered in this light, the different religious traditions
may be seen as proposing the moral values by which human beings ought to
live. Keith Ward suggests that in the religious traditions—or "ethical
systems," as he says—of Confucianism, Buddhism, and Christianty "a
certain group of values is selected as constituting an 'ideal' of human life;
and this ideal is usually paradigmatically presented in the form of a perfect
human exemplar of the ideal—Confucius, the Buddha or Jesus, in the
examples just cited." The ideal in the case of Christianity, exhibited in the

---

64. Richard of St. Victor, *The Twelve Patriarchs*, in *Richard of St. Victor*, trans. and intro. Grover
A. Zinn (New York: Paulist Press, 1979), 106–7.

life of the historical Jesus, is "that of the man of unlimited charity, humility, courage and temperance," Ward suggests.[65] For Ward, Christians refer their "interpretation of the moral life back to the historical Jesus in two distinct though related ways."[66] The values embodied in the life of Jesus are accepted by Christians on the authority of Jesus. And also Jesus' life, by embodying the perfectly realized ideal to be pursued by Christians, helps Christians understand what a realization of unlimited charity—love—humility, courage, and temperance requires.

There is something very right in Ward's suggestion, it seems to me. There is a sense in which religious adherents, and Christians in particular, do or might hold before themselves an ideal exemplar of the life they would lead. However, perhaps contrary to appearances, such a moral practice does not in itself amount to following a religious shame morality. It does not because the ideal that is pursued may not operate as an ego ideal. Consider Buddhism. The moral teachings of the Buddha are embodied in the Noble Eightfold Path, and the ideal attainment of those teachings is the Buddha himself. A Buddhist, then, could follow Buddhist teachings by seeking to approach the ideal exemplified by the Buddha. But he or she would not be following a shame morality unless the pursued ideal had become an internalized ego ideal, and it would not be that unless shame were felt at failure and pride were felt at success. Instead, sorrow might be felt at failure, and peace might be felt as one began to attain to the ideal. Buddhism, as a religion oriented toward the goal of nirvana, may be understood as involving what I earlier (in Chapter 10) called a "path morality." In seeking to draw near to the ideal of the Buddha, a Buddhist may simply and purely be seeking to follow the path to nirvana laid out by the Buddha. We cannot infer that merely because an ideal is pursued, a shame morality is present.

The same is true in regard to Chrisitianity: we cannot reason that if a Christian ideal is pursued by Christians, they are therefore following a religious shame morality. In the case of Christianity, as compared with Buddhism, there are other reasons why a shame morality would not be present. For Christians, the single, preeminent ideal must be that of Jesus. Saint Paul in fact says, "Be imitators of me, as I am of Christ" (1 Cor. 11.1), and "be imitators of God, as beloved children. And walk in love, as Christ loved us and gave himself up for us." (Eph. 5.1–2). This theme of imitating Christ, or holding before oneself Christ as a model of perfection,

65. Ward, *Ethics and Christianity*, 93.
66. Ibid., 154.

was taken up in the late Middle Ages by the author of *The Imitation of Christ*. Neither Paul nor the author of *The Imitation of Christ* is espousing that Christ be taken as a model identity in a shame morality. All is vanity, says the author of the *Imitation*, "except to love God and serve Him only." And doing so, in the categories of the *Imitation*, requires a kind of dying to self and being grounded in true humility, as opposed to serving one's own ideal.

Imitating God or Christ in this way is not only different from but incompatible with having Christ as a model identity or ego ideal in a shame morality—something that is possible to do, but only at the cost of the tension we have identified. They are incompatible because of the role of pride in shame morality, on the one hand, and, on the other hand, the requirement of humility in the Christian ideal, as implicitly found in Paul and explicitly found in the *Imitation* and in Ward's formulation of the values of the Christian ideal.

Holding before oneself the life of Jesus as an ideal, though incompatible with taking Jesus as an ego ideal within a shame morality, is compatible with following a religious sin morality. For one thing, pursuing an ideal is in accord with sin morality's character as a scale morality, since one in pursuing an ideal can begin to draw near to the ideal and yet draw nearer. This point, though, can equally well be made regarding a shame morality, which also is a scale morality. What shows that imitating Christ, or pursuing the ideal of the historical Jesus, is compatible with religious sin morality is this: for Christians, Jesus, as the embodiment of Christian values perfectly realized, is the primary, or a primary, exemplification of perfectly living as one ought in God's eyes. That is, He is, on the view of religious sin morality, taken as the primary, or a primary, exemplification of living perfectly within a fully realized God-relationship. The life of Jesus shows Christians what truly living in that relationship requires. Pursuing the ideal of Jesus, then, is one way to draw nearer to realizing the requirements of one's relationship to God.

The main point that I am making here, it should be noticed, applies to other religious ideals that Christians might follow in an effort to live in accord with a relationship to God. Following a religious ideal other than the life of Jesus, like following the ideal embodied in the life of Jesus, does not in itself amount to following that religious ideal as an ego ideal in a shame morality and may even be incompatible with doing so. There are other possible Christian ideals, of course, ideals patterned after the lives of other exemplars of Christianity or ideals that are composed of those virtues and spiritual attributes that are seen as defining an ideal Christian life. There may be several possible ideals of this latter sort. There are two in particular that we should note, for they seem initially to be at odds with both the ideal of Jesus, as Ward presents it, and with my main point about Christian religious ideals. The particular ideals that I have in mind are those that some liberation theologians and some feminist theologians might bring forward as an ideal of the Christian life.

We find such an ideal embodied in the theological reflections of Gustavo Gutiérrez. For Gutiérrez, the Christian ideal that presents itself to our contemporary world is one that may still be seen as embodied in the life of Jesus.[67] But it is an ideal of social commitment to the exploited social classes. It is an activist ideal devoted to the removal of poverty and injustice in the structure of society. While voluntarily assuming poverty can be an act of love and of solidarity with the poor,[68] allowing poverty is an expression of sin and the negation of love.[69] It is a sin because it constitutes a "breach of friendship with God and with other men."[70] And in order to oppose poverty and to love concretely we must become practically commit-ted, even to the point of not avoiding confrontations.[71]

Much in Gutiérrez' vision, we might observe, is in accord with, and very nearly in the language of, sin morality—notably the characterization of sin as a breach in our relationship with God and with other persons. Of course, some is not, as when, citing Genesis, he proclaims and accepts the idea that God has given the earth to human beings to dominate[72] (this is the Dominion Theory, about which, more in Chapter 15). As far as I can see, however, this element of Gutiérrez' thinking is not essential to a formulation of his liberation ideal. Our present concern is whether the liberation ideal Gutiérrez brings forward is contrary to the more traditional Christian ideal as Ward formulates it or contrary to the point I argued for relating to shame morality. It is contrary to neither, I submit. To the extent we sense a conflict between the more traditional Christian ideal and Gutiérrez' activist ideal, we do so, I suspect, because we think that Christian love is not compatible with the kind of social activism Gutiérrez' ideal entails. Gutiér-rez' ideal involves activity, confrontation, commitment, opposition to politi-

---

67. Gustavo Gutiérrez, A *Theology of Liberation*, ed. and trans. Sister Caridad Inda and John Eagleson (Maryknoll, N.Y.: Obris Books, 1973), 225 ff.
68. Ibid., 330.
69. Ibid., 295.
70. Ibid., 175.
71. Ibid., 275.
72. Ibid., 159 and 295.

cal powers—and love. It is not therefore inconsistent, however. Confrontation need not be violent, and in itself it does not contradict love, as Gutiérrez says. In fact it can be argued that not opposing injustice is a failure of love, a failure of love toward not only the oppressed but toward the oppressors as well, for the oppressors by their wrongful exercise of power alienate themselves from others, and so harm themselves as well as others. [73] If poverty is seen as a product of social injustice, and if love of neighbor is understood as requiring us to oppose injustice, then working to eliminate poverty is in accord with the kind of Christian ideal Ward presents. And, to speak to the second part of our question, if love—love of neighbor, charity in the full Christian sense—is a part of Gutiérrez' Christian ideal, then this ideal cannot be an ego ideal in a shame morality. One cannot love others for their sake in fulfillment of our relationship to others and in accord with the religious ideal if one loves for the sake of meeting one's own ego ideal (just as we saw that Lord Jim, following his ego ideal, finally cannot have the virtue of courage in the full sense).

The other religious ideal that seems to be at odds with a more traditional Christian ideal is a feminist religious ideal. Valerie Saiving writes:

> The temptations of woman *as woman* are not the same as the temptations of man *as man*, and the specifically feminine forms of sin—"feminine" not because they are confined to women or because women are incapable of sinning in other ways but because they are outgrowths of the basic feminine character structure—have a quality which can never be encompassed by such terms as "pride" and "will-to-power." They are better suggested by such items as triviality, distractability, and diffuseness; lack of an organizing center or focus; dependence on others for one's own self-definition; tolerance at the expense of excellence; inability to respect the boundaries of privacy; sentimentality, gossipy sociability, and mistrust of reason—in short, underdevelopment or negation of the self. [74]

Since these words were written, it has come to be widely recognized—and is regarded as a commonplace among feminist thinkers—that while pride may be the primary sin for men, negation of the self, or self-abnegation, is

---

73. Ibid., 275–76.
74. Valerie Saiving, "The Human Situation: A Feminine View," *Womanspirit Rising*, ed. Carol P. Christ and Judith Plaskow (San Francisco: Harper & Row, 1979), 37 (Saiving's emphasis).

the primary sin of women.[75] The ideal women should strive toward, because it corrects the kind of sin that tempts them more than men on this feminist analysis, is, or centrally includes, self-realization.

Does this implicit ideal contradict the more traditional Christian ideal? To the extent it seems to, it does so because self-realization seems to be contrary to the element of humility. We need to ask, then, What is the relationship between humility and self-abnegation? First, what is humility? Is it pusillanimity? Is it conformity or servility? Is it acceptance of what is unjust and degrading? Humility is none of these things, I suggest—although many who have had humility may have had these other attributes too. The humility of Christ, for Ward, we will recall, goes with courage, and he is right in his implicit affirmation of their compatibility. Self-abnegation, or the form of it of concern to Saiving and others, on the other hand, does express itself in pusillanimity, servility, and in those other modes of passivity Saiving names. Self-realization, then, requires overcoming these modes of passivity, but it does not for this reason require rejecting humility.

What humility opposes is not self-realization but pride, in accord with what we saw earlier (in Chapter 11). It opposes, specifically, the private pride that one feels when one draws near one's ego ideal, or model identity, in a shame morality. It we avoid pusillanimity and do not conform when there is reason not to and work to attain excellence, need we take pride in our efforts or success? Not at all. And we will not, in the relevant sense of pride, if these attainments are not sought on behalf of an internalized ego ideal.

The feminist point before us is *not* that humility is a sin for women or that pride is a virtue for women. Saiving's point, we should bear in mind, is that pride does not cover the gamut of sin, and it misleads us regarding women's experience to think that it does. The greater temptation for women is the temptation to weakness and self-negation due, as she says, to the "basic feminine character structure." She is clear that her point is not that men are never tempted in the way of self-anegation or that women are never tempted in the way of pride. Her point, then, allows that both women and men can sin either through the negation of self or through pride. This feminist point allows also, it is worth our noting, that sin is a violation of a relationship. When women—or men—practice to excess obedience, conformity, and other forms of passivity, as Judith Plaskow puts it, they

75. Cf. Judith Plaskow, *Sex, Sin, and Grace* (Lanham, Md.: University Press of America, 1980), 2–3.

"undermine" or violate the "self's relationship to itself and ultimately to God."[76] Notice how Plaskow sees self-abnegation as in part an undermining or violation of the relationship that one has to oneself. In the language of sin morality, it violates the person/person relationship one has to oneself; it does so because it denies or undermines the inherent worth one has as a person. Self-realization, as required by respect for oneself as a person, as a being with inherent worth, must oppose self-abnegation, we can say, for self-abnegation denies one's inherent worth. But self-realization does not therefore oppose humility.

So, finally, there is no tension between self-realization, which is central to the ideal feminist thinkers advance as the relevant religious ideal for women, and humility in the traditional Christian ideal. Though the feminist ideal opposes and is a corrective for self-abnegation, that does not make it a recommendation of pride or a repudiation of humility. In this way the feminist Christian ideal that addresses women's experience is not incompatible with the traditional Christian ideal—even if at odds with the way many have applied the traditional ideal to women and to men, namely those who have understood humility as requiring servility and blind conformity. Could the feminist ideal of self-realization be an ego ideal in a shame morality? If the ideal is self-realization in accord with one's inherent worth, then such an ideal may or may not be made part of a shame morality. But it need not be, and it would not be if such an ideal were pursued in order to respect one's relationship to oneself and to draw nearer to realizing one's relationship to God—in accord with Plaskow's thinking. To follow this ideal, then, is not ipso facto to follow a shame morality and may instead be an element of human sin morality or religious sin morality, or both.

The main thing that I have tried to show in this chapter is that human sin morality and religious sin morality are not only compatible but are continuous with one another. Yet, as we have seen, they are also independent morally and epistemologically. While the relationship between human sin morality and religious sin morality has been our main concern, before taking up this concern we examined various notions of sin in order to defend the concept of sin integral to sin morality. And finally we have tried to show how religious guilt morality and religious shame morality, though possible morality forms, must, unlike either human sin morality or religious sin morality, be in tension with religious commitment.

76. Ibid., 2.

14

Sin/Relationship Morality and the Adam and Eve Story

Human sin morality and religious sin morality, I argued in the last chapter, are continuous. Both are forms of relationship morality, or of what we may, combining our descriptive designations, call "sin/relationship morality." And, I argued in the last chapter, there is an essential opposition between religious sin morality and a religious shame morality. In the same or a similar way, I argued earlier (in Chapter 12), there is a tension between shame morality and sin morality, human sin morality. Not that a person cannot in some manner follow both a shame morality and sin morality in different areas of his or her life. A person could even follow both, in some manner, where the two conflict. We cannot argue that because two morality forms conflict, no person could follow both at once: we human beings are too capable of living with confusion and tension for such an argument to be sustained. The tension, however, would remain. In this chapter I want to look at the tension between shame morality and sin morality, or relationship morality, through a different lens. I want to look at the biblical story of Adam and Eve and draw out of it both its sin element and its shame element, for both are present in the biblical account taken as a whole.

In my treatment of the Genesis story of Adam and Eve the primary thing I want to do is to distinguish and discuss two separable elements of the story of Adam and Eve, one having to do with their attaining moral knowledge and one having to do with their shame at their nakedness. The significance of these two elements, as will emerge, is best understood by bringing to bear on the Adam and Eve story, or stories, what we have seen of the contrast between sin morality and shame morality. And finally, in this chapter I shall reflect on the implications of what will have emerged for our understanding of loss of innocence.

Though sin morality and shame morality are in some ways similar, ultimately sin morality vividly opposes shame morality. For our purposes in this chapter, we need to keep in mind certain of their irrevocable differences. Let me then set forth again, in outline, the relevant elements of the logics of the two moralities:

Shame Morality
1. One serves, seeks to attain, one's ego ideal or model identity.
2. It is not a fault morality.
3. Failure in it is a matter of shame; success is a matter of pride.

Sin Morality
1. One seeks to live in accord with one's relationships.
2. It is a fault morality.
3. Failure is sin, a violation of a relationship; success is living within and respecting one's relationships.

However, as we have seen, there are two continuous forms of sin morality: human sin morality and religious sin morality. Our concern in this chapter focuses on the religious form. Accordingly, here in outline are the relevant elements of the logic of religious sin morality:

Religious Sin Morality
1. One seeks to live in accord with one's relationship to God.
2. It is a fault morality.
3. Failure is sin, a violation of a relationship; success is living within and respecting a relationship, one's relationship with God.

Now let us turn to the story of Adam and Eve as found in the first three chapters of Genesis. Here it is in summary:

> God creates Adam in His own image. He puts Adam in the garden of Eden, but commands him not to eat of the tree of the knowledge of good and evil. God creates Eve, and the man and his wife are both naked and not ashamed. However, the serpent says to Eve that if she eats of the forbidden tree, her eyes will be opened, and she will be like God, knowing good and evil. Eve sees that the wisdom of the tree is to be desired. She eats of the tree and gives its fruit to Adam, who eats also. Their eyes are opened, and they

know they are naked, and they cover themselves. When God calls to Adam he is afraid. He tells God that he has eaten of the tree. God says, "Behold, the man has become like one of us, knowing good and evil." Having made garments for them, God banishes Adam and Eve from the garden of Eden, lest they eat of the tree of life.

How are we to understand this story? As we know, there are two creation stories in Genesis, but furthermore, I find two distinct and very different elements within the Genesis story of Adam and Eve after they have been placed in the garden of Eden: one is their coming to be ashamed of their nakedness; the other is their gaining knowledge of good and evil. It is almost as though two stories were being told together, their elements intermingled. I will not speculate that there are two merged stories with perhaps two separate sources. Such a speculation is beyond my concern. My concern is with these two separable elements of the Adam and Eve story, however they came to be incorporated into the story.

Adam and Eve do something wrong. What is this wrong thing they do? Is it their gaining moral knowledge? How can it be? Surely gaining moral knowledge per se, gaining knowledge of good and evil per se, is good. Our coming to appreciate how we can unintentionally hurt others is a part of valuable moral growth, one would think. So too is our coming to appreciate how certain habits we may have allowed to develop in ourselves are open to moral improvement. So too is our coming to appreciate how we may have the capacity to do evil. And so too is our coming to understand and appreciate the legitimate demands of justice that may be put forward on the part of those half a world away. All these seem to be, or to involve, valuable increases in moral knowledge. In any case, I want to start with an acknowledgment of what must strike many as a correct intuition: gaining moral knowledge, in itself, cannot be morally wrong. Knowledge, or gaining knowledge, *ceteris paribus*, is a moral good, and it is especially good if the knowledge is moral knowledge.

Let me offer a caveat, so that this point is not misunderstood. The intuitive point that moral knowledge is good, is a moral good, does not imply that a life of seeking knowledge is the best life or even that all knowledge is sunny and good. Accepting it does not require us to side with the Enlightenment and its bright-faced naïveté regarding the heart of darkness. Perhaps, in accord with a suggestion we noted in Chapter 8, there are some truths about ourselves that we are better off not knowing at certain points in our lives. Perhaps, perhaps not. To say knowledge of good and evil is good leaves it open whether all knowledge is good.

But does God not punish Adam and Eve for gaining knowledge of good and evil? I do not think so. In fact Adam and Eve had some knowledge of good and evil before they ate of the tree. They must have in order to have received and understood God's command as a moral command about what they ought not to do. In the understanding of many, going back at least to Clement of Alexandria, Adam's sin was disobedience, that is, doing what God had commanded him not to do.[1] Herbert Morris, however, in his reflections on Adam and Eve, suggests that though they are guilty of disobeying God, they have no moral culpability in disobeying.[2] Morris says this because, on his view, before they eat of the tree, they have no moral knowledge: they are like children who do what is wrong but do so in all innocence, without moral understanding, and so are not morally blameworthy for their acts. Given the internal structure of the story, I do not think that this interpretation can be right. If it were, Adam and Eve would not be morally culpable, and hence not deserving of punishment. But their being banished from the garden of Eden looks very much like God's punishment of Adam and Eve.

So Adam and Eve were morally culpable, and so they did have at least some moral knowledge in receiving God's command. Thus, in eating of the tree they are not gaining a first knowledge of good and evil. But, moreover, if knowledge of good and evil in itself is good, it is not gaining further knowledge of good and evil, not this in itself, that is their wrongful act for which they are punished.

Their wrongful action, in its full dimensions, begins to become clear when we enquire into the other element in the Genesis story: the shame that Adam and Eve have of their nakedness, their newly acquired shame.

They sin by disobeying God, that is, on the view of religious sin morality, they violate their relationship to God by disobeying Him, for a requirement of their relationship to God is obedience. But, moreover, they disobey God in their desire to have God's knowledge of good and evil, to have God's wisdom, to be like God. In the story the serpent beguiles Eve by exciting her desire to be like God. When Adam and Eve eat of the tree, they desire to be like unto God in having His knowledge of good and evil, as opposed to merely desiring to attain increased knowledge of good and evil per se.

1. Elaine Pagels, *Adam, Eve, and the Serpent* (New York: Random House, 1988), xxiii.
2. Herbert Morris, "Lost Innocence," in *On Guilt and Innocence: Essays in Legal Philosophy and Moral Psychology* (Berkeley and Los Angeles: University of California Press, 1976), 141.

They are already in the image of God, but now they have acquired an ego ideal, which is to be godlike, a very different thing. With it comes a new acute form of self-consciousness that goes with aspiring toward this—or any—model identity.

In the story we are told that the eyes of Adam and Eve are opened, and they know that they are naked. But when their eyes are opened to their nakedness, they do not come to see that being naked is morally wrong. Seeing that they are naked with their new eyes is not an instance of increased knowledge of good and evil. They do not discover that all along it was evil or wrong for them to be naked. They could not discover this, because it was not wrong for them to be naked. God did not forbid their being naked, and in fact He instituted their nakedness by leaving them thus before one another in His creation. Nor, as far as I can see, did it become wrong or evil for them to be naked after eating the fruit. True, God clothes Adam and Eve when He banishes them. But this is not tantamount to God's regarding as wrong their being naked after eating of the tree: He may have clothed them out of compassion for the shame they would feel unclothed or merely to help them withstand the rigors of their new life. No, their eyes are opened to their nakedness in a different sense: they begin to see or become aware of their nakedness in a new self-conscious way, in the way of shame and pride. Hence they react in the way of shame by covering up.

Their eyes are opened to their nakedness as something at odds with their new ego ideal. Not being naked is a part of this ideal, and they see their nakedness as they had not seen it before. They see self-consciously that they are naked. And they are ashamed. For now not being naked is a part of the ideal they would attain. Now they will be proud of being thus and so (approaching their model identity), but ashamed of not being thus and so (being at odds with their model identity), which is symbolized by nakedness. Nakedness in the story represents or symbolizes much beyond itself. It is an instance of something like metonymy, I suggest, so that nakedness represents all that they will be ashamed of—their nakedness, but also not being wise and, in general, not being like God. Their nakedness is a psychologically well-chosen symbol, for we can well imagine one's being ashamed of one's nakedness and proud of being clothed in any cultural setting in which being clothed imparts a certain status and being unclothed is lowly; in the same way, we can easily imagine one's being proud of the fineness of one's clothes in a setting in which all are clothed. Of course, we should not infer that being clothed is an attribute of God, as wisdom is a traditional attribute of God, although being clothed may be a part of how Adam and Eve think of being godlike or lordlike.

Notice that it does not follow from this interpretation that we today who would not consider going about naked are ashamed of our nakedness. Rather, such nakedness would be embarrassing, not to mention in poor taste and, in public, a violation of law. In a nudist community, though, it would be a matter neither for shame nor for embarrassment. The purpose of the myth, or story, on this interpretation, is not to teach us something about the inherent shamefulness of nakedness, or the inherent wrongness of nakedness or of gaining moral knowledge. Rather, the story teaches us something about shame and pride and about rebellious disobedience and sin.

It is not wrong, then, for Adam and Eve to come to appreciate better moral rightness; it is not wrong to become more sensitive to the require- ments of morality, which, from the perspective of sin morality, is a matter of appreciating better what violates relationships—in particular, in religious sin morality, what would violate one's relationship to God. Nor is it wrong for them to be naked before one another. The wrong thing they do in part is to disobey God, but more than that, it is their disobeying God in their desire to be like God. In doing so they take up a shame morality. They acquire an ego image of themselves that they are ashamed of not attaining. And now their service will be, at least in part, to a shame morality informed by their ego ideal, and, as I argued in the last chapter, a shame morality is in tension with a religious sin morality, even if the ego ideal is religious. In pursuing their new ego ideal, to the extent they do so, they will seek to attain a godlike stature, of which they can be proud, in tension with and in opposition to their serving God in their relationship to God.

The Adam and Eve story in Genesis is also a story of loss of innocence. And the sin and shame aspects of the Adam and Eve story are reflected in this dimension of the story as well. I want now to take up this dimension of the story because our doing so will allow us to bring into relief in a different way the sin and shame aspects of the story.

The phrase "loss of innocence" can refer to several rather different human phenomena, several of which may be seen as symbolized by the Adam and Eve story, but not all of which are relevant to our present concern. For instance, loss of innocence in one form, it may be said, occurs as a function of biological maturation and the natural emergence of sexual desire: the child matures, becomes a young adult, and in so doing loses the sexual innocence of childhood. This is a clear and coherent sense, although this particular sense does not fit the Adam and Eve story very well, it seems to me. For Adam and Eve are one flesh before they decide to eat of the tree: they do not gain sexual maturity as a result of eating of the tree. Also, there is the lust interpretation of loss of innocence. On this interpretation, loss of innocence is the awakening of lust, as distinguished from sexual maturation. In the Genesis story Adam and Eve were husband and wife before they ate of the tree, and presumably a part of their conjugal relationship was sexual. But, on this interpretation, as long as they are innocent, they do not lust after one another. Adam and Eve may have lost innocence in this sense; arguably this sense fits the story. And there may be other interpretations that can be sustained. But there are two interpretations of the human phenomenon of loss of innocence, or two forms of loss of innocence, that particularly relate to our concern, for they correlate with the sin and shame aspects of the Adam and Eve story:

(1) Loss of innocence occurs when moral knowledge is acquired. This interpretation has two versions. (1a) Loss of innocence occurs when we come to realize that we have moral obligations hitherto innocently unrecognized, and (1b) loss of innocence occurs when we gain an experiential knowledge of evil. The other interpretation that we must consider and juxtapose to the first is that (2) loss of innocence is acquiring a kind of self-consciousness, a shame consciousness.

1. The first interpretation sees loss of innocence as the result of gaining new or deeper moral knowledge. Both versions of this interpretation deserve our attention. For (1a), we lose our innocence when it comes home to us that we have obligations, especially obligations to others, that we had in all innocence not recognized. For this version, loss of innocence is a loss of ignorance of good and evil understood primarily as an ignorance of what is right and wrong, what we ought to do and ought not to do. This version seems to me to be coherent and applicable to our moral experience and, indeed, to apply to various spheres of human affairs. We at times speak of someone innocently mistaking one person for another or innocently thinking that something is true when it is false. In these cases we regard as innocent the ignorance that leads to the mistake, rather than accuse someone of being naïve, which carries with it the attribution of an ignorance that ought to have been corrected. In such cases—when we innocently mistake one person for another or think that something true is false—that which we learn and which brings about a loss of innocence is not that we have an obligation we had not recognized, although the judgment that we made an innocent mistake is the moral judgment that we are not blamewor-

thy. In these two cases the loss of innocence is not precisely a loss of *moral* innocence, however. The loss of innocence identified by (1a), we may say, is this species of a loss of innocence as it is found in the moral sphere, where it occurs just when we come to realize we have obligations to which we were innocently oblivious. This version of the first interpretation, according to which loss of innocence is the result of gaining this kind of moral knowledge, may fit the Adam and Eve story fairly well. Their eating the fruit symbolizes their, and our, gaining a depth of moral knowledge regarding obligations to one another and responsibility for one another that marks their, and our, departure from the moral innocence of childhood. The judgment that this interpretation fits the story is supported by the reflection that Adam and Eve's quickly accomplished act of eating the fruit can symbolize something very different from itself, namely the very long and perhaps tortuous process of gaining moral knowledge, a finer appreciation of our obligations to those near us and a new appreciation of our obligations to those neighbors who are strangers; and it is supported by the reflection that the knowledge gained by Adam and Eve need not be a first moral knowledge (which, I have argued, they had before eating the fruit) but, rather, further moral knowledge, removing their innocent ignorance about matters whose moral dimension now comes home to them.

1b. In this version of the first way of understanding loss of innocence Adam and Eve lose their innocence by gaining moral knowledge of a very different kind, which, moreover, they must learn in a particular way. Morris suggests and develops such a construction, and here too I will draw upon his account, although I will amend it somewhat.[3] Morris is interested in a kind of moral innocence that children, but perhaps not only children, may have. In this state of innocence children may perform acts that are wrong, for which they are responsible, but for the performance of which they bear no moral culpability. An instance of this may occur when a child, in all innocence, in a loud voice gratuitously announces to a guest the undeniable truth "You're fat!" The child is not being malicious and may well be unaware of the wounding nature of such an observation; the child may well think of himself or herself as following the parental instruction "Always tell the truth." Such a child would have moral innocence, at least to an extent, that is, at least regarding some matters; and it is a state of innocence that is lost when moral knowledge is acquired. This much holds for both this version and the first version of loss of innocence seen as gaining moral

---

3. Morris develops his account of loss of innocence in "Lost Innocence."

knowledge, where gaining moral knowledge is gaining knowledge of our obligations. Loss of innocence in the definite sense Morris goes on to develop, however, comes not with a knowledge of what is right and wrong but with "a knowledge of evil and the set of dispositions to act and feel that are connected with this knowledge."[4] For Morris, the child in my example would not suffer a loss of innocence by learning it is wrong to tell people that they are fat. For Morris, one may know what is right and wrong, even be sophisticated about giving reasons why certain actions are right and certain actions are wrong, and still remain innocent. Loss of innocence of the sort we now want to clarify, in the case of the child in my example, would come with learning that the infliction of such suffering is evil and that he or she has the capacity and disposition to inflict such evil. For Morris, such knowledge must come in a certain way: we cannot just be told. Such knowledge as we acquire when we are told, and come to believe, that an action is evil and that we have a capacity to inflict such evil, may remove ignorance, he allows, but not innocence.[5] What marks the end of moral innocence, for Morris, is the painful experience of evil in one or more of three ways: one becomes aware of oneself as an object of evil (one comes to see that one has been manipulated by someone who was trusted), or one experiences through "empathetic identification" evil done to others (one identifies with those who are tortured or those who suffer social injustice), or one experiences oneself as the subject or potential subject of evil (one feels in oneself the powerful temptation to take revenge, or, as with the child in my example, one feels one's capacity to do evil by saying what is true).[6] There is more to Morris' analysis of loss of innocence, but we can use this much to mark out a second version of loss of innocence as the gaining of moral knowledge.

This version of the loss of innocence also is coherent, I believe, and arguably is applicable to the Adam and Eve story. Adam and Eve's eating of the tree of the knowledge of good and evil may be understood as symbolizing their, and our, losing moral innocence in this way; when they eat of the tree, they gain painful new moral knowledge, knowledge of themselves as objects and subjects of evil, and they gain a new capacity to apply the moral category of evil to themselves. So this sense of loss of innocence—loss of innocence through gaining moral knowledge—may apply in both versions to the Adam and Eve story; in one version it involves a wider acceptance of

---

4. Morris, "Lost Innocence," in *On Guilt and Innocence*, 154.
5. Ibid., 152.
6. Ibid., 155–56.

obligation and moral responsibility, and in the other version it involves a deeper moral sensitivity regarding one's capacity for evil.

Loss of innocence in this interpretation, in either version, involves a loss of easiness and spontaneity. Before loss of innocence in this sense the child does just what the child wants, unburdened by moral reflection. After the acquisition of moral knowledge or further moral knowledge this spontaneity is replaced by deeper moral consideration of obligations, consideration of one's capacity to hurt others, and reflection on relationships to others and the moral demands of those relationships. Yet loss of innocence in this sense, in either version, or in both versions, is a good thing: it is a matter of moral maturation.

And, be it noted, loss of innocence in this sense, in either version, is eminently understandable in terms of sin, or sin/relationship, morality. For the first version, we lose our innocence by gaining a greater knowledge of our obligations to those around us and to those not in our immediate ken. For sin/relationship morality, this occurs when we begin to perceive that we have various relationships to persons and that we are capable of violating those relationships. For the second version, we lose our innocence through gaining an experiential knowledge of ourselves as the objects or subjects of evil. Again, such moral knowledge is gained because our relationships to others are such that we are capable of wounding others and they are capable of wounding us. In my example the child who announces, "You're fat!" comes to experience himself as the subject of evil, as one who can inflict pain on another, just because of the relationship between himself and the other.

2. So much for the first interpretation of loss of innocence that relates to our concern with the two aspects of the Adam and Eve story. Now let us turn to the second interpretation that is relevant to our concern. As the first interpretation of loss of innocence corrolates with the sin aspect of the Adam and Eve story, seeing loss of innocence as the gaining of moral knowledge, so the second interpretation correlates with the second, shame aspect of the Adam and Eve story, seeing loss of innocence as acquiring a shame consciousness. Given our discussion of shame and shame morality in earlier chapters, I think that I can be brief.

Loss of innocence in this second interpretation—the shame sense of loss of innocence—occurs when a person begins to feel ashamed before himself or herself for some lack of attainment or for an aspect of his or her character or for something else that is seen as reflecting on the person that he or she would be. Loss of innocence in this shame sense, in itself, has nothing to do with gaining increased moral understanding, nothing to do with gaining a better appreciation of obligation to others or to God, and nothing to do with the painful realization that one has the capacity to do evil.

True, one can do what is morally right in service to one's ego ideal, as Lord Jim does in Conrad's novel. But note that while there is intense self-consciousness in such a case, there may be no appreciation of one's capacity to do evil, and there may be no moral knowledge of right and wrong grounded in experience. Jim, we are told, wants to be like a hero in a book, to be courageous, to do his duty unflinchingly. However, if he understands what his duty is, he may do so from a book. If so, while he may have understanding enough to do his duty to an impressive extent, he would not understand from his own experience what makes his duty his duty. In a sense, regarding knowledge of good and evil as knowledge of what is right and wrong, he would still be innocent. He would be if the gaining of moral knowledge required experiential acquaintance, something like what Cardinal Newman called "real assent." Has the child learned that it is wrong to pull the cat's tail, when he or she is told so by a parent, most often refrains from the practice, and sternly repeats the dictum to a young sibling? Or must there also be some felt sense of the inherent wrongness, the evil, of needlessly inflicting pain? If the latter, doing what is right in service to one's ego ideal would not in itself reflect moral knowledge, and a Lord Jim who does much that is morally right and even is morally heroic would still be innocent regarding moral knowledge. He would not, of course, be innocent in the shame sense, something his very self-conscious demeanor makes clear. In any case, Jim's model identity, with its internal sense of moral duty, is only one instance of a model identity. A model identity may have little or nothing to do with what is morally right, as in the case of those who feel ashamed only of their bald spot or of their tennis game—or of their nakedness. When this is the case, it is abundantly clear that the self-consciousness related to shame has no direct connection to gaining moral knowledge.

Loss of innocence in the shame sense, like the loss of innocence that comes with attaining moral knowledge, involves a loss of spontaneity, but in a different sense. Spontaneity is not lost to a need for moral reflection and consideration, but is replaced by a self-conscious awareness of oneself, not in relation to others, but in relation to one's ego ideal. This sense of loss of innocence is also found in the Adam and Eve story: its presence is indicated by their covering up.[7] Arguably this is their unhappy and wrongful loss of innocence, for their loss of innocence in the shame sense distances them from God and from one another. Losing their innocence in this sense marks their ceasing to live purely in a morality defined by a relationship to God and a relationship to each other and marks their taking up a service to their individual ego ideals.

If I am right, then, we find two very different kinds of loss of innocence represented in the Genesis story of Adam and Eve: loss of innocence in a good sense, through gaining a knowledge of good and evil, and loss of innocence in an unhappy sense, through coming to a shame consciousness. No doubt part of the power of the Genesis story derives from its interweaving the threads of the positive loss, which is gain, and the negative loss, which is truly loss. In the human condition, reflective of the Adam and Eve story, both kinds of loss of innocence are present. Moreover, the two kinds of loss of innocence may accompany one another in the human condition, but logically and psychologically they need not, as they need not morally.

---

7. Morris includes in his analysis of loss of innocence, as one experiences loss of innocence in oneself, the advent of a self-consciousness "captured by the imagery of Adam and Eve covering their nakedness" (ibid., 149). He wants this element at least in part because he believes that "the knowledge Adam and Eve acquire of good and evil first reflects itself in their learning of their nakedness" (142). While he keeps separate the knowledge of good and evil and the knowledge of nakedness, he sees the former as essential for the latter (151). But if what I have argued is correct, Morris is mistaken on this point. Knowledge of good and evil, whether original or deeper knowledge of our obligations to others or knowledge of our own capacity for evil, is sharply different from a shame consciousness.

Morris' construction of loss of innocence, in which he makes this shame element a requirement for gaining knowledge of good and evil, does not really fit the Adam and Eve story, it seems to me. Morris himself comes close to seeing that this is so. He says that "there does not appear to be any logical connection between Adam and Eve covering up and their recognition of the wrongfulness of disobedience" (153). (The recognition of the wrongfulness of their disobedience, for Morris, they come to only after eating the fruit—a point I have challenged; but set that aside.) In allowing that there is no logical connection between their covering up and their recognition of the wrongfulness of disobedience, Morris is allowing that there is no conceptual connection between their fault reaction, which accompanies knowledge of good and evil, and their shame reaction to nakedness. He is right: there is no such connection, although there should be on his analysis. On my view, there is no such connection because they are two very different and separable elements of the story, one having to do with moral knowledge, the other having to do with shame consciousness.

PART VI

IMPLICATIONS
OF
SIN/RELATIONSHIP
MORALITY

15

The Worth of Persons and Animal Rights

We live in an age of moral activism. In recent years social prejudice has been challenged in several of its dimensions, and as a result we have become more deeply aware of the residual and sometimes blatant racism, sexism, ageism, and discrimination against the disabled that many in society suffer. In a clear way, I believe, sin/relationship morality, with its identification of a universal person/person relationship, can provide a groundwork of support for these efforts to remove social injustice. There is another front along which moral activism has sought reform: our immoral treatment of animals. Here too there has been an effort to heighten our moral awareness, and here too a form of prejudice has been challenged, a prejudice against species other than Homo sapiens, which has been called "speciesism."[1] Here, however, it is not so clear that sin/relationship morality can provide a groundwork of support. Relationship morality—or sin/relationship morality, as we are now calling it—may take two forms, as we have seen. In one form it is human sin morality, for which relationships between human persons are foundational; in the other form it is religious sin morality, for which our relationship with God is foundational. Initially, then, it may seem that relationship morality cannot even recognize the rights of animals or human obligations toward animals. But despite initial appearances, it can, and it can in a way that justifies reform, not only in our treatment of animals but in the way we treat the environment.

The contemporary concern with the rights of animals has arisen not so much because there are isolated instances of cruelty to individual animals,

1. Peter Singer, *Animal Liberation*, 2d ed. (New York: New York Review, 1990), 6.

as when someone abuses a pet, but because there is a systematic cultural cruelty to animals, found by animal activists in the laboratory testing on animals, the raising of animals for food, and the killing of animals for their pelts. What is argued for is a recognition that animals are covered by the moral principle of equality. Philosophers who have developed the case for animal rights appreciate that there is a cultural and intellectual history in the West that tends to justify or condone the mistreatment of animals. Certainly Peter Singer appreciates this history.[2] In fact in the West there have been a number of rather different attitudes toward animals and toward nature. At one extreme is the Dominion Theory, which we had occasion to note in Chapter 7. On this view, God gave human beings dominion over all other creatures to do with as they will. Singer sees this view as having a great influence in the West. Regarded as sanctioned by God (Gen. 1.26), it was defended by Aquinas in the thirteenth century, but it has had its contemporary exponents as well. Paul Ramsey, for instance, in the context of a larger discussion, has it that "lower animals" "have no *rights* which we should not infringe. Since animals have feelings, no one approves of needless cruelty to them. Nevertheless we do not renounce our dominion over them, the dominion, which, according to Genesis, God gave man over the brutes. We simply exercise our dominion with as little brutality as possible."[3] Ramsey at least allows that animals can feel pain, something that Descartes denied, as Singer points out.[4] Though he denounces "needless cruelty" to animals, Ramsey affirms the dominion of human beings over animals. This sort of view is not unrelated to a more general view of humanity's relation to nature, sometimes associated with John Locke, according to which nature is something to be mastered or exploited. Daniel Defoe's Robinson Crusoe may be seen as a literary exponent of this view of our relation to nature. A very different view is expressed in the sensibilities of a Rousseau. Jean-Jacques Rousseau presents nature not as something to be exploited but as a source of what is pure, what is healing, in accord with the Romantic vision of nature. Singer observes, however, that the "kinship" with animals engendered by Rousseau's Romanticism was "in no sense egalitarian."[5] A Romantic might commune with nature, while denying any animal rights.

2. Ibid., chap. 5.
3. Paul Ramsey, "Dostoevski: On Living Atheism," *Nine Modern Moralists* (Englewood Cliffs, N.J.: Prentice-Hall, 1962), p. 24.
4. Singer, *Animal Liberation*, 200.
5. Ibid., 203; and cf. Allan Bloom, *The Closing of the American Mind* (New York: Simon & Schuster, 1987), 167 ff., esp. 172, where Bloom contrasts Locke's and Rousseau's views on "man's relation to nature."

Singer could hardly be more opposed to the Dominion Theory, but neither does he hold the Romantic view. His argument, like that of others concerned with animal rights, notably Tom Regan, is for the moral equality of animals. The contention is that just as the principle of equality covers human beings, so it covers nonhuman animals. Just as it is a bias to deny equality to women and to minorities, so it is a bias to deny equality to animals. While both Regan and Singer, as Singer acknowledges, "argue for a new ethical status of animals by considering the basis of the principle of equality,"[6] their arguments differ significantly on the status of *moral rights*. Regan argues that "like us [human beings], animals have certain basic moral rights, including in particular the fundamental right to be treated with the respect that, as possessors of inherent value, they are due as a matter of strict justice."[7] Singer, though, is suspicious of the concept of a moral right. He is "not . . . convinced that the notion of a moral right is a helpful or meaningful one, except when it is used as a shorthand way of referring to more fundamental moral considerations."[8] He seems to agree with Jeremy Bentham's view of rights, which he sympathetically quotes. "Bentham," he observes, "famously described 'natural rights' as 'nonsense' and 'naural and imprescriptable rights' as 'nonsense upon stilts' "; Bentham too "talked of rights" as a kind of "shorthand."[9] For Singer, the "more fundamental moral considerations" that we might use the term "rights" to refer to are the *interests* of sentient beings. So it is that at one point Singer says, "The claim that all animals ought to come within the scope of equal consideration of interests is, in my view, on firmer ground than Regan's claim that all animals have an equal right to life."[10] However, this is not to say that Singer does not speak of animal rights. He does, in his qualified way, while Regan unabashedly and more literally claims that animals have moral rights. In this way both often carry on the discussion in terms of the rights of animals.

Both Singer and Regan reject speciesism. "To avoid speciesism," says Singer, "we must allow that beings who are similar in all relevant aspects have a similar right to life—and mere membership in our own biological

---

6. Peter Singer, "Ten Years of Animal Liberation," *New York Review of Books*, January 17, 1985, 48.

7. Tom Regan, *The Case for Animal Rights* (Berkeley and Los Angeles: University of California Press, 1983), 329.

8. Peter Singer, "Animals and the Value of Life," in *Matters of Life and Death: New Introductory Essays in Moral Philosophy*, ed. Tom Regan (New York: Random House, 1980), 238.

9. Singer, *Animal Liberation*, 8.

10. Singer, "Animals and the Value of Life," 247.

species cannot be a morally relevant criterion for this right."[11] In "Animals and the Value of Life" Singer argues that under the assumption that self-consciousness is the criterion for being a person (an assumption that Singer makes, as we saw in Chapter 7), nonhuman animals, notably chimpanzees, qualify as persons, and so, if persons have a right to life, these animals "have a serious right to life, of the same kind as the right to life of an adult human."[12] Although Singer does not do so in "Animals and the Value of Life," it would be possible to mount parallel arguments using alternative criteria for personhood. Justin Leiber, in *Can Animals and Machines Be Persons?* in effect provides us with the material for such parallel arguments. The book has the form of a dialogue: in the futuristic dialogue Leiber constructs, members of the "United Nations Space Administration Commission" hear a case presented on behalf of Washoe-Delta, a chimpanzee, and AL, a highly advanced computer. Washoe-Delta and AL are scheduled to be "terminated" for economic reasons, and in the case brought on their behalf it is argued that Washoe-Delta and AL "think and feel," that they are therefore persons, and that hence their termination would violate their rights as persons.[13] The circle of consideration expands to include the criteria of acting, being self-conscious, experiencing thought, desire, and meaning, making choices, and having intelligence—or alternatively these are seen as aspects of thinking and feeling. In any case, Leiber's dialogue provides us with the makings for one or more arguments parallel to Singer's.

At least Leiber's implicit argument is more or less parallel. There is one difference to be noted. Singer is arguing that *consistency* requires us to count some nonhuman animals as persons *if* we count humans as persons on the basis of self-consciousness. Singer does, as a matter of fact, define a "person" as a self-conscious being, as we have seen. But his argument does not require this premise. The argument or arguments implicit in Leiber's dialogue, however, do seem to contain a premise that Washoe-Delta and AL *are* persons by virtue of their being thinking and feeling beings (or by virtue of some such criterion). Still, we can adjust the argument so that it becomes a consistency argument. Adjusted, the main argument would be as follows: Washoe-Delta and AL think and feel; and so, if thinking and feeling is the criterion we use to count humans as persons, then we must count Washoe-Delta and AL as persons; and if they are persons, their termination would

---

11. Singer, *Animal Liberation*, 19.
12. Singer, "Animals and the Value of Life," 242–43.
13. Justin Leiber, *Can Animals and Machines Be Persons?* (Indianapolis: Hackett, 1985), 4.

violate their rights. Revised in this way the argument in Leiber's dialogue becomes completely parallel to Singer's.

In *Animal Liberation* Singer provides us with another argument of the same type:

> Whatever criteria [for the right to life or having a valuable life] we choose . . . we will have to admit that they do not follow precisely the boundary of our own species. We may legitimately hold that there are some features of certain beings that make their lives more valuable than those of other beings; but there will surely be some nonhuman animals whose lives, by any standard, are more valuable than the lives of some humans. A chimpanzee, dog, or pig, for instance, will have a higher degree of self-awareness and a greater capacity for meaningful relations with others than a severely retarded infant or someone in a state of advanced senility.[14]

This argument is similar to the other that Singer gives us in "Animals and the Value of Life" and to the revised argument in Lieber's dialogue, except this argument is generalized to cover any criterion, or reasonable criterion, that we may choose; and in this argument, that for which the chosen feature is to be a criterion is not personhood but the right to life or having a valuable, or more valuable, life.

These consistency arguments are related and may be combined without violence to their intent. When they are combined, we get this reasoning: on any reasonable criterion for being a person or having a right to life or having a valuable or more valuable life, certain nonhuman animals will qualify, and sometimes qualify better than certain humans; and so consistency requires us to recognize that some nonhuman animals are persons or have the right to life or have a valuable or more valuable life. Before I comment on this reasoning, let me condense it slightly. While a concern of these arguments is the right to life, this right is seen as flowing either from personhood or from the value—the inherent value—of a being's life. Thus the criteria considered are either for personhood or for the inherent value of life. Compressed, the reasoning is this: on any reasonable criterion for being a person or having inherent value, certain nonhuman animals will qualify, and sometimes qualify better than certain humans; and so consistency requires us to recognize that some nonhuman animals are persons or have inherent value.

14. Singer, *Animal Liberation*, 19.

Now a comment. This reasoning does not require that the criterion for personhood or for inherent value be this or that feature: what the chosen criterion is, is left open. However, the argument does assume that there must be *some* criterion for personhood or for inherent value. It assumes, that is, that there is a strong criterion for personhood or for inherent value (using "strong criterion" in the sense of a defining, or necessary and sufficient, feature). But if what I argued in Chapter 7 is right, then there is no strong criterion for personhood or for the inherent value that persons have. As we saw, neither consciousness nor self-consciousness nor any other venerable candidate will do as a criterion for personhood or as a criterion for inherent worth. The concepts of person and the inherent worth of persons are not defined by a strong criterion; rather, they are "polythetic" concepts. So these arguments, and the reasoning they share, are undermined by their assumption that personhood, or inherent value, must be determined by some "criterion." This in itself, of course, does not mean that no nonhuman animals are persons or that no nonhuman animals have inherent value, and, for reasons I shall present later in the chapter, the claim that nonhuman animals have inherent value seems to me to be right.

For Singer, as opposed to Regan, the underlying moral consideration should always be the *interests* of human and nonhuman beings. "The basic element—the taking into account of the interests of the being, whatever those interests may be—must, according to the principle of equality, be extended to all beings, black or white, masculine or feminine, human or nonhuman."[15] At one point, however, Singer seems quite sympathetic to a form of utilitarianism that he calls "preference utilitarianism." Preference utilitarianism is the view that "an action contrary to the preference of any being is, unless this preference is outweighed by stronger contrary preferences, wrong." This form of utilitarianism, Singer believes, has an advantage over "classical utilitarianism" (that is, hedonistic utilitarianism, which judges the moral rightness or wrongness of actions by their tendency to maximize pleasure or minimize pain). It does because preference utilitarianism can recognize as wrong the killing of a person who prefers to live, even if the death is painless, and it can recognize this wrong as a direct wrong to the individual killed, without appealing to the anxiety his or her death might cause other persons in order to account for the wrongness of the act. Preference utilitarianism, says Singer, holds that "taking the life of a person will normally be worse than taking the life of some other being, since a

15. Ibid., 5.

being that cannot see itself as a distinct entity with a possible future existence cannot have a preference about its own future existence." This, however, does not commit the view to speciesism, for, as Singer maintains, beings other than human beings, such as chimpanzees, have self-consiousness and so are "persons." There are some problems with this view in Singer's elaboration of it, I think. One has to do with what he says about preferences. He thinks that only "persons"—by which he means self-conscious beings—can have preferences. But this seems wrong. He allows that a fish (which on the criterion of self-consciousness is not a person, he suggests) struggling to get free of a barbed hook manifests "no more than a preference for the cessation of a state of affairs," being hooked, and such a struggle does not indicate that "the fish is capable of preferring its own future existence to nonexistence."[16] Well, maybe not, but the fish is, on Singer's own account, manifesting a preference "about its future existence": it prefers an existence free of the hook. I am not sure how serious this problem is for the view, but another problem seems far more serious. Are all preferences equal in moral value? Might not some preferences in fact be evil—quite independently of how strongly they are felt? In any case, neither problem may be a problem for Singer, since he, finally, distinguishes his own position from that of the preference utilitarian.[17]

Singer's central moral category is interests, not preferences. His rejection of speciesism, and his affirmation of animal rights, or of the moral need of the liberation of animals, rests on the moral necessity of taking into account, and treating in accord with the principle of equality, the *interests* of humans and nonhumans. The rejection of speciesism does not mean, for Singer, that all lives are of equal worth[18] or that all interests weigh equally.[19] It does require, for Singer, giving equal weight to like interests and not dismissing the interests of any being simply because that being is not a member of Homo sapiens.[20] The principle of equality requires that our concern for others and our consideration of their interests should not depend on what abilities thay have. But our actions in accord with their interests, under the principle of equality, may vary according to the characteristics of those affected by our actions. What tends to the well-

16. Singer, "Animals and the Value of Life," 238.
17. Ibid., 252. Regan, however, in *The Case for Animal Rights*, sees Singer as a preference utilitarian (142–43).
18. Singer, *Animal Liberation*, 20.
19. Singer, "Ten Years of Animal Liberation," 50.
20. Singer, *Animal Liberation*, 5.

being of pigs is different from what tends to the well-being of children, to use Singer's example. So far, on this score, there is not much to argue with, it seems to me.

However, as we found problems with the way Singer understands preferences, so, when we turn to the exact way Singer understands interests, we again find problems, or at least questions. Singer argues that we cannot count the suffering of a pig less than the suffering of a human being simply because of the species differences, and he then goes on to say "the only relevant boundary to the equal consideration of interests is the limit of sentience, beyond which one cannot meaningfully speak of interests at all."[21] This latter claim is more than dubious. It is almost as though Singer has in mind preferences again. For, arguably, sentience or consciousness is necessary for having a preference. But preferences are distinguishable from interests: one may have a preference for what is not in one's interest. Regarding interests, it may be that the sentience or consciousness of a being is required for that being to be interested in something, but it is not necessary for that being to have interests. As I argued against Cranford and Smith in Chapter 7, permanently unconscious human beings may yet have interests that we ought to consider. Perhaps, though, Singer means that we can meaningfully speak of the interests only of *the kind* of being that normally is sentient or has consciousness. This is a different claim, but it too is at least dubious. If harm can be done, not just to animals, but to the natural environment, and if we can speak of the flourishing of the natural environment as its good, then perhaps we can speak of the interest of the environment. It is in the interest of the trees of the forest not to be deprived of water, we may say. I acknowledge, however, that not all who would hold that we have moral obligations toward the environment unequivocally allow that we can speak of the interests of plants and rivers.[22] And Singer is surely among those not tempted in this direction. (Later in this chapter we shall take up the related issue of whether we can speak of the *rights* of plants and of the environment.)

A larger problem for Singer's view of interests is posed by the not insignificant question, What are the true interests of animals, human and nonhuman? We can agree with much of what Singer says about considering the interests of nonhuman animals, and about considering like interests equally, and still have a question about what those interests are. It must be

21. Singer, "Ten Years of Animal Liberation," 48.

22. See William T. Blackstone, "The Search for an Environmental Ethic," in *Matters of Life and Death*, 299–335 and esp. 322–25, for an exploration of this and related issues.

granted and insisted upon that it is in the interests of animals that they not be tormented. Moral activists like Singer and Regan have done much to bring it to our attention that animals are systematically tormented in pharmacological experiments designed to test the toxicity of drugs and cosmetics and in the "factory" conditions that are imposed on them when they are raised for food. However, is it in the interests of animals to keep them alive? This is another question, and in affirming that it is in the interests of animals that they not be tormented, we do not answer this question. It is relevant to reflect that even in the case of human beings it is not always in their interest to be kept alive. Such was Socrates' austere judgment regarding his own life when he chose to give up his life in order not to corrupt that more valuable part of himself "that is improved by just actions and destroyed by unjust actions."[23] And, as I argued earlier (in Chapter 7), there may be times when maintaining the physiological life of one who is terminally ill for some few hours or longer does not contribute to the good of that person. Singer, in recognizing that euthanasia may be justified in the case of stray animals, concedes that it is not always in the interests of a being to have its life maintained.[24] It may still generally be in the interests of animals to have their lives maintained, but this does not follow from the moral necessity of considering equally the like interests of all animals.

However the interests of humans and nonhuman animals are determined, Singer is a utilitarian, and the way he wants us to weigh interests is in accord with a utilitarian consideration of consequences: actions that maximize benefits, understood as realized interests, are morally right. Given this utilitarian orientation, Singer has a problem regarding the replaceability of animals. The "replaceability argument" is provided by Singer himself. Leslie Stephen, he observes, once wrote, "The pig has a stronger interest than anyone in the demand for bacon." "The thought here," says Singer, "is that animals are replaceable, and that although meat eaters are responsible for the death of the animals they eat, they are also responsible for the creation of more animals of the same species. The benefit they thus confer on one animal cancels out the loss they inflict on the other. We shall call this the replaceability argument."[25] Singer takes the challenge posed by this argument seriously. He must, as a utilitarian. For utilitarianism, "benefits" to some beings can cancel out "losses" for others, and if some action or policy

23. *Crito* 47d–48b.
24. Singer, "Animals and the Value of Life," 253.
25. Ibid., 249.

maximizes benefits by producing benefits to some that outweigh losses to others, even if only slightly, then that action or following that policy becomes a moral duty. So, if by killing thousands we make it possible to cause to be born equal thousands plus one, it becomes our duty to kill the thousands. Clearly this conclusion is distasteful to Singer. At one time he followed Henry S. Salt and thought the argument was fallacious because it compared existent and nonexistent beings, but he has come to have second thoughts about this criticism, he says in one place.[26] Or, as he says in another place, he is not so sure that it is nonsense to believe that "it is possible to benefit a nonexistent being."[27] Singer may do well to have second thoughts about this matter. He allows that "most of us would agree that it would be wrong to bring a child into the world if we knew, before the child was conceived, that it would have a genetic defect that would make its life brief and miserable," and, he says, "to conceive such a child is to do it harm." But if so, he asks rhetorically, "can we really deny that to bring into the world a being who will have a pleasant life is to confer on that being a benefit?"[28] Our not being able to deny this implies that it is possible to benefit a child-yet-to-be while it is a nonexistent being. Further, as we will recall from our discussion of rights in Chapter 9, it does not seem to be nonsense to speak of the rights of future generations. Certainly James Sterba does not think so. And respecting the rights of those yet unborn is a way of benefiting them. It seems, then, as Singer himself finally allows, that the replaceability argument cannot be dismissed on the grounds that it compares existent and nonexistent beings and assumes that it is possible to benefit nonexistent beings.

Singer has other criticisms of the replaceability argument, but he senses that "they do not go to the heart of the matter."[29] Nel Noddings, it seems to me, begins to get to the heart of the matter when she says, "On this view [that of the replaceability argument], we ought to kill animals (as painlessly as possible, of course) in order to allow space for animals reproduced and, thus, increase the total pleasure or happiness experienced by animals. We have already made an odd move when we talk this way. We are no longer considering how we shall meet the particular other but how we shall treat a

---

26. Ibid., 250. Singer says here that he is no longer sure of the view he shared with Salt when he wrote (the first edition of) *Animal Liberation*. His reference is to page 154 of the 1975 New York Review edition.

27. This is the way Singer puts it in the edition of *Animal Liberation* I have been citing, the second edition, published in 1990, 228.

28. Ibid.

29. Singer, "Animals and the Value of Life," 250; and cf. *Animal Liberation*, 228–30.

vast group of interchangeable entities."[30] Noddings makes her point under the assumption that the benefits produced will take the form of pleasure; however, her main point remains intact if the benefits are realized interests (or any other good). What she draws to our attention is the moral repugnance of the interchangeability of animals that is assumed by the replaceability argument.

The replaceability argument is a utilitarian argument and as such is committed to this interchangeability. It cannot consider the inherent worth that individual animals may have. In true utilitarian manner, it considers only effects ("benefits," construed as pleasure, happiness, realized interests, or some other good; and "losses," construed as the opposite). And it is accepted that a maximization of the identified good is the right-making criterion, while individuals are regarded as morally neutral receptacles for the designated good. Singer is so troubled by this argument because it proceeds from the same utilitarian principles that inform his own utilitarian approach.

Singer appreciates that "if we had a clear basis for saying that all sentient creatures have a right to life . . . then it would be easy to say why killing a sentient creature is a kind of wrong that cannot be made good by creating a new creature," but, he says, "such a position has its own deep philosophical and practical difficulties," thus reiterating his objection to the notion of rights.[31] By way of contrast, Regan, who recognizes the inherent worth of animals and the rights of animals, deals with the replaceability argument with dispatch. "The grounds for finding unjust any practice that treats individuals who have inherent value as renewable resources," he says, "are distinct from considerations about the consequences of such a practice." And "to treat farm animals as renewable resources is to fail to treat them with the respect they are due as possessors of inherent value."[32] Considerations of justice, which require us to respect the rights of animals, make it morally wrong to treat animals as interchangeable receptacles of benefits, Regan argues. We have seen that Singer maintains that lives have value and that some lives have more value than others, and we have seen that Singer argues consistency requires us to recognize that certain nonhuman animals, as much as humans, have a right to life or have inherent value. But Singer is careful not to affirm that either animals or humans have

30. Nel Noddings, *Caring: A Feminist Approach to Ethics and Moral Education* (Berkeley and Los Angeles: University of California Press, 1984), 154.

31. Singer, *Animal Liberation*, 229.

32. Regan, *The Case for Animal Rights*, 344 and 345.

rights in the literal sense or that animals or humans have an inherent value that entails rights in the literal sense. Given his utilitarianism, Singer cannot countenance any inherent value of individual animals by virtue of which animals have rights independently of consequences—which is just what Regan argues. Regan, on his side, affirms the inherent value of animals (and even the equal inherent value of animals) and assumes that the inherent value animals have entails their right to life, which makes it contrary to justice, and hence wrong, to take the lives of animals. I shall return to the question of the inherent value of animals and its connection to animal rights shortly.

Before I turn to these matters and, in general, what sin/relationship morality has to say about animal rights, there is one other element of Singer's thinking, and also of Regan's thinking, that requires comment. Both moral philosophers reject speciesism, but this does not mean that, for either, *all* animal life is clearly of equal value. Singer, in *Animal Liberation*, says this: "While self-awareness, the capacity to think ahead, and have hopes and aspirations for the future, the capacity for meaningful relationships with others and so on are not relevant to the question of inflicting pain—since pain is pain, whatever other capacities, beyond the capacity to feel pain, the being may have—these capacities are relevant to the question of taking life. It is not arbitrary to hold that the life of a self-aware being, capable of abstract thought, of planning for the future, of complex acts of communication, and so on, is more valuable than the life of a being without these capacities." Taking the life of a being with these capacities involves a kind of loss not involved in taking the life of a being without these capacities, Singer says, and since on utilitarian principles we should minimize loss, he concludes that "normally this will mean that if we have to choose between the life of a human being and the life of another animal we should choose the life of the human being."[33]

What is worthy of note here is that the criterion for a more valuable life that Singer names—essentially self-awareness, filled out with a reference to such capacities as the capacity for abstract thought and the capacity to plan for the future—in effect keeps in place the higher moral status of humankind. It does so, not because humans alone have these characteristics, but because they most clearly have them. That is, typically they most clearly have them, even though not all human beings have them.

We find something similar in Regan's thinking. It emerges in Regan's

33. Singer, *Animal Liberation*, 20 and 21.

formulation of "the subject-of-a-life criterion." Individuals are subjects of a life, on Regan's criterion, "if they have beliefs and desires; perception, memory, and a sense of the future, including their own future; an emotional life together with feelings of pleasure and pain; preference-desires and goals; a psychophysical identity over time; and an individual welfare in the sense that their experiential life fares well or ill for them logically independently of their utility for others and logically independently of their being the object of anyone else's interests. Those who satisfy the subject-of-a-life criterion themselves have a distinctive kind of value—inherent value—and are not to be viewed or treated as mere receptacles."[34] There are some differences between Regan and Singer, to be sure. For one thing, for Regan, as opposed to Singer, dogs, pigs, and humans have equal inherent value. What about nonmammalians? Regan is not sure, although he says that even if some nonmammalians are not the subjects of a life, they still may experience pain, which is enough to make them subjects of moral consideration; and, he says, we do not know enough to dismiss the idea that frogs, for instance, may be the subject of a life.[35]

For Regan, as for Singer, it is not human beings alone that meet the criterion for a valuable life (that would come close to speciesism). But for Regan, as for Singer, the crucial consideration for determining the value of a life is one that is most clearly met by human beings. This, I think, is not accidental but a reflection of a deep moral intuition that is embodied in our moral experience. It is this moral intuition that explains why Singer gives more moral value to "higher" animals than to "lower" animals and why Regan allows that "higher" animals more clearly than "lower" animals qualify as having equal inherent value. It is this underlying intuition that explains why neither moral philosopher puts forward, as the criterion for a valuable life, say, having an exoskeleton or having appetites or being able to grow. We and they intuitively reject these criteria as a criterion for equal inherent value or for a more valuable life. Sin/relationship morality has an explanation of the basic moral intuition that is at work here, as we shall see.

However, let me enlarge the present point—that Singer and Regan, in their thinking about the value of life, give a central place to criteria that apply best or most clearly to human beings—by considering how Singer and Regan, respectively, treat what may be called "the moralist's delight": the overcrowded lifeboat case. Regan sets the stage: "Imagine five survivors are

34. Regan, *The Case for Animal Rights*, 243.
35. Ibid., 366–67.

on a lifeboat. Because of limits of size, the boat can only support four. All weigh approximately the same and would take up approximately the same amount of space. Four of the five are normal adult human beings. The fifth is a dog. One must be thrown overboard or else all will perish. Who should it be?"[36] Singer's answer is straightforward. For Singer, the human beings have "a greater interest in living than the dog, either because of the greater benefit that continued life will be to them, or because they, but not the dog, have plans, hopes, and desires for the future which will be thwarted if they do not continue to live."[37] Human lives are more valuable, Singer affirms in *Animal Liberation*, and, for the utilitarian Singer, this comes to their having more to gain by living and more to lose by dying—hence their greater interest in living.

For Regan, though, the dog as well as the humans is a subject of a life, and so the dog has equal inherent value. Nevertheless, Regan's conclusion is the same as Singer's, although of course his reasoning is different. The dog is the one that should perish, for Regan, not because its life has less value, but because "the harm that death is, is a function of the opportunities for satisfaction it forecloses," and though the death of the dog is a harm, the death of any of the humans would be a much greater harm. The loss caused by the death of any one of the humans, other things being equal, is much greater than the loss caused by the death of the dog. And, for Regan, it would not matter if it were several or even a million dogs whose lives must be lost in order to save the life of one human being—since to reason that the harm done to a million dogs by causing their deaths outweighs the harm done to one human by causing that human's death requires us to set the sum of the losses of the million dogs against the loss of the one human. Such aggregative reasoning is contrary to respecting the equal inherent value of subjects of a life, for Regan, because such respect requires us to compare the harm done individually, and the harm done to any one of the humans would be greater than the harm done to any one of the million dogs.[38]

Now let me raise some questions. Why, for Regan, is it a greater harm to the human to take the human's life? Because the human's death is a greater loss. This is the same point Singer made in his reasoning. All right. But

36. Ibid., 285. Regan, in an endnote, cites W. R. Carter, "Once and Future People," *American Philosophical Quarterly* 17 (1980): 66. Carter's case is similar to Regan's and, like Regan's, is in a long tradition of limited-resources cases.

37. Singer, "Ten Years of Animal Liberation," 50.

38. Regan, *The Case for Animal Rights*, 324–25.

why is the loss greater? Not, for Regan, because a life of greater value is lost, whereas for Singer, this does seem to be the reason. So, of Regan we may ask, Why is there a greater loss? And of Singer we may ask, Why is there a greater value to each human's life? I am not suggesting that they are wrong in these judgments. In fact they seem to me to be intuitively right. And again, sin/relationship morality has an explanation for their rightness, as we are about to see.

What does sin/relationship morality have to say about the rights of animals? Can sin/relationship morality, which finds the source of obligations and of moral rights in relationships between *persons*, including the person/person relationship, have anything to say about the rights of animals? First, let us remind ourselves that sin/relationship morality does not hold the brief that only human beings are persons. Persons are those beings into whose presence as persons we can enter. Now or in the future it may be possible to enter the presence of nonhuman persons, even fabricated persons. Yet, as I have suggested, in our moral lives as we in fact live them it is human beings who are preeminently experienced as persons.

Say that this is right. Say, moreover, that we do not experience animals as persons. Still, nonhuman animals may have their own unique and inherent value. Furthermore, we may understand their inherent value on analogy with the inherent value of human persons. As animals are like human persons, so they have an inherent value like that possessed by human persons. In this way higher animals, like chimpanzees, which are very like human persons, would have an inherent value very like that of human persons, while lower animals would have an inherent value less like that of human persons.

Such a scale of inherent value, ranging downward from human persons, would explain why Singer is justified in attributing more value to human lives than to the lives of other animals—all other animals—as he suggests in *Animal Liberation*, and why he is justified in attributing more value to the lives of chimpanzees than to, say, the lives of lizards, as he either suggests or comes close to suggesting in "Animals and the Value of Life."[39] In any case, his thinking seems to imply the latter: that the lives of chimpanzees have more value than the lives of lizards. Given his claim that sentience is the limit beyond which we cannot meaningfully speak of interests but up to which we can, he would allow that lizards have interests, if they are sentient,

39. Singer, "Animals and the Value of Life," 243–44.

as they are. But if so, lizards have something to gain from living, and accordingly—if I have Singer right—Singer would say that lizards have at least some interest in living and that hence their lives have at least some value. In Singer's apparent view, then—bringing together the two points—the lives of lizards have some value, though not as much as the lives of chimpanzees, and the lives of human beings have the greatest value. For Singer, it seems, as I have noted, the greater value of a human being's life is a matter of human being's having more to gain from living than other animals and so "a greater interest" in living. But why a greater interest? Presumably it is not because the interest is more strongly felt or different in its immediate object from a lesser interest—since this would not always make the interests of humans "greater" than those of nonhuman animals. Somehow, as I say, for Singer, the greater interest human beings have in living connects to the greater value human lives have (or normally have). Thus, if we explain the greater value of human life, we explain what Singer sees as the greater interest humans have in living. Keeping in mind this connection, sin/relationship morality can explain the greater value of human life, sensed by Singer, in accord with an abiding moral intuition. It is because humans are persons and animals are only analogous to persons. Again, the life of the chimpanzee is more valuable than the life of the lizard because the chimpanzee is more closely analogous to a person than is the lizard.

In the same way, the analogy between human persons and animals, and between the inherent value of human persons and the inherent value of animals, can explain why Regan sees a greater loss in the death of a human than in the death of a dog. Regan reasons that in a case where we must choose between the life of a dog and the life of a human, the dog, rather than any human, ought to perish, even though the dog, as much as a human, is a subject of a life, on the grounds that a lesser harm is done to the dog because the loss is less. The harm that death is, he says in what I quoted above, "is a function of the opportunities for satisfaction it forecloses." Presumably the consideration here is not the number of satisfactions foreclosed. Closer to what makes the opportunities for satisfaction foreclosed by death greater for humans, I would suppose, is something like the quality of the satisfaction involved. If so, one can hardly not think of Mill and his pronouncement that "it is better to be a human being dissatisfied than a pig satisfied; better to be Socrates dissatisfied than a fool satisfied."[40] Mill meant

40. Mill, *Utilitarianism*, 10.

that the pleasures appropriate to humans and pursued by humans like Socrates are worth more morally.[41] Nevertheless, for Mill, other things being equal, it would be better to save a healthy dog than to save a demented human being (one unable to attain the intellectual pleasures of a Socrates or even very much in the way of appetitive pleasures), while this would not be so for Regan, I think. For Regan, in some other way the moral significance of a human's satisfaction is different from that of a dog, and different in a way that makes its loss greater.

It may be unfortunate that Regan has fastened onto the term "satisfaction," for it suggests that his thinking is more hedonistic than it is. A better term here might be "fulfillment," so that the harm death imposes is a function of the lost opportunity for fulfillment. The loss occurs if the *opportunity* is lost, we should observe. That is, the loss occurs even if the opportunity is not acted upon. What it comes down to, then, is that for Regan the loss imposed by death is the loss of those opportunities that a continued life allows, and in the case of humans, as compared with dogs—and other animals, we may assume—that loss is greater. Why is that loss greater? As far as I can see, Regan gives no answer to this question. Sin/relationship morality does provide an answer, however. Ultimately the reason for the loss being greater, sin/relationship morality can say, is that a person's life is lost when a human's life is lost, while this is not the case when a dog's life is lost. We may well experience dogs and other animals as having an inherent value, but we preeminently experience human beings as persons and as having the inherent value of persons. "No reasonable person would deny that the death of any of the four humans [in Regan's overcrowded lifeboat case] would be a greater prima facie loss . . . than would be true in the case of the dog," says Regan.[42] Sin/relationship morality not only can agree with this claim about our deep moral intuition but can give an explanation of its basis in a way that Regan cannot.

Accepting that we in our moral lives experience only humans as persons does not deny that humans may have an important moral likeness to certain animals. We may, if we wish, follow Regan and place humans and other animals like chimpanzees and dogs and other more or less higher animals in the category of subjects of a life and, at the same time, allow, first, that within this category humans are persons and the other members are only

41. This is what Mill means if he means by "better," better morally, as it appears he does. Whether it is open to a hedonistic utilitarian like Mill to intend such a meaning is, of course, another question, and one that need not concern us here.
42. Regan, *The Case for Animal Rights*, p. 324.

analogous to persons and, second, that the nonhuman members may vary among themselves in being more or less analogous to persons. Regan, though, wants to say that all subjects of a life have *equal* inherent value. All subjects of a life have the same inherent value whether they are "moral agents," as most human beings are, or "moral patients," as some human beings and many animals are. (In Regan's terminology "moral agents" are those beings who can do what is right or wrong and thus act in a way open to moral praise and blame, while "moral patients" are those beings, including animals, who are incapable of doing what is right or wrong but who nevertheless may have moral rights or be affected morally by moral agents.)[43] Why does Regan think that all subjects of a life, whether human or nonhuman, have the same inherent value? He does so, apparently, because, as he sees it, if we deny equal inherent value to all subjects of a life, inevitably we will do so confusedly and arbitrarily. To argue that beings that are "moral agents" have more inherent value than other beings that are "moral patients" on such grounds as "the comparative value of their experiences" or because they have certain "virtues," such as intellectual or artistic excellence, or have greater utility for others is, for Regan, to confuse inherent value with these other matters.[44] Also, Regan wants us to see, it is arbitrary to tie the degree of inherent value that "moral patients" have to some valuable or desirable feature they have to a lesser extent than "moral agents." "Since the inherent value of moral agents does not wax or wane depending on *their* comparative happiness or *their* total of pleasures-over-pains, it would be arbitrary to maintain that moral patients have less inherent value than moral agents because *they* (i.e., moral patients) have less happy lives or because *their* total of pleasures-over-pains is less than that of moral agents—even if this were true."[45] Surely Regan is right that the inherent value of "moral agents" does not vary with their quotient of happiness. Indeed, as I argued in Chapter 7, the inherent value that persons have as persons does not hinge on (and so would not vary with) any natural feature that persons may have. And we can agree with Regan that it would be arbitrary to say that "moral patients"—enfeebled human beings and various animals—have less inherent worth when they experience less happiness or pleasure. Moreover, we can add, since we do not, or should not, allow that the inherent value of "moral agents" varies with the degree of any of the features Regan names or with the degree of any other natural

43. Ibid., 151 ff.
44. Ibid., 240.
45. Ibid. (Regan's emphasis).

feature, it would be arbitrary to hold that the inherent value of "moral patients" varies with the degree of any such feature. So far, so good for Regan's equality case.

But what Regan fails to consider is the possibility that in our actual moral experience we experience some beings as persons and do not experience other beings as persons. If this is so, then those beings we can experience as persons, those beings into whose presence we may enter in our moral experience, will have equal inherent worth, and other beings, who are not persons, while they may well have inherent worth, will have a lesser degree of inherent worth. This is not a matter of persons meeting some criterion and nonpersons failing to meet it: there is no such criterion, I have argued. And it is not a matter of persons more fully measuring up to some such nonexistent criterion. It is a matter of our individual moral experience, in accord with what we have seen in earlier chapters.

Regan conceives of inherent value as a "categorical value, admitting of no degrees." He can if he wants to, but it need not be so conceived. To be sure, the inherent value of one *person* will not be more or less than that of another person. Since all persons equally are persons, they equally have the inherent value they have by virtue of being persons. But when the category of inherent value is extended to various kinds of beings, some of which are persons and some of which are analogous in some degree to persons, it is not an implication that all beings with inherent worth will have the same inherent worth. "The subject-of-a-life criterion identifies a similarity that holds between moral agents and patients," Regan says. Say that Regan has identified a relevant moral similarity. Still, such a similarity does not entail that all moral agents and moral patients, all the beings in his subject-of-a-life category, have *equal* inherent value. Regan, in arguing that his subject-of-a-life criterion is intelligible and nonarbitrary, gives as one of his grounds for this claim the following: "Since inherent value is conceived to be a categorical value, admitting of no degrees, any supposed relevant similarity must itself be categorical. The subject-of-a-life criterion satisfies this criterion. This criterion does not assert or imply that those who meet it have the status of a subject of a life to a greater or lesser degree, depending on the degree to which they have or lack some favored ability or virtue (e.g., the ability for higher mathematics or those virtues associated with artistic excellence)."[46] Nevertheless, his criterion for being a subject of a life (quoted in full above) does admit of degrees: it does allow that one being

46. Ibid., 244–45.

can more fully meet the criterion than can another. For instance, memory and the ability to initiate action, which are elements of his criterion, admit of degrees in this way. It is not accidental that Regan's proposed criterion admits of degrees, I suggest. If animals have inherent value by virtue of their greater or lesser analogy with persons, then the best criterion that Regan can come up with for his category of subjects of a life, as he strives to define the category, will admit of degrees because his category includes both persons and beings that are in some degree like persons. By way of contrast, the category of person is already operative in our moral experience and discourse and does not need a criterion. Further, not only is a criterion for being a person superfluous, but any attempt to formulate a strong criterion for personhood seems doomed to failure, as we have seen (in Chapter 7).

Both Singer and Regan are right to maintain that nonhuman animals have valuable lives or inherent value, and sin/relationship morality explains that value on the basis of the analogy between nonhuman animals and human persons. Again, Singer and Regan are right that we have moral obligations toward animals, as each maintains on different grounds. Sin/ relationship morality justifies the moral treatment of all animals on analogy with the moral treatment of human persons. Singer recognizes that humans have rights—in his sense of "rights"—that nonhumans do not (a dog, for instance, he points out, does not have the right to vote, since it cannot vote), a difference that Singer attributes to the difference between humans and other animals.[47] And Singer recognizes that we have different obligations toward different species with their different needs and capacities.[48] Sin/relationship morality's justification of the moral treatment of animals on analogy with the moral treatment of human persons does not contradict these points but goes beyond them. It explains and justifies why we have a greater moral responsibility to human beings than to nonhuman animals. It explains and justifies why we have a greater obligation to a human being than to a dog in the overcrowded lifeboat case that Singer and Regan consider.

This brings us to the subject of speciesism: giving moral favor to one's own species over all others. Regarding the overcrowded lifeboat case, Singer and Regan agree that the dog's life, rather than any human life, ought to be sacrificed. Neither, however, thereby commits himself to speciesism, for neither is arguing that the human being *precisely because he or she is a human being* ought to have his or her life preserved at the cost of the dog's life. Sin/

---

47. Singer, *Animal Liberation*, 1–2.
48. Singer, "Ten Years of Animal Liberation," 50.

relationship morality agrees in the rejection of speciesism. It is not by virtue of belonging to Homo sapiens, by virtue of being human beings, that we are persons, even if, as things are, human beings are the only persons we encounter. And, furthermore, for sin/relationship morality, even if human beings are the only beings we morally experience as persons, the boundary of required moral consideration is not marked by the boundary of Homo sapiens. Sin/relationship morality agrees with Singer and Regan that we have direct duties to animals that are not merely indirect duties to human beings (as Kant thought).[49] For sin/relationship morality, what these duties are is illuminated by considering the analogy between nonhuman animals and human persons.

The closer animals are to human persons in their character and capacities, the more our obligations toward them will be like the obligations we have toward human persons by virtue of the person/person relationship. While we have an obligation not to torment any animals capable of feeling pain, that obligation takes different forms regarding different species. What counts as torment of a chimpanzee or a dog may be very different from what counts as torment of a chicken. Though much that would inflict pain on a chicken would also inflict pain on a chimpanzee or a dog, as well as on a human being, a chimpanzee or a dog in our care may be made to suffer from a lack of our companionship in a way that a chicken cannot be. Some animals may be very like human beings, even to the point of having self-awareness, while others may have consciousness but not self-awareness, and yet others—oysters, perhaps, or single-celled animals—may lack consciousness. Our obligations toward the different species of animals, and the form of our obligations, for sin/relationship morality, are determined by the analogy between those species and human persons. Analogy, then, determines both the inherent value of nonhuman animals and our obligations toward them. We human persons are not only related to all persons by virtue of the person/person relationship, we are as well related to the various kinds of nonhuman animals by virtue of an analogue, or a series of analogues, of the person/person relationship.

Also, the analogy between human persons and nonhuman animals explains how we can speak of animal rights (using "rights" to mean moral rights, as Regan does): just as the rights of persons are required by and in accord with the inherent value of persons, so the rights of nonhuman animals are required by and in accord with the kind of inherent value

---

49. Singer, "Animals and the Value of Life," 232; Regan, *The Case for Animal Rights*, 189.

possessed by the animal species in question. So it is that Regan is closer to being right on the replaceability issue than is Singer. Regan sees that animals have an inherent value that generates rights of a sort that forbid treating them as replaceable receptacles—something Singer does not see and which his utilitarian commitment does not allow him to acknowledge. But Regan infers from the inherent value of animals, or those animals that are subjects of a life, a right to life that makes it wrong to raise animals for human consumption. Regan is right that if animals have inherent worth, we are under an obligation to respect their worth, but for reasons we have seen, it does not immediately follow that respecting the inherent worth of a being requires us to maintain the life of that being. We can agree with Regan that animals have an inherent value and that we ought to respect that value and that that value generates certain rights, without agreeing that one of those rights is the right to have their life maintained. Whether animals have a right to life, and which animals do, is another question. And sin/relationship morality, as a matter of its internal logic, offers no answer to that question. It does, however, offer a way of approaching the question: rights are in accord with the inherent value of a species, and if we violate the inherent value of an animal by taking its life, then it has a right to life.

Now let me turn to some further ramifications that help to show the essential rightness of thinking of the ethical status of animals on analogy with the ethical status of persons, under the assumption that we preeminently experience human beings as persons in our moral lives. For one thing, our preeminently experiencing human beings as persons would explain why Singer and Regan provide the criteria they do for one life's having more value than other lives (Singer) or being a subject of a life and having inherent value for that reason (Regan). Their cirteria, each of which is an elaboration of self-consciousness, apply best or most clearly to adult human beings, as we have seen. Starting with the moral intuition that human beings have more value or have inherent value, each proposes a criterion that fits that intuition.

Of course, Singer seems to make the unhappy assumption that the feature he names functions as a strong criterion—a necessary and sufficient condition—for being a person or having a more valuable life. Regan avoids making this assumption. His criterion for being a subject of a life functions as "a sufficient condition of making the attribution of inherent value intelligible and nonarbitrary," but not as a necessary condition for inherent value.[50] Singer's thinking, though not Regan's, then, carries the implication

50. Regan, *The Case for Animal Rights*, 245–46.

that certain humans—very young infants, say—may have a less valuable life than certain animals. Both Singer and Regan try to show how their views are in accord with our strong moral intuitions. Here, however, Singer's view is quite unintuitive, and this has not gone unnoticed.

Noddings, who proposes an ethic of care, or caring (and whose concept of care we had occasion to discuss in Chapter 5), says that such an ethic "strives consistently to capture our human intuitions and feelings," and, against Singer, states, "We cannot accept an ethic that depends upon a definition of personhood if that definition diminishes our obligation to human infants. An ethic that forces us to classify human infants with rats and pigs is unsettling."[51] Noddings' point is well taken. For Singer, infants, rats, and pigs, have the same value if they have the same relative incapacity for self-consciousness, while a chimpanzee, which has self-consciouness, qualifies as a person, unlike a human infant. The basis for Noddings' intuition, in the light of which Singer's suggestion is so unsettling, I suggest, is that humans, including infants, are persons, while rats and pigs are not. On the other hand, Noddings may not fully appreciate the dimensions of our obligations to animals. She recognizes that one with a pet cat has entered a kind of relationship with one's pet and that by virtue of that relationship one has certain obligations toward one's cat.[52] So far what she says seems right: the relationships persons can enter with nonhuman beings can generate obligations. Furthermore, she says, if a stranger-cat comes to her door, she cannot ethically drive it away. This too sounds right. But, she asks, what if it were a rat? She might, she says, kill the rat as efficiently as she could. Her reason is not that the rat might carry disease and so on, but rather that she does not have a caring relation to the rat, as she does to her cat and other cats. What, then, if a stranger-cat comes to the door of someone who has no pet cat? That person, unlike her, she says, may have no ethical responsibility toward cats. Noddings is right, I think, that the close relationship one has with, say, a cat or a dog may be marked by caring and reciprocity, and that relationship will carry obligations for the human party (though not for the cat or dog). What she seems not to recognize, though, is that in the absence of such a close relationship, we still have obligations toward animals, be they cats or rats. Of course, such obligations are prima facie and may be overriden, but as Singer and Regan are keenly aware, they are not nonexistent, and they do not depend on personal

51. Noddings, *Caring*, 151.
52. Ibid., 156.

acquaintance. In Nodding's defense, however, it should be noted that she does acknowledge a general obligation to spare animals pain and that she is as much aware as Singer or Regan that working to save the whales, the seals, or the condors solely for the sake of future generations of human beings is not acting morally toward the animals in question.[53]

What emerge here are two distinct points regarding the ethical status of animals: we have moral responsibility toward animals even though we may have no close personal relationship to the animals in question (a point that Singer and Regan agree upon, and Noddings too, at least regarding a general obligation to spare animals pain); and, second, the responsibility we have toward a human infant is greater than that we have toward a fully grown higher nonhuman animal (a point that Noddings draws to our attention, with which Singer apparently cannot agree and with which Regan may be able to agree). Both points, I suggest, are intuitively right, and both are explained by sin/relationship morality. Under the assumption that we have the person/person relationship to all humans, but not to nonhuman animals, the first point is explained by our having a relationship to farm animals, animals used in experiments, and animals in the wild, even though we have never seen them, by virtue of the inherent value they have—a relationship analogous to, but not the same as, the person/person relationship. The second is explained in the same way: our relationship to a human infant is the person/person relationship, while we have only an analogous relationship to even more developed nonhuman animals.

We come now, and finally in this chaper, to one further area of ethical concern on which a moral analogy with the inherent value of persons may shed some light: the area of environmental ethics. Strictly, this takes us beyond a concern with animal rights, but a short excursus is in order. At issue here is the inherent value of inanimate life (plants and trees) and the inherent value of natural objects (rivers and mountain ranges) and the inherent value of ecological systems, as opposed to individual beings or single natural objects. Secondarily at issue are our obligations toward such entities and the moral rights of such entities.

In order to hold that on whatever criterion for a valuable life we choose, some nonhuman animals will qualify as having a valuable life, as Singer

53. Ibid., 150 and 158. Another feminist thinker who is acutely aware that we have obligations toward animals with which we have no close relationships, and that our caring should extend to them, is Rita Manning; see chap. 6, "Caring for Animals," in *Speaking from the Heart: A Feminist Perspective on Ethics* (Lanham, Md.: Rowman & Littlefield, 1992).

does, it is not necessary to hold that all life has value. And, Singer tells us, he does not believe that all life, "whether animal or plant, conscious or not, has value."[54] For Singer, apparently, as self-consciousness is necessary for being a person and having the more valuable life of a person, so sentience (which, for him, having interests requires) is necessary for a being's life to have even some value.

But think about a case in which a man is killing fish in a tank or opening oysters and letting them die or killing larvae—not for food and not to protect himself or others from danger, but out of a perverse pleasure. Why is this killing morally repugnant? It is in part because what the man is doing is degrading to himself, we might say. And this seems right: he is violating his person/person relationship to himself by allowing himself to indulge in such a pleasure. Take away this element of self-degradation, however, and still there is something that strikes us as very wrong about what the man is doing. Why, let us ask ourselves, is his pleasure so repugnant morally? It is in great part, I submit, because such pleasure derives from an action that evinces a complete lack of respect for life. But such respect reflects a value that life has, which we ought to respect. And this intuitive point remains in place even if the oysters or the larvae lack sentience. It would change nothing that relates to the present point if the man were gratuitously cutting down trees out of a sense of perverse pleasure.

One ethical thinker who believed that all life has value was Albert Schweitzer. For him, the lives of human beings, nonhuman animals, and plants all have a value of their own, and, moreover, "the ethic of reverence for life makes no sharp distinction between higher and lower, more precious and less precious lives."[55] At the same time, though, Schweitzer allowed that some killing is "necessary"—so observes Blackstone, who offers a critique of Schweitzer's reverence-for-life view. Consequently, as Blackstone sees it, Schweitzer faces a problem. "This problem of the necessity of killing is made all the more acute by Schweitzer's claim that there is no objective ground for judging to what degree various life forms are inherently valuable. If all forms of life are equally valuable, then it should be just as wrong to kill a daisy as it is to kill a person. This is a position that must strike us as incredible, and it is reasonably clear that Schweitzer himself did not have any such position in mind. . . . But the problem remains of how to account

54. Singer, "Animals and the Value of Life," 255 n. 2.
55. Albert Schweitzer, *The Teaching of Reverence for Life,* trans. Richard Winston and Clara Winston (New York: Holt, Rinehart & Winston, 1965), 47; quoted by Blackstone, "The Search for an Environmental Ethic," 306.

for the hierarchy of inherent value various kinds of life are supposed to possess."[56] It is, I think, reasonably clear that Schweitzer must have distinguished between more and less valuable life forms. He would have to if only to maintain aseptic conditions in the hospital he established in West Africa. This is so even if, as I once heard from one who visited Schweitzer's hospital in Gabon before his death, Schweitzer prohibited killing flies. How, then, to account for "the hierarchy of inherent value various kinds of life are supposed to possess"? The answer, or account, that sin/relationship morality would propose is by now evident. As nonhuman animals have inherent value on analogy with the inherent value of persons, so inanimate life forms have inherent value on analogy with the inherent value of persons. The closer the analogy, the greater the value, and the less the analogy, the less the value.[57]

This explanation accounts for our moral repugnance at the gratuitous killing of any living thing and for our sense that the lives of human persons have more value. It also accounts for our having prima facie obligations toward all living things and allows that all living things have moral rights.

What, though, shall we say about natural objects? They are not alive. Do they have inherent value that generates rights and obligations? Some have said so. Aldo Leopold, who proposes the idea of a "land ethic," provides us with such a view. "All ethics so far evolved," he believes, "rest upon a single premise: that the individual is a member of a community of interdependent parts," a claim that applies fairly well to guilt morality, at least. "The land ethic," he says, "simply enlarges the boundaries of the community to include soils, waters, plants, and animals, or collectively, the land." And thus, "a land ethic changes the role of Homo sapiens from conqueror of the land-community to plain member and citizen of it. It implies respect for his fellow-members, and also respect for the community as such."[58] Leopold's thinking need not be construed in guilt-morality terms, I suggest. When he speaks of "respect" for members of the community and for the community itself, if he means respect for inherent value, he is pointing beyond guilt

---

56. Blackstone, "The Search for an Environmental Ethic," 308–9.

57. Schweitzer says, "[W]hen we establish hard and fast gradations in value between living organisms, [we are] judging them in relation to ourselves, by whether they seem to stand closer or farther from us. This is a wholly subjective standard" (*The Teaching of Reverence for Life*, 47). But if such "gradations" are based on our actual moral experience of human beings as persons and of nonhuman animals as only analogous in some degree to persons, the "standard" is not subjective—if "subjective" means lacking in any basis.

58. Aldo Leopold, *A Sand County Almanac*, enl. ed. (New York: Oxford University Press, 1966), 119–20.

morality. In any case, Leopold allows that not only animals but nonliving members of the land-community, like soils and waters, have moral rights.[59] And, he holds, we human beings have obligations toward the living and nonliving members of the land-community and toward the community as a whole.

Both Blackstone and Regan have considered Leopold's land ethic. Blackstone observes, "It is plain from what Leopold says that he regards a land ethic (in the broad sense, including any use of the environment), an ethic in which ethically relevant entities are not just human, but soils, waters, plants, and animals, as a *higher* form of ethics."[60] This seems to be right. To put the point differently: for Leopold, living and nonliving entities in fact have rights, and we humans in fact have obligations toward them, and any understanding of morality that denies this is mistaken.

It is a part of Leopold's thinking that not only individual animals, plants, rivers and land areas but also systems or collections of such individual entities have moral rights, and we have moral responsibilities toward systems and collections, including that collection that is the whole of nature. At times Leopold seems to give moral preference to the welfare of systems over that of individuals. He says, "A thing is right when it tends to preserve the integrity, stability, and beauty of the biotic community. It is wrong when it tends otherwise."[61] His concern is with land use, and he is urging that "decent"—morally proper—land use cannot be determined solely by economic factors. However, his claim about rightness, which seems to promulgate a kind of utilitarian standard for moral rightness, puts the rights of individual entities at risk. As Regan, who quotes the above passage, observes, "the implications of the view include the clear prospect that the individual may be sacrificed for the greater biotic good."[62] Regan seems right about this, but Leopold has this problem only because of his utiliarian-sounding standard—a problem of the same sort Mill has regarding the rights of persons, given the utilitarian standard for moral rightness he proposes. It would not change that much or diminish the spirit of Leopold's thinking, it seems to me, if we understood him as saying that a relevant ethical concern in determining what is right is always "the integrity, stability, and beauty of the biotic community," as well as the rights of individuals within that community.

59. Ibid., 226 and 219.
60. Blackstone, "The Search for an Environmental Ethic," 317 (Blackstone's emphasis).
61. Leopold, *A Sand County Almanac*, 240.
62. Regan, *The Case for Animal Rights*, 361.

The larger question, perhaps, is whether it is permissible to speak of the rights of systems, collections, or communities, as opposed to the rights of individuals. Regan raises this concern,[63] as well as a concern about what the criterion for the inherent value of, say, an oak tree would be.[64] Let me say a word about each concern, starting with the second. Regan allows that a criterion can be given for when an oak tree is good of its kind, a good oak tree, but then we can do the same for cancer cells or murderers, he observes. So this kind of criterion will not do as a criterion of inherent value. Nor will his criterion for being a subject of a life, since it presupposes consciousness. So what criterion can be advanced? But Regan may be misguided in having this concern. True, he only wants a sufficient condition for inherent value (strictly a sufficient condition for the intelligible and nonarbitrary attribution of inherent value), not a necessary and sufficient condition. However, it is not clear to me that even such a criterion as this is required. Instead of advancing some statement of features that we use to identify entities with inherent value, we can say that those beings we experinece as having inherent value in some degree are beings with inherent value—and they happen to have the various features they in fact possess.

Regan's other concern is with the permissibility of speaking of the rights of collections, as opposed to the rights of individuals, as we would do if we spoke of the right of a forest of trees, as opposed to the right of an individual tree. Regan, we should be clear, does not argue that it is impermissible or confused to speak of the rights of collections of entities, but he does see a certain unclarity or difficulty in such an attribution. He does so, I think, because rights, as generally understood, are rights of individuals. As he says, "paradigmatic rights-holders are individuals." Nevertheless it may be that less typical rights-holders are collections or communities. And, I think, Regan points the way to our understanding how this may be so. "The rights view [that is, Regan's own view,]," he says, "does not deny the possibility that collections or systems of natural objects might have inherent value."[65] However, the possibility of inherent value, I suggest, entails the possibility of rights. The moral rights of persons, on the view we have developed (in Chapter 9), are in accord with and required by the inherent value of persons. By extension, the rights of beings or entities that are not persons, including collections such as biotic communities or ecosystems, would be in accord with and required by their inherent value. Perhaps various rights

63. Ibid., 362.
64. Ibid., 245–46.
65. Ibid., 362.

possessed by such entities, like various human rights, could be overridden, but like the moral right to be treated as a person, the moral right of an entity to be treated in accord with its inherent value would be truly inalienable. Accordingly, if natural entities have some degree of inherent value, they have at least some moral rights. And while, once again, sin/relationship morality as such has no list of rights to propose, it is clear that if nonliving natural entities have inherent value, they, like living beings, have those rights that are consonant with their inherent value, whether those natural entities are individuals or communities of individuals.

But do natural objects have inherent value? What does sin/relationship morality have to say about the inherent value of nonliving natural objects like mountain ranges and deserts? Let me use here the same line of reasoning I used above in reflecting on the inherent value of animals without consciousness and the inherent value of inanimate living things. Consider cases in which a beach or a landscape is despoiled, as by a negligent oil spill or by deliberate strip mining. Why is such a thing so morally repugnant, aside from the waste of resources? Again, in part, it may be because such actions are degrading to the persons who perform them, and it may also be because, in these cases, there is great animal suffering and loss of life. However, let us set aside these elements as much as we can. To the extent there yet remains a sense of moral repugnance, its source is in the sense that something of value in the natural nonliving environment has been violated. To use one of Leopold's terms, the "integrity" of a natural setting has been violated. Using the lanugage of sin/relationship morality, the inherent value of a setting has been violated. I would suppose that in most cases of environmental atrocity there is a great element of animal suffering and loss of life, both animal and inanimate, but perhaps not always. Putting a billboard in a pasture may be an example. Our moral sensibility that in these cases there has been a lack of respect for the inherent value of a natural entity or a natural system can be explained by sin/relationship morality. The explanation is that the analogy with persons extends, though with lessening force, from human persons to higher animals, to lower animals, to plants, and to nonliving natural objects.

In effect, such an explanation points to a dimension, or several related dimensions, of our potential moral experience. As we can come into the presence of persons and thereby discover their inherent value as persons, so too we can come into the presence of nonhuman animals, into the presence of inanimate but living beings, like an oak tree, and into the presence of nonliving natural entities—natural settings like a pasture or a mountain range or a desert—and thereby discover an inherent value analogous to that possessed by persons. Whether this is right, to be sure, is contingent on the actual nature of our moral experience, or potential moral experience, but then I have never maintained otherwise. If this point is correct, what is discovered is the inherent value of various entities, and this inherent value does not reduce to some set of natural features. It surely does not reduce to some value that entities have for human use, but also it does not reduce to a property or a set of properties of the entity in question—just as the inherent value of persons does not reduce to the value of rationality or consciousness. To think otherwise is to insist on a will-o'-the-wisp strong criterion for inherent value. It follows that it is not necessary to think that every entity that has inherent value has it by virtue of some *shared* natural property. Blackstone is wrong, then, when he suggests that if we think that all animals have rights, we must "see all of life as a continuum in which there are different degrees of consciousness"[66]—just as he is wrong in suggesting, as he apparently does, that if we think that "nonsentient nature" has rights, we must in some way see it as having a degree of consciousness.

What, though, would it be like to come into the presence of a natural setting? There are, of course, various ways that we can react to or respond to a natural setting. We all, I suppose, have been moved by natural vistas. Our breath may be taken away by the sheer beauty of a place, a secluded dell or a canyon reaching away from a ridge. Or we may find a place fascinating. Or we may find a place intriguing and want to return to it to learn more about it. But these ways of experiencing a place need have no moral aspect. True, if we experience the beauty of a place, we may come to feel a moral commitment toward it. Perhaps this is invariably so for many, as it must have been for Leopold. But, unhappily, one can experience the beauty of a place without being moved morally. On the other hand, coming into the presence of a place is an experience with a distinct moral dimension. It involves a discovery of the integrity of the place, to use Leopold's category, and, as a part of that discovery, an affective dimension resulting in a kind of moral sympathy for the place or a respect for the integrity of the place. (Perhaps any one of several like affective states may be involved, as with coming into the presence of persons [see Chapter 5]; however, I shall not pursue that question.) When one has such an experience and discovers the integrity of a natural setting, one comes to have

66. Blackstone, "The Search for an Environmental Ethic," 329.

respect for the integrity of the place and to appreciate the appropriateness of that respect.

A question that may occur to some at this point is whether we can come into the presence of a nonnatural setting as well as that of a natural setting. Can we come into the presence of a setting created by human industry or artistic endeavor, a city's skyline as opposed to a mountain range's ridgeline, a magnificent bridge or a cathedral, such as the Cathedral of Florence? Again, the question is not whether we can experience the beauty of such places. Do they possess an integrity that we can experience, which we thereby come to respect? I think that we must allow that they do if natural settings do. If we allow this, we can understand why some argue on moral, as well as esthetic, grounds that new buildings in a city setting or on a university campus should be architecturally compatible with the already existing structures. Our noting that we may well be able to experience the integrity of nonnatural settings if we can experience the integrity of a natural setting, though, is essentially an aside. Our present concern is with the character and possibility of coming into the presence of a place that is a natural setting. Such an experience of a natural setting, I suggest, is a possibility within our moral lives, although, as with the discovery of the inherent worth of persons, I have no proof to offer. Ultimately, once again, my appeal is to our actual or potential moral experience.

In any case, that respect for the integrity of a place which follows upon coming into the presence of a place, if there is such an experience, should not be confused with respecting a property owner's rights. Nor should it be confused with respecting God's right of Lordship regarding His creation. If we have obligations of stewardship to God in respect to His creation, such obligations are to God, but what discovering the integrity or inherent value of a place amounts to, or involves, is discovering the basis of direct obligations to a natural setting. Of course, this is not to deny that both sorts of obligations might exist, and, in fact, I would suggest that among the obligations to God that arise from our relationship to God in a religious sin morality, there are obligations regarding our treatment of God's creation. Furthermore, it may be that we can come into the presence of a place just because in doing so we are reacting to the glory of God's creation, though it may be unrecognized as such by many. I would not wish to deny this. But even so, there is a difference between the Psalmist's experience of coming into the presence of God when he lifts his eyes up to the hills and the moral experience of the presence of a place. The difference, of course, is that for the Psalmist, but not for one who experiences the presence of a place, there necessarily is a felt sense of the presence of God or of the Divine.

Early on in this chapter I suggested that sin/relationship morality could provide a kind of groundwork or justification for moral activism on behalf of animals. We are now in a position to see why this is so, and why sin/relationship morality can as well provide a justification for moral activism on behalf of the environment. For sin/relationship morality, as we can come into the presence of persons, so we can come into the presence of nonhuman animals, even if they are not persons, and into the presence of natural nonliving objects and settings. In so doing we discover a kind of inherent value that they possess, on analogy with the inherent value persons possess. The rights of animals and of natural objects and settings, and our obligations toward them, can be understood in relation to their inherent value. As we can violate the inherent value of persons, which we do when we violate the person/person relationship we have with persons, so we can violate the inherent value of animals and natural objects and settings, which we do when we violate our fundamental relationship to them. In this way it is possible for us to sin against animals and to sin against the environment.

Sin/relationship morality, like other morality forms, such as guilt morality, has what I have called a person-scope. And, we will recall from our earlier discussion (in Chapter 12), a morality form has a person-scope in two aspects, or dimensions: it has, on the one hand, a responsibility-scope, consisting of all those who are responsible or accountable under that morality form; and, on the other hand, it has an obligation-scope, consisting of all those toward whom one has obligations under that morality form. The person-scope of sin morality—that is, of human sin/relationship morality—I said is universal in both of its aspects. So it is. That is, for sin/relationship morality, all persons are included in each of the two dimensions of its person-scope. Moreover, only persons are included in its responsibility-scope. Only persons are morally accountable, that is to say. To use Regan's categories, only persons are "moral agents." And thus, under the assumption that only human beings are persons, only human beings are morally accountable. But even under that assumption, the other dimension of sin/relationship morality's person-scope is another matter. What we have seen in this chapter is that if we experience only human beings as persons, still the obligation-scope of sin morality includes many beings and entities who are not persons. Many beings and entities are "moral patients," in Regan's terms. The obligation-scope of sin/relationship morality includes many nonpersons by virtue of the analogy between the inherent value of human persons and the inherent value of nonhuman animals and the further analogy with the inherent value, or integrity, of nonliving natural objects and settings.

16

The Fruits of Sin/Relationship Morality: Practical Implications

If a main thesis of this book is correct, relationships between persons are foundational to morality—to obligations, to virtue, and to the other mansions of morality in the first sense of "morality." If a second main thesis of this book is correct, relationship morality, viewed as sin morality, more deeply reflects our moral experience than does either guilt morality or shame morality. If these theses are both correct, then sin/relationship morality is the fundamental morality that we live. At the deepest level our moral lives are constrained by and enlivened by our relationships, including the person/person relationship. This is not to say, however, that the underlying role of relationships is fully and explicitly appreciated by all who in some way respond to their relationships in their moral lives. As we have seen, it is possible to act morally on the basis of principle, and it is possible to follow a conventional form of guilt morality. Yet, I have argued, even in these cases, the source of obligation and of the moral rules that are followed, if they are proper, is relationships between persons. Relationships are foundational to the morality we live, even if that morality is conventional. At the same time, as we have seen at points in earlier chapters, if we come to appreciate the foundational role of relationships, we will come to appreciate not only the fuller demands of our obligations but the reason our obligations extend to all persons and even to nonpersons. We have, that is to say, already seen some of the practical implications of sin/relationship morality. In this final chapter I want to bring into high relief the greater practical implications of sin/relationship morality—greater because they press hardest against conventional morality.

Some way back (in Chapter 6) I cited and illustrated the distinction between acting morally on the basis of principle and acting morally on the basis of an appreciation of the inherent worth of persons and the person/ person relationship we have to persons, and I argued that there is an ultimate and enduring difference between principled behavior grounded in an appreciation of the validity of a moral principle and moral behavior consciously grounded in an appreciation of the inherent worth of persons and our person/person relationship to them. We need not be thinking of the inherent worth of persons every minute or every time we act in order for our moral behavior to be grounded in an appreciation of the inherent worth of persons. Well-informed action can be spontaneous and need not be deliberated upon. We can be aware of something without thinking of it constantly. Yet it may be that we do not think of the inherent worth of persons, and of our person/person relationship to other persons, as much as we ought and that for this reason our morality is not all that it can be or ought to be. The main implications that I want to draw out in this chapter are implications of our being in a person/person relationship to persons.

It is an implication of sin/relationship morality that, by virtue of being a person, each of us shares with each a fundamental relationship, which is foundational to obligation and to the moral rights of persons. This relationship, the person/person relationship, underlies and supports the obligations generated by other relationships between persons, and it would generate many basic obligations even in the absence of other more familiar relationships. Close personal relationships, family relationships, and relationships that turn on ethnicity and nationality exist and generate obligations. But they are not our fundamental relationship to persons. When family, ethnicity, and nationality recede as a strongly felt basis of moral commitment or, alternatively, strongly assert themselves and their moral demands, it is well to keep in mind the fundamental relationship we have to persons by virtue of their being persons. For one thing, it is from this relationship that our basic obligation to practice justice toward all derives. In a shrinking world where more and more the decisions of nations, corporations, and even individuals affect others beyond our immediate ken, it is particularly important to keep vivid our appreciation of our relationship to all other persons and its moral requirements. John Donne wrote, in Devotion XVII, "No man is an *Island,* intire of it selfe; every man is a piece of the *Continent,* a part of the *maine;* if a *Clod* bee washed away by the *Sea, Europe* is the lesse, as well as if a *Promontorie* were, as well as if a *Manner* of thy *friends* or of *thine owne* were; any mans *death* diminishes *me,* because I am involved in *Mankinde.*" We need never send to know for whom the bell tolls: we are "involved in *Mankinde*," but not only the mankind of Europe, and not only *man*kind; we are, Donne means, involved in humanity, with every person. Sin/relationship morality identifies that involvement and shows us that in the form of the person/person relationship, it not only survives, or would survive, the dissolution of every other personal relationship, but is the source of our obligation to practice justice toward all quite independently of any other personal relationships.

As sin/relationship morality carries an implication for the way we should understand our basic obligation to practice justice, so it carries an implication for how we should regard war. It does so, again, because of what the person/person relationship entails regarding just treatment of persons. However, in this case the relevant area of justice is not distributive justice but that part of justice that requires us to respect the rights of persons. If there were a paramount duty of justice that required us not to engage in warfare, then even though a war might be fought for just ends, still this paramount duty of justice would be overriding. Arguably this is just the case. Sometimes the rights of individuals come into conflict, and then it must be decided which right takes moral precedence, that is, which right justice requires us to respect in our actions. In such cases we should respect the more basic, if one of the conflicting rights is more basic than the other. That is, in cases where one right derives from another we should respect the more fundamental, underlying right. It is not always clear when this is so. In fact, I will allow, it is rarely clear. When it is clear, though, the more basic right takes moral precedence. Now, one right in particular can make a fair claim to be the most basic right, namely the right of persons to be treated as persons. This right, it seems, is *the* underlying right of human beings, upon which the others rest.

Engaging in war, though, is at odds with respecting this basic right of persons. It is because, while all that this right entails may not be clear, it is clear that it entails not dismissing the inherent worth of others. It entails not viewing and treating human persons merely as obstacles in our path, to be got around or climbed over. War, unlike staying the hand of an assailant, involves viewing and treating the enemy with hostility and, often, even as dehumanized. But these ways of viewing and treating other human beings renders them objects, as mere obstacles, and so these ways of viewing and treating others are in themselves a violation of the right of persons to be treated as persons.

This is so whether or not the war is fought according to rules and whether or not efforts are made to keep the war "gentlemanly." Though certain rules are followed and civilities exchanged, the tendency of those engaged, even before the fighting begins, but especially after it has begun, is to view the enemy with hostility. Or worse, after the civilities, the enemy may be treated, not with hostility, but as so many dehumanized targets. For combatants, this tendency is deepened by the use of weapons that do not require face-to-face contact. For the opposed civilian populations, the process is encouraged by each side's propaganda effort. Perhaps the violation of the right of persons to be treated as persons is clearest when the enemy is dehumanized and treated as material objects to be obliterated or neutralized. But treating the enemy with utter hostility also violates this right.

Some, however, it must be admitted, would challenge this last claim. For, they would argue, to treat persons with hate is still to treat them as persons. In a sense, this is true. Hate of another is a personal attitude, as opposed to one's attitude toward the chilliness of the day or the grayness of the sky. And being someone's enemy can be an intensely personal relationship in that the relationship can feed on knowledge about the other's personality or the history of the other's actions. However, acting with hate toward another person does not entail respecting any of that person's rights, let alone his or her basic right to be treated as a person. If anything, it is in tension with respecting his or her rights. A related point is that hostility can be personally directed, and, as Thomas Nagel argues, in warfare we would in a sense treat individuals as persons if we intentionally directed our hostility toward them as subjects with the intention that they receive it as subjects (as opposed to a dehumanized "bureaucratic operation," as he puts it.)[1] But, again, to direct hostility toward individuals as subjects is not therefore to treat them as persons in the way required by their fundamental right to be treated as persons. True, it is to treat them as knowing, conscious beings, as opposed to material objects or dehumanized targets. But still it is to treat them as mere obstacles in one's path—though they be regarded as conscious, knowing obstacles—whose removal or neutralization is a means to one's end. It is possible to view persons with contempt, even a kind of hate, and to respect their rights, even their basic right to be treated as persons, as a matter of principle. This we have seen. But to view and treat others with utter hostility—to allow hostility to be the crystallizing focus of one's regard for others—is to regard them as mere obstacles or objects who

---

1. Thomas Nagel, "War and Massacre," *Philosophy and Public Affairs* 1 (1972); reprinted in *Ethics and Public Policy*, ed. Tom L. Beauchamp (Englewood Cliffs, N.J.: Prentice-Hall, 1975), 224. For a fuller discussion of the ethical status of pacifism than I provide here, see my "A Defense of Pacifism," *Faith and Philosophy* 4 (1987).

by virtue of being mere obstacles have forfeited their basic right to be treated as persons.

Thus, since war requires treating the enemy as dehumanized or at least with this kind of overriding hostility, even though a particular war may be fought for just ends (to oppose atrocities, say), it will of necessity violate the underlying right of those designated "the enemy " to be treated as persons. And since war requires us to violate this most basic right of persons, it requires us to violate the paramount duty of justice, and this makes our engaging in war incompatible with our practice of justice.

It is another implication of sin/relationship morality that it provides a basis for moral reform. The person/person relationship and its moral requirements, particularly regarding justice, provide the basis for opposition to racism, sexism, ageism, and other forms of social prejudice. In this way, as in other ways, sin/relationship morality opposes what was until recently, and may still be with many, the received morality. Also, as we saw in the last chapter, sin/relationship morality provides a basis for the moral rejection of speciesism. As it is wrong to practice prejudice against persons on the basis of race, gender, or age, so it is wrong to practice prejudice against nonhuman animals on the basis of species membership. For sin/relationship morality, speciesism is to be rejected because human persons have a relationship to nonhuman animals analogous to the person/person relationship. So, for sin/relationship morality, while it may be that moral responsibility is, strictly, limited to persons (because nonpersons are not morally blameworthy or praiseworthy for their actions, and hence do not come under the categories of moral judgment), the obligations that persons have extend to nonpersons. Our obligations extend to any number of beings that are not persons, beings that, by virtue of their analogy to persons, may have moral rights. Moreover, sin/relationship morality provides a rationale for the recognition that the scope of our obligations extends to the nonliving environment and to the recognition of environmental rights. Never send to know for whom the bell tolls, Donne advises us. Each death diminishes each of us. For Donne, each of us is "involved in *Mankinde,*" in humanity. And, we should add, each of us is involved in more than humanity—in the lives of nonhuman beings and in the natural world in which all our lives are embedded.

To sum up so far: It is a practical implication of sin/relationship morality that, by virtue of the person/person relationship, we have obligations to all other persons and that we are morally required to consider the rights of all others, regarding justice in particular, but not justice alone. Similarly it is a practical implication of sin/relationship morality that, by virtue of their analogy to persons, we have obligations toward many nonhuman beings, including nonliving natural objects, and must morally consider their rights. These two main implications arise from and apply to the person-scope of sin/relationship morality. Now let us look at an implication that arises from and applies to its action-scope.

We have had occasion to consider how the action-scope of sin/relationship morality includes perhaps hitherto disregarded interior actions, such as harboring wishes and desires (we saw this in Chapter 4). I want now to focus on certain further interior actions demanded by the person/person relationship. If the person/person relationship obtains, one morally required interior action is our having love or respect for persons, or, if not love or respect, some like attitude. If we are all related through our personhood, we ought to love or respect all persons or have some like attitude toward all persons, by virtue of the inherent value all persons share. Indeed, persons have the right to be loved or to be respected as persons or to have some like attitude manifested toward them. The point here is not that if we come into the presence of persons and thereby discover their inherent worth and our person/person relationship to them, we shall, as part of that discovery, come to have love or respect or some like attitude toward persons. Though this is true (as I tried to bring out in Chapter 5), the present point is that we have a duty to love or respect persons or to have a like attitude toward persons, a duty, or obligation, that is not contingent on our discovering the inherent worth of persons but that flows directly from persons having inherent worth as persons. Here, then, is one implication of sin/relationship morality for our interior actions. In fact, it should be familiar to us (we identified it back in Chapter 4). What I want to do now is to explore the further demands of this duty, in particular its requirements regarding belief and hope.

The duty to love our neighbor, with its connection to belief and to hope, is recognized in the Christian tradition. Saint Paul, in his First Letter to the Corinthians, says that "Love . . . believes all things, hopes all things" (1 Cor. 13.7). Our concern, of course, is not to argue that we have a duty to love because God commands it, or to argue that love involves belief and hope because Paul says so. Still, it will be helpful to draw upon religious, particularly Christian, reflection, and I shall use the thought of Kierkegaard on our duty to love as a heuristic aid. Kierkegaard, to be sure, is maintaining that we have a duty to *love*, while the duty that arises from human sin/relationship morality is the duty to have an affective attitude toward persons in the respect/love range; and in that range there is respect for persons as persons and an attitude of caring, as well as love. But what Kierkegaard helps us see is involved in love is also involved in like attitudes.

Kierkegaard, in *Fear and Trembling*, we will recall (from our discussion in Chapter 10), gives us the category of "the ethical," or "the universal." The universal, as the morality that is open to our common sense, is commonly accepted and "universally" understandable and as such, I suggested, coincides with conventional guilt morality. But elsewhere Kierkegaard allows a different perspective on morality. In *Works of Love*, which he wrote without the insulation of pseudonym, when Kierkegaard speaks of the "duty to love," he has in mind morality in its highest sense—which, for him, is Christian ethics. In any event, however he is thinking of morality, Kierkegaard is acutely aware of the interior dimensions of the duty to love, which he gets at in part by reflecting on Paul's claim that "Love . . . believes all things, hopes all things."

With the aid of Kierkegaard's reflections, I want to explore how the duty to love involves further duties to believe and to hope. With Kierkegaard, I shall consider hoping and believing to be interior acts. One can, in at least some settings, try to believe that something is true, or try to hope that something is so, and on these occasions one may or may not succeed. Hoping and believing, then, in at least some settings, seem to be more or less within our voluntary control (whether or not, ultimately, our being able to believe or hope in trying circumstances is a gift). We may, accordingly, consider voluntary those hopes that we want to have and try to have. However, though I think this is right, I am not going to insist upon it. It will not seriously affect my discussion if beliefs and hopes are involuntary but still blameworthy if they are wrong.[2] Our question, and Kierkegaard's, is, What does our duty to love require us to believe and to hope? Kierkegaard divides the question: What does love require us to believe? And what does love require us to hope?

Let us start with belief. "Love," says Paul, "believes all things." We may at this point hear from offstage the question of the mocking literalist: Are we to believe all possible propositions, then, even those that are obviously self-contradictory? Clearly not. The term "all things" has a context, and that context puts what is to be believed in the vicinity of those who are loved. And even then, as Kierkegaard brings to our attention, love's believing all things should be distinguished from frivolity's believing every-

---

2. It will not, for the reason that came out in our examination of Robert Adams' category of "involuntary sins" in Chapter 13.

thing that is said, from vanity's believing everything flattering that is said, and from spite's believing everything evil that is said.[3] Love's believing all things must not make it embrace frivolity, vanity, or spite. What, then, in the vicinity of those loved, must love believe in order to believe all things? Finally, it is this question that we must answer in our effort to shed light on the interior demands of love. However, I shall turn the question slightly to accommodate Kierkegaard: How shall we understand the saying that love believes all things? I find several threads running through Kierkegaard's reflections, three of which I want to separate. The third will be most helpful to us, but we cannot disregard the other two.

The first thread relates to the hiddenness of human motivation and intention. How inventive hidden inwardness can be! Kierkegaard observes. May it not be true that one person never completely understands another? But if one person "does not understand the other completely, then it always remains possible that what is most indisputable could still have a completely different interpretation which, mark well, would be the true interpretation." With this understanding we would do well to judge others sparingly or not at all. These comments are embedded in a paragraph set off as a quotation, and of what is said therein Kierkegaard himself says "it is completely ambiguous." It is "ambiguous" in that it could have been said equally well by "the most mistrustful and the most loving person." Still, Kierkegaard does not dispute that it is "knowledge." As knowledge, for Kierkegaard, it is "impersonal" and "places everything in the category of possibility."[4] To get past such mere knowledge we must make a "decision" to believe—to believe all things—and so we move to a second position, one that corresponds with the second thread in Kierkegaard's reflections. To it we shall turn shortly, but before we move on, there are implications of this first way of thinking that we should trace.

This way of thinking allows us to believe much. It allows us to believe that the most obviously cruel act may yet turn out to be not a cruel act at all. It allows us to believe that in every case, however heinous the act may be, it still is possible that "the true interpretation" of that act will speak well of the person whose act it was. This way of thinking, then, though Kierkegaard does not make it explicit, allows us to believe "all things" in a sense. It allows us to believe that in every case of an obvious betrayal or otherwise evil act, it *is possible* that what was done was good, although it

3. Søren Kierkegaard, *Works of Love*, trans. Howard V. Hong and Edna H. Hong (New York: Harper & Row, 1962), 214.

4. Ibid., 216, 217, and 218.

does not allow us to believe that in every case what was done *was* good. Involved in this way of thinking is an epistemological assumption. It is something like this: We can never be absolutely certain of the evil nature of human actions. Is this assumption correct? If it is, then we must say that, for instance, Hitler's adoption of his genocidal death-camp policy may possibly have been a good act, and we must say something similar of Dostoyevsky's general in *The Brothers Karamazov*. In that novel Ivan recounts to his brother Alyosha a number of cruelties done to children. In one of the cases Ivan has collected, a landowner, a general, sets his dogs on a serf boy, a child of eight, for throwing a stone and hurting the paw of one of his favorite hounds. While his mother is made to watch, the general's dogs run down the boy and literally tear him to pieces.[5] It is not precisely because this assumption and its implications are so hard to accept that Kierkegaard moves to a second dialectical position. In fact, he does not identify this assumption or consider its implications. He does, however, move on.

And so we come to the second thread in Kierkegaard's reflections. The theme of this thread is that "love believes all things—and yet is never deceived."[6] And here more than possibilities are believed in: the lover will believe that things are just as the one loved presents them to be. Amazingly, reflects Kierkegaard, though love believes everything, it is never deceived. This is amazing, for one would think that it is the person who believes nothing who would never be deceived. But, says Kierkegaard, by believing everything and making oneself "fair game for all deception and deceivers," one precisely thereby "assure[s] oneself infinitely against every deception."[7] "The deceiver wants to trick him [the lover] out of his love," but "this cannot be done." Kierkegaard falls back on an a analogy: as one who freely gives away his money cannot be swindled out of it, so one who gives his love cannot be tricked out of it.[8] And it would not matter if it should turn out "in eternity" that the lover "really had been deceived."[9] If love is "the highest good and the greatest blessedness," then the lover cannot be deceived in time or in eternity.

It is important for this theme that love in and for itself is "the highest

---

5. Fyodor Dostoyevsky, *The Brothers Karamazov*, trans. Constance Garnett (New York: Modern Library, n.d.), 251–52.

6. Kierkegaard, *Works of Love*, 213 ff. This is the title of Kierkegaard's chapter on love and belief.

7. Ibid., 221.

8. Ibid., 228.

9. Ibid., 229 (emphasis deleted).

good and the greatest blessedness." Such love is given freely and unconditionally: it is not given on the condition that love be returned. Indeed, it is
not offered with the demand that there be anything given in return—thus
the impossibility of being swindled out of love. "True love, love in and for
itself," Kierkegaard recognizes, stands in contrast with "a lower conception
of love," according to which love demands that it be reciprocated.[10] Love
in this "lower conception" can be taken advantage of and deceived; and
precisely when it is deceived, such love, not being reciprocated, is aban-
doned. Kierkegaard's distinction between these two conceptions of love,
we might note in passing, parallels the distinction between Agape and
"transactional" forms of love that we found it necessary to acknowledge in
Chapter 5. The distinction, then, is viable. Does Kierkegaard's use of it
allow him to make out a sense in which love is never deceived? In a way it
does. It is, I think, fairly clear what Kierkegaard is saying here. If love is
freely and unconditionally given, then it cannot be "deceived" in the sense
that it cannot be disappointed or destroyed—for it is given regardless of lies
and fraud. And if, in its simply being given, it is the greatest blessedness,
then, again, lies and fraud cannot deny the lover that blessedness. That
love is a blessedness for the one who loves is a relevant Christian idea (cf.
the Beatitudes: "Blessed are those who mourn, for they shall be comforted,"
Matt. 5.4). But by dwelling on this point Kierkegaard provides a kind of
prudential justification for believing everything, something he is normally
averse to doing.[11] At the same time, he does not provide a reason for
regarding such belief as a duty. (It would be a curious epistemic duty to
believe what we clearly perceive to be a lie.) Moreover, this construction
allows that the lover who believes all things will be deceived in the
straightforward sense of being led to believe what is false.

This brings us to the third thread in Kierkegaard's thinking about love's
duty to believe all things. It is embodied in the theme that "love is the very
opposite of mistrust."[12] "Mistrust," Kierkegaard says, "believes nothing at
all," and so "does just the opposite of what love does."[13] What this theme
brings out is that trust, as faith in someone, is a kind of belief, a belief *in* a
person. What is it to trust or believe in a person, or in all persons, in this
way? For sin/relationship morality it is, first, to believe in the lovability of
persons and, second, to believe that it is in persons to act and to be in their

10. Ibid., 223.
11. Cf., e.g., ibid., 214
12. Ibid., 216.
13. Ibid., 214.

hearts and minds in accord with their inherent worth. This belief we should carefully distinguish from the belief that all everyone has done may possibly turn out to be good (the construction of the first thread). And we should of course distinguish it from the belief that all everyone has done *is* good or *is* as those loved present it (the construction of the second thread). For this third thread of Kierkegaard's thinking, in the denouement provided by sin/ relationship morality, the one who loves can be deceived about whether his or her love is returned, about the story he or she is told, and about much else. But the one who loves can never be deceived about the inherent lovability of the person loved. Love believes everything in believing in each person's worthiness of love and also in the possibility of goodness in accord with that worth, though not necessarily in the probability or even the possibility of manifested moral goodness of every person in every setting. What is believed in and trusted in is not an inner core of actual morality in every person, but an inherent worthiness of love and, in accord with their inherent worth, the ultimate possibility of goodness. This love truly cannot be deceived, because it does not depend on any reciprocation or on any contingent feature of those loved, moral or otherwise.

"Love . . . believes all things, hopes all things," says Paul. The remaining half of the question we have set before ourselves is, What does our duty to love require us to hope? Here, in pursuing this part of our question, it is once more useful to distinguish three threads in Kierkegaard's reflections. The first identifies the hope of love with the hope that finally in this life there is the possibility of the good manifesting itself in the life of the other person. The one who loves, says Kierkegaard, "hopes in love that possibility is present at every moment, that the possibility of the good is present for the other person, and that the possibility of the good means more and more glorious advancement in the good from perfection to perfection or resurrection from downfall or salvation from lostness and thus beyond."[14] The "lover hopes all things," that "there is even at the last moment the possibility of the good."[15] This thread is not unlike the first thread of Kierkegaard's reflections on love's believing all things. Each affirms a possibility. Here, though, as befits hope, the focus in on the future, even up to "the last moment." And here too there is an assumption: that no human life is so ensnarled with evil that there is no possibility of turning toward the good.

14. Ibid., 237.
15. Ibid., 240.

The second thread develops dialectically from the first and again is not unlike the second thread relating to belief. It is that "love hopes all things—and yet is never put to shame."[16] Even though the hope of the lover is not realized, it is not put to shame. So, even if the story of the prodigal son ran differently and "the prodigal son were dead in his sins and consequently lay in a grave of shame," his father would not be put to shame. The prodigal son's father hopes all things for his son, and though "the concerned father thinks least of all about honour," he "nevertheless . . . stands indeed with honour."[17] That is, I gather, the father's hope is not "put to shame" in the sense that it is in itself an "honour," whether the hope is realized or not. "In eternity," says Kierkegaard, "it is not the result that determines honour and shame, but the expectation itself."[18]

Again, as with understanding what love requires us to believe, it is the third thread in Kierkegaard's reflections that is most helpful to our understanding what love requires us to hope. In the case of love's hoping all things, however, the third thread is slightly harder to draw out. Kierkegaard stresses that love hopes for only one thing. "Holy Scriptures," he says, "do not use the name *hope* for each and every expectation, the whole crowd of expectations. They recognize only one hope, the hope, the possibility of the good."[19] Here, as in the first thread, there is the crucial phrase "the possibility of the good." But in my construction of the first thread I understood the possibility of the good—which is present at every moment—as the possibility that the one for whom love hopes all things might at any moment manifest the good. For the third thread we need a different understanding of the possibility of the good, so that hoping for the good is hoping for one thing, and not a "crowd of expectations." How does Kierkegaard understand the good, that which love hopes for? Does he understand the one hope to be a hope for resurrection, as many do, including Peter Geach?[20] I think not. The "highest good" for Kierkegaard, in *Works of Love*, is "the God-relationship."[21] This Kierkegaardian idea is not limited to *Works of Love*; it is found in the pseudonymous corpus as well. "Essentially it is the God-relationship that makes a man a man," he says in *Concluding Unscientific Postscript*.[22] Kierkegaard was resolutely a

---

16. Ibid., 233 ff. This is the title of Kierkegaard's chapter on love and hope.
17. Ibid., 245.
18. Ibid., 246.
19. Ibid., 245 (emphasis in the text).
20. Peter Geach, *The Virtues* (Cambridge: Cambridge University Press, 1977), 45 ff.
21. Kierkegaard, *Works of Love*, 222.
22. Søren Kierkegaard, *Concluding Unscientific Postscript*, trans. David F. Swenson and Walter Lowrie (Princeton: Princeton University Press, 1941), 219.

"religious author"[23] and remained focused on the requirements of a "God-relationship," which, for Kierkegaard, in the *Postscript*, as in other works, is a faith relationship to God that is consciously chosen and lived *in this life*. For Kierkegaard, then, the one hope required by love is a distinctly religious hope, but for this life.

The third thread in Kierkegaard's reflections helps us to understand what love requires us to hope for. Love requires one hope, a hope for the possibility of the good for persons. For sin/relationship morality—human sin/relationship morality—that good is in accord with the inherent worth of persons. The good for persons that love must hope for is that they may live in tune with their own inherent worth and may attain a fulfilled person/person relationship to all others and to themselves; and here, because hope is different from belief, hope includes the hope that any person may even at "the last moment" turn toward the good. Does the good include—or, put better, is it embraced by—a faith relationship to God? This question I shall not try to answer. Its answer depends on whether there is a God to be related to. However, in Chapter 13 we saw that human sin/relationship morality and religious sin/relationship morality are continuous in such a way that in sinning against persons we may, if there is a God, also sin against God. And I did argue that if one gains a better understanding of the requirements of one's relationships to other persons, one may thereby gain a better understanding of the requirements of one's relationship to God, even if such a relationship is denied. In effect, then, in living in accord with our relationships to persons, including the person/person relationship, we may be following the requirements of a God-relationship and so may enter, if not a conscious faith relationship to God, a relationship of a sort to God.[24]

For sin/relationship morality, the moral ground for the hope that any person and all persons may live in tune with their inherent worth is that persons as persons do in fact have a real inherent worth, and the source or our obligation to have this hope for all persons is the person/person relationship each person has to every person by virtue of that very inherent worth. By virtue of their inherent worth, or personhood, all persons deserve our hope, deserve not to be given up on. This hope for the ultimate goodness of persons rests on the potential for goodness that resides in the inherent worth of persons, and this hope remains a duty of love even though

23. Søren Kierkegaard, *The Point of View for My Work as an Author*, in *Kierkegaard Anthology*, ed. Robert Bretall (Princeton: Princeton University Press, 1946), 326.

24. See note 62 to Chapter 13.

it may be all too plain in many cases that it will be thwarted by the accretion of habit and acquired disposition in conspiracy with circumstance. As long as persons have inherent worth, there is the possibility of turning toward the good in the sense required by hope, even if in any number of instances any real chance of that possibility of being realized has been cut off.

Though Kierkegaard's reflections can be used as a heuristic aid to our getting out the interior demands of love as sin/relationship morality understands them, it is too much to claim that Kierkegaard shares our concept of the deep nature of morality. Still, it is worth noting that Kierkegaard's concept of love is close to the concept of love or Agape we identified earlier (in Chapter 5). We have already seen that Kierkegaard distinguishes "true love" from a "lower conception" of love that demands reciprocation, and we have observed that his distinction accords with one we found between Agape and "transactional" love. Moreover, he is clear that there is a duty to find "in the world of actuality those we can love in particular and in loving them to love the men we see." "When this is the duty," he says, "the task" is not to find a "lovable object" but "to find the object already given . . . lovable, and to be able to continue to find him lovable, no matter how he becomes changed."[25] Kierkegaard's comment on this aspect of love relates, as he says, precisely to "love in particular," to love for particular persons met in the world, which he opposes to "love to one's neighbour."[26] For sin/relationship morality, all persons may be found to be lovable as they are "given" because all persons *are* lovable as they are, not by virtue of their merit or by virtue of any other attractive but changeable feature, but by virtue of simply being a person. And this holds for those we have met in the world and those half a world away. There is no limit to love, says Kierkegaard.[27] Love is giving and seeks nothing in return. Again, this is in accord with Agape in the conception we developed. This does not mean, we should appreciate, that the duty to love requires us to approve of all things. (And here I reiterate a point I sought to emphasize in Chapter 5.) Kierkegaard's "true love," like Agape, need not always be approving, nice, easy, or comfortable.

But Kierkegaard's reflections on the duty to love are also in some ways at odds with sin/relationship morality. For one thing, the duty to love "men," or persons, for him, seems to be a duty to God. That is, Kierkegaard seems to allow that even though the duty to love requires us to find persons lovable

25. Kierkegaard, *Works of Love*, 158. On the previous page Kierkegaard refers to 1 John 4.20.
26. Ibid., 157.
27. Ibid., 164.

as they are, this is a duty we have to God, not to "men." Though we are to strive to find persons lovable, we are to do so for the sake of God, as a part of a God-relationship, not for the sake of persons, as a part of our relationship to persons. For sin/relationship morality the duty to love is a duty to persons, although it may also be a duty to God. Persons are lovable by virtue of their personhood, and our duty to love them, to love persons for their own sake, is a duty that has a sufficient source in the fundamental relationship we have to persons as persons. Also, for sin/relationship moral- ity, the duty that flows from the person/person relationship is the duty to love or the duty to respect persons as persons or to have some like attitude toward persons. In order to fulfill this duty we need not have love toward all persons, although we must have some like attitude. Of course, if we follow a religious sin/relationship morality, and if it is God's commandment that we love all persons, which our relationship to God requires us to obey, then we will try to have love for persons and not some like attitude. But this is true only for those who follow a religious sin/relationship morality and who understand the commandment to love our neighbors as excluding like attitudes. And even for them, if their religious sin/relationship morality is continuous with a human sin/relationship morality, the duty to love is as well a duty to persons, and it is a duty to love persons for their own sake and not for the sake of God alone.

In any case, Kierkegaard helps us see what further interior actions— specifically belief and hope—are involved in our duty to love. For sin/ relationship morality, while we may respect persons and not love them, respect and its kindred attitudes, as much as love, carry the same obligations for belief and hope. This is because all of the attitudes in the respect/love range are alike in being a response to the requirements of the person/person relationship, and, at bottom, it is that relationship that requires our believing and hoping all things.

What we have just seen is an implication of sin/relationship morality in the area of its action-scope, and it is an implication that can be derived from our person/person relationship to persons, irrespective of any relationship to God that we may have. As an implication of sin/relationship morality, it makes the distance between sin/relationship morality and conventional morality seem unbridgeable, as perhaps it is. There are as well other hard implications carried by sin/relationship morality. One in particular is at odds with conventional moral understanding, although it is not for that reason at odds with our deepest moral intuitions.

The implication I now want to identify corresponds to a moral claim that is given expression in *The Brothers Karamazov*. When Dostoyevsky articulates it, as he does through the voice of Father Zossima's brother Markel, he does so in conjunction with other moral claims, which also are implications of sin/relationship morality. In earlier chapters I had occasion to quote some of what Zossima and Markel say in the novel. Let me quote from them again. The monk in his seclusion, Zossima says, must realize "that he is responsible to all men for all and everything, for all human sins, national and individual."[28] And Markel says, in a similar vein, "Every one of us has sinned against all men, and I more than any other. [And] every one is really responsible to all men for all men and for everything."[29] I find in what Zossima and Markel proclaim four moral claims relevant to our present concern. I shall express them as follows:

1. We all are morally responsible *to* all persons.
2. We all are morally responsible *for* all persons.
3. We all are morally responsible for *everything*.
4. We all have sinned against *all* persons.

(There is a fifth claim—that we all have *sinned* against all persons—which we discussed earlier, in Chapter 12. But we are now well acquainted with the idea that we can sin against persons. It is the further idea that we can and do sin against *all* persons that we must now examine as an implication of sin/relationship morality.) The first three claims are embodied in what Zossima says and in what Markel says. The fourth claim is expressed only in what Markel says, and it is this fourth claim that corresponds to the particular hard implication that I do not want to escape our attention. Before we turn to it, let me say something about the first three claims, since they also correspond to implications of sin/relationship morality.

The first claim is that all of us have obligations to all persons (not only to some). This is implied by sin/relationship morality by virtue of its recognition that the person/person relationship not only morally binds all persons but includes all persons in its obligation-scope. We are morally responsible to all persons in that it is possible to sin against each and every person by violating our person/person relationship to them. It is not merely that when

28. Dostoyevsky, *The Brothers Karamazov*, 170; quoted in Chapter 4.
29. Dostoyevsky, *The Brothers Karamazov*, 301; quoted in part in Chapter 4 and in part in Chapter 12.

we sin against any one person we are answerable to all persons: we can sin against all persons. The second claim is that we have obligations for all persons, for their welfare or good (not merely obligations to all persons for the welfare or good of some persons). This is implied by sin/relationship morality by virtue of the demands of the person/person relationship. The person/person relationship is the source of an obligation that we all have for the good of all persons. Moreover, we have responsibilities to and for beings who are analogous to persons by virtue of the relationship we have to them. Our responsibility, sin/relationship morality implies, is not only for humanity; and, of course, so far as it extends to humanity, it is by virtue of human beings being persons, not by virtue of human beings being human beings.[30]

The third claim is that we all are responsible for everything. We all are responsible for "all human sins," Zossima says. This claim, then, relates to the wrongs committed by human beings. It asserts that we all are morally responsible for all wrongs done by persons. Herbert Morris, who reflects on the first three claims, finds this third moral claim especialy problematic, but also the most intriguing of the three. In the essay in which he considers this third claim, he observes that "the claim that we are all responsible for everything, particularly when tied to narrower cases, say, being told that as whites we are responsible for the condition of the black man, responsible even for the evils perpetrated before our birth, produces not just intellectual disagreement, not just critical analysis but unquestionably, in the case of some people, considerable anger, sometimes anger of such intensity that we may become suspicious and wonder what nerve the claim has touched."[31] Morris senses that there is something true at the root of the third claim, but as it stands, he believes that it is in need of clarification and qualification. Accordingly, he suggests that the claim be understood as asserting neither a causal connection to all wrongdoing nor legal responsibility for all wrongdoing, but rather moral responsibility (an understanding our formulation of the claim makes explicit); and he suggests that the claim be understood as asserting shared moral responsibility for all *types* of wrongdoing, as opposed to all instances of all types.[32] With these qualifications in mind, Morris discovers four ways in which we may be responsible for much more than we would like to think, ways that would begin to justify the claim that we share

30. Cf. Herbert Morris, "Shared Guilt," in *On Guilt and Innocence: Essays in Legal Philosophy and Moral Psychology* (Berkeley and Los Angeles: University of California Press, 1976), 111–12.
31. Ibid., 116.
32. Ibid., 120–21.

moral responsibility for the wrongs done by others. He directs our attention to accepting desires and intentions to do what is hurtful—which is an instance of the kind of interior action we have discussed. Such states of mind, he points out, even if not acted upon, can harm a relationship of love or a friendship and so constitute wrongs.[33] This much shows that we are responsible for more than many of us would have thought, but it does not show that we share responsibility for wrongs done by others. In showing this much, Morris is trying to broaden the way we think of our moral responsibility in order to "loosen up objections" to the moral claim that we are responsible for everything.[34] He goes further, though. Certain states of mind may bring upon us complicity in the wrongdoing of others, such as recklessness or negligence in aiding a wrongdoer or, we may add, a lack of concern or care for those affected by the actions of others. Second, he points out that we may have complicity in the wrongdoing of others by substantially contributing to it through our unwise decisions—as when we do not provide greater financial support for education, to use one of his examples; or we may have complicity in the wrongdoing of others by profiting from it—as when, under a tax law that we did not initiate and may even have opposed, we enjoy paying a lower tax that unjustly favors our economic class. Third, we may share responsibility in at least some wrong-doing through our failure to act—as when we do not speak out or stand up in order to prevent evil.[35] And, fourth, we may share responsibility in wrongdoing simply by remaining alive in some instances. Morris' example, borrowed from Karl Jaspers, is the Germans' reaction to the Holocaust in the Nazi era. Morris quotes Jaspers: "When our Jewish friends were taken away, we did not go into the street and cry aloud until we also met our death."[36]

In these four ways, Morris suggests, we may indeed share moral responsibility for the wrongs done by others. Bearing in mind Morris' qualifications of the third claim, sin/relationship morality implies that we share moral responsibility for "everything" in accord with each of Morris' four ways that this may be so. The person/person relationship is violated by our state of mind when we fail to care for those near to us or those half a world away who are the sufferers of others' evil. The person/person relationship, and perhaps not it alone, is violated when we act with insufficient concern or

33. Ibid., 125.
34. Ibid., 128.
35. Ibid., 130–33.
36. Ibid., 133. The quotation is from Jaspers' *The Question of German Guilt.*

wisdom and when we fail to act to prevent or oppose evil. And it may be that there are cases of horrendous evil where the person/person relationship requires us to express our solidarity with those who are oppressed by giving up our lives with them, so that if we continue to live, we violate this fundamental relationship and share responsibility with the oppressors for their evil acts.

But now we come to the fourth claim, the claim that we all have sinned against *all* persons. It is this claim that deserves our particular attention, for it asserts more than the others and, from the perspective of conventional moral understanding, is more paradoxical. It claims more than that we *can* sin against all persons. It claims that we *have* sinned against all persons. Unlike the first and second claims, it asserts more than that we are morally responsible to and for all persons. It asserts that we all have violated our responsibility to and for all persons. And unlike the third claim under Morris' construction, it asserts that we share responsibility for wrongs done to each and every person. Is this fourth moral claim implied by sin/relationship morality? I think that it is. Once more I shall call upon Kierkegaard for heuristic assistance.

At the end of *Either/Or* Kierkegaard provides an "Ultimatum," or a final word. Its title is "The Upbuilding That Lies in the Thought That in Relation to God We Are Always in the Wrong."[37] The thought that we are always in the wrong relates to Zossima and Markel's sense that we are responsible to all persons for all persons and for all things, but it goes further and captures, or nearly captures, the claim that we have sinned against all persons. The thought that we are always in the wrong is "upbuilding," Kierkegaard says. How contrary this is to conventional thinking! he observes. For normally we strive to think of ourselves as being in the right. It is painful to think of ourselves as being in the wrong. Yet the thought that we are always in the wrong is upbuilding. The two thoughts together form a "contradiction," Kierkegaard acknowledges. The explanation is "that in the one case you loved, in the other you did not." Kierkegaard directs our attention to the fact that there are some persons to whom we "are drawn by a more fervent love than to others." "Now," Kierkegaard says, "if such a person who is the object of your love were to do you a wrong, is it not true that it would pain you, that you would scrupulously examine everything but that you would say: I know for sure that I am in the right; this thought will

37. Søren Kierkegaard, *Either/Or*, II, trans. Howard V. Hong and Edna H. Hong (Princeton: Princeton University Press, 1987), 339.

calm me? Ah, if you loved him then it would not calm you. . . . You would wish that you might be in the wrong; you would try to find something that could speak in his defense." And Kierkegaard goes on to say that "wishing to be in the wrong is an expression of an infinite relationship [of love], and wanting to be in the right, or finding it painful to be in the wrong, is an expression of a finite relationship [that is not a relationship of love]."[38]

Kierkegaard's reflections here are helpful, I think, for they do remind us of a movement in our love that we find recognizable. But, of course, he has in mind instances of "fervent love," love we have for someone who is close to us. In such instances our loving concern for the other may understandably lead us to wish to defend him or her at our own cost. Say that we had such love for everyone. Then we would understandably wish to be in the wrong in our relationship to each person and to all persons. Love fulfills the affective requirement of the person/person relationship that we have to all persons; however, such love—Agape—should probably be distinguished from the fervent love we have for those close to us. That is, while our fervent love for those close to us can be Agape, the Agape we have or might wish to have for those we shall never in fact see is distinguishable from fervent love. Let us grant this. Still, Agape is love and shares with fervent love the giving character that allows Kierkegaard to make his case. In this way, then, sin/relationship morality implies that for the sake of others we should wish to be in the wrong. At least it does so when the affective attitude that fulfills the requirement of the person/person relationship is love. Does it as well when the affective attitude is not love, but some other attitude in the respect/love range? This is less clear. Perhaps respect for persons as persons, for instance, will not sustain this implication.

What we have gathered from Kierkegaard's reflection so far, though, is only support for the implication that we ought to wish to be in the wrong. We so far have found nothing that supports the implication that we *are* always in the wrong, that we *have* sinned against all men. What about sin/relationship morality implies that this is so? If sin/relationship morality is right, the source of all our obligations toward persons, and of all the mansions of morality, is in relationships between persons. Morality is fundamentally a matter of living up to our relationships, including the person/person relationship. Living up to our relationships is something we can do to a greater or lesser extent. It is something that by its nature admits of degrees. For this reason, we will recall, sin/relationship morality is a

38. Ibid., 347–48.

"scale" morality (something we saw in Chapter 12). What this means is that there is always more that we can do to fulfill those relationships with others that underlie morality. There is always more that we can do to fulfill the requirements of the person/person relationship in particular. But, sin/relationship morality implies, to the extent we do not fulfill our relationships, we are in the wrong and have wronged, sinned against, the persons in those relationships. And this holds for the person/person relationship as much as for closer relationships. In this way sin/relationship morality does indeed carry the hard implication that we have sinned and continue to sin against all persons. The main reason that it is upbuilding to think that we are always in the wrong is that it is true.

This implication, like the others, in a significant way hinges upon the person/person relationship. In connection with this point it is important to return to Kierkegaard and comment on an element of his thinking that is apparently discomfiting to my argument. The thought that is upbuilding, for Kierkegaard, is that we are always in the wrong *in our relation to God*. Kierkegaard says, "If it were a person whom you loved . . . you would . . . be in a continual contradiction, because you would know you were right, but you wished and wished to believe that you were in the wrong. If, however, it was God you loved, could there be any question of such a contradiction, could you then be conscious of anything else than what you wished to believe?"[39] For Kierkegaard, we are always in the wrong in our relation to God, but not so in our relation to persons. Kierkegaard, as a religious author, is acutely aware that the demands of a God-relationship can never be fully met and that we, therefore, are always in the wrong in our relation to God. What he fails to see, though, is that the same logic applies to various relationships between persons, including the person/person relationship.

Because there is always more that we can do to fulfill the person/person relationship, we have sinned against all persons. Many may see this implication of sin/relationship morality as bitter fruit. And I suppose it is, if our tastes are conditioned by conventional morality. Does sin/relationship morality imply, then, that we should have a crippling sense of guilt or worthlessness? No, no such sense is necessitated or made appropriate by this implication. The implication before us does not further imply that we have sinned in every intention or act or that sin is unavoidable at every turn. There is always more that we can do to fulfill our relationships, but there

39. Ibid., 348–49.

may be much that we have done to fulfill our relationships. Drawing ever nearer to fulfilling our relationships, including the person/person relationship, is compatible with ever failing to fulfill them. And, in any case, our sin does not and cannot destroy or lessen the inherent worth we have as persons. But there are further implications of the implication before us that may also be distasteful to many. Our sinning against *all* persons implies that there was more that we ought to have done and, in the present, more that we ought to do to prevent the criminal's failure, the homeless child's hunger, the colleague's shortness of temper, and to correct our lack of compassion for the world. There was more we could have done, and there is more we can do, to fulfill the requirements of the person/person relationship we have to each and every person.

There are two other implications of sin/relationship morality that we should identify. Each is an implication for forgiveness. The first, quite simply, is this: we ought to forgive all who have in any way wronged us. The second is that we ought always to accept forgiveness. I shall discuss the first at some length and then treat the second more briefly.

All of us, I suppose, have the sense that at times in our lives we as individuals have been wronged by others. Sometimes, we may feel, the wrongs we have suffered are slight, sometimes grievous. Moreover, if what we have just seen implied by sin/relationship morality is true—that we, all of us, are always in the wrong and have sinned against all persons—then all of us are also the sufferers of wrongs done to us by all persons. With this implication in place, there is much for each person to forgive, but even without it, as I say, we all have the sense that we have at times been wronged by others. In every case, sin/relationship morality implies, we ought to forgive those who have wronged us. The only limitation on forgiveness recognized by sin/relationship morality is the conceptual limitation that allows us to forgive persons only for wrongs that are done to ourselves. As Ivan Karamazov puts it, the mother "has no right" to forgive the general who set his dogs on her son, that is, no right to forgive him for the suffering he caused her son. She may forgive him for her mother's suffering, but only the child himself can forgive the general for the harm and pain the general inflicted on him.[40] In fact, this is a conceptual point: logically the mother cannot forgive her child's oppressor for what he did to her child. It is not that she "has no right" to forgive the general but that

---

40. Dostoyevsky, *The Brothers Karamazov*, 254.

she might exceed her rights and do so anyway. So far as this conceptual point goes, however, it is possible, conceptually possible, for all of us to forgive every person for any and all wrongs done against ourselves— conceptually possible, but not therefore psychologically possible and not therefore morally proper. What sin/relationship morality implies is that in every instance it is morally proper, and not merely morally allowable, but a duty.

Now I think that it is counter to the way we conventionally think of forgiveness to say that we invariably have a duty to forgive those who have wronged us. Forgiveness must be earned, it is said. And, we conventionally believe, some forgiveness is improper. Nevertheless, sin/relationship moral- ity implies that there is this duty. And if the person/person relationship obtains, we do have such a moral duty, as sin/relationship morality implies. In order to see why this is so—why, given the person/person relationship, we ought to forgive all who have wronged us in any way—we shall need to reflect further on the character of forgiveness, its conceptual character, and also on some of the issues that have been raised regarding the ethical status of forgiveness.

First, then, some reflections on the conceptual character of forgiveness.

1. Forgiveness presupposes a wrong: there must be something to forgive (or, at any rate, the one offering forgiveness must believe that he or she has been wronged). As Aurel Kolnai says, forgiveness "presupposes an affront, injury, transgression, trespassing or offence committed by one person against the other and consequently the other's readiness or refusal to 'forgive.' "[41]

2. Forgiveness is not just forgetting the wrong that has been done to one. In fact, says Kolnai, "Forgiving is not only *not* 'forgetting' . . . but [is] incompatible with forgetting."[42] Forgiveness presupposes a recognition of the wrong done. It is different from the granting of amnesty, which is a kind of "forgetting" or wiping the slate clean. When a general amnesty is granted for, say, all that was done during a time of war, the power granting the amnesty is saying, in effect, We forget all that you did, right or wrong, and we will not hold you accountable.

3. Forgiveness in some way addresses and lessens the guilt of the wrong- doer. It involves some kind of "absolution from guilt," as Jean Hampton suggests.[43] Or, as Richard Swinburne puts it, the guilt of the wrongdoer is

---

41. Aurel Kolnai, "Forgiveness," *Proceedings of the Aristotelian Society*, n.s., 74 (1973–74): 92.

42. Ibid., 100 (Kolnai's emphasis).

43. Jean Hampton, "Forgiveness, Resentment, and Hatred," in Jeffrie G. Murphy and Jean Hampton, *Forgiveness and Mercy* (Cambridge: Cambridge University Press, 1989), 83.

"remitted." The act of the wrongdoer is "disowned" by both the wrongdoer and the "victim" in the ideal case, says Swinburne.[44] But Swinburne also suggests that forgiveness "removes guilt," causes it to disappear.[45] This way of putting it is at best misleading. Forgiveness does not transmogrify the wrong done so that it is no longer something of which the wrongdoer is guilty. Yet forgiveness, if accepted, can in some way lessen the felt burden of guilt. It sets aside the guilt, we may say; it absolves the wrongdoer from guilt without denying the guilt from which the wrongdoer is absolved.

4. Not actions but persons are forgiven, though persons are forgiven for what they did or failed to do, or thought or felt or failed to think or feel.

5. Forgiveness is some way "reapproves"[46] or "re-accepts"[47] a person. Forgiveness takes away the force of the wrong that alienates the wrongdoer from the person wronged and makes it possible for the wronged person to once again accept the person who committed the wrong.

6. Related to the last point, forgiveness in some way restores a relationship between persons.

7. Forgiving is in some way something we do. It is something we often do verbally. When we say, "I forgive you," that has a performance force and, at least at one level, constitutes granting forgiveness. If others witness my saying these words to another, they can affirm that I forgave the other. A boy who is urged by a parent to forgive his sister will do what is requested by saying to his sister, "I forgive you, sister." But at the same time, we are inclined to say that true forgiveness, or genuine forgiveness, involves more than perfunctorily uttering the words, "I forgive you." True forgiveness must be from the heart, we feel, and if we at first resent the wrongdoer and the wrong that was done to us, we must have a change of heart toward the person who has wronged us, in order truly to forgive that person.[48]

These conceptual features of forgiveness should strike us as familiar, or at

---

44. Richard Swinburne, *Responsibility and Atonement* (Oxford: Clarendon Press, 1989), 87.

45. Ibid., 85.

46. Hampton, "Forgiveness, Resentment, and Hatred," in *Forgiveness and Mercy*, 83.

47. Kolnai, "Forgiveness," 104.

48. Herbert Morris says that forgiveness is "not a doing and therefore not a voluntary doing *in the usual understanding of these concepts*" (my emphasis). He allows, however, that expressions such as "please forgive me" "suggest an element of agency at its very core." Forgiving someone, we may say, is more or less voluntary (about which, more later). Morris, "Murphy on Forgiveness," *Criminal Justice Ethics* 7 (1988): 17.

See Marilyn McCord Adams, "Forgiveness: A Christian Model," *Faith and Philosophy* 8 (1991): 294, for the distinction between performative forgiveness and forgiveness from the heart. P. Twambley, whom she cites, brings out the performative character of forgiveness in his "Mercy and Forgiveness," *Analysis* 36 (1976).

least as identifiable upon reflection. More could be said about these features of forgiveness and about their interconnectedness; however, we have seen enough, I think, to proceed. We want next to note two issues regarding forgiveness, for our appreciation of these issues will also, in its way, help us to see why forgiveness is such that sin/relationship morality implies that we ought to forgive all who have wronged us.

The first issue takes the form of a paradox, the "paradox of forgiveness," which arises because forgiveness has to be distinguished from condonation, on the one hand, and from our readjusted positive attitude toward the reformed person, on the other hand. The paradox is easily stated once its terms are clarified. Both of the attitudes that must be distinguished from forgiveness require a comment, particularly condonation. In cases of condonation, as Kolnai elaborates the notion, a wrong is recognized and disapproved of, but no opposition is registered: "condonation *acquiesces* in the offence."[49] Hampton provides a slightly different definition: it is "the acceptance, without moral protest (either inward or outward), of an action which ought to warrant such protest, made possible, first, by ridding oneself of the judgement that the action is wrong, so that its performer cannot be a wrongdoer, and, second, by ridding oneself of any attendant feelings (such as those which are involved in resentment) which signify one's protest of the action."[50] The essence of condonation is that one treats the wrong action as all right—whether or not one judges it to be wrong. One may not approve of the action, but one might as well have. Strictly, condonation can apply to wrongs not done against oneself, but when the wrong is against oneself, condonation can look like forgiveness in that it too seems to set aside whatever guilt there may be arising from a wrong one has received. The difference is that forgiveness, unlike condonation, must recognize and insist upon the full impermissibility of the wrong done.

Forgiveness is not condonation, but it is also not our taking up a new positive attitude toward the person who has renounced his of her wrongful act and made amends. Our new attitude of approval toward the reformed person is not in itself forgiveness and may come about without our forgiving the person. Now we are ready for the paradox of forgiveness. It takes the form of a dilemma. In Kolnai's original statement it is this: "Either the wrong is still flourishing, the offence still subsisting: then by 'forgiving' you accept it and thus confirm it and make it worse [which is condonation]; or

49. Kolnai, "Forgiveness," 95 and 96 (Kolnai's emphasis).
50. Hampton, "Forgiveness, Resentment, and Hatred," in *Forgiveness and Mercy*, 40.

the wrongdoer has suitably annulled and eliminated his offence, and then by harping on it further you would set up a new evil and by 'forgiving' you would only *acknowledge* the fact that you are no longer its victim. Briefly, forgiveness is either unjustified or pointless."[51] Kolnai, however, has a solution to the paradox he has discovered. He tries to salvage a place for proper forgiveness by finding a middle ground for it between the two extremes. For one thing, even if the wrongdoer has reformed and "eliminated his offence," there may still be a point to forgiveness in that one's forgiveness may have the beneficial effect of making the reformation "more explicit, definitive and fruitful."[52] But the point and moral value of forgiveness do not turn on effects, for Kolnai. There are times, he says, when "I might . . . see a meaning in forgiving X, who has gratuitously 'wronged' me, without condoning his offence but also without hoping for an improvement of his character." Kolnai continues, "It is possible to 're-accept' somebody—the essence of forgiveness—without exculpating him and without hoping for anything like a thoroughgoing repentance on his part [even though] we should *wish* for such a change of heart." And, lastly, for Kolnai forgiveness has value because, although he denies "that a virtuous person forgives every wrongdoer," he allows that "the more virtuous I am the more *disposed* I am to forgive."[53] We shall return to the paradox of forgiveness, and to Kolnai's solution to it. But now let us look briefly at a second issue that forgiveness faces.

The second issue is over the deep character of forgiveness. It relates in particular to the role of resentment in forgiveness. Is forgiveness an overcoming of resentment against the one who has wronged us? Is the change of heart often spoken of in connection with forgiveness just this overcoming of resentment? Is resentment, then, a necessary prelude to forgiveness? For Bishop Butler, as Jeffrie Murphy reminds us, forgiveness is the forswearing of resentment.[54] However, this does not mean that ceasing to have resentment always constitutes forgiveness. We will no longer resent those wrongs that we have forgotten, but mere forgetting is not forgiving, Murphy argues. Nor are we happy with the idea that a *selfish* forswearing of resentment is forgiveness of another, as Murphy also argues. To use a variant of the case Murphy presents, we do not seem to have a case of forgiveness if an

---

51. Kolnai, "Forgiveness," 98–99 (Kolnai's emphasis).
52. Ibid., 102.
53. Ibid., 104 (Kolnai's emphasis).
54. Jeffrie G. Murphy, "Forgiveness and Resentment," in *Forgiveness and Mercy*, 15. Murphy cites Sermons 8 and 9 in Butler's *Fifteen Sermons* (London: S.P.C.K., 1970).

individual who is told that his health is being undermined by his feelings of resentment undertakes to banish his resentment and does so through a judicious use of drugs. In the same way, we might be dubious about the forgiveness offered by someone with a committed shame morality who is forgiving precisely because his or her ego ideal demands it and for no other reason. Our ceasing to resent does not constitute forgiveness, Murphy suggests, unless we forswear our resentment for a "moral reason"—such as the wrongdoer's repenting or really having meant well.[55] (Murphy maintains that in each case a moral reason for forgiveness involves a "divorce of the evil act from the wrongdoer.")[56]

Often forgiveness does seem to involve the forswearing or the letting loose of resentment, for often our resentment can stand in the way of the change of heart toward the wrongdoer that will allow forgiveness. However, as Hampton observes, Murphy and Butler "try to characterize that change of heart by focusing on what the forgiver must overcome in order to have it."[57] For Murphy, the forswearing of resentment is forgiveness only when done for a moral reason, but for him, as for Butler, it is essentially a kind of overcoming of resentment. For Hampton, this characterization of the change of heart in forgiveness may be right as far as it goes, but it misses "the essence of forgiveness." In order to elucidate the essence of forgiveness Hampton directs her attention to a further characterization of the change of heart found in forgiveness. Much that she goes on to say helps us to understand forgiveness, it seems to me. Moreover, her reflections will help us in our present endeavor to show that sin/relationship morality implies that we have a duty to forgive all who have wronged us and that we do indeed have that duty if the person/person relationship obtains. Accordingly, I shall use as a means of pursuing our endeavor an examination of Hampton's analysis of the concept of forgiveness.

The definition of forgiveness, and of its change of heart, that Hampton comes to is this: "The forgiver who previously saw the wrongdoer as someone bad or rotten or morally indecent to some degree has a change of heart when he 'washes away' or disregards the wrongdoer's immoral actions or character traits in his ultimate moral judgment of her, and comes to see her as still *decent, not* rotten as a person, and someone with whom he may be able to renew a relationship."[58] Several elements in Hampton's definition

55. Ibid., 22–23.
56. Ibid., 25 ff.
57. Hampton, "Forgiveness, Resentment, and Hatred," in *Forgiveness and Mercy*, 43.
58. Ibid., 83 (Hampton's emphasis).

merit our attention. It is an effort to "capture the forgiver's change of heart," as she says, and her characterization of the change of heart in forgiveness is richer than the characterization of it as what allows overcoming resentment. What it involves is one's coming to see the wrongdoer as "decent," as "not rotten as a person." It allows the possibility of a renewal of "a relationship." Hampton goes on immediately to say, "When one has a change of heart towards one's wrongdoer, one 'reapproves' of her."[59] All of these elements are in accord with one or another of the conceptual features of forgiveness we identified earlier.

There is one other element that is crucial for Hampton's analysis. For her, as for Kolnai, forgiveness need not wait upon the wrongdoer's reformation. "Instead," she says, "the forgiver *trusts* that, although [the wrongdoer] has undergone no rebirth, he is still 'good enough' despite what he has done."[60] And so, Hampton concludes, "forgiveness is . . . the *decision* to see the wrongdoer in a new, more favorable light."[61] This decision, for Hampton, is a decision to believe, "to have faith in a decent core within, even if it is a core which we are completely unable to see."[62] It is a decision to have faith in the ultimate "value" of others—and in our own value, too, Hampton sees.[63] But what about, say, Hitler or the general who sets his dogs on the child in *The Brothers Karamazov*? Do they have an inner core of decency? Hampton admits that "the idea that I should have faith that people such as Dostoevsky's General have some inherent decency despite their action sticks in my craw."[64] And she has a similar sense about Hitler, Stalin, and Charles Manson, "who really may not have any decency left in them—nor even any possibility of decency."[65] Nevertheless, in their cases too we should believe in their inherent decency, despite a lack of evidence. "The [Christian] injunction to forgive," she suggests, "is not merely the injunction to encourage in oneself the reapproval of others based on real evidence of decency, but also the injunction to reapprove of others through faith in their decency despite a lack of evidence for it."[66] Faith and a decision to believe come into it, for Hampton, because the evidence is not adequate to

59. Ibid., 83.
60. Ibid., 84 (Hampton's emphasis).
61. Ibid. (my emphasis).
62. Jean Hampton, "The Retributive idea," in *Forgiveness and Mercy*, 151.
63. Ibid., 148.
64. Ibid., 153.
65. Hampton, "Forgiveness, Resentment, and Hatred," in *Forgiveness and Mercy*, 81.
66. Hampton, "The Retributive Idea," in *Forgiveness and Mercy*, 155.

justify our belief. And what we are to believe is that wrongdoers have "a decent core within" despite what we see of their lives.

Hampton sees, and sees clearly, that our having a sense of the value of the wrongdoer makes it possible for us to forgive him or her. But she identifies this value with an inner core of moral decency. And of course one immediately thinks of such persons as Hitler and Ivan Karamazov's general, who seem to lack any moral decency. Certainly we have no reason to believe in their moral decency, and so Hampton falls back on faith-without-evidence. Notice what happens, though, if we understand the value of the wrongdoer to be, not an inner core of moral decency, but the inherent value the wrongdoer has as a person. On this understanding a concern with the wrongdoer's moral status or goodness ceases to be relevant for forgiveness. What is relevant is that the wrongdoer is a person and as a person has inherent worth. But the worth that persons have by virtue of being persons is not contingent on moral merit: as long as persons are persons, they have the inherent worth of personhood, irrespective of their moral status. And so it is no longer necessary to "decide" to believe in the undetectable moral decency of a distinctly evil wrongdoer in order to forgive that wrongdoer. Moreover, if the value of the wrongdoer is understood in this way, we may have an abundance of evidence for his or her value. Coming into the presence of persons involves making a discovery of the inherent worth of persons, and of our fundamental relationship to others as persons. Such a discovery—if it is indeed a discovery—is by definition a realization of what is the case, a seeing of what is true. If we have made a universal discovery of the person/person relationship, if, that is, we have entered into the presence of *all* persons, then we will appreciate the inherent value of even the person who has done a wrong against us, regardless of the enormity of that wrong. Or if we have entered into the presence of only some persons, but the person who has wronged us is included, then again we will have discovered his or her inherent value, irrespective of what wrong has been done against us. Hampton is right, I think, in finding near the heart of forgiveness a sense of the value of the one to be forgiven. If we understand that value as the inherent worth persons have as persons, then we do not need to hold a belief in the moral decency of those who wrong us, a belief for which, in some cases, there may be no evidence. We need, rather, to believe in the inherent worth that those who wrong us have as persons, and this belief, in every case, may have an abundance of evidence upon which to rest.

With Hampton's help we have made headway, I think, and are closer to seeing why sin/relationship morality implies a moral duty to forgive all who wrong us. However, before I say explicitly why this is so, let us return to the two issues regarding forgiveness that I identified. Our seeing what sin/ relationship morality entails for them will help us appreciate why sin/ relationship morality implies a duty to forgive. The first issue regarding forgiveness takes the form of the paradox of forgiveness. This is the paradox formulated by Kolnai, and we have already seen how he resolves it. Hampton also has a resolution of the paradox. Let us look at her resolution and then turn to what sin/relationship morality has to say. Hampton criticizes Kolnai's resolution on the grounds that it does not completely escape condonation. For Kolnai, as she says, forgiveness does not condone the wrongs that were done by wrongdoers. But, Hampton says, for Kolnai, we are "forgiving that within them which led them to perform the action," that is, their bad character traits. And, asks Hampton, "why doesn't forgiveness of people with bad character traits amount to a condonation of their traits?"[67] For Hampton, as we saw in her definition of forgiveness, the forgiver has a change of heart and " 'washes away' or disregards the wrongdoer's immoral actions or character traits." But since disregarding is not condoning, the forgiver, in granting forgiveness, does not end up condoning either wrong actions or bad traits, on Hampton's account. She does, however, as we have seen, insist that one who has a change of heart and forgives a wrongdoer "reapproves" of the wrongdoer. For Hampton, then, there still is condona-tion, since in granting forgiveness we approve of the *person*, though we do not approve of the person's actions or traits. It is perhaps this element in Hampton's analysis that leads her to understand a person's value as that person's core of moral decency (which would be something we could appropriately approve of). And it would then be this element that leads in turn to the problem she has in understanding how Hitler and others like him can have value as persons.

For sin/relationship morality, forgiveness is not, and does not involve, such moral approval—not of actions, not of traits, and not of persons. Forgiveness is not the condonation of persons as basically decent. Instead, it involves the acceptance of persons as persons, with the inherent value of personhood. It involves the acceptance of persons as they are. (Here we might recall Kierkegaard: we are to love the persons we see, persons as they are.) Persons, by virtue of their inherent value as persons, deserve not to be rejected. A part of the resolution of the paradox of forgiveness, for sin/ relationship morality, is this: forgiveness is or involves a form of accepting

---

67. Hampton, "Forgiveness, Resentment, and Hatred," in *Forgiveness and Mercy*, 83 n. 32.

or reaccepting persons, which, as persons, they deserve; but this acceptance does not amount to either approving of or not disapproving of wrong acts, bad traits, or evil persons. This partially resolves the paradox in that it shows how forgiveness is not condonation, and the horn of the dilemma that traps Kolnai, according to Hampton, and traps Hampton herself is the possibility that forgiveness is a form of condonation. How forgiveness escapes the second horn of the dilemma, how it is not "pointless" but has a positive value, Kolnai and Hampton have already helped us see. Part of what makes forgiveness valuable, even when a resolutely evil person is forgiven, has to do with the connection between that acceptance of persons embodied in forgiveness and the concepts of faith and hope. For Kolnai—for whom, as we saw, to reaccept somebody is "the essence of forgiveness"— when we forgive, we need not *hope* for the wrongdoer's repentance, though we should *wish* for the wrongdoer's change of heart. For Hampton, forgiveness involves *faith*, but it is faith in an invisible core of moral decency. For sin/relationship morality, forgiveness and its acceptance of persons are made possible by faith or trust in the inherent worth of persons, though it is faith that may have its source in a realization-discovery and so may be well grounded. And this faith allows us to hope that the wrongdoer may come to act and be in accord with his or her inherent worth. (What more sin/relationship morality may have to add regarding this second horn of the dilemma, we shall see shortly.)

The second issue regarding forgiveness has to do with the relationship between forgiveness and resentment. Does forgiveness presuppose resentment or indignation or taking offense on the part of the one wronged? For some, like Butler and Murphy, the opportunity for forgiveness requires a resentment to be overcome. Kolnai similarly sees forgiveness as presupposing a "primary indignation and retributive attitude."[68] Does forgiveness presuppose resentment or indignation or taking offense, so that forgiveness would not be possible unless the one wronged had such a retributive attitude in the first place? I suggest not. And we can see that it does not, I believe, by considering a progression of three cases.

1. A believes that he has wronged B, but B does not think so. A asks for B's forgiveness. B says in all seriousness, "There is nothing to forgive." This, as Kolnai sees, is not a case of forgiveness.

2. A has wronged B. B is aware of this and resents the wrong. B is at first alienated from A, but B has a change of heart and forgives A. This, we may

68. Kolnai, "Forgiveness," 94.

say, is a normal case of forgiveness. It is the familiar kind of case that Kolnai, Murphy, and Hampton seem to have in mind.

3. A has wronged B. B knows this, but does not hold it against A—maybe B knows B's own weakness. A asks for B's forgiveness. Here B can give A forgiveness for the sake of A, without overcoming any sense of indignation or resentment. And B's forgiveness can be from the heart, although B has had no *change* of heart.

In this connection we should think about blaming persons for their blameworthy acts. Earlier (in Chapter 13) I observed that we can recognize that an action is blameworthy and not blame a person for that act. There are four points that should be made here and related to forgiveness.

1. If an action is wrong in type, it still may not be blameworthy. Though an action is wrong in the sense that we would not morally encourage it or approve of it, it still may not be blameworthy. Wrongs committed by innocents are in this category. The child who innocently announces, "You are fat," may have committed no blameworthy action (to use my example from Chapter 14). In some cases where we see a wrong has been done—a hurtful remark made, someone's property taken—we should not judge that the action was blameworthy, and would not if we appreciated the agent's innocence or motive or the degree of compulsion present or what the agent justifiably believed. Such cases as this substantiate the moral advice in Matt. 7.1 that we should not judge others, and provide part of its point.

2. If an action is blameworthy, it may not be our place to blame the person, to pronounce a condemnation. Our blaming the person, though only with the words "What you did was wrong," may be pointless or worse in many cases. And these cases also substantiate and provide part of the point of Matt. 7.1.

3. If an action is blameworthy and it is our place to blame the person for his or her action, still this is not to judge that the person is evil. Say that a person elicits from us our opinion of his or her action; then we might say, "Yes, what you did was wrong. I hope that I am never faced with such a choice." Such a judgment, clearly, does not judge the person to be evil. In *The Cloud of Unknowing* we find the following: "no man should be judged by others here in this life, neither for the good nor the evil that they do. Of course it is lawful to judge whether the deeds are good or evil, but not the men."[69]

69. *The Cloud of Unknowing*, ed. James Walsh, S.J. (New York: Paulist Press, 1981), chap. 29, 178.

4. Even if we cannot avoid the judgment that the person is evil, this is only the judgment that he or she is morally evil. It is not the judgment that he or she lacks inherent worth as a person. Even though we see that the person is evil, as many say that we can see that Hitler or Ivan Karamazov's general is evil, still love and the belief and hope entailed by love need not be renounced. Here I think that we approach the nub of Saint Augustine's urging us to "Hate the sin, love the sinner."

Now, how does all this relate to forgiveness? Conceptually we *can* blame people for acts against others—not just appreciate that what they did was wrong and blameworthy but blame them, pronounce a condemnation—while, conceptually, we can forgive others only for blameworthy acts against ourselves. So there are differences. Let us recast these four points so that they address forgiveness.

1. Here, in the adjusted case, though a wrong has been committed against us, the person who committed the wrong is not blameworthy. There is for this reason no appropriate place for forgiveness. It is in cases like this that we should try to show the person that he or she should not feel guilty.

2. When an action is a blameworthy wrong against ourselves, it still may not be our place to blame the person—to pronounce blame—and, similarly, it may not be our place *overtly* to grant forgiveness. Maybe the wrongdoer is a stranger, and the wrong is helpfully pointed out to him or her by a friend. If the wrongdoer heeds what the friend has said, our "forgiving" him or her may only "harp on" the wrong in an unnecessary and hurtful way, as Kolnai suggests. This, however, does not mean that we ought not to forgive the wrongdoer in our heart. We may have a duty to forgive in our heart when there is no duty to forgive openly and indeed a duty not to.

3. When an action is a blameworthy wrong against ourselves and it is our place to pronounce blame, then we must give our honest judgment and so pronounce blame, if only with the words "What you did was wrong." Perhaps we are in such a relationship to the person who has committed a wrong against us because we are a parent or a friend, or because our opinion is seriously sought. Here our being required to pronounce blame does not rule out our also having the duty to forgive. And in this kind of case the forgiveness that we ought to give will be overt forgiveness that is communicated, although, if it is true forgiveness, it must also come from the heart. Such forgiveness need not come after overcoming resentment. A mother may want to emphasize to her child the wrongness of what the child did, and then may quickly forgive the child, without any sense of resentment or indignation. Her attitude is not one of condonation: she may say sternly

and seriously that what the child did was very bad. But her moral attitude may not be, will not be, resentment toward her child or the child's action, but hope for the child's moral maturation. And, clearly, she need not judge her child to be evil.

4. If we are the victim of Ivan Karamazov's general or of a Hitler, then we may be dishonest if we do not judge the person to be evil. Even so, we can still forgive what is done to us. It is still possible, even if it is beyond most of us to forgive from the heart one we perceive to be evil. Again, even in this kind of case, resentment is not necessitated morally, although it may be humanly inescapable. Those who say that we should love our enemies are saying we can and should still love the person, even in this kind of case.

Now I think that we are in a position to see why sin/relationship morality implies there is a duty to forgive. It is a duty to forgive from the heart all who have wronged us, even if only sometimes a duty to make our forgiveness explicit. But, some may say, surely some wrongdoers are more forgivable than others. This may be. What this means, though, is only that some are *easier to forgive* than others, not that we have an obligation to forgive only some. But do we not ask those who have wronged us to *earn* forgiveness? I think that we sometimes do, and when they make an effort to earn forgiveness, that makes our granting forgiveness easier. It does not follow from this that we have no obligation to forgive those who do nothing to earn forgiveness. Some, more than others, it may be said, *deserve* forgiveness. Also, it is said, some may not deserve to be forgiven and then, through their repentance, come to deserve it. What, though, if all deserve to be forgiven simply because they are persons? This is just the case, for sin/relationship morality, for if all persons have inherent value simply by virtue of being persons, then all persons deserve forgiveness as they are. Persons *deserve* the acceptance of forgiveness. And this entails that we *ought* to forgive all who have wronged us, for *we ought to give what is deserved*. Equivalently, the person/person relationship we have to all persons requires of us that we forgive all who have wronged us. In not forgiving another person for the wrong that person has done to us, we in effect reject that person; and this rejection violates our person/person relationship to that person. The opposite of that rejection is acceptance, or reacceptance if we must overcome resentment. It of course is not moral approval of anything, and it is not "reapproval" of a person, unless that is understood as reacceptance of a person.

There is a connection to virtue here. While forgiving a person is something we do, being forgiving is something we are. Forgiveness, in the sense of being forgiving, is a trait, or disposition of character, and as such is a moral virtue. Forgiveness, as a disposition, has just the interior aspect that it should as a virtue. The forgiveness that we give must be from the heart—or involve a change of heart if there is resentment to be overcome. This means that forgiving a person is or embodies an interior action, in the sense of that term we have consistently employed. If it does not require a *change* of heart, it requires our not giving ourselves over to resentment or indignation. Forgiveness, as the disposition to forgive from the heart, accordingly has the interior dimension that is generally recognized to belong to the virtues. That forgiveness is at least *sometimes* a virtue, several have acknowledged. Murphy is one. For Murphy, forgiveness is permissible when there is a "moral reason" that justifies it, but also, he says, "if forgiveness is a virtue, then it must be that sometimes it is not merely permissible that I forgive but that I *ought* to forgive." After consideration, he suggests that "we sometimes *ought* to forgive others . . . [and] forgiveness is . . . sometimes a virtue."[70] But, for Murphy, we ought to forgive only when there is the kind of moral reason he identifies—something that serves to divorce the agent from the act, as in repentance; otherwise forgiveness is not permissible. Kolnai, as we have seen, says something similar: while he does not believe that a "virtuous person" forgives every wrongdoer for every wrong received, he does believe that the "more virtuous" the person is the more he or she is disposed to forgive. Kolnai, then, like Murphy, allows that there are times when we are not obligated to forgive. Forgiveness, he says, however "duty-like" it may be is never "a strict obligation," though he allows that forgiveness is "a *quasi*-obligation" when there is a change of heart, or repentance, in the wrongdoer.[71] Otherwise, for Kolnai, it is not even a quasi-obligation. For Murphy and Kolnai, forgiveness is only sometimes a virtue, because there are times when we are not obligated to forgive or, more severely, we ought not to forgive. They think as they do because each thinks that there must be some kind of moral reason in the area of repentance in order for it to be a duty, or duty-like, to forgive. For sin/relationship morality, there is always a sufficient moral reason for forgive-

70. Murphy, "Forgiveness and Resentment," in *Forgiveness and Mercy*, 29 and 30 (Murphy's emphasis). Murphy offers an argument for forgiveness sometimes being a virtue, but the argument turns on forgiveness overcoming resentment. Two further arguments he offers, which he says he associates with the Christian tradition, seem to be arguments for forgiveness always being a virtue: (1) we should forgive in order to reform the wrongdoer, and (2) we should forgive because we ourselves need to be forgiven (p. 30).

71. Kolnai, "Forgiveness," 101 and 105 (Kolnai's emphasis).

ness: persons as persons deserve to be forgiven, and our not forgiving them violates our relationship to them. We need no further moral reason. Forgiveness, then, is *always* a virtue.

Just here let us return briefly to Kolnai's paradox of forgiveness. In order to escape its dilemma he must show that forgiveness is neither condonation nor pointless. Part of the reason it is not pointless, for Kolnai, as we have seen, is that forgiveness is a virtue. That is, for him, as for Murphy, forgiveness is *sometimes* a virtue. Sin/relationship morality can argue more strongly that forgiveness is not pointless because it is, not merely sometimes, but always a virtue. And it is not pointless and is always a virtue because it is always an obligation we have to those who have wronged us. Also, we may add, going beyond the kind of reason that Murphy and Kolnai give us, forgiveness is not morally pointless, because it not only meets an obligation to persons that we have but helps us live in a keenly explicit awareness of that fundamental relationship between persons that is the source of the obligation to forgive. Forgiveness, as a response to the worth of persons, is in accord with love[72] and in accord with other like attitudes. And the state of our heart in forgiveness, or its change of heart if it issues from a change of heart, is not inimical to that lifting of selfish passion that may open our eyes to the presence of persons (see Chapter 3). So it is that our belief in the inherent worth of persons, which makes forgiveness possible, may be grounded in our realization of the worth of persons and, conversely, that the state of our heart, or change of heart, found in forgiveness may help us come to the moral discovery of the inherent worth of persons.

The obligation to forgive all who have wronged us is implied by sin/relationship morality, given our person/person relationship to all persons. If that relationship obtains, we do indeed have this universal obligation. It is possible, though, to recognize the universal obligation to forgive, while denying that the person/person relationship is its source. For Marilyn McCord Adams, we have a universal obligation to forgive. But, as we might expect from what we have seen of her view of sin (in Chapter 13), she may well understand its source differently. For her, we will recall, "God and creatures are ontologically incommensurate," as she says in "Sin as Uncleanness."[73] As she puts her point in "Forgiveness: A Christian Model," "from a metaphysical point of view, creatures are 'almost nothing' when compared

---

72. Cf. Bishop Butler, in Sermon 9, where he speaks of forgiveness and love together. *Butler's Fifteen Sermons*, 80–81.

73. Adams, "Sin as Uncleanness," *Philosophical Perspectives* 5 (1991): 7. Cited in Chapter 13 above.

to God." Yet in a way creatures have value. Adams, I think, shares the intuition that a sense of the value of persons makes possible our forgiveness. However, she says, the source of the worth of "created persons" is "Divine love and generosity"; it is a "positive value *conferred*" by Divine love.[74] Now, there are two ways to understand this theological idea: (1) in creating persons, God in His love created beings with inherent worth; and (2) God created persons without inherent worth and then, by loving them, imparted a worth to them. We discussed these two constructions in Chapter 5 in connection with Anders Nygren's understanding of Agape, it may be recalled. The first in no way contradicts the idea that persons have *inherent* worth: it only adds that God created persons, those beings with the inherent worth of persons. The second construction, though, does deny that persons have a worth *in themselves*. I am not clear which Adams intends, but the way she understands our obligation to forgive suggests that she tends toward the second. While there is an obligation to forgive, the wrongdoer has no "correlative right" to be forgiven. She does not seem to see persons as *deserving* forgiveness. For Adams, "forgiveness is a peculiarly Christian obligation."[75] This is because "for the Christian, the obligation to forgive arises out of his/her fundamental commitment to God, his/her call to see as God sees and love as God loves; it is an obligation to be generous as God is generous."[76] As Adams sees it, then, the source of our obligation to forgive is not the deserving nature of persons as persons, not our relationship to human persons, but our relationship to God. Our obligation to forgive persons is not an obligation we have to them; it is an obligation we have to God. I shall not deny that we have such an obligation to God. But I would point out that our having such an obligation to God does not deny that we also have the obligation to persons, human persons, to forgive all who have wronged us. Human sin/relationship morality and religious sin/relationship morality are continuous in the way we have seen (in Chapter 13). And if sin/relationship morality is correct, and the person/person relationship obtains, even without an obligation to God, we have a sufficient moral reason to forgive all who have wronged us.

We have at this point advanced and defended our announced thesis regarding forgiveness: sin/relationship morality implies that we ought to forgive all

74. Adams, "Forgiveness: A Christian Model," 291 (Adams' emphasis).
75. Ibid., 300.
76. Ibid.

who have wronged us. And we have seen, I hope, that if we do in fact stand in the person/person relationship to all persons, then we do have this obligation toward all who have wronged us. There are, however, two further aspects of our obligation to forgive that merit our attention. Also, beyond the obligation to forgive those who have wronged us, sin/relationship morality implies that we have the obligation to accept forgiveness; and we must discuss this obligation as well. First, though, the two further aspects of our obligation to forgive.

One has to do with the restoration of a relationship. As I indicated, it is a conceptual feature of forgiveness that forgiveness in some way restores a relationship between persons. When one person forgives another, a relationship between them is *in some way* restored. Hampton speaks to this feature of forgiveness when she makes it a part of her definition of forgiveness and its change of heart that the forgiver "may be able to renew a relationship." Notice that she says, *"may* be able." Marilyn Adams observes that a "hesitancy on the victim's part to renew and restore" a close personal relationship does not necessarily "signal a limitation on his/her willingness to forgive." "Parties to a painful divorce may genuinely forgive one another, but realize that . . . any sort of close personal interaction is inadvisable," she points out.[77] This seems to me to be right. Forgiveness may restore a friendship or some other close relationship, but it may not. Forgiveness does not require us to want to associate with those forgiven or even to like them. However, forgiveness does restore a relationship. For sin/relationship morality, the relationship restored is one of *acceptance of the wrongdoer as a person.* That is, if this relationship has been lost or undermined, as it would be if the one wronged resented and rejected the wrongdoer, forgiveness restores the relationship of acceptance. It is not the person/person relationship that is restored, for that relationship was there all along. However, it may need to be rediscovered or again acknowledged, as it would be if the person wronged, through his or her forgiveness, turned from rejection to acceptance of the wrongdoer.

The relationship of acceptance, it should be noticed, is restored in cases of self-forgiveness as much as in cases of one person forgiving another. Herbert Morris notes that Murphy leaves self-forgiveness unexamined.[78] Murphy is not alone in not heeding self-forgiveness. Kolnai, in fact, thinks that forgiveness of oneself is "a fairly dubious concept." It is, he thinks,

77. Ibid., 299.
78. Morris, "Murphy on Forgiveness," 16.

"because a person cannot 'wrong' himself, *i.e.*, infringe his own rights."[79] But persons can infringe their own basic right to be treated as a person. Persons have it in their power to violate the person/person relationship to themselves and so to wrong themselves. And if I do so, if I fail to respect my worth as a person and degrade myself, then I may not forgive myself. Such bitter self-rejection is overcome and made right by the same forgiveness that one person may grant to another. If we have an obligation to forgive others for the wrongs they have done to us, we have the same obligation to forgive ourselves for the wrongs we have done to ourselves—and for the same reason.

The other aspect of our obligation to forgive has to do with the question of its voluntary nature. On the one hand, we *can* endeavor to forgive others, and we do at times succeed; this suggests that forgiveness is voluntary. But we can also want to forgive and not be able to; and this suggests that forgiveness is not voluntary.[80] That we can be asked to forgive and can try to forgive—and that we have an obligation to forgive—all suggest that forgiveness is at least more or less voluntary, more or less within our power. However, though this be so, it still may be that, as Morris says, forgiveness is "a gift."[81] Or, as Adams says, "actual forgiveness is a manifold miracle."[82] None of what we have seen denies that our being able to forgive another, or ourselves, is a miraculous gift. It may be that we are obligated to forgive, or to try to forgive, but that invariably when we do forgive, it is by God's grace. Any who have felt that they ought to forgive another, have tried and failed, and have then somehow found themselves able to forgive, to forgive from the heart—any who have experienced this—will have a sense of what is referred to as grace. Grace being present in our forgiving does not rule out our having a sufficient moral reason for always forgiving those who have wronged us. Its presence allows us to do what we have a sufficient reason for trying to do.

It remains to trace and discuss one further implication of sin/relationship morality. It too identifies an obligation that has to do with forgiveness: the obligation to accept forgiveness. This obligation is the mirror image of the other, being both the like and the opposite of the obligation to forgive. And in a way it is the harder implication of the two.

79. Kolnai, "Forgiveness," 106.
80. Morris, "Murphy on Forgiveness," 17.
81. Ibid., 19.
82. Adams, "Forgiveness: A Christian Model," 295.

If it is true that we, all of us, have sinned against all persons, as Markel claims and as I have argued sin/relationship morality implies, then we not only have wronged all persons but have been wronged by all persons. Even if we set aside this severe implication, we have the sense that we have, upon occasion, wronged other persons and been wronged. To the extent we have been wronged by others, we ought to forgive them. And to the extent that we have wronged others, they ought to forgive us. So much we have seen, or, at least, so much I have argued sin/relationship morality implies. But say that forgiveness is offered. Must it be accepted? Sometimes in the human scheme of things forgiveness is accepted, happily accepted, but sometimes it is rejected. Sometimes people prefer to be unreconciled. They feel the forgiveness has been too slow in coming, or they have settled into the role of the alienated and misunderstood wrongdoer. Sin/relationship morality, however, implies that we always ought to accept forgiveness.

Markel's claim that we have sinned against all persons entails that others have sinned against all others, including him. But the point of his claim is that we have sinned against all persons, that we are in the wrong, and it is to confess that *he* in particular has sinned against all persons. His claim in effect confesses that we all are in need of forgiveness, and that he is in particular. In this way, Markel's words point more to the second obligation of forgiveness than to the first. Not that Markel formulates our obligation to accept forgiveness. He does not any more than he formulates the first obligation of forgiveness. However, it is clear that he accepts forgiveness. For he says, ". . . if I have sinned against every one, yet all forgive me, too, and that's heaven."[83] Markel accepts the universal forgiveness that he feels he is offered, but that does not mean that, in general, forgiveness is easy to accept, or that Dostoyevsky thought that it was. Kolnai gives us one paradox of forgiveness. Dostoyevsky gives us another. It is that it is harder to be forgiven than to forgive.[84] It is harder to accept forgiveness than it is to grant forgiveness. In *The Possessed* Stavrogin wants to be forgiven, but only by Tikhon and perhaps one or two others he deems to be his equals: he does not want forgiveness from "all the others"; and, finally, he says, "I want to forgive myself myself."[85] Stavrogin cannot abide accepting forgiveness from others (even though this may be his deepest wish, unacknowledged to

83. Dostoyevsky, *The Brothers Karamazov*, 302.

84. This Dostoyevskian paradox is noted by A. Boyce Gibson in his *The Relgion of Dostoevsky* (Philadelphia: Westminster Press, 1973), 57.

85. Fyodor Dostoyevsky, *The Possessed*, trans. F. D. Reeve (New York: Dell, 1961), 729 and 731 in the appended chapter "At Tikhon's" (or "Stavrogin's Confession").

himself—but that is another matter). Part of what Dostoyevsky sees here has to do with pity. Stavrogin does not want "universal pity." As Nietzsche appreciated, it is harder to receive pity than to give pity. But pity is not forgiveness. Why is it harder to accept than to give forgiveness? For one thing, for Dostoyevsky, our accepting forgiveness may wound our pride. In the terms of shame morality, one may have a model identity, or ego ideal, that requires one to be "above" either seeking or accepting forgiveness from others. Stavrogin may be seen as having just such an ego ideal. Alternatively, or also, it may be harder to be forgiven because to be forgiven, to accept forgiveness, is to admit one's fault. Granting forgiveness carries no such implication, and so the one who forgives can remain on high, above the sinner who is granted forgiveness. The antidote, for Dostoyevsky, is to affirm "solidarity in sin with the forgiven."[86] This one does by acknowledging that one oneself has sinned—and indeed, sinned against all persons. Finally, we all need forgiveness. So it is that Tikhon tells Stavrogin that he will forgive him—provided that Stavrogin will forgive him.[87] For sin/relationship morality, affirming solidarity in wrongdoing is not an exaggeration but a proper and accurate acknowledgment that, as I argued earlier, we all have sinned against all others in not fully living up to the demands of our relationships to them, the person/person relationship in particular. So we should grant that the affirming of such solidarity is in order, and, of course, its affirmation makes it easier for the one offered forgiveness to accept it. While the affirming of such solidarity will make it easier for those who are offered forgiveness to accept it, often when we are in need of forgiveness, such solidarity may not be affirmed by the one who offers forgiveness. Nevertheless, even then, and whenever we stand in need of forgiveness and it is offered, sin/relationship morality implies that we ought to accept the forgiveness that is offered.

Why does sin/relationship morality imply that we all have an obligation to accept forgiveness? It has this implication, again, by virtue of the person/person relationship that it posits. When we forgive a person, we continue to accept, or we reaccept, that person and so do not deny his or her value as a person. But also, when we accept forgiveness, we accept the one who gives us forgiveness. Accepting forgiveness accepts the forgiver, just as granting forgiveness accepts the wrongdoer—if acceptance is not merely performative but from the heart. Not accepting forgiveness rejects the one who offers the forgiveness. It does not merely reject a close personal relationship with the forgiver or say that the forgiver is not likable. Our not accepting forgiveness from someone in effect says that we do not value a relationship to that person as one who accepts us. It rejects him or her as a person whose forgiveness is valuable. But as persons deserve to be forgiven, so they deserve to have their forgiveness accepted, and not accepting forgiveness consequently violates our person/pereson relationship to the one who offers forgiveness.

This is not to say that accepting forgiveness is always or ever easy. It is only to say that sin/relationship morality implies an obligation to accept forgiveness and that if sin/relationship morality is correct in its positing of the person/person relationship, we always have this obligation. Again, this does not mean that it is always in our power to accept forgiveness. Morris says, "Forgiveness is, at once, a gift to the forgiven and to the forgiver. For the forgiven still another gift is required, the capacity to accept another's forgiveness."[88] Our obligation is to try, whether the forgiveness offered is by another or by ourselves.

88. Morris, "Murphy on Forgiveness," 19.

Afterword

All of morality in one way or another rests upon relationships if relationship morality—or, as we have come to call it, sin/relationship morality—is right. Obligations of various sorts are in their specific demands determined by the relationships we have to others: our spouses, our friends, those with whom we interact as speakers and hearers, and so on. We stand in a myriad of relationships to others, and our obligations are created by and are given the form they have by this webbing of relationships. But, moreover, if sin/relationship morality is right, the fundamental relationship that obtains between persons is the relationship we all have to one another, and to ourselves, by virtue of being persons. Obligations, justice, virtues, and rights all are determined by or have their source in this fundamental relationship.

This relationship, the person/person relationship, can, like our other relationships with persons, be violated. As we can violate the person/person relationship, so we can endeavor to live up to it. Perhaps we can never truly fulfill this relationship, for there is always more that we could have done and more that we can do: sin/relationship morality is a scale morality. Still, in the vision of morality given to us by sin/relationship morality, to the extent we live fully in accord with the person/person relationship to all others and to ourselves, we will ipso facto respect the rights of others, be virtuous, and keep our obligations. Given that there is the person/person relationship in the conception that I have developed—but only given that there is the person/person relationship in this conception—respecting the rights of persons, being virtuous, and keeping our obligations are all a matter of living in accord with the demands of this fundamental relationship between persons. This I have tried to show. The vision of morality given to us by sin/relationship morality, then, is contingent on there in fact being the person/person relationship between persons.

Is there the person/person relationship? If we enter into the presence of persons, we thereby discover their inherent worth as persons. In so doing we discover that we have this relationship to persons, defined by our shared personhood; and if we enter into the presence of *all* persons, we discover that we indeed have this fundamental relationship to all persons. One main thesis of this book has been that the entirety of the complex of morality rests upon the person/person relationship of each to each, discoverable by each in individual moral experience. Seeing that sin/relationship morality is right rests on a discovery of the person/person relationship, a discovery that, sin/relationship morality avers, lies in our potential moral experience.

The basis upon which sin/relationship morality rests is not faith-without-evidence in the inherent worth of persons, nor does it rest upon a mere "foundational assumption" that persons have inherent worth.[1] Sin/relationship morality rests upon a potential *discovery*—and if that discovery is made, one comes to see an abundance of evidence for the inherent worth of persons and our consequent person/person relationship to persons. The discovery is a realization-discovery, a "calm, clear insight," as Royce says, although I have argued that it has an affective side. It amounts to seeing in what is familiar to us all, the familiar presence of persons, the moral significance of their presence. The evidence is all about us, but its significance as evidence must be realized. Hence the discovery is a realization-discovery.

Is there such a discovery of the person/person relationship open to us? That there is such a discovery perhaps cannot be proven. It may be that, by the nature of the case, no logical demonstration can show us what is discoverable in our moral experience—although, if we have come into the presence of some persons, we may be able to imagine what it would be to come into the presence of other persons. On the other hand, for those who have experienced the discovery, any offered proof would be redundant—or worse. A careful argument, rich in neurological detail, may prove to someone who has never felt pain that there is the sensation of pain; however, that person's actually coming to feel pain not only makes the

1. Cf. Louis P. Pojman, "A Critique of Contemporary Egalitarianism: A Christian Perspective," *Faith and Philosophy* 8 (1991): 487–89 and 500, where Pojman critically discusses the ideal that *equal* worth, or egalitarianism, may be regarded as a "foundational assumption" without supporting evidence.

proof unnecessary but provides an understanding of what pain is that makes the neurological proof seem ludicrously off the mark.

If the discovery of the person/person relationship has not been made by someone, then, for that person, the foundation of our argument will not be in place. But if the discovery has been made by a person, then, for that person, if I am right, all in our first main thesis will follow as a natural upward unfolding of our moral experience. All that is really necessary for there to be the discovery of the person/person relationship is that this discovery has been made at least by one individual. From the fact that many do not make the discovery it does not follow that there is no discovery to be made, while from its being the case that but one person has truly made this discovery it does follow that there is such a discovery to be made.

As sin/relationship morality sees morality, when morality is informed by a full consciousness of its grounding it is like an inverted pyramid. Morality stands on the needlepoint of an experience, the experience of coming into the presence of persons, and falls away upward from that experience.

It is perhaps at this point that many will want to ask again, What counts as a person? The best answer to this question, I suggested, is that persons are those beings who are experienceable as persons, those beings into whose presence as persons we can come. But, some may say, What counts as a person varies across communities. In a way this is right, and in a way this is wrong. What a community chooses to count as a person is indeed up to that community. A community can choose to count "barbarians" or slaves or the demented as nonpersons. But this is only to say that it is in the power of communities to deny not only the legal but the moral status of some persons. On the other hand, what *is* a person is not up to a community. Persons are persons whether or not that fact is acknowledged, although community attitudes can make it hard or next to impossible for individuals in a community to enter the presence of those persons the community casts out of the family of persons.

Something similar may be said about nonhuman animals and other beings. In our moral experience human beings alone are experienced as persons or are preeminently experienced as persons. Given that we morally experience only human beings as persons and do not experience nonhuman animals and other beings as persons, it is still the case that nonhuman animals and other beings may have inherent value. And, again, beings have what inherent value they have irrespective of anyone's acknowledging it, although, to be sure, our failure to acknowledge the inherent value of animals and natural entities can cut the heart out of our morality toward animals and the environment.

If sin/relationship morality is right, our experience of persons as persons brings us to a discovery of the foundation of morality as it relates person to person, and an analogous experience, or set of experiences, brings us to a discovery of the foundation of morality as it relates human persons to other beings in our world. And, sin/relationship morality allows, a further experience of the presence of God can bring us to a discovery of the foundation of morality as it relates human persons to the Divine.

Sin/relationship morality is an explanatory ethical theory: it offers a foundational thesis about the nature of morality. But it is an explanatory ethical theory with a vengeance. For it has strong practical implications regarding our obligations. Sin/relationship morality entails that we have a number of specific, perhaps unsuspected, obligations, some of which are severe: these are the normative "fruits" of sin/relationship morality. At the same time, sin/relationship morality offers no strong criterion for moral rightness and argues that there is none. True, it offers a kind of test: actions are morally right when they are in accord with our relationships and, ultimately, with the inherent worth of persons by virtue of not violating the person/person relationship. Also rights, goods, and virtues are in accord with the inherent worth of persons.

How can we tell what is in accord with the inherent worth of persons? It has been a theme of our discussion that in many cases the desire for a strong criterion is misplaced. This is so regarding a "definition" of personhood and also regarding a criterion for moral rightness and a criterion for being in accord with the inherent worth of persons. There is no simple informative rule to follow that will invariably guarantee accordance with the worth of persons. There is no strong criterion for being in accord with the inherent worth of persons, nothing like "If and only if it prolongs life, it is in accord with inherent worth." In the end it is a matter of judgment what is and is not in accord with the inherent worth of persons. This is not to be lamented. Our judgments here need not be baseless. If we are sensitive to our relationships—our close relationships, our general relationships, and our relationship to persons by virtue of their being persons—our judgments will be well grounded. This, of course, does not provide a rule or strong criterion. The old desire for a rule that will mechanically unwind, through a series of logical implications, into a full statement of each and every obligation, virtue and right, or just into a statement of every obligation, is the result of an overly intellectual picture of both morality and ourselves. On the understanding of morality offered in our discussion, the mansions of morality are not so rigidly structured. Moreover, morality, understood most broadly, is complex and even confused. And this brings us back to our second main thesis.

The larger phenomenon named by "morality" is not one entity, simple or complex, but a series of different morality forms, not all of which give a place to obligation or virtue or rights, and which together, in the compass of our humanity, set up a dissonance of confusing voices. Sin/relationship morality, under this aspect of reflection, becomes but one morality form. Even so, it can be seen to underlie or account for more of our moral lives than other morality forms. This has been our second main thesis. And if it is correct, as I have tried to show it is, then relationships underlie morality in this second way as well.

In these two ways, then, if sin/relationship morality is right, our relationships are foundational to morality. Ultimately the foundation of morality is that fundamental relationship between each and each, the person/person relationship, in which our other relationships are grounded. We are, as it were, wedded to one another in our shared personhood. We are all, as John Donne said, "involved in *Mankinde*," and, indeed, in more than "Mankinde." For this reason we should "Never send to know for whom the *bell* tolls."

Works Cited

Adams, Marilyn McCord. "Forgiveness: A Christian Model." *Faith and Philosophy* 8 (1991): 277–304.

———. "Sin as Uncleanness." *Philosophical Perspectives* 5 (1991): 1–28.

Adams, Robert Merrihew. "Common Projects and Moral Virtue." *Midwest Studies in Philosophy* 13 (1988): 297–307.

———. "Divine Commands and the Social Nature of Obligation." *Faith and Philosophy* 4 (1987): 262–75.

———. "Involuntary Sins." *The Philosopher's Annual* 8 (1985): 1–29.

Aristotle. *Nicomachean Ethics*. Trans. W. D. Rose. In *Introduction to Aristotle*, ed. Richard McKeon. New York: Modern Library, 1947.

———. *Nicomachean Ethics*. Trans. J.A.K. Thomson, revised by Hugh Tredennick. In *The Ethics of Aristotle*. New York: Penguin Books, 1976.

Atwell, John E. "Are Kant's First Two Moral Principles Equivalent?" *Journal of the History of Philosophy* 7 (1969): 273–84.

Audi, Robert. "Self-Deception, Action, and Will." *Erkenntnis* 18 (1982): 133–58.

———. "Self-Deception and Rationality." In *Self-Deception and Self-Understanding: New Essays in Philosophy and Psychology*; ed. Mike W. Martin. Lawrence: University of Kansas Press, 1985.

Austin, John. "Three Ways of Spilling Ink." *Philosophical Review* 75 (1966): 427–40.

Baier, Kurt. "The Meaning of Life." Reprinted in William T. Blackstone, ed. *Meaning and Existence*. New York: Holt, Rinehart & Winston, 1971.

Baynes, Kenneth. "The Liberal/Communtarian Controversy and Communicative Ethics." In *Universalism Vs. Communitarianism*, ed. David Rasmussen. Cambridge: MIT Press, 1990.

Bernard of Clairvaux, St. *On the Necessity of Loving God*. In *The Wisdom of Catholicism*, ed. Anton C. Pegis. New York: Random House, 1949.

Bernstein, Richard J. "Nietzsche or Aristotle? Reflections on Alasdair MacIntyre's *After Virtue*." In *Philosophical Profiles*. Philadelphia: University of Pennsylvania Press, 1986.

Blackstone, William T. "The Search for an Environmental Ethic." In *Matters of Life and Death: New Introductory Essays in Moral Philosophy*, ed. Tom Regan. New York: Random House, 1980.

Bloom, Allan. *The Closing of the American Mind.* New York: Simon & Schuster, 1987.

Blum, Lawrence. "Gilligan and Kohlberg: Implications for Moral Theory." In *An Ethic of Care: Feminist and Interdisciplinary Perspectives*, ed. Mary Jeanne Larrabee. New York: Routledge, 1993.

Brandt, R. B. "The Structure of Virtue." *Midwest Studies in Philosophy* 13 (1988): 64–82.

Brook, J. A. "How to Treat Persons as Persons." In *Philosophy and Personal Relations*, ed. Alan Montefiore. London: Routledge & Kegan Paul, 1973.

Brümmer, Vincent. *What Are We Doing When We Pray?* London: SCM Press, 1984.

Buber, Martin. *I and Thou.* Trans. Walter Kaufmann. New York: Charles Scribner's Sons, 1970.

Butler, Joseph. *Butler's Fifteen Sermons.* London: S.P.C.K., 1970.

Camus, Albert. *The Plague.* Trans. S. Gilbert. New York: Modern Library, 1948.

Catherine of Genoa, *Purgation and Purgatory.* In *Catherine of Genoa: Purgation and Purgatory, The Spiritual Dialogue*, trans. Serge Hughes. *The Classics of Western Spirituality.* New York: Paulist Press, 1979.

———. *The Spiritual Dialogue.* In *Catherine of Genoa: Purgation and Purgatory, The Spiritual Dialogue*, trans Serge Hughes. *The Classics of Western Spirituality.* New York: Paulist Press, 1979.

The Cloud of Unknowing. Ed. James Walsh, S.J. *The Classics of Western Spirituality.* New York: Paulist Press, 1981.

Cranford, Ronald E., and David Randolph Smith. "Consciousness: The Most Critical Moral (Constitutional) Standard for Human Personhood." *American Journal of Law and Medicine* 13 (1987): 233–48.

Donne, John. Devotion XVII. In *The Complete Poetry and Selected Prose of John Donne and the Complete Poetry of William Blake.* New York: Modern Library, 1941.

Dostoyevsky, Fyodor. *The Brothers Karamazov.* Trans. Constance Garnett. New York: Modern Library, n.d.

———. *The Brothers Karamazov.* 2 vols. Trans. David Magarshack. Baltimore: Penguin Books, 1958.

———. *Crime and Punishment.* Trans. Constance Garnett. New York: Modern Library, 1950.

———. *The Possessed.* Trans. Constance Garnett. New York: Dell Publishing Co., 1961.

Drengson, Alan. "Critical Notice: Herbert Fingarette, *Self-Deception.*" *Canadian Journal of Philosophy* 3 (1974): 475–84.

Dreyfus, Hubert I., and Stuart E. Dreyfus. "What Is Morality? A Phenomenological Account of the Development of Ethical Expertise." In *Universalism Vs. Communitarianism*, ed. David Rasmussen. Cambridge: MIT Press, 1990.

Dworkin, Ronald. *Taking Rights Seriously.* Cambridge: Harvard University Press, 1977.

Edwards, Jonathan. *Original Sin.* Ed. Clyde A. Holbrook. Vol. 3 of *Works of Jonathan Edwards*, ed. John E. Smith. New Haven: Yale University Press, 1970.

Endo, Shusaku. *Silence.* Trans. William Johnston. New York: Toplinger Publishing Co., 1960.

Evans, Donald. *Faith, Authenticity, and Morality.* Toronto: University of Toronto Press, 1980.

Ewing, A. C. *Ethics.* New York: Macmillan, 1953.

Feinberg, Joel. *Social Philosophy.* Englewood Cliffs, N.J.: Prentice-Hall, 1973.

Ferrara, Alessandro. "Universalism: Procedural, Contextualist, and Prudential." In *Universalism Vs. Communitarianism*, ed. David Rasmussen. Cambridge: MIT Press, 1990.

Fingarette, Herbert. *Self-Deception.* In *Studies in Philosophical Psychology*, ed. R. F. Holland. New York: Humanities Press, 1969.

Flanagan, Owen, and Kathryn Jackson. "Justice, Care, and Gender: The Kohlberg-Gilligan Debate Revisited." In *An Ethic of Care: Feminist and Interdisciplinary Perspectives*, ed. Mary Jeanne Larrabee. New York: Routledge, 1993.

Fletcher, Joseph. "Humanness." In *Humanhood: Essays in Biomedical Ethics*. Buffalo, N.Y.: Prometheus Books, 1979.

———. "Indicators of Humanhood: A Tentative Profile of Man." *Hastings Center Report* 2 (1972): 2–4.

Foot, Philippa. *Virtues and Vices and Other Essays in Moral Philosophy*. Berkeley and Los Angeles: University of California Press, 1978.

Frankena, William. *Ethics*. 2d ed. Englewood Cliffs, N.J.: Prentice-Hall, 1973.

Freuchen, Peter. *Book of the Eskimo*. New York: World Publishing Co., 1961.

Friedman, Marilyn. "Beyond Caring: The De-Moralization of Gender." In *An Ethic of Care: Feminist and Interdisciplinary Perspectives*, ed. Mary Jeanne Larrabee. New York: Routledge, 1993.

Geach, Peter. *The Virtues*. Cambridge: Cambridge University Press, 1977.

Gibson, A. Boyce. *The Religion of Dostoevsky*. Philadelphia: Westminster Press, 1973.

Gide, André. *Les Caves du Vatican*. Published in English as *Lafcadio's Adventures*. Trans. Dorothy Bussy. New York: Random House, 1953.

Gilligan, Carol. *In a Different Voice: Psychological Theory and Women's Development*. Cambridge: Harvard University Press, 1982.

———. "Reply to Critics." Reprinted in *An Ethic of Care: Feminist and Interdisciplinary Perspectives*, ed. Mary Jeanne Larrabee. New York: Routledge, 1993.

Grimshaw, Jean. *Philosophy and Feminist Thinking*. Minneapolis: University of Minnesota Press, 1986.

Gutiérrez, Gustavo. *A Theology of Liberation*. Ed. and trans. Sister Caridad Inda and John Eagleson. Maryknoll, N.Y.: Orbis Books, 1973.

Hampton, Jean. "Forgiveness, Resentment, and Hatred." In Jeffrie G. Murphy and Jean Hampton, *Forgiveness and Mercy. Cambridge Studies in Philosophy and Law*, ed. Jules Coleman. Cambridge: Cambridge University Press, 1988.

———. "The Retributive Idea." In Jeffrie G. Murphy and Jean Hampton, *Forgiveness and Mercy. Cambridge Studies in Philosophy and Law*, ed. Jules Coleman. Cambridge: Cambridge University Press, 1988.

Hawthorne, Nathaniel. *The Scarlet Letter*. In *The Portable Hawthorne*, ed. Malcolm Cowley. Rev. ed. New York: Viking Press, 1969.

Hazlitt, Henry. *The Foundations of Morality*. Princeton: D. Van Nostrand, 1964.

Hoagland, Sarah Lucia. "Some Thoughts About 'Caring.' " In *Feminist Ethics*, ed. Claudia Card. Lawrence: University Press of Kansas, 1991.

Hohfeld, Wesley Newcomb. *Fundamental Legal Conceptions*. New Haven: Yale University Press, 1919.

Jaeger, Werner. *Paideia: The Ideals of Greek Culture*. Vol. 1. Trans. G. Highet. 2d ed. New York: Oxford University Press, 1962.

Julian of Norwich. *Showings*. In *Julian of Norwich: Showings*, trans. and ed. Edmund College and James Walsh. *The Classics of Western Spirituality*. New York: Paulist Press, 1978.

Kant, Immanuel. *Groundwork of the Metaphysic of Morals*. In H. J. Paton, *The Moral Law or Kant's Groundwork of the Metaphysic of Morals*. 3d ed. New York: Barnes & Noble, 1956.

Kaufmann, Walter. *Nietzsche: Philosopher, Psychologist, Antichrist*. 4th ed. Princeton: Princeton University Press, 1974.

Kekes, John. *The Examined Life*. Lewisburg: Bucknell University Press, 1988.

———. "Shame and Moral Progress." *Midwest Studies in Philosophy* 13 (1988): 282–96.

Kellenberger, J. *The Cognitivity of Religion: Three Perspectives*. London: Macmillan; and Berkeley and Los Angeles: University of California Press, 1985.

———. "The Death of God and the Death of Persons." *Religious Studies* 16 (1980): 264–82.

———. "A Defense of Pacifism." *Faith and Philosophy* 4 (1987): 129–48.

———. *God-Relationships With and Without God*. London: Macmillan; New York: St. Martin's, 1989.

———. *Religious Discovery, Faith, and Knowledge*. Englewood Cliffs, N.J.: Prentice-Hall, 1972.

Kierkegaard, Søren. *Concluding Unscientific Postscript*. Trans. David F. Swenson and Walter Lowrie. Princeton: Princeton University Press, 1941.

———. *Either/Or*. 2 vols. Trans. Howard V. Hong and Edna H. Hong. Princeton: Princeton University Press, 1987.

———. *Fear and Trembling* and *Repetition*. Ed. and trans. Howard V. Hong and Edna H. Hong. Princeton: Princeton University Press, 1983.

———. *The Point of View for My Work as an Author*. In *A Kierkegaard Anthology*, ed. Robert Bretall. Princeton: Princeton University Press, 1946.

———. *The Sickness Unto Death*. Trans. Howard V. Hong and Edna H. Hong. Princeton: Princeton University Press, 1980.

———. *Works of Love*. Trans. Howard V. Hong and Edna H. Hong. New York: Harper & Row, 1962.

King-Farlow, John, and Richard Bosley. "Self-Formation and the Mean (Programmatic Remarks on Self-Deception)." In *Self-Deception and Self-Understanding: New Essays in Philosophy and Psychology*, ed. Mike W. Martin. Lawrence: University Press of Kansas, 1985.

Kohlberg, Lawrence. *The Psychology of Moral Development*: Vol. 2 of *Essays on Moral Development*. San Francisco: Harper & Row, 1984.

Kolnai, Aurel. "Forgiveness." *Proceedings of the Aristotelian Society*, n.s., 74 (1973–74): 91–106.

Lampert, Laurence. *Nietzsche's Teaching*. New Haven: Yale University Press, 1986.

Leiber, Justin. *Can Animals and Machines Be Persons?* Indianapolis: Hackett, 1985.

Leopold, Aldo. *A Sand County Almanac*. Enlarged ed. New York: Oxford University Press, 1966.

Locke, John. *An Essay Concerning Human Understanding*. Vol. 1. New York: Dover, 1959.

Lynd, Helen Merrell. *On Shame and the Search for Identity*. New York: Harcourt, Brace & Company, 1958.

MacIntyre, Alasdair. *After Virtue*. 2d. ed. Notre Dame, Ind.: University of Notre Dame Press, 1984.

Maclagan, W. G. "Respect for Persons as a Moral Principle I." *Philosophy* 35 (1960): 193–217.

———. "Respect for Persons as a Moral Principle II." *Philosophy* 35 (1960): 289–305.

Malcolm, Norman. *Wittgenstein: A Memoire*. London: Oxford University Press, 1958.

Manning, Rita C. *Speaking from the Heart: A Feminist Perspective on Ethics*. Lanham, Md.: Rowman & Littlefield, 1992.

Martin, Mike W. *Self-Deception and Morality*. Lawrence: University of Kansas Press, 1986.

McGinn, Colin. "My Wicked Heart." *London Review of Books* 12, November 22, 1990, 8–10.

Mill, John Stuart. *Utilitarianism*. Indianapolis: Hackett, 1979.

Mitchell, Basil. "How Is the Concept of Sin Related to the Concept of Moral Wrongdoing?" *Religious Studies* 20 (1984): 165–73.

Moore, G. E. *Principia Ethica.* London: Cambridge University Press, 1968.

Morris, Herbert. "Guilt and Suffering." In *On Guilt and Innocence: Essays in Legal Philosophy and Moral Psychology.* Berkeley and Los Angeles: University of California Press, 1976.

———. "Lost Innocence." In *On Guilt and Innocence: Essays in Legal Philosophy and Moral Psychology.* Berkeley and Los Angeles: University of California Press, 1976.

———. "Murphy on Forgiveness." *Criminal Justice Ethics* 7 (1988): 15–19.

———. "Persons and Punishment." In *On Guilt and Innocence: Essays in Legal Philosophy and Moral Psychology.* Berkeley and Los Angeles: University of California Press, 1976.

———. "Shared Guilt." In *On Guilt and Innocence: Essays in Legal Philosophy and Moral Psychology.* Berkeley and Los Angeles: University of California Press, 1976.

Mouw, Richard J. *The God Who Commands.* Notre Dame, Ind.: University of Notre Dame Press, 1990.

Murphy, Jeffrie. "Forgiveness and Resentment." In Jeffrie G. Murphy and Jean Hampton, *Forgiveness and Mercy. Cambridge Studies in Philosophy and Law,* ed. Jules Coleman. Cambridge: Cambridge University Press, 1988.

Nagel, Thomas. "War and Massacre." Reprinted in *Ethics and Public Policy,* ed. Tom L. Beauchamp. Englewood Cliffs, N.J.: Prentice-Hall, 1975.

Nakhnikian, George. "Love in Human Reason." *Midwest Studies in Philosophy* 3 (1978): 286-317.

Needhan, Rodney. "Polythetic Classification: Convergence and Consequences." *Man,* n.s., 10 (1975): 349–69.

Newman, John Henry. *A Grammar of Assent.* Notre Dame, Ind.: University of Notre Dame Press, 1979.

Nietzsche, Friedrich. *The Antichrist.* Trans. Walter Kaufmann. In *The Portable Nietzsche.* New York: Viking, 1954.

———. *Beyond Good and Evil.* Trans. Helen Zimmern. In *The Philosophy of Nietzsche.* New York: Modern Library, 1954.

———. *The Dawn.* Trans. Walter Kaufmann. In *The Portable Nietzsche.* New York: Viking, 1954.

———. *The Gay Science.* Trans. Walter Kaufmann. New York: Random House, 1974.

———. *The Genealogy of Morals.* Trans. Horace B. Samuel. In *The Philosophy of Nietzsche.* New York: Modern Library, 1954.

———. *Thus Spoke Zarathustra.* Trans. Walter Kaufman. In *The Portable Nietzsche.* New York: Viking, 1954.

———. *Twilight of the Idols.* Trans. Walter Kaufmann. In *The Portable Nietzsche.* New York: Viking Press, 1954.

Noddings, Nel. *Caring: A Feminist Approach to Ethics and Moral Education.* Berkeley and Los Angeles: University of California Press, 1984.

Nygren, Anders. *Agape and Eros.* Trans. Philip S. Watson. New York: Harper & Row, 1969.

Otto, Rudolf. *The Idea of the Holy.* Trans. John W. Harvey. 2d ed. London: Oxford University Press, 1950.

Pagels, Elaine. *Adam, Eve, and the Serpent.* New York: Random House, 1988.

Parfit, Derek. *Reasons and Persons.* Oxford: Oxford University Press, 1986.

Phillips, D. Z. *Faith After Foundationalism.* London: Routledge, 1988.

Pico della Mirandola, Giovanni. *Oration on the Dignity of Man.* Trans. A. Robert Caponigri. Chicago: Henry Regnery, 1956.

Piers, Gerhart, and Milton B. Singer. *Shame and Guilt.* Springfield, Ill.: Charles C. Thomas, 1953.

Plaskow, Judith. *Sex, Sin, and Grace*. Lanham, Md.: University Press of America, 1980.

Plato. *Crito*. Trans. Hugh Tredennick. In *Plato: The Collected Dialogues*, ed. Edith Hamilton and Huntington Cairns. Bollingen Series 61. Princeton: Princeton University Press, 1961.

———. *Euthyphro*. Trans. G.M.A. Grube. In *The Trial and Death of Socrates*. Indianapolis: Hackett, 1975.

———. *Laws*. Trans. A. E. Taylor. In *Plato: The Collected Dialogues*, ed. Edith Hamilton and Huntington Cairns. Bollingen Series 61. Princeton: Princeton University Press, 1961.

———. *Republic*. Trans. Paul Shorey. In *Plato: The Collected Dialogues*, ed. Edith Hamilton and Huntington Cairns. Bollingen Series 61. Princeton: Princeton University Press, 1961.

Pojman, Louis P. "A Critique of Contemporary Egalitarianism: A Christian Perspective." *Faith and Philosophy* 8 (1991): 481–504.

Ramsey, Paul. "Dostoevski: On Living Atheism." In *Nine Modern Moralists*. Englewood Cliffs, N.J.: Prentice-Hall, 1962.

Rashdall, Hastings. *The Theory of Good and Evil*. 2 vols. 2d ed. London: Oxford University Press, 1924.

Rasmussen, David. "Universalism v. Communitarianism: An Introduction." In *Universalism Vs. Communitarianism*, ed. David Rasmussen. Cambridge: MIT Press, 1990.

Regan, Tom. *The Case for Animal Rights*. Berkeley and Los Angeles: University of California Press, 1983.

Richard of St. Victor, *The Twelve Patriarchs*. In *Richard of St. Victor: The Twelve Patriarchs, The Mystical Ark, Book Three of the Trinity*, trans. and intro. Grover A. Zinn. *The Classics of Western Spirituality*. New York: Paulist Press, 1979.

Richardson, Alan, ed. *A Dictionary of Christian Theology*. Philadelphia: Westminster Press, 1969.

Rorty, Amelie O. "Belief and Self-Deception." *Inquiry* 15 (1972): 387–410.

Ross, W. D. *Foundations of Ethics*. Oxford: Clarendon Press, 1939.

———. *The Right and the Good*. Oxford: Clarendon Press, 1930.

Rossi, Alice S., ed. *The Feminist Papers: From Adams to de Beauvoir*. New York: Columbia University Press, 1973.

Royce, Josiah. *The Religious Aspect of Philosophy*. New York: Harper & Brothers, 1968.

Saiving, Valerie. "The Human Situation: A Feminine View." In *Womanspirit Rising*, ed. Carol P. Christ and Judith Plaskow. San Francisco: Harper & Row, 1979.

Schweitzer, Albert. *The Teaching of Reverence for Life*. Trans. Richard and Clara Winston. New York: Holt, Rinehart & Winston, 1965.

Singer, Irving. *The Modern World*. Vol. 3 of *The Nature of Love*. Chicago: University of Chicago Press, 1987.

Singer, Peter. *Animal Liberation*. New York: New York Review, 1990.

———. "Animals and the Value of Life." In *Matters of Life and Death: New Introductory Essays in Moral Philosophy*, ed. Tom Regan. New York: Random House, 1980.

———. "Ten Years of Animal Liberation." *New York Review of Books*, January 17, 1985, 46–52.

Soble, Alan. *The Structure of Love*. New Haven: Yale University Press, 1990.

Stack, Carol B. "The Culture of Gender: Women and Men of Color." In *An Ethic of Care: Feminist and Interdisciplinary Perspectives*, ed. Mary Jeanne Larrabee. New York: Routledge, 1993.

Stefansson, Vihjalmur. *My Life with the Eskimo*. New York: Collier Books, 1962.

Stell, Lance K. "The Just Society and Lifeline." Address delivered to a conference sponsored by the North Carolina Utilities Commission, June 28, 1978.

Sterba, James P. *The Demands of Justice.* Notre Dame, Ind.: University of Notre Dame Press, 1980.

Strawson, P. F. "Freedom and Resentment." In *Studies in the Philosophy of Thought and Action*, ed. P. F. Strawson. New York: Oxford University Press, 1968.

Strong, Augustus. *Systematic Theology.* Valley Forge, Pa.: Judson Press, 1907.

Swinburne, Richard. *Responsibility and Atonement.* Oxford: Clarendon Press, 1989.

Taylor, Charles. "The Diversity of Goods." In *Utilitarianism and Beyond*, ed. Amartya Sen and Bernard Williams. Cambridge: Cambridge University Press, 1982.

———. *Sources of the Self.* Cambridge: Harvard University Press, 1989.

Taylor, Gabriele. *Pride, Shame, and Guilt.* Oxford: Clarendon Press, 1985.

Twambley, P. "Mercy and Forgiveness." *Analysis* 36 (1976): 84–90.

Wallace, James. *Virtues and Vices.* Ithaca, N.Y.: Cornell University Press, 1978.

Walzer, Michael. *Spheres of Justice.* New York: Basic Books, 1983.

Ward, Keith. *Ethics and Christianity.* London: George Allen & Unwin; New York: Humanities Press, 1970.

Wellman, Carl. *A Theory of Rights.* Totowa, N.J.: Rowman & Allanheld, 1985.

Wisdom, John. "Gods." In *Philosophy and Psycho-analysis.* Oxford: Blackwell, 1964.

Wittgenstein, Ludwig. *Philosophical Investigations.* Trans. G.E.M. Anscombe. New York: Macmillan, 1953.

Wurmser, Léon. *The Mask of Shame.* Baltimore: Johns Hopkins University Press, 1981.

Index